COOKING for the FAMILY
in colour
MARGUERITE PATTEN

Evans

Evans Brothers Limited

Introduction

I hope you enjoy cooking as much as I do, for it gives me an enormous amount of pleasure to see my family and friends enjoy dishes I have prepared.

There are occasions of course when shopping and cooking seem a very time-consuming and tiresome task, but I am sure that is the time when we should take a new look at our menus and decide that we will experiment with new ideas. This will provide a challenge, it may well save money and it will be a change from the familiar routine. I think the family often appreciate a new look to their meals.

We are living in times when new ideas on food and new developments in the kitchen are happening all the time and most of us like to keep abreast of these. It is for this reason that I have given quite a lot of space to advice on freezing various foods and dishes. It may be that you have no freezer but this could give you an indication of the scope of this appliance and maybe help you to decide whether it would be of value in your home.

Metrication is something with which we shall all soon become familiar. To help you accept this new way of weighing and measuring and to enable you to compare it with our familiar Imperial weights and measures every recipe gives them side by side. In most cases I have followed the recommended practise of using 25 g. as the equivalent of 1 oz., but occasionally I have used the more accurate metric conversion as I found it gave a better result in that particular recipe. Recipes give the equivalent of 1 lb. as 500 g.; this is to be consistent with other metric measures used. If however you are buying vegetables, meat or other foods it may well be that you will be dealing with $\frac{1}{2}$ kilo which is the same as 500 g.

Do not let the thought of metrication worry you for it is surprisingly easy to deal with and since all ingredients are converted strictly in proportion you will have just as satisfactory results as when dealing with the 'old' Imperial system.

This book has been planned for family living, so it carries a mixture of economical and special occasion dishes. I hope it will give you as much pleasure to use as it gave me to prepare.

Marguerite Patten

This edition produced in 1977 by Octopus Books Limited for Evans Brothers Limited
Evans Brothers (Nigeria Publishers) Limited, Jericho Road, P.M.B. 5164, Ibadan, Nigeria
Evans Brothers Limited, c/o B.D.L., P.O. Box 47610, Nairobi, Kenya
Evans Brothers Limited, Montague House, Russell Square, London WC1B 5BX
ISBN 0 237 45002 X
© 1976 Octopus Books Limited
Produced by Mandarin Publishers Limited, 22a Westlands Road, Quarry Bay, Hong Kong
Printed in Hong Kong

The publishers would like to acknowledge the help of the following in providing photographs:
Angel Studios pages 21 and 91; Birds Eye Foods Ltd. page 73; Cadbury Schweppes Food Advisory
Service page 155; Danish Agricultural Producers pages 74 and 119; The Flour Advisory Bureau
pages 135 and 149; Lawry's Foods Inc. page 77; The National Magazine Company pages 19, 24,
35, 38, 46, 49, 53, 59, 78, 80, 93, 123, 137, 139, 163, 173; New Zealand Lamb Information Bureau
page 64; Taunton Cider Company page 150; John West Foods Ltd. page 22; China shown on
endpapers by Wedgwood, from Gered of Regent Street.

Family Needs

Good food undoubtedly plays a part in keeping all members of the family healthy, from the youngest to the eldest. I am a great believer in family meals being a pleasant 'get together', so that they may be enjoyed not only for their food but for the fact that the family can relax; this is why you will find that I have concentrated on family type meals. This does not mean they are all rather plain, for some of the dishes that seem elaborate are very simple to make. I have also given sections, as you will see, on various types of entertaining, for most of us enjoy this.

If your family has varied meals you will undoubtedly be giving them a well balanced diet. It is, however, worthwhile checking now and again to make certain that every member of your family is having the right kind of food.

Proteins
This particular nutrient is found in all meat, poultry, game, in every kind of fish and in cheese, eggs and milk. It is also present in some vegetables such as peas, beans and lentils and in nuts. It is essential to produce strong healthy babies and children and to maintain health throughout our lives. When you allocate money for housekeeping, therefore, this is one of the most important things to consider: is your family having enough protein?

Fats
Some kind of fat is important for producing a feeling of warmth in the body. Butter, margarine, suet and other fats and oils give us this, together with the fat you find on meat and some kinds of fish, such as herrings. Most of us eat sufficient, but not too much, fat and the only time you may need to reduce the amount of fat you eat is if you are on a slimming diet which is based upon calories, as fats are very high in calories.

Carbohydrates
Two kinds of food come under this heading:
starch and sugar. Starches are in certain vegetables, such as potatoes, peas and beans, in flour and all the foods that are made with flour, which range from pasta to biscuits and cakes; other food such as rice also contains starch.

Sugar is in sugar itself of course and anything made with sugar; jam, cakes, puddings, etc. It is present in honey, treacle and golden syrup.

It is fashionable today to condemn carbohydrates but most of us need a certain amount as they promote energy. If you are on a slimming diet you must cut down, or even cut out, carbohydrates for a time, then quite possibly eat a restricted amount.

Children should not be given too many sweet things as it spoils their appetite for the more important food and can harm their teeth.

Vitamins and Minerals
There are certain vitamins that we all need to keep us well. If you eat a varied diet including fresh foods you will automatically have these; for example fresh fruit and vegetables give us Vitamin C (ascorbic acid) which is often called the protective vitamin as it builds up resistance to colds and influenza and also helps us to recover after an illness.

In addition to vitamins you will read of the importance of minerals and these also are present in many of our everyday foods. Two of the most important are calcium and iron as calcium keeps teeth and bones healthy and severe lack of iron causes anaemia. The best source of calcium is cheese and it is also added to white bread, so a meal of bread and cheese is a healthy *and* enjoyable one. Iron is found in all meat, especially liver, heart and kidneys, and it is also obtained from watercress, spinach, dried apricots and other dried fruit.

As you see, it is not difficult to plan the kind of meals your family enjoy and at the same time 'keep an eye' upon their nutritional needs.

Modern Kitchen Developments

All around us there are modern developments, but possibly some of the biggest changes have come in our homes, and in no place more than in the kitchen.

The refrigerator
This is the one place in your home where food is kept at an absolutely safe temperature. Even if you have a good larder it is not a perfect storage place for perishable food, as the temperature is often too high, even in Winter, and it is affected by humidity, steam, etc. Cover food in the refrigerator to prevent inter-mingling of odour and store food with a strong smell as near the freezing unit as possible. Frozen foods should be stored in the freezing compartment.

The freezer
There are certain important things to remember when using your freezer.
The food you freeze: a) Check that everything you freeze is really fresh.
b) Although most foods freeze well, there are certain foods that can give problems, e.g. cooked eggs become hard and 'rubbery'. Sauces, especially if they are creamy, may separate out (curdle) during freezing and reheating. I find this is less likely to happen if you use potato flour or cornflour instead of ordinary flour see page 54.
I would not choose to freeze mayonnaise, which also has a tendency to separate, but I have frozen left-over dishes containing some mayonnaise without dire results.
Lettuce and other salad vegetables lose their crisp texture. Some flavours lose a certain potency in freezing, e.g. garlic and wine. Either make allowance for this or, if possible, add after freezing. Many people feel pastry dishes are better frozen before cooking. In my own home I find it convenient to have both cooked and uncooked pastry dishes.
c) For best results do not keep foods in the freezer longer than the recommended period.
The way to freeze: Follow the manufacturers' recommendations at all times on the care and use of your freezer with special regard to:
a) The part of the freezer in which to place food for rapid freezing and the amount of food to freeze at one time. The faster the food is frozen the better the results.
b) Take the trouble to pack food carefully. Efficient wrapping is important to retain both the fresh flavour and the texture of each food. Tight wrapping and the exclusion of air from packages promotes fast freezing. Certain foods *are* frozen before wrapping, i.e. decorated cakes etc., but wrap immediately they are firm. There is a wide choice of packaging materials available: waxed cartons, aluminium foil, *thick* polythene bags, sheets and containers etc. It may seem expensive to invest in these, but many can be used over again.
c) Keep a record of where the food is stored and the date it is frozen.

After freezing: a) Plan ahead so you allow adequate time to defrost food. Some foods can be cooked from the frozen state. To hasten defrosting stand the wrapped article in cold (*not* hot) water.
b) Reheat carefully. Allow yourself adequate time to warm the mixture, to prevent burning or curdling.
c) When frozen foods are thawed out they become as perishable as fresh foods.

Commercially frozen food
When you have your own freezer or an adequate compartment in a refrigerator you can store commercially frozen foods. Remember these foods have been selected and frozen under ideal conditions and in many cases you will find it better to buy commercially frozen vegetables, for the variety grown has been specially selected for freezing.

Many of the prepared meat and fish dishes are created and cooked by experienced chefs. Follow the recommendations given on the packet at all times, for this will ensure your frozen food keeps in perfect condition.

The mixer

Use the whisk and/or beater for creaming, beating and whisking processes. You will find this invaluable, as it saves time and effort.

Use the same techniques for blending mixtures as you would when mixing by hand, i.e. whip cream on a slow speed, *do not* overbeat; add the eggs *gradually* to a creamed mixture to avoid curdling. I always fold in the flour by hand when making cakes.

The blender (liquidizer)

Use a blender instead of a sieve to make purées of fruit, vegetables, soups. In most cases you will have a perfectly smooth purée, but the blender does not deal with the tiny hard pips in raspberries and similar fruits. The blender can also be used for making milk shakes and other drinks, stuffings and mayonnaise.

Sometimes you will be advised to add the ingredients gradually, with the motor running. If you try to do this without a cover on the goblet you may well have the ingredients splashing out. Some blenders have a removable 'cap' in the lid for this purpose, but if yours does not, the solution

is simple. Make a foil cover for the blender with a hole in the centre, or make a funnel of foil and fit this into the top of the goblet. You can then 'feed-in' the ingredients gradually.

Never over-fill the goblet, particularly with hot liquids, as the mixture often rises and could force off the lid. It is also wise to start the process of blending on a low speed, then move on to a higher one.

The term used for dealing with food in a blender is to emulsify.

The pressure cooker

When you use a pressure cooker you shorten cooking times appreciably. For example a beef stew that normally takes $2\frac{1}{2}$ hours gentle simmering needs only 15 minutes at 15 lb./7 kilo pressure but it naturally takes time to bring the ingredients up to the desired pressure. The manufacturer provides detailed information on using the pressure cooker and cooking times for various dishes, but do watch the timing carefully. Even 2–3 minutes over-cooking at pressure can spoil vegetables. You will find the pressure cooker invaluable for making stocks, soups, stews. etc.

11

Appetizers

Do not imagine a meal starter or hors d'oeuvre is an extravagance; it can turn a light meal into one that is well balanced nutritionally and more sustaining and interesting. Do not be too conservative about the dishes you choose to start a meal, some countries have cheese at the beginning rather than at the end of a meal and I have included an interesting recipe using cheese on page 16.

When you have a fairly filling main dish, appetizers based upon fruit are a wise choice. If your main dish is fish, try having pâté, salami or other cold meat, see pages 22–24. You can adapt many of the recipes in the fish and egg sections of this book to serve at the beginning of a meal, simply by giving smaller portions than you would if they were main courses, and page 18 gives some ideas for making the most of smoked fish.

To freeze: Have a selection of hors d'oeuvre in your freezer to bring out in the event of unexpected guests. Pack fruit juices into waxed containers with ½-inch/1-cm. 'head-room' to allow for expansion of the liquid as it freezes.

Put grapefruit segments in small waxed or polythene containers; I would not sweeten the fruit, then everyone can add as much or as little sugar as they require when eating this.

Dice melon and freeze in syrup, page 185. If you buy avocado pears that are perfect for eating but you cannot use them at once, store in your refrigerator (as far away from the freezing compartment as possible) for one or two days, or freeze, so they do not become over-ripe. Thaw out at room temperature and *use on the same day.*

Pâtés can be frozen in well wrapped containers.

More information on freezing is given on page 10 and storage time for each dish under the relevant recipe.

Economical Appetizers: One of the secrets of economy in menu planning is to use foods when in season. At that time most foods are at their cheapest.

Fresh fruit makes a good hors d'oeuvre, so in addition to the more familiar melon, grapefruit and avocado pear recipes in this section, try:

Orange and onion salads: Cut thin slices of skinned orange, remove the pips. Arrange on a bed of shredded lettuce and top with finely chopped spring onions or rings of raw onion and a well-flavoured oil and vinegar dressing.

Fruit Supreme: Mix together fresh fruit in season, including fairly sharp citrus fruit. Flavour with a little dry sherry and serve well chilled.

Many countries serve vegetables and salads as separate courses, rather than as an accompaniment to main dishes and this idea can be used to make good meal starters.

Garden salad: Serve plates of wafer-thin slices of cucumber, tomato, red and green peppers (discard core and seeds), top with an oil and vinegar dressing and a generous amount of chopped parsley, chives, basil and/or tarragon.

Cauliflower salad: Divide a cauliflower into small evenly-sized sprigs (flowerets). Cook in boiling salted water until just softening; do not over-cook. Strain and blend while still warm with mayonnaise and chopped chives and parsley. Cool and top with more chopped parsley and chopped hard-boiled eggs.

Avocado prawn cockt

Avocado Prawn Cocktail

To make: 10–15 minutes   **No cooking**   (Serves 4)

8 oz./200 g. large prawns
2 avocado pears
For the French dressing:
6 tablespoons olive oil
2 tablespoons white wine vinegar
1 tablespoon lemon juice
1 teaspoon sugar
¼ teaspoon dry mustard
½ teaspoon salt
freshly ground black pepper
2 teaspoons chopped chives
2 teaspoons chopped parsley
To garnish:
few extra prawns
Quick tip:
Use 4 oz./100 g. ready peeled prawns
and bottled mayonnaise.

Peel the prawns and place in a bowl. Place all the remaining ingredients, except the extra prawns and avocado pears, in a screw-top jar and shake until well mixed. Pour the dressing over the prawns and leave to stand for 10 minutes. Cut the avocado pears in halves lengthways and remove the stones. Pile the prawns in the centre of each avocado pear half.
To serve:
Slightly chilled, garnished with the extra small prawns. If preparing some little time before serving, sprinkle the halved avocado pears with lemon juice.
To vary:
Use any other shelled fish and substitute mayonnaise or sauce under Prawn Cocktail, page 17. Serve filled just with the dressing in the recipe.
To freeze:
Do not freeze this dish, if using frozen prawns thaw out at room temperature.
To economize:
Use a mixture of flaked white fish and prawns.

Grapefruit & Melon Cocktail

To make: 10 minutes   **To cook:** 3–4 minutes   (Serves 4–6)

2 oz./50 g. sugar
¼ pint/1½ dl. water
1 tablespoon sherry
little ground ginger
2 large grapefruit
½ small melon

Quick tip:
Use canned grapefruit and nearly
¼ pint/1½ dl. syrup from the can;
flavour this with sherry and
ginger.

Make a syrup by boiling together the sugar and water. Flavour with the sherry and ginger. Take the segments from the grapefruit, remove the skin and seeds from melon and dice. Mix together and put into glasses. Spoon the syrup over and chill.
To serve:
As the first course of a meal or a dessert.
To vary:
Mix other fruit with the grapefruit and/or melon.
To freeze:
This freezes well. Use within 3–4 months as melon tends to lose some texture.
To economize:
This is an excellent way of using inexpensive melons or one that is slightly damaged.

Melon & Grapes

To make: 10 minutes   **No cooking**   (Serves 4–6)

1 small melon (honeydew or
    cantaloup)
1 tablespoon caster sugar
1 lemon
1 small bunch grapes

Quick tip:
Use bottled lemon juice or dry
sherry.
To economize:
Choose a time when melon is
cheapest.

Carefully remove the skin and seeds from the melon and cut the melon flesh into cubes, or into balls with a vegetable scoop. Place in a serving bowl, sprinkle with the sugar and squeeze the lemon juice over. Add the skinned and de-seeded grapes.
To serve:
Chilled as an hors d'oeuvre or dessert.
To vary:
Mix other fresh fruit with the melon.
To freeze:
Follow the directions on page 185 and see note above.

Melon and grap
Grapefruit and melon cockta

14

Stuffed peaches

Avocado Fruit Cocktail

To make: 10 minutes   **No cooking**   **(Serves 4–6)**

Choose a dressing, see opposite
2 avocado pears
1 grapefruit
1 orange
1 small lettuce

Quick tip:
Use canned grapefruit and orange
segments.
To economize:
See To vary:

Place the dressing in a basin. Halve the avocado pears, remove the stones and skin. Dice the fruit neatly and place in the basin immediately so the pears do not discolour. Cut away the peel and pith of the grapefruit and orange, dice and add to the avocado mixture. Shred the lettuce finely, put into glasses and top with the avocado mixture. Chill before serving.
To vary:
Use other fruit in season with the avocado pears or use diced celery and other salad ingredients.
To freeze:
See comments page 12.

Stuffed Peaches

To make: 8–10 minutes   **No cooking**   **(Serves 4)**

2 large ripe peaches or 4 halved
   canned peaches
lemon juice (see method)
2 tablespoons sultanas
little boiling water
6 oz./150 g. cream cheese
2 tablespoons chopped walnuts
few lettuce leaves

Quick tip:
Use canned peaches
To economize:
Use finely grated left-over hard
cheese; moisten with a little milk.

If using fresh peaches, halve and sprinkle the cut surface with lemon juice to prevent discolouration. Put the sultanas on a plate. Cover with the water, leave for 4–5 minutes then drain. Mix the cheese, sultanas and nuts and make into about 12 small balls. If these balls are very soft, chill the mixture in the refrigerator for a short time. Arrange the peach halves on lettuce leaves and place three cheese balls into each.
To serve:
Well chilled as a light snack or an unusual hors d'oeuvre.
To vary:
Use pears instead of peaches.
To freeze:
Better served freshly made.

16

Green pepper and prawn cocktail

Shellfish Cocktails

Most shellfish can be used for these. Crab or lobster should be flaked, but leave prawns and shrimps whole. Mix with a dressing (see below), put on finely shredded lettuce and serve as cold as possible.

Marie Rose

Mix enough tomato ketchup or tomato purée (fresh or from a tube or can) with mayonnaise to give a delicate tomato flavour. Add seasoning, a few drops of Worcestershire sauce, a squeeze of lemon juice and/or a little sherry, and any other flavouring desired.

Cream Dressing

Blend equal quantities of lightly whipped double cream and mayonnaise. Add a little extra seasoning, a few drops of Tabasco sauce (be careful, this is very hot) and any other flavourings required.

Yoghourt Dressing

This is ideal for slimmers. Season the yoghourt, flavour with fresh tomato purée and add a little chopped parsley and lemon juice to flavour.

Green Pepper & Prawn Cocktails

To make: 10 minutes   **No cooking**   **(Serves 4–6)**

4–6 oz./100–150 g. peeled prawns
3 tablespoons mayonnaise (see
    page 23).
1 large green pepper
2–3 sticks celery, chopped
lettuce
To garnish:
lemon

Quick tip:
Use ready prepared mayonnaise.
Buy ready peeled prawns.
To economize:
Mix cooked white fish with a smaller
amount of prawns.

Mix the prawns, mayonnaise, diced green pepper (discard core and seeds) and the chopped celery. Shred the lettuce finely and put into glasses or on individual dishes. Top with the prawn mixture and garnish with slices of lemon.
To serve:
As cold as possible, with brown bread and butter.
To vary:
Grapefruit and Prawn Cocktail: Use segments of fresh or well drained canned grapefruit instead of the pepper and celery.
Use diced melon or melon balls in place of the celery. Omit the lettuce.
Add a little fresh tomato purée, tomato ketchup or concentrated tomato purée to the mayonnaise.
To freeze:
Although the cocktail cannot be frozen, you can use frozen shelled prawns. Thaw these out at room temperature or see page 10.

Seafood Ramekins

8 oz./200 g. white fish
$\frac{3}{4}$ pint/4$\frac{1}{2}$ dl. milk
2 oz./50 g. mushrooms
1$\frac{1}{2}$ oz./40 g. butter
1 oz./25 g. flour
4 oz./100 g. prawns or shrimps
seasoning
juice of $\frac{1}{2}$ a lemon
4 tablespoons soft breadcrumbs
2–4 tablespoons grated cheese

To garnish:
$\frac{1}{2}$ lemon
1–2 tomatoes

Quick tip:
Omit the mushrooms, butter and flour and use a can of condensed cream of mushroom soup instead. Simmer the fish in $\frac{1}{4}$ pint/1$\frac{1}{2}$ dl. milk.

Cut the white fish into neat pieces and simmer in the milk for only 5 minutes. Meanwhile wash, but do not peel, the mushrooms and toss in the hot butter for 2–3 minutes. Stir in the flour, then add the strained liquid from cooking the fish, stir over a low heat until a coating consistency. Add the white fish, the prawns or shrimps, then season well and add the lemon juice. Spoon into 4 individual dishes or scallop shells, top with the crumbs and cheese and brown under a hot grill. Garnish with lemon and tomato slices and serve at once.

To vary:
Pipe a border of creamed potatoes round the edge of the dish, then spoon the fish mixture into the centre and place under the grill.
Make short crust pastry, roll out and line scallop shells, then bake 'blind', see page 140. Fill with the fish mixture. Brown in the oven, NOT under the grill.

To freeze:
This freezes well for a period of one month.

To economize:
Use all white fish; do not waste stale bread or dry cheese, use for toppings as above.

Smoked Trout Mousse

2 large smoked trout
black pepper
pinch cayenne pepper
$\frac{1}{2}$ teaspoon finely grated lemon rind
$\frac{1}{2}$ tablespoon lemon juice
6 tablespoons double cream
3 tablespoons single cream

Quick tip:
Put the fish into a blender and make a smooth purée.

To economize:
Substitute the cheaper bloater, buckling or kipper for trout.

Remove the skin from the trout and flake the fish, being careful to take away all the bones. Pound the fish until very smooth, then add the peppers, lemon rind and juice, and double and single cream, *lightly* whipped together. Put into small individual dishes and chill thoroughly.

To serve:
With wedges of lemon and brown bread and butter.

To vary:
Use any other smoked fish, see To economize.
Flavour the mousse with a little horseradish cream.
To make an even lighter texture, simmer the fish skin in about $\frac{1}{2}$ pint/3 dl. water with seasoning to taste for 10 minutes.
Strain and save $\frac{1}{4}$ pint/1$\frac{1}{2}$ dl. Soften, then dissolve 1 teaspoon powdered gelatine in this liquid, add 1 tablespoon dry sherry. Allow to cool and stiffen slightly, then fold in the flaked fish then the rest of the ingredients as the recipe above.

To freeze:
The first version, without the gelatine, freezes best. Use within 4–6 weeks.

Sardine Salad

1 large can sardines in oil
1 small lettuce
French dressing (see below)
chopped parsley
grated Parmesan
   cheese

To garnish:
2 tomatoes
1 lemon

Quick tip:
Use ready-grated cheese.

Open the can of sardines, drain off the oil (this can be used in the French dressing). Arrange the sardines on a bed of shredded lettuce and spoon over the French dressing. Top each sardine with an equal quantity of chopped parsley and Parmesan cheese and garnish the dish with slices of tomato and lemon.

To vary:
Use any other canned or cooked fish in place of sardines.

To freeze:
Left-over sardines could be frozen for 1–2 weeks; do not freeze salad.

Note: French or Vinaigrette dressing is used in many recipes. Avocado Prawn Cocktail (page 14) gives the usual proportions of oil and vinegar; vary as wished or add chopped herbs.

Seafood Quiches

For the flan cases:
12 oz./300 g. plain flour
pinch salt
8 oz./200 g. butter
1 egg yolk
water to mix

For the filling:
6 oz./150 g. smoked salmon
4 oz./100 g. peeled prawns
1 tablespoon lemon juice
4 large eggs
$\frac{1}{4}$ pint/$1\frac{1}{2}$ dl. single cream
$\frac{3}{4}$ pint/$4\frac{1}{2}$ dl. milk
seasoning
chopped parsley

To garnish:
few whole prawns (optional)

Quick tip:
Use ready frozen pastry or packet pastry mix.

Sieve the flour and salt together. Rub in the butter until the mixture resembles fine breadcrumbs. Bind with the egg yolk and water. Knead the pastry lightly on a floured surface, divide into 6 and roll into pieces large enough to line 5-inch/13-cm. deep flan cases. Prick the base of each pastry case with a fork and flute the edges. Cut the smoked salmon into 1-inch/2-cm. pieces. Mix with the peeled prawns and sprinkle with lemon juice. Whisk the eggs, cream and milk together, season. Divide the salmon and prawn mixture between the pastry cases, cover with the egg mixture. Bake in the centre of a moderately hot oven, 400°F./200°C., Gas Mark 6, for 15 minutes. Reduce the temperature to 325°F./170°C., Gas Mark 3, and cook for about a further 20 minutes. Sprinkle with chopped parsley before serving. Garnish with a few whole prawns, if wished.

To serve:
Hot or cold as an hors d'oeuvre or light supper dish.

To freeze:
These quiches freeze very well, use within 6 weeks. Reheat from frozen state. If preferred, prepare the pastry, put in the filling and freeze. Cover well then cook from the frozen state.

To economize:
Use flaked cooked white fish or canned pink salmon in place of smoked salmon and prawns.

Seafood quiches

Kipper Pâté

To make: 15 minutes   **To cook:** 5 minutes   (Serves 4–6)

2–3 large kippers or 4–6 kipper
  fillets
water
pepper
1 clove garlic
2 oz./50 g. butter
juice of 1 lemon
little single cream

To garnish:
few lettuce leaves
lemon
Quick tip:
Use uncooked kipper (see To vary).
To economize:
Use top of the milk instead of cream.

Put the kippers into a large container. Pour over boiling water to cover and leave for 5 minutes only. Remove from the liquid and take out any bones, then flake finely, or put into the blender to make a smooth mixture. Do not try to put too much fish into the blender at one time. Add the pepper, finely crushed garlic and melted butter and beat well, then add the lemon juice and enough cream to make a soft consistency. Put into small individual containers or one larger dish. Chill thoroughly.
To serve:
Turn out and garnish with lettuce and wedges of lemon.
To vary:
Use any other smoked fish instead of kippers. While you can cook bloaters as suggested above, you naturally would not cook smoked eel, buckling or cod's roe, and kippers can also be used without cooking.
Omit the cream and blend the cooked, flaked kipper with 4 oz./100 g. cream or cottage cheese and finely diced gherkins. This makes a delicious pâté.
To freeze:
Wrap well and freeze. Use within 4–6 weeks.

Spanish Salad

To make: 15 minutes   **To cook:** 20 minutes   (Serves 4–6)

1 tablespoon olive oil
4 oz./100 g. long grain rice
generous ½ pint/3 dl. cold water
seasoning
1 green pepper
1 red pepper
little mayonnaise
few stuffed olives
3 tomatoes
4–6 oz./100–150 g. canned
  anchovies, prawns, cooked
  chicken, ham or other cooked
  meat (see method)
few lettuce leaves

Quick tip:
Cook extra rice when serving boiled
rice hot, save and reheat for a salad.

Heat the oil and toss the rice in the hot oil, then add the water and seasoning. Bring the liquid to the boil, stir briskly, cover the pan, lower the heat and simmer for 15 minutes, by which time most of the liquid should have evaporated. Remove from the heat. Dice the peppers (discarding the cores and seeds) and add to the rice with the mayonnaise while the rice is still hot. Allow to cool then stir in the sliced olives, skinned sliced tomatoes, chopped anchovies, prawns and any cooked chicken, ham or other meat. This is a salad in which you can have a mixture of fish and meat. Serve on a bed of lettuce.
To vary:
Omit the peppers and add cooked diced carrots and cooked peas.
To freeze:
The rice mixture can be frozen, see page 102.
To economize:
Use small portions of left-over fish, etc.

Mediterranean Stuffed Tomatoes

To make: 10 minutes   **To cook:** 15 minutes   (Serves 4–6)

4 large or 6 medium-sized firm
  tomatoes
seasoning
2 oz./50 g. soft breadcrumbs
1 medium-sized onion
1 clove garlic
2 oz./50 g. mushrooms
8 blanched almonds
1 tablespoon chopped parsley
1 oz./25 g. butter

To garnish:
black olives
Quick tip:
Use about 2 oz./50 g. packet sage
and onion stuffing and mix with
the mushrooms, nuts and parsley.

Cut the tomatoes in half and scoop out the insides. Season the insides and turn the tomatoes upside down on a board or plate to drain while preparing the stuffing. Chop the tomato pulp finely and blend with the breadcrumbs, grated onion, crushed garlic, finely chopped mushrooms, almonds and parsley, season well. Pile the mixture into the tomato cases. Put a small knob of butter on top of each stuffed tomato and place in an ovenproof dish. Bake, uncovered, in the centre of a moderate oven, 350°F./180°C., Gas Mark 4, until golden brown. Garnish each tomato with a whole or halved olive.
To serve:
As a starter or light supper dish.
To vary:
Omit the mushrooms and add grated Cheddar cheese.
To freeze:
Do not freeze this dish.
To economize:
Use 1 oz./25 g. peanuts in place of the almonds.

Meat Appetizers

There are many ways in which meat can be served at the beginning of a meal. It is often a good way to use up small portions of meat that would be insufficient for a main dish.

Chopped liver: Buy chickens' livers or other tender liver, i.e. calves' or lambs'. Slice thinly and fry in hot chicken fat or butter with a finely chopped onion for a few minutes. Season, then chop very finely and blend with chopped hard-boiled egg yolks. Put on to lettuce and top with the chopped hard-boiled egg whites.

Ham mousse: Follow the directions for the Smoked Trout Mousse on page 18, but flavour with mustard as well as lemon juice. If using the recipe with gelatine, dissolve this in $\frac{1}{4}$ pint/$1\frac{1}{2}$ dl. tomato juice or stock that is not too salt.

Ham rolls: Spread thin slices of cooked ham or boiled bacon with cream cheese or mayonnaise, flavoured with mustard or horseradish. Lay an asparagus tip on the ham and roll up firmly. Serve on a bed of lettuce. This can be varied, as you will see from the recipe opposite. Another good filling for the rolls would be a home-made or canned pâté.

Old fashioned potted beef: Simmer minced stewing steak in enough seasoned water to cover. When nearly tender, remove the pan lid, so the excess liquid evaporates. Blend each 1 lb./500 g. beef with 2 oz./50 g. butter, grated nutmeg and sherry or brandy to flavour. Anchovy fillets are a traditional addition to potted beef; simmer the beef with pepper, but little, if any salt, add the butter and chopped anchovy fillets.

Salami cornets: Blend cream cheese with finely chopped walnuts or pickled walnuts. Spread on slices of salami, then twist into cornet shapes. Secure with tiny cocktail sticks until just ready to serve.

Sour sweet tongue: Dice cooked tongue neatly (the canned lambs' tongues are ideal). Blend with equal quantities of a sweet chutney and finely chopped cocktail onions or vinegar pickle. Serve on a bed of lettuce and garnish with 'fans' of gherkin.

Sour sweet sausages: Use sliced cooked sausages or frankfurters instead of the tongue above.

Ham, tuna and fennel appetizer

Ham, Tuna & Fennel Appetizer

To make: 10 minutes **No cooking** (Serves 4)

4 large slices lean ham
1 small can tuna
$\frac{1}{4}$ pint/1$\frac{1}{2}$ dl. mayonnaise
3 level tablespoons grated or finely
    chopped fennel
12 black olives
1 canned red pepper
To garnish:
parsley

Quick tip:
Grate the fennel, instead of chopping this.
To economize:
Use boiled bacon, canned ham or luncheon meat and cut into neat fingers.

Tuna combines with most other ingredients and here is teamed with aniseed-flavoured fennel and mild, lean ham for an interesting salad. Halve the slices of ham, roll neatly and put on to a flat serving dish. Drain the tuna and break the flesh into smallish chunks. Stand in a line on top of the ham. Combine the mayonnaise and fennel together. Spoon over the tuna then stud with olives. Cut the pepper into thin strips and decorate the rolls with a criss-cross of pepper strips. Garnish with parsley.
To serve:
As a light main dish or starter to a meal.
To vary:
Spread the slices of ham with cottage or cream cheese, blended with chopped olives, then roll.
To freeze:
Do not freeze this dish, although you could use frozen boiled bacon or ham, see page 74.

Devilled Crab

To make: 15–20 minutes **To cook:** 3–4 minutes (Serves 4)

1 medium-sized can crabmeat or
    1 large crab
2 oz./50 g. butter
1 teaspoon made mustard
pinch curry powder
$\frac{1}{2}$ teaspoon Worcestershire sauce
2 oz./50 g. soft breadcrumbs
3 tablespoons mayonnaise
seasoning

Quick tip:
Use the canned crabmeat

Open the can of crabmeat, remove the fish and discard any liquid, or dress the crab. Mix the fish with half the softened butter, the mustard, curry powder, Worcestershire sauce, half the breadcrumbs and the mayonnaise. Season very well. Put into one shallow dish or four individual scallop shells and top with the remaining crumbs and butter. Brown steadily under a moderate grill and serve hot.
To vary:
Omit mustard and curry powder and add tomato purée to taste.
To freeze:
Prepare, but do not cook; freeze then cover. Use within 1 month.
To economize:
Use a mixture of flaked white fish and a small quantity of crab.

Home-made mayonnaise
If making this by hand or with an electric whisk put 1 egg yolk into a dry basin with seasoning to taste, a good pinch of sugar and $\frac{1}{2}$–1 teaspoon made mustard. Add up to $\frac{1}{4}$ pint/1$\frac{1}{2}$ dl. oil drop by drop, whisking steadily or beating with a wooden spoon. Beat in 1–2 tablespoons vinegar or lemon juice plus $\frac{1}{2}$ tablespoon hot water. If making in a blender put in the egg yolk, seasonings and vinegar or lemon juice. Switch on for few seconds, then add the oil steadily through the hole in the cap or foil funnel, see page 11, at medium speed, adding the water at the end.

Bacon & Prawn Kebabs

To make: 10 minutes **To cook:** 5–6 minutes (Serves 4)

8 long rashers streaky bacon
32 cooked peeled prawns
To garnish:
few lettuce leaves
lemon

Quick tip:
It is not quicker to cook in the oven but much easier for a party. Balance skewers over a dish so the excess fat runs away. Cook quickly without turning.
To economize:
Use cooked mussels instead of prawns

Remove the rinds from the bacon. Stretch the rashers by stroking them firmly with the back of a knife, then divide each rasher into 4 pieces. Roll each piece around a prawn. Put on to 4 metal skewers and cook under a moderately hot grill until the bacon is crisp, turning once or twice during cooking. Serve hot, garnished with lettuce and wedges of lemon.
To vary:
Devils on Horseback: Roll halved bacon rashers round prunes and cook as above. Serve on toast as a savoury.
Angels on Horseback: Roll halved bacon rashers round well seasoned oysters. Serve on toast as a savoury.
Note: Secure the bacon round the prunes or oysters with small wooden cocktail sticks or put on to skewers as the recipe for kebabs.
To freeze:
Use frozen prawns and thaw out before cooking. Do not freeze the cooked dish.

23

Pâtés

Pâtés are an interesting hors d'oeuvre which can be prepared well ahead.

Quick tip:
Put the ingredients into a blender to mix. Remember though to emulsify small amounts at a time and to put in any liquid (such as melted butter) before the solid liver.

To serve:
With hot toast and butter.

To freeze:
Cover the top of the cool pâté with melted butter, wrap and freeze. Use within 6 weeks. The tongue pâté only freezes when the eggs are emulsified; even chopped hard-boiled eggs become like rubber when frozen.

To economize:
Simmer cheaper ox-heart in a little stock, when tender mince finely and use in the pâté. Follow the recipe, but use double the amount of butter to give a richer flavour.

Liver Pâté

To make: 10 minutes   **To cook:** 6–10 minutes   (Serves 5–6)

12 oz./300 g. calf's, lamb's, pig's or mixed livers
3–4 oz./75–100 g. butter
1 clove garlic
1 small onion
2–3 tablespoons stock
2–3 tablespoons single cream
1 tablespoon sherry
seasoning
To garnish:
parsley

If you are not using a blender, mince the raw liver or chop very finely. If you are using a blender, see Quick tip, given above. Heat half the butter in a large pan and toss the minced liver in this for about 5 minutes, together with the crushed clove of garlic and grated onion; add the stock during cooking so the liver keeps very moist. Tip out of the pan, into a large basin, then add the rest of the butter, cream, sherry and seasoning. Mix very thoroughly, cover and allow to set. If you have a blender you can cut the liver into thin slices, cook, then emulsify as directions above. Turn into 1 large or several smaller dishes and garnish with parsley.

Tongue Pâté

To make: 10 minutes   **To cook:** 10 minutes   (Serves 5–6)

2 eggs
8 oz./200 g. cooked tongue
2 oz./50 g. butter
3 tablespoons single cream
1 tablespoon finely chopped chives
1 tablespoon brandy
seasoning

Put the eggs on to hard-boil then plunge into cold water at the end of 10 minutes to prevent a dark line forming around the yolks. Try to use them while warm as they are easier to blend. Cut the tongue into small pieces and soften the butter. Put the tongue, butter and chopped eggs into a bowl and bind together, then add the cream, chives and brandy. Season to taste. If preferred, use a blender see Quick tip, above.

Speedy Liver Pâté

To make: 10 minutes   **No cooking**   (Serves 4–6)

8 oz./200 g. liver sausage
1 oz./25 g. butter
2 oz./50 g. cream cheese
2–3 gherkins
2–3 cocktail onions
½–1 teaspoon made mustard

Soften the liver sausage and blend with the butter and cream cheese. Add the finely chopped gherkins and onions, together with the mustard. Press into a buttered dish, cover with foil and chill. If preferred, use a blender, see Quick tip above.
To vary:
Use freshly cooked minced liver instead of the liver sausage. Add chopped parsley or other chopped herbs.

Russian Salad

To make: 25 minutes   **To cook:** 20–25 minutes   (Serves 4–6)

1 lb./500 g. mixed root vegetables
seasoning
¼ pint/1½ dl. mayonnaise (see page 23)
1–2 tablespoons chopped parsley

Quick tip:
Use cooked frozen or well drained canned vegetables.
To economize:
Use the cheaper swedes, carrots, turnips.

Prepare and dice the vegetables. Cook in boiling salted water until just tender; do not over-cook as the vegetables soften slightly as they cool. Drain well, blend with the mayonnaise and half the parsley. Allow to cool and top with more parsley.
To serve:
As part of an hors d'oeuvre.
To vary:
The original Russian salad had diced cooked tongue added and this makes a sustaining first course. You can also add diced cooked ham and chopped hard-boiled eggs.
To freeze:
While you can freeze the cooked vegetables, see page 100, it is not satisfactory to freeze the salad.

Herring Salad

4 rollmop herrings
2 dessert apples
2–3 gherkins or piece cucumber
2 teaspoons capers
2 tablespoons French dressing
    (see page 14)
2 tablespoons mayonnaise (see
    page 23)
few lettuce leaves
To garnish:
watercress
diced beetroot

Quick tip:
Grate rather than dice the apples
and cucumber.
To economize:
Use cooked, rather than rollmop
herrings, or make your own pickled
herrings (see page 52).

Drain the herrings and cut into narrow strips, peel and dice the apples, cut the gherkins or cucumber into small neat pieces. Mix the herrings, apples, gherkins or cucumber and capers together and toss in the dressing and mayonnaise. Spoon on to the lettuce just before serving and garnish with watercress and diced beetroot.
To serve:
By itself or as part of an hors d'oeuvre.
To vary:
Use cooked herrings with rather more French dressing.
To freeze:
The salad cannot be frozen.

Russian salad

Egg Dishes

Eggs form an essential part of most mixed hors d'oeuvre. They can be hard-boiled, sliced and topped with mayonnaise, or served whole with a coating of mayonnaise and garnished with strips of canned red pepper, anchovy fillets or smoked salmon, as in Nova Scotia Eggs.

Scrambled eggs can be blended with mayonnaise or cream as in Stuffed Mushrooms.

Bake eggs in individual dishes with seasoning, cream, diced smoked or cooked salmon, asparagus tips, or grated cheese, or cook in tomato cases as in Cheese and Tomato Meringues, opposite.

Crunchy Tomato & Egg Pie

To make: 15 minutes **To cook:** 10 minutes **(Serves 6)**

For the pie crust:
6 oz./150 g. cornflakes, crushed
seasoning
3 oz./75 g. butter
1½ oz./40 g. grated Cheddar cheese
For the filling:
3–4 eggs
generous ¼ oz./8–9 g. powdered
    gelatine
2 tablespoons cold water
just under ½ pint/3 dl. tomato juice
3–4 spring onions or 1 small onion,
½ small cucumber
3 oz./75 g. grated Cheddar cheese
Quick tip:
Stand the tomato mixture on a bed of crushed ice to set quickly, or place the mixture into the freezer for about 20–30 minutes; do not forget it, as the eggs and cucumber are spoiled by freezing.

Mix the crushed cornflakes, seasoning, slightly softened butter and cheese. Press into a flan shape on an ovenproof dish or pie plate. Bake for approximately 10 minutes in the centre of a moderate oven, 350–375°F./180–190°C., Gas Mark 4–5. Allow to cool. Meanwhile hard-boil the eggs. Soften the gelatine in the cold water, then stand over a pan of hot water, stirring until dissolved. Add the tomato juice, leave until thickened slightly, then stir in the finely chopped onion, diced cucumber, cheese and two of the eggs, finely chopped. Put into the pie shell. Leave to set. Chop the remaining egg white and yolk separately, and arrange round the edge of the flan.
To freeze:
This dish cannot be frozen as the chopped hard-boiled eggs would become tough, and the cucumber and onion would lose their crisp texture.
To economize:
This is a very good way of using small pieces of cheese, a few onions, etc. that are left over. If you have some left-over tomatoes, warm these with a little water, then rub through a sieve and use in place of the tomato juice.
Another way to give a tomato flavour is to blend 1 tablespoon concentrated tomato purée, from a tube or can, with chicken stock or water and ½ a chicken stock cube. This gives a pleasantly piquant taste.

Nova Scotia Eggs

To make: 5 minutes **To cook:** 4–5 minutes **(Serves 4)**

4 eggs
4 thin slices smoked salmon
juice of 1 large lemon
approximately 6 tablespoons
    mayonnaise
2 tablespoons double cream
To garnish:
shredded lettuce
sliced lemon

Quick tip:
Poach eggs for 2 minutes instead of boiling.
To serve:
With shredded lettuce around each egg and a slice of lemon.
To freeze:
Do not freeze this dish, although frozen smoked salmon can be used, see page 52. Hard-boiled eggs are one of the foods that cannot be frozen, they become very 'rubbery'.

Place the eggs gently in a pan of boiling water and boil gently for 4–5 minutes. Plunge into a bowl of cold water immediately. When cold, remove shells carefully. Lay slices of smoked salmon on to individual plates, sprinkle with half the lemon juice. Place an egg on the centre of each slice of smoked salmon. Blend the mayonnaise and cream, flavour with remaining lemon juice. Coat each egg neatly with 2 tablespoons mayonnaise mixture. Refrigerate until ready to serve.
To economize:
Use portions of smoked kipper or trout instead of salmon.
To vary:
Eggs Benedict: A simplified version of this classic dish can be made by putting the shelled eggs on to a slice of ham and coating them with mayonnaise. The classic dish is made by coating hot poached eggs or lightly boiled shelled eggs with Hollandaise sauce.
To make enough Hollandaise sauce to coat the eggs: Put 2 egg yolks, ½–1 tablespoon lemon juice or white wine vinegar and seasoning into a basin. Stand over a pan of hot water, whisk sharply until thick and creamy. Gradually beat 1½–2 oz./40–50 g. softened butter into the sauce.
Paprika eggs: Blend ½–1 teaspoon paprika into mayonnaise or Hollandaise sauce, made as above, then spoon over the boiled eggs. Serve on slices of smoked salmon or ham and garnish with strips of canned red pepper.

Stuffed Mushrooms

To make: 10 minutes **To cook:** 10 minutes **(Serves 4–6)**

about 16–18 good-sized mushrooms
2–3 oz./50–75 g. butter
seasoning
3 eggs
2 tablespoons mayonnaise or double
    cream
little grated cheese (optional)
2 teaspoons chopped chives

Quick tip:
Use well drained canned mushrooms
and spoon the egg mixture over the
top of them.

Wash the mushrooms, but do not peel them. Remove the stalks and chop finely. Heat half the butter in a pan, fry the mushrooms until tender, season and keep hot. Melt the remaining butter and fry the stalks for 2–3 minutes. Pour in the beaten and seasoned eggs and scramble lightly. Add the rest of the ingredients when the eggs are nearly set. Spoon the mixture into the mushroom caps. Serve at once.

To vary:
Serve cold. Sprinkle well drained mushrooms with French dressing, page 14. Arrange on a bed of salad, then fill with egg mixture; make this a little more moist as it stiffens as it cools.

To freeze:
Do not freeze the cooked dish, but you can use frozen mushrooms.

Cheese & Tomato Meringues

To make: 10 minutes **To cook:** 15 minutes **(Serves 4)**

4 large tomatoes
1 oz./25 g. butter
4 eggs
seasoning
4 tablespoons grated Parmesan
    cheese
1 tablespoon chopped chives or
    parsley

Quick tip:
Buy ready grated Parmesan.

Make sure the tomatoes stand quite firmly, then cut a slice from the top of each tomato. Scoop out the pulp with a teaspoon, chop this finely and mix with the softened butter, egg yolks and seasoning. Add half the cheese and half the herbs. Pour the mixture back into the tomato cases. If you have a little too much mixture, put the extra into a small dish. Put the tomatoes into an ovenproof dish, cook for 10 minutes towards the top of a moderately hot oven, 400°F./200°C., Gas Mark 6. Whisk the egg whites until stiff, fold in the seasoning and remaining cheese and herbs. Bring the tomatoes out of the oven, top with the meringue, lower the heat to moderate, 350°F./180°C., Gas Mark 4, and cook for a further 5 minutes. Serve at once.

Cheese and tomato meringues

Soups

While there are excellent ready made soups on the market, it is both easy and economical to make some soups at home. This chapter gives interesting and varied recipes.

Take advantage of vegetables in season to produce nutritious soups, which can be made in minutes and try new ideas with fish or meat. Remember too that chilled soups can be delicious.

A blender saves valuable time as when a recipe states 'sieve' the ingredients, you can make a smooth purée in the goblet. It does not, however, remove all traces of skin and pips from tomatoes, etc.

Some soups depend upon stock for flavour; it is easy to make this, simply cover bones with water, add seasoning, herbs and vegetables to flavour (although these are not essential). Simmer gently for several hours. To save fuel make the stock in a covered container in the oven when you are cooking other dishes at a low temperature.

Stock is highly perishable so store in the refrigerator and use as soon as possible, particularly if it contains vegetables. Boil thoroughly when using this.

To freeze: Most soups freeze well but use within the time recommended in the recipe. Freeze stock, as the picture below. Make the stock, strain, cool and pour into freezing trays, as though making ice cubes. When frozen remove the cubes and store in a suitable container. Add as many as required to flavour the soup. Use frozen stock within 3 months.

Vegetable Soups There are so many good soups to be made with vegetables and every month of the year produces a different variety to use. Treat the vegetable soup recipes (pages 30–36) as basic ideas and change the vegetables according to the season.

Remember to taste as you make the soup, and season wisely; add enough well flavoured vegetables (onions, leeks, etc.) for a good definite taste in vegetable soups. Use a *bouquet garni* in many soups; this is a selection of herbs, tied either into a small bunch or in a muslin bag. Remove these before you serve the soup, although they can be sieved or put into the blender (without the muslin bag or string) with the rest of the vegetables if you feel the soup needs the extra interest. Garlic not only adds its own taste but helps to 'bring out' the flavour of onions and other ingredients.

The picture opposite shows one of the best known vegetable soups, the classic French Onion Soup. You will find the recipe on page 30.

If you are in a hurry grate the prepared vegetables so they cook quickly and retain the maximum flavour.

Economical soups: Never waste left-over meat, fish or vegetables, for they can form the basis of interesting soups; the recipes in this section will give you ideas for using these.

French onion so

10 Minute Vegetable Soup

To make: 15 minutes   **To cook:** 10 minutes   (Serves 4–6)

1 lb./500 g. mixed vegetables
1¼ pints/7½ dl. chicken stock or
    water and 1–2 chicken stock
    cubes
bouquet garni
seasoning
1 tablespoon chopped parsley

Quick tip:
Use the blender (see method) or use
frozen mixed vegetables.
To economize:
Choose vegetables in season.

Peel the vegetables. Either grate, put through a shredder or drop into the blender goblet (use a small quantity of the liquid, and follow the manufacturer's instructions to give tiny pieces of vegetable). Meanwhile bring the stock or water to the boil. Add the vegetables, stock cubes, if using these, *bouquet garni* and seasoning. Cook quickly for 6–7 minutes or until the vegetables are tender. Remove the *bouquet garni*. Top with parsley and serve very hot.
To vary:
Purée the soup, cook as above and sieve or put into a blender. There is no need to make the vegetables into such small pieces if puréeing.
To freeze:
The soup freezes well. Use within 3 months.

Creamed Vegetable Soup

To make: 20 minutes   **To cook:** 15–20 minutes   **Serves 4–6**

1 lb./500 g. vegetables*
2 oz./50 g. butter or margarine
1 pint/6 dl. chicken stock or water
    and 1 chicken stock cube
bouquet garni
seasoning
1 oz./25 g. flour
generous ½ pint/3 dl. milk
little single cream
1 tablespoon chopped parsley

Quick tip:
Use the blender to make the purée.
To economize:
Use inexpensive vegetables –
carrots, potatoes, turnips.
*If using very starchy vegetables
such as potatoes, and making a purée,
reduce this quantity to just over
8 oz./200 g., otherwise the soup will
be too thick.

Prepare and dice the vegetables; if you do not want to make a purée, follow the directions for grating in the recipe above. Toss the vegetables in half the butter or margarine then add the stock or water and stock cube, and *bouquet garni*. Season lightly and simmer for about 15 minutes. When the vegetables are tender, sieve or put into the blender. Remove the *bouquet garni* or sieve or emulsify with the vegetables. Meanwhile make a white sauce with the rest of the butter or margarine, flour and milk, see page 55. Mix the vegetables and liquid, or the vegetable purée, with the hot sauce and reheat; add extra seasoning if desired and the cream. Top with parsley and serve hot.
To freeze:
This soup can separate out during freezing. It is better to freeze the vegetable mixture and complete the soup before serving.

French Onion Soup

To make: 15 minutes   **To cook:** 35–40 minutes   (Serves 4–6)

3 large onions
2 cloves garlic (optional)
1 oz./25 g. butter
1 tablespoon olive oil
2 pints/1¼ litres beef stock or water
    and 2–3 beef stock cubes
seasoning
4–6 rounds French bread
2 oz./50 g. grated Gruyère or
    Cheddar cheese

Quick tip:
Cook dehydrated onions in canned
beef consommé or in water and
stock cubes. Top with bread and
cheese as the recipe.
To economize:
Never waste good beef bones (or
other bones); simmer to give stock.

Peel the onions and cut into thin slices, then chop these slices so the portions of onion are easy to eat. Peel and crush the garlic, if using this. Heat the butter and oil and toss the onions and garlic in this until a pale golden brown. Add the stock or water and stock cubes and seasoning; for this soup it is important to have a well flavoured stock. Cover the pan and simmer for 25–30 minutes. Meanwhile toast the bread, then top with the cheese. Spoon the soup into a flameproof dish, top with the bread and brown for 1–2 minutes under the grill. Serve hot.
To vary:
When the onions are cooked the soup could be sieved or emulsified in a blender.
To freeze:
This soup is excellent when frozen although some people find the garlic loses its potency, see page 10, so add crushed garlic when reheating if you require a stronger flavour.

Bortsch

1 clove garlic
1 onion
1 tablespoon oil or margarine
4–6 oz./100–150 g. stewing beef
2 pints/1¼ litres cold water
seasoning
1 bay leaf
½–1 tablespoon chopped fresh
    thyme or ½–1 teaspoon dried
    thyme
1 carrot
½ small turnip
¼ cabbage
2 raw medium-sized beetroot
2 tomatoes
few drops vinegar or lemon juice
little soured cream or yoghourt

Quick tip:
Use cooked beetroot, peel, grate
and add to soup with the tomatoes
(see variations)

To vary:
Omit the meat and use beef stock or
water and 1–2 beef stock cubes.
This means the cooking time can be
reduced by 1 hour.

Ten-minute Bortsch: Put
1½ pints/9 dl. beef stock or water
and 2 beef stock cubes into a pan.
Add 2 large grated cooked
beetroot, 1 grated onion, 1 grated
carrot, 1 crushed clove garlic,
seasoning, a little lemon juice or
vinegar, pinch dried thyme and
celery salt. Simmer fairly quickly
for 10 minutes. Serve hot or cold.

Cranberry Bortsch:
Russian cooks make a delicious
soup with cranberries instead of
beetroot. Follow recipe for
Ten-Minute Bortsch.

To freeze:
This freezes well, use within
3 months; add soured cream or
yoghourt when serving the soup.
Use within 2 months, if making and
freezing the quick Bortsch.

To economize:
Make larger quantities of this soup
when beetroot are at their cheapest
and freeze.
You save time and money on fuel
if you cook this soup in a pressure
cooker. Use just over half the amount
of water in the recipe and allow 25
minutes at 15 lb./7 kg. pressure.
Allow pressure to drop at room
temperature.

Peel and chop the garlic and onion. Fry slowly in the oil or margarine until
golden. Remove fat and coarse tissues from beef and cut into ½-inch/1-cm.
cubes. Add the meat to the pan and fry lightly until brown. Add the cold
water, seasoning, bay leaf and thyme, cover and bring to the boil. Reduce
heat and simmer gently for 30 minutes. Meanwhile, slice the carrot, turnip
and cabbage, peel and grate the raw beetroot and add to pan. Return to the
boil and simmer for 1 hour. Skin and chop the tomatoes, add to the pan and
simmer for a further 20 minutes. Flavour the soup with vinegar or lemon
juice.

To serve:
Hot or cold, topped with soured cream or yoghourt.

Bortsch

8 oz./200 g. haricot beans
8 oz./200 g. salted pork belly
1 onion
2 cloves garlic
4 pints/2¼ litres beef stock or water
  and 4 beef stock cubes
2 carrots
2 sticks celery
seasoning
4 oz./100 g. peas, fresh or frozen
4 oz./100 g. green beans
2 tomatoes
¼ cabbage
4 oz./100 g. macaroni
2 tablespoons chopped parsley

To garnish:
2–4 oz./50–100 g. grated
  Parmesan cheese

Quick tip:
Omit the dried haricot beans and
add canned haricot beans or baked
beans in tomato sauce to the soup
towards the end of the cooking
period.

To freeze:
This soup freezes well for a limited
period, after this the pasta tends to
lose its texture. Use within
2 months. If, however, you make
the soup without the macaroni you
can store it for 4 months. Add a
little cooked macaroni when
reheating the soup, or add a little
extra water or stock to the soup
when heating, put in the uncooked
macaroni and continue cooking
until this is tender.

To economize:
Serve generous portions of this
soup as a light main meal with a
generous amount of cheese to
provide the protein. Use up
left-over pieces of cheese instead of
buying Parmesan cheese.

Speedy Minestrone:
Heat ½ pint/3 dl. water in a good-
sized pan, add 1 beef stock cube.
Tip in 12 oz./300 g. frozen
vegetables, cook until nearly
tender. Add the contents of a small
to medium-sized can of both baked
beans and spaghetti in tomato
sauce (chop the spaghetti into
smaller pieces). Heat well, then top
with chopped parsley.
Do not try to freeze this version
of Minestrone soup for the
ingredients would become over-soft
with storage. It also is pointless since
the soup is prepared so quickly.

Soak haricot beans in cold water overnight or for 12 hours. Drain, place in
a clean pan with cold water to cover, put a lid on the pan and simmer for
1½ hours. Drain well.

Remove skin from the pork and cut pork into ½-inch/1-cm. cubes. Place
diced pork in a large heavy-based pan, cover and fry in its own fat until
brown, shaking the pan occasionally. Add the chopped onion and garlic
and fry until soft. Add the stock or water and beef stock cubes, drained
haricot beans, sliced carrots and celery and seasoning; do not add too much
salt. Cover and bring to the boil, reduce heat and simmer the soup for 1½
hours. Add peas, green beans broken into large pieces, skinned and
chopped tomatoes, shredded cabbage and macaroni (long macaroni should
be broken into pieces). Simmer for a further 15–20 minutes or until the
macaroni is tender. More water may be added at this stage if the soup is too
thick. Taste the soup and add more seasoning if necessary. Stir in the
chopped parsley just before serving.

To serve:
Hot, sprinkled with Parmesan cheese.
This is the type of soup that can be served as a light main dish, for it is
very satisfying and the peas, beans and cheese provide an adequate
amount of protein.

To vary:
Use half stock and half tomato juice for a more pronounced tomato flavour
and a very pleasant colour to the soup. The fresh tomatoes could then be
omitted.

Minestrone soup

Tomato Chowder

2–3 rashers fairly fat streaky
  bacon
2–3 medium-sized onions
1¼ pints/7½ dl. water
2–3 medium-sized potatoes
4 large tomatoes
pinch dried basil or ½–1 tablespoon
  chopped fresh basil
seasoning
little double cream
To garnish:
chopped chives

Quick tip:
Use 1–2 tablespoons dehydrated
onions, canned potatoes and
canned tomatoes (use liquid from
can and less water).

Remove the rinds and chop the bacon into small pieces. Heat the rinds to give a little extra fat then remove and fry the bacon and chopped onions for a few minutes. Add the water, bring to the boil, then put in the diced potatoes, skinned and chopped tomatoes, herbs and seasoning. Cook steadily until the vegetables are tender (approximately 12 minutes). Spoon into hot soup cups (this is a very thick soup, almost like a stew) and top with cream and chives.
To serve:
Hot with crisp rolls or toast.
To vary:
Use less potatoes and add cooked or canned sweetcorn.
Fry 1–2 cloves crushed garlic with the bacon and onions.
To freeze:
Although this soup can be frozen, I prefer the texture when it is freshly cooked and served.
To economize:
Use any 'odd' pieces of bacon and buy less perfect shaped tomatoes (which are always slightly cheaper).

Tomato & Onion Soup

2 large onions
1–2 cloves garlic (optional)
2 tablespoons oil or 2 oz./50 g.
  butter or margarine
1 red pepper
1½ pints/9 dl. brown or white stock
  or water
3 large tomatoes
2–4 oz./50–100 g. mushrooms
seasoning
To garnish:
chopped herbs, grated cheese or
  croûtons

Quick tip:
Use canned tomatoes, 2 tablespoons
dehydrated onion and 1 canned
red pepper.

Peel the onions and cut into narrow strips. Peel and crush the garlic cloves, if using. Heat the oil, butter or margarine and toss the onion and garlic in this until nearly transparent; take care the onions do not brown. Discard the core and seeds from the pepper, and cut the flesh into small strips. Blend with the onion but do not fry if you like a firm texture. Add the stock or water, bring steadily to the boil. Skin and chop the tomatoes, slice the mushrooms and add to the pan. Continue cooking until the vegetables are soft, season well.
To serve:
While very hot. Garnish with chopped fresh herbs, grated cheese or croûtons.
To vary:
Use all onions.
Use all mushrooms.
To freeze:
Excellent, use within 3 months.
To economize:
Omit red pepper. Turn this into a light, complete meal by adding any tiny pieces of left-over cooked chicken.

Cucumber Soup

2 small or 1 large cucumber
1 onion
2 oz./50 g. butter
1½ pints/9 dl. stock or water and
  2 chicken stock cubes
seasoning
¼ pint/1½ dl. double cream

Quick tip:
Put the stock and large pieces of
vegetables into the blender, switch
on for a few seconds only, then
continue as the recipe.
To economize:
Use white sauce instead of cream.

Peel and chop nearly all the cucumber. Put a small piece on one side to slice for garnish and retain a small portion of the peel to give colour and additional flavour to the soup; too much peel gives a bitter taste. Peel and chop the onion. Toss the vegetables in the hot butter for a few minutes; take care they do not brown. Add the stock or water and stock cubes, the pieces of cucumber peel and a little seasoning. Simmer for 20 minutes, then emulsify in a blender or sieve. Cool, then blend in the cream.
To serve:
Hot, or chill well.
To vary:
Add a pinch of curry powder to the soup.
Use a little white wine in place of some of the stock.
To freeze:
While this soup can be frozen for 2–3 weeks, it is not the most satisfactory soup for this purpose.

Cold Soups

Many soups are equally good hot or cold, some rather surprinsingly, such as Mulligatawny which is delicious ssrved well chilled. Most cold soups can be topped with soured fresh cream or yoghourt just before serving.

Cucumber Yoghourt Soup

To make: 10 minutes   **No cooking**   (Serves 4–6)

1 small cucumber
½ pint/3 dl. yoghourt
milk or stock (see method)
seasoning

Peel and grate the cucumber, blend with the yoghourt and enough milk or stock to give the consistency of single cream, season well. Chill.
To vary:
Flavour the soup with chopped spring onions or chives, curry powder or a little chopped mint.

Chilled Avocado Soup

To make: 10 minutes   **No cooking**   (Serves 4–6)

2 large or 3 medium-sized ripe
   avocado pears
juice of 1 lemon
15 oz./420 g. can consommé or use
   nearly 1 pint/6 dl. home-made
   beef or chicken stock or water
   and stock cubes
¼ pint/1½ dl. yoghourt
seasoning
To garnish:
chopped chives or spring onions.

Quick tip:
Use the blender as suggested
in the recipe.
To economize:
Often one can buy avocado pears
that are slightly damaged or over-
ripe at a cheaper price; discard
damaged part and use remainder.

Halve the avocado pears, scoop out the flesh and rub through a *nylon* sieve, using a wooden spoon. Blend in the remaining ingredients at once, except the chives or spring onions, and season well.
If preferred, place all the ingredients (but not the chives or onions) in a blender and set at high speed until the mixture is smooth.
To serve:
Chilled, topped with a few chopped chives or chopped spring onions.
To vary:
Flavour with a little curry powder or Tabasco sauce.
To freeze:
This freezes excellently; use within 2–3 months. If the mixture shows signs of separating when it defrosts, whisk sharply.

Orange & Apple Soup

To make: 15 minutes   **To cook:** 5 minutes   (Serves 4)

1 medium-sized onion
¼ pint/1½ dl. chicken stock
½ pint/3 dl. dry cider
½ pint/3 dl. orange juice
little sugar (see method)
seasoning
1 stick cinnamon or pinch ground
   cinnamon
To garnish:
2 dessert apples

Quick tip:
Use 2 teaspoons dehydrated onion
and canned orange juice.
To economize:
Use stock with a little lemon juice
instead of cider.

Chop the onion and heat for 5 minutes in the stock. Cover the pan and leave until the stock is cold then strain the liquid into the cider and orange juice. Add a little sugar and enough seasoning to make an interesting taste. Add the cinnamon and chill until ready to serve. Remove the cinnamon stick.
To serve:
In cold soup cups, topped with finely diced peeled apple. Serve rye bread with the soup.
To freeze:
Although you can freeze the soup it is better freshly made; you can, how-ever, use frozen orange juice, see page 12.

Chilled avocado so

Chilled Asparagus Almond Soup   To make: 10–15 minutes   To cook: 25 minutes   (Serves 6)

approx. 1 lb./500 g. asparagus
seasoning
2½ pints/1½ litres chicken stock or
    water and 2 chicken stock
    cubes
2 oz./50 g. ground almonds

Quick tip:
Use canned asparagus and freshly
blanched and ground almonds for
a good flavour. However, if you
use commercially prepared
almonds, this soup is very quick to
make.

Cook the asparagus in well seasoned water until tender. Reserve some of
the asparagus tips for garnish. Put the remaining asparagus and half the
chicken stock or water and stock cubes in a blender and mix to a purée, or
sieve the asparagus and blend with the stock. Place purée, remaining stock,
ground almonds and seasoning in a large pan. Cover, bring to the boil and
simmer for 1 minute. Strain soup and chill thoroughly.
To serve:
In chilled soup bowls garnished with reserved asparagus tips.
To freeze:
This soup freezes well. Use within 2–3 months.
To economize:
Use cooked leeks in place of asparagus.

Mulligatawny Soup   To make: 25 minutes   To cook: 1½ hours   (Serves 4–6)

2–3 pieces scrag or middle neck of
    lamb
2 pints/1¼ litres water
2 onions
2 carrots
1 small apple
seasoning
1 tablespoon sultanas
1 oz./25 g. fat or dripping
1 oz./25 g. flour
½–1 tablespoon curry powder
1 teaspoon lemon juice

Quick tip:
Use a pressure cooker (see method)
and emulsify in a blender.

Put the meat into a pan with the water, chopped onions and carrots, sliced
apple, seasoning and sultanas. Cover the pan and simmer gently for 1¼
hours. Lift the lamb from the pan and remove the meat from the bones.
Sieve or emulsify the meat and vegetables to give a smooth purée. Heat the
fat or dripping, stir in the flour and curry powder then blend in the purée.
Bring to the boil, stir over a low heat until thickened. Add the lemon juice
and any extra seasoning required.
To serve:
As a hot or cold soup; it is particularly good served cold.
To vary:
Use less stock and a little single cream or milk.
To freeze:
A good soup for freezing. Use within 2 months.
To economize:
Use up the stock after cooking Spring Lamb, page 71, and omit the pieces
of meat.
To serve with Mulligatawny Soup:
If cold top with diced green pepper, (discard core and seeds) finely
chopped spring onions, desiccated coconut or sprigs of raw cauliflower.
The same garnishes can also be used for hot soup, together with crisp
toasted or fried croûtons of bread.

Chilled Fish Cream   To make: 15 minutes   To cook: 15 minutes   (Serves 4–6)

1 small plaice
¾ pint/4½ dl. water
bouquet garni
seasoning
1 small can red salmon
few drops Tabasco sauce
juice of ½–1 lemon
¼ pint/1½ dl. single cream
To garnish:
little chopped parsley or fennel
    leaves

Quick tip:
Use all canned salmon and flavour
the water with anchovy essence.
To economize:
Use inexpensive huss or other
white fish, instead of plaice.

Fillet and skin the fish, or ask the fishmonger to do this for you. Put the
bones and skin into the water with the *bouquet garni* and seasoning and
simmer for 10 minutes, strain and return the fish stock to the pan. Cut the
plaice fillets into very small pieces and simmer in the stock for 5 minutes,
then add the flaked salmon, seasoning, Tabasco sauce and the lemon juice.
To serve:
Very cold. Whisk in the cream just before serving and top with the parsley
or fennel.
To vary:
Use prepared prawns or other shelled fish instead of the salmon.
Add a very little curry powder to the other ingredients.
Sieve or emulsify the soup with the cream before adding the garnish.
Add tiny matchsticks of cucumber and red pepper just before serving.
Heat the soup, then whisk in the cream just before serving.
To freeze:
The soup is better freshly prepared, but frozen fish can be used.

Frosted Tomato Soup

To make: 10 minutes   **To cook:** 5 minutes   **(Serves 4)**

½ pint/3 dl. chicken stock or
    water and ½ chicken stock cube
1 lb./500 g. tomatoes, skinned
1 teaspoon Worcestershire sauce
2 teaspoons sherry
seasoning
To garnish:
soured cream, chopped chives,
    chopped parsley

Heat the stock or water and stock cube, put in the tomatoes and heat for 1–2 minutes only. Sieve or emulsify; if you want a very smooth mixture you must sieve to get rid of all the pips. Add the Worcestershire sauce, sherry and seasoning. Cool, pour into a freezing tray and frost very lightly.
To serve:
In chilled soup cups, topped with soured cream and the herbs.
To vary:
Use a generous 1 pint/6 dl. tomato juice and omit stock and tomatoes.

Watercress Soup

To make: 20 minutes   **To cook:** 20 minutes   **(Serves 4)**

4 oz./100 g. sprigged watercress
1 tablespoon oil
1 pint/6 dl. chicken stock or water
    and 1 chicken stock cube
½ oz./15 g. cornflour
¼ pint/1½ dl. milk
seasoning
3 tablespoons cream (double or
    single)

Quick tip:
Fry watercress as method, add
canned cream of chicken soup and
dilute with milk. Heat or chill, add
cream to taste.
To economize:
Omit cream and use extra milk.

Wash the watercress, reserving some small sprigs to garnish the soup, and chop the remaining leaves coarsely. Fry slowly for 2–3 minutes in the hot oil. Add the stock or water and stock cube, bring to boiling point, stirring, then simmer for about 15 minutes. Do not overcook as the flavour of the watercress will be lost. Rub through a sieve or emulsify in a blender and return to the pan. Mix the cornflour smoothly with the milk, add to the purée and cook for 3 minutes, stirring well until thick. Add seasoning. Just before serving stir in the cream and garnish with sprigs of watercress.
To vary:
This soup is very good made with ham stock.
Chilled watercress soup: Use only ¾ pint/4½ dl. chicken stock or water and 1 chicken stock cube. Cook and sieve as the recipe above then chill. Blend with ½ pint/3 dl. single cream, a little lemon juice and seasoning. Garnish with sprigs of watercress and serve as cold as possible.
To freeze:
Make the watercress purée, freeze this and use within 3–4 months. Add the cornflour mixture or cream after defrosting.

Chilled asparagus almond soup

Fish Soups

No soup is more neglected in this country than the fish soup, but these are extremely popular in many Continental countries and many are made with inexpensive fish.

A fish soup is an ideal dish for the elderly or someone who is ill, for you have a meal in a soup bowl which is easy to eat and digest.

The recipes that follow are basic ones that you can adapt by adding additional flavourings, such as a pinch of saffron, a few drops of Tabasco sauce, or anchovy essence.

Shrimp chowder

Shrimp Chowder

To make: 20 minutes   **To cook:** 30 minutes   **(Serves 4)**

1 large onion
½ oz./15 g. butter
¼ pint/1½ dl. boiling water
3 medium-sized potatoes
seasoning
1 pint/6 dl. shrimps
1 pint/6 dl. milk
1–2 oz./25–50 g. grated cheese
1 tablespoon chopped parsley

Quick tip:
Use 4–6 oz./100–150 g. ready peeled shrimps, or small prawns.

Peel, slice and fry the onion in the butter for 5 minutes, until soft but not coloured. Add the boiling water, diced potatoes and seasoning. Cover and simmer gently for 15–20 minutes, or until the potatoes are just cooked. Add the peeled shrimps and the milk and reheat. Stir in the grated cheese and parsley.
To serve:
Hot with crusty bread or toast.
To freeze:
Do not freeze this dish, although frozen shrimps could be used.
To economize:
Cook diced skinned white fish with the potatoes, then add a small quantity of shrimps or prawns.

Spiced Fish Soup

To make: 15 minutes **To cook:** 25 minutes **(Serves 4–6)**

8–10 oz./200–250 g. white or
　　smoked fish
1 onion
2 oz./50 g. butter or margarine
1 tablespoon flour
good pinch ground cinnamon
good pinch curry powder
1¼ pints/7½ dl. water
1 teaspoon Worcestershire sauce
2 tomatoes
seasoning
1–2 slices toast

Quick tip:
Use dehydrated onion.

Cut the fish into small pieces, peel and chop the onion. Heat the butter or margarine and turn the fish and onion in this until golden coloured. Stir in the flour, with the cinnamon and curry powder, then blend in the water. Bring to the boil and stir until the flour is well blended. Add the Worcestershire sauce, skinned and chopped tomatoes and seasoning. Simmer for 10 minutes. Cut the toast into small croûtons.
To serve:
Top the soup with the toast just before serving.
To vary:
Add diced celery and pepper (discard core and seeds) with the tomatoes.
To freeze:
This soup freezes well. Use within 1 month.
To economize:
Choose the least expensive fish.

Salmon Bisque

To make: 15 minutes **To cook:** 20 minutes **(Serves 4–6)**

1 lemon
1 onion
1½ pints/9 dl. milk
2 oz./50 g. butter or margarine
2 oz./50 g. flour
8 oz./200 g. cooked or canned
　　salmon
seasoning
3–4 tablespoons single cream

To garnish:
little cucumber
Quick tip:
Use a little dehydrated onion and
canned salmon.

Peel away some of the rind from the lemon; do not use any of the bitter white pith, just the yellow 'zest'. Peel the onion and halve. Put the lemon rind and onion into the milk, bring the milk to boiling point, then strain. Heat the butter or margarine, stir in the flour, then gradually blend in the strained milk. Stir over a moderate heat until thickened, add the flaked salmon, seasoning and cream. Heat gently, but do not boil. Add a very little juice from the lemon and season to taste.
To serve:
Pour into hot soup cups and top with matchstick pieces of cucumber.
To vary:
Use any other fish in place of salmon.
To freeze:
This is not a good soup to freeze, but is an ideal way of using frozen salmon.
To economize:
Use canned pink salmon.

Smoked Haddock Broth

To make: 15 minutes **To cook:** 25 minutes **(Serves 4–6)**

1 small smoked haddock
1–2 onions
1 pint/6 dl. milk
½ pint/3 dl. water
pepper
1 tablespoon long-grain rice
1–2 eggs
To garnish:
1 tablespoon chopped parsley

Quick tip:
Use fillets of smoked haddock
which are quicker to flake, and
dehydrated onion.
To economize:
Use cheaper white fish (see To
vary) and add salt to the milk.

Remove the fins and tail from the fish. Cut the haddock into 2 or 4 portions. Peel and chop the onion(s). Put the fish and onion(s) into the milk and water with pepper to taste. Poach for about 10 minutes, or until the fish is cooked. Remove from the liquid and flake the fish finely. Meanwhile add the rice and simmer until soft. Hard-boil, shell and chop the egg(s). Add the fish and egg(s) to the soup and heat for 2–3 minutes only.
To serve:
Top with parsley.
To vary:
Use white fish instead of smoked haddock and add a pinch of saffron powder to the liquid.
Stir a little cream into the soup before serving.
To freeze:
This freezes moderately well. I would only freeze to prevent any soup being wasted. Use within 3–4 weeks.

Garnishes for Soups

Soups look more interesting garnished with chopped herbs or tiny fried or toasted diced bread (known as croûtons). Yoghourt, cream or chopped nuts are nourishing toppings.

Meat Soups

The stock from cooking meat is particularly good to give a definite flavour to a soup, but in addition there are many soups based upon meat. Some of the most practical ones are given on these two pages.

The recipes can also be adapted to use other meats, for example the recipe for Turkey Purée Soup could be followed with beef, lamb or veal bones, or a game carcass, using any meat on the bone. The Chicken Consommé with Meat Dumplings is equally as good with beef, using beef bones instead of a chicken carcass.

Oxtail Soup:

A recipe for cooking oxtail is given on page 81. Generally there is quite an amount of liquid left over in this recipe as one must cover the pieces of oxtail to prevent them from drying. I put this, plus any vegetables left, into the blender or through a sieve to give a thick soup. If, however, you want to make a thinner soup, follow the recipe for cooking oxtail on page 81, but use only half the amount of meat and vegetables then sieve or emulsify.

Kidney and bacon soup

Kidney & Bacon Soup

8 oz./200 g. ox kidney
2 onions
2 rashers streaky bacon
1 oz./25 g. fat or beef dripping
1¼ pints/7½ dl. beef stock or water
    and 1–2 beef stock cubes
seasoning
1 level tablespoon flour
1 carrot (optional)

Quick tip:
Use canned kidneys. Chop and
simmer in stock with onion to
flavour.

To economize:
Use bacon or ham pieces.

Cut the kidney and peeled onions into very small pieces. Remove the bacon
rinds and chop the rinds and bacon. Fry the bacon with the bacon rinds
until the bacon is cooked. Lift out of the pan but continue frying the rinds
until they are crisp (like potato crisps). Remove these and put with the
bacon. Heat the fat or dripping and toss the kidney and onions in this for
5 minutes. Add most of the stock, or water and stock cubes, with seasoning.
Cover the pan and simmer gently for 1 hour. Blend the flour with the
remaining stock, stir into the soup and cook until slightly thickened. Peel
and grate the carrot, add to the soup and cook for 5 minutes (this could be
omitted).

To serve:
Topped with the bacon and bacon rinds.

To freeze:
This freezes well, use within 6 weeks.

Chicken Consommé with Herb Dumplings

1 chicken carcass
water
bouquet garni
seasoning
1–2 chicken stock cubes (see
    method)
about 8 oz./200 g. mixed
    vegetables
For the dumplings:
2 oz./50 g. self-raising flour (or
    plain flour with ½ teaspoon
    baking powder)
pinch salt
1 oz./25 g. shredded suet
¼–½ tablespoon chopped chives
¼–½ tablespoon chopped parsley
water to mix
2 tomatoes
1–2 tablespoons chopped parsley

Quick tip:
Use water and stock cubes with
frozen vegetables.

Put the chicken carcass into a large saucepan with water to cover. Add the
bouquet garni and seasoning; stock cubes can be added for extra flavour
later. Simmer steadily for 2 hours then strain the liquid. Return this to the
pan (any tiny pieces of chicken could be removed from the bones and
added with the tomatoes). Prepare and dice the vegetables. add to the stock
and bring to the boil. Sieve the flour or flour and baking powder with the
salt. Add the suet and herbs and bind with water to a soft rolling consistency. Roll into tiny balls (the size of a hazel nut) with floured fingers and
drop into the boiling liquid. Cook for 10 minutes then add the skinned,
finely chopped tomatoes and parsley and heat for a further 5 minutes.
Serve hot.

To vary:
Beef bones or other poultry could be used.

To freeze:
This soup, plus the dumplings, freezes well. Use within 2 months.

To economize:
This is an excellent way of using the bones of chicken which are so often
wasted.

Turkey Purée Soup

1 turkey carcass
water
seasoning
vegetables to taste, e.g. onions,
    carrots, turnips
double or single cream

Quick tip:
Use a pressure cooker (see method).

To economize:
This is a very good way to make
sure none of the turkey is wasted.

Put the turkey carcass into a large pan with water to cover, seasoning and
vegetables. Simmer the liquid for 2–3 hours then lift the bones from the
liquid. Cool sufficiently to handle, then take all the tiny pieces of meat from
the bones. Sieve the meat or emulsify with some of the stock, adding the
cooked vegetables as well. To save cooking time use a pressure cooker at
15 lb./7 kg. pressure for about 1 hour, see page 11. Put the turkey purée
into a pan and dilute with enough stock to make the consistency of single
cream. Any stock left over can be used in cooking, or see Chicken Consommé above. Heat with any extra seasoning required.

To serve:
Top each portion with a little cream.

To freeze:
An excellent soup for freezing. Use within 2–3 months.

Fish

We are very fortunate in having a wide choice of fish and most of this can be cooked in a variety of ways, as the following pages show.

The basic methods of cooking are all given in this section together with newer ideas to give a pleasant change to fish cookery.

As fish has a delicate taste you can make the dish more interesting by the wise use of herbs and sauces. Some of the best herbs to use with fish are fennel, dill and tarragon as well as the better known parsley.

Whatever method you select there is one golden rule—*never* over-cook fish, as it loses its moist texture and much of its flavour.

Check carefully when you buy fish to make sure it is really fresh. It should smell pleasant, with no trace of the odour of ammonia, the scales and eyes should be bright, and the fish feel firm.

Avoid buying fish, particularly herrings and plaice, when the fishmonger tells you they are not in season, for this means they tend to be very 'watery' and have large roes, so there is a very little flesh to cook. Check the weight of crab and lobster by the size of the fish. If they feel surprisingly light they are 'watery' and poor value.

Economical fish dishes: There are a number of inexpensive dishes in this section, but one way to save money is to choose fish that is plentiful and cheaper. Buy frozen fish when fresh fish is expensive due to bad fishing conditions.

There is also a good range of frozen fish available today; store this as directed on the packet. You will find that most frozen fish does not need defrosting and can be cooked from the frozen state. Hints on freezing fish dishes are given under the recipes, and on page 48.

To fry fish One of the best and most popular ways to cook fish is by frying it. The coating of flour or flour plus beaten egg and crumbs or batter keeps the fish flesh moist, while allowing the outside to become crisp and brown. The method of coating with batter is on page 44, and this is particularly suitable for deep frying.

To coat fish with egg and crumbs Dry the fish, then coat in a little seasoned flour. Beat an egg with a little water, then brush this over the fish. Coat in fine breadcrumbs. The easiest and tidiest way to coat the fish is either to put the crumbs on a sheet of greaseproof paper and lay the fish on this, pressing the crumbs firmly against both sides of the fish with a broad-bladed knife, or to put the crumbs into a large bag, drop the fish into the bag and shake vigorously until the fish is coated.

The only drawback about using a bag for coating fish is that you tend to spoil the shape of rather large fillets, so I would reserve this method for smaller pieces of fish or fairly substantial cutlets or portions which will retain their original appearance.

Secrets of good shallow frying Heat a little oil or knob of fat in a large frying pan. Make sure this is hot then put in the coated fish. Fry quickly until crisp and brown, turn and fry quickly on the second side. Thin fillets of fish take only about 4 minutes, so would be cooked at the end of this time. Thicker fish cutlets or whole fish need about 8 minutes, so lower the heat and complete cooking more slowly. Drain on absorbent kitchen paper and serve with lemon, tartare sauce, page 55, and fried potatoes, page 104.

Frying f

Fish and bacon whirls

To Coat Fish in Batter

If you prefer to deep fry fish, you may coat in egg and crumbs, as page 42, or in batter.

To coat 4–6 portions of fish

Sieve 4 oz./100 g. plain or self-raising flour with a pinch of salt. Beat in 1 egg and ¼ pint/1½ dl. milk, to give a fairly thick batter. This is ideal for solid portions of fish, see opposite, but to coat fillets of fish or scampi, add 3–4 tablespoons extra milk or water to give a more delicate coating.
Coat the fish in seasoned flour, then batter.

Secrets of Deep Frying

Half-fill the pan with oil or fat, with the frying basket in position. Heat the oil or fat carefully, then test with a cube of day-old bread. It should turn golden in under 1 minute.

Lower the coated fish into the basket and fry steadily. Allow about 3 minutes for fillets or scampi, 6–7 minutes for thicker portions.

Lift out the basket slowly, so the oil or fat drains back into the pan. Drain the fish on absorbent paper and serve as shallow fried fish, page 42.

Fish to Fry

Most fish can be fried, either in shallow or in deep fat. Here are some of the best fish to fry and methods of coating.

White fish

Cod, hake, turbot, plaice, sole: Coat in egg and crumbs or batter and shallow or deep fry as pages 42 or 44. The more luxurious sole is also delicious cooked as Fish Meunière, below.

Oily fish

Herrings: Coat in seasoned flour or seasoned oatmeal and shallow fry. Trout can be cooked as Fish Meunière, opposite.

Shell fish	Large prawns, known as scampi, can be coated in seasoned flour, then egg and crumbs or a thin coating of batter. While they can be shallow fried, they are nicer cooked in deep oil or fat, see above. Oysters, mussels or scampi can be prepared and fried in the same way. Do not over-cook shellfish.
Fish cakes	Mix equal quantities of mashed potatoes and flaked cooked fish, season and flavour with chopped parsley. Add egg to bind and form into round cakes. Coat in seasoned flour, egg and crumbs and shallow fry as page 42.

Fish & Bacon Whirls

To make: 10 minutes   **To cook:** 10 minutes   (Serves 4)

4 portions white fish
1 tablespoon flour
seasoning
1 egg
2 oz./50 g. crisp breadcrumbs
4 rashers long streaky bacon
4 tomatoes
To fry:
little oil or fat

Quick tip:
Buy ready-coated portions of fish
and fry from the frozen state.
To economize:
Use the most inexpensive fish,
such as coley.

Dry the fish and coat in the flour, mixed with the seasoning, then in beaten egg and crumbs. Fry in hot oil or fat until nearly cooked (approximately 4–5 minutes for fillets of plaice and 6–7 minutes for thicker pieces of cod or fresh haddock). Remove from the pan on to a plate. Cut off the rind of the bacon, cut each rasher in half lengthways and twist round the portions of fish. Secure with wooden cocktail sticks. if necessary. Return the fish to the pan with halved seasoned tomatoes and cook for a further 2–3 minutes, turning once, so the bacon becomes crisp.
To serve:
Hot with a green vegetable or salad.
To vary:
Use whole small herrings. Remove heads and backbones, as directions on page 46. Coat in seasoned flour, but omit the egg and crumbs. Fry as above or grill if preferred.
To freeze:
Although you can use frozen fish, it is better to prepare and freeze, rather than cook and freeze, as this dish is better served immediately after cooking.

Fish Meunière ✗

To make: 10 minutes   **To cook:** 6–12 minutes   (Serves 4)

seasoning
4 portions white fish (sole, turbot,
    etc.), or fresh trout, scampi or
    scallops
3–4 oz./75–100 g. butter
½–1 tablespoon lemon juice
½–1 tablespoon chopped parsley
1–2 teaspoons capers

To economize:
Use vinegar instead of lemon juice.

Season the fish. Fry in the hot butter until cooked, then remove from the pan and keep hot. Heat butter remaining in pan until golden, add lemon juice, parsley and capers and heat for 1–2 minutes.
To serve:
Spoon the butter mixture over the fish.
To vary:
Fish in Riesling cream: Fry the fish as above, allow the butter to turn golden, then add ¼ pint/1½ dl. Riesling and ¼ pint/1½ dl. single cream, heat *without boiling*, add parsley and capers and serve.
To freeze:
Do not freeze the cooked dish, but frozen fish can be used. Cook without defrosting it first.

Trout with Almonds

To make: 10 minutes   **To cook:** 10 minutes   (Serves 4)

4 large trout
1 tablespoon flour
seasoning
3 oz./75 g. butter
1–2 oz./25–50 g. blanched
    almonds
2 teaspoons lemon juice
To garnish:
watercress

To economize:
Use filleted herrings or mackerel.

If using frozen trout there is no need to defrost these. Mix the flour and seasoning, coat the fish with this and fry in the hot butter until just cooked. Add the almonds during cooking and fry these with the fish. Lift the fish and nuts on to a hot dish. Heat the lemon juice with any butter in the pan, spoon over the fish and serve at once, garnished with watercress.
To vary:
Use fillets of sole or portions of turbot or see 'To economize'.
Substitute small pieces of tomato, lemon and green pepper for the almonds.
To freeze:
Cook lightly, freeze, reheat for a short time. Use within 1 month.

Sole and grapes

To Grill Fish

Many of the fish that can be fried are equally as good when grilled. In addition to the fish listed on page 44 you can grill both kippers and bloaters.

Secrets of grilling fish
Always pre-heat the grill before putting the fish underneath, this makes certain it cooks quickly and does not dry.

Brush the fish with melted butter or oil before and during cooking. It is also advisable to oil the grid of the grill pan before putting on the fish; this prevents the fish sticking.

Season the fish, add a little lemon juice or chopped herbs to the butter or oil, then coat the fish. Cook thin fillets of fish for 4–5 minutes without turning. Turn thicker pieces of fish and lower the heat after both sides are golden coloured.

Plaice with mushrooms and tomatoes
Put halved seasoned tomatoes and mushroom caps on the grid of the grill pan with the fish. Brush with melted butter and cook quickly.

Sole and grapes
Grill whole sole and when nearly cooked add peeled grapes coated with melted butter and heat for 1–2 minutes only. Garnish with parsley and lemon slices.

Moules au Gratin

To make: 15 minutes **To cook:** 12 minutes **(Serves 4)**

4 pints/2¼ litres mussels
   (prepared and cooked as
   page 48)
2½ oz./65 g. butter
1½ oz./40 g. flour
wine from preparing mussels
3–4 tablespoons single cream
4 tablespoons grated cheese
4 tablespoons breadcrumbs
To economize:
Use cider in sauce (see page 48).

Prepare the mussels as method under Moules Americaine (page 48); strain and save the wine. Heat 1½ oz./40 g. butter in a pan, stir in the flour and cook for several minutes, then gradually blend in nearly ¾ pint/4½ dl. of the cooking liquid. Bring the sauce to the boil, stirring well, and cook until thickened over a low heat; add mussels and heat for 2–3 minutes. Remove from the heat and stir in the cream. Spoon into a flameproof dish, top with the cheese and crumbs, dot with the remaining butter and brown under the grill for a few minutes.
To serve:
As soon as cooked, as an hors d'oeuvre or main dish.

Norfolk Herrings

To make: 15 minutes **To cook:** 10 minutes **(Serves 4)**

4 large fresh herrings
3 oz./75 g. butter or margarine
1 tablespoon mustard
1 large onion
seasoning
1 tablespoon chopped parsley
To garnish:
lemon
watercress

Quick tip:
Top canned herrings with the flavoured butter in the recipe, grill for 2–3 minutes.
To economize:
Mix soft breadcrumbs with the filling to make it go further.

Bone the herrings, if the fishmonger has not done this. To bone herrings, split under the stomach, remove the roes and intestines, save the roes and chop finely. Insert the knife into the herrings and cut into the fish towards the centre until they can be opened out flat. Lay the cut side downwards on to a board, run your finger firmly down the centre backbone, then turn over again and lift away the bones. Cream 2 oz./50 g. butter or margarine with the chopped roes, mustard, grated onion, seasoning, and parsley. Spread over the inside of the herrings. Place under a preheated grill and cook for 4–5 minutes. Remove from the grill, fold the herrings over and brush with the remaining 1 oz./25 g. butter, which should be melted and mixed with seasoning. Continue to grill steadily until cooked.
To serve:
With wedges of lemon and watercress. These are also very good when cooked and served cold.
To freeze:
Prepare, but do not cook, wrap and freeze. Use within 6 weeks.

Grilled plaice with mushrooms and tomatoe

To Freeze Fish

Many people are keen fishermen and are therefore able to obtain fairly large quantities of fish. It is well worth freezing any that cannot be cooked at that time. Fish **must** be very fresh to freeze well.

Prepare the fish, cut into convenient-sized portions, separate fillets etc., see page 185. Wrap well. Use white fish within 6 months; oily fish (salmon, herrings etc.) within 4 months and shell fish within 2 months. See page 52 for freezing smoked fish.

Secrets of Poaching Fish

Poaching fish is often described as 'boiling' but this term really is incorrect, as if fish *is* boiled rapidly it is spoiled in both texture and flavour. The liquid should simmer gently. Fish can be poached just in seasoned water; in water flavoured with lemon juice with a sliced carrot and sliced onion; in white wine or dry cider; in fish stock (this is made by simmering fish skin and bones in seasoned water); or in a court bouillon. To make this mix equal quantities of wine and water, add a bay leaf and any other herbs you like (e.g. fennel, lemon thyme) and a carrot and onion. The fish can be placed into cold liquid to cover; this is then brought to simmering point. If using this method shorten the times given below by 2–3 minutes in each case. If preferred, bring the liquid to simmering point, add the fish and time as follows:

Allow 7 minutes per lb./500 g. for fillets of fish or thin steaks or 10 minutes per lb./500 g. for whole fish or large portions.

If cooking small portions to serve cold, follow the method for poaching salmon steaks below.

To Poach Salmon Steaks

Large pieces of salmon or the whole fish should be cooked as above, allowing 10 minutes per lb./500 g., but making quite certain there is only an occasional bubble on the surface of the water.

Small slices (often called steaks or cutlets) of salmon can be cooked in the same way, but I find a better method is as follows:

Make a large square of greaseproof paper for each portion of fish or use a polythene cooking bag. Butter the paper or bag well. Lay the fish on this, season and flavour with lemon juice, seasoning and a little butter or oil. Wrap the 'parcel', tie with fine string or seal the bag. Put into cold water, bring this to boiling point slowly. Remove from the heat when the water comes to the boil, cover well, leave fish in the water until cold.

If serving hot follow timing under poaching.

Moules Americaine

To make: 30 minutes To cook: 20 minutes (Serves 4–6)

4 pints/2¼ litres mussels
½ pint/3 dl. white wine
¼ pint/1½ dl. water
seasoning
bunch parsley
1 lb./500 g. tomatoes
little chopped parsley
little chopped basil

Quick tip:
Heat bottled mussels in wine and tomato mixture.
To economize:
Use cider in place of wine.

Scrub the mussels thoroughly, discard any that do not close when tapped sharply; this is very important, as it could mean that the fish has been dead for some time. Put into a large heavy pan with the wine, water, seasoning and bunch of parsley. Cook over a medium heat for 6–8 minutes until the shells are open; discard any that remain closed. Cool slightly so you can handle the fish, remove the mussels from the shells. Meanwhile slice the tomatoes (skin if wished) and add to the liquid in the pan. Simmer for about 10 minutes, remove the bunch of parsley and add the chopped herbs and a little more seasoning. Put the mussels into the liquid and heat for 1 minute only.
To serve:
With green salad and French bread. A good hors d'oeuvre or main dish.
To freeze:
Freeze for 2–3 weeks only; heat gently to serve.

Coquilles St. Jacques

Coquille St Jacques

To make: 15 minutes   **To cook:** 25–30 minutes   **(Serves 3–6)**

6 large scallops in their shells
¾ pint/4½ dl. milk plus a little extra
  (see method)
seasoning
1 lb./500 g. peeled potatoes
3 oz./75 g. butter
little single cream or milk
  (see method)
2 oz./50 g. flour
To garnish:
lemon
parsley

Quick tip:
Use condensed cream of mushroom
soup instead of making the sauce.
To economize:
Use diced white fish with fewer
scallops.

Remove the scallops from their shells and add the small amount of liquid from the shells to the milk. Wash the shells and put on one side. Either leave the scallops whole or cut into several pieces. Put into the pan with the milk and a little seasoning. Simmer steadily for just 10 minutes, no longer. Meanwhile cook the potatoes in boiling salted water, strain, then mash with 1 oz./25 g. butter and a very little cream or milk. Melt the remaining butter in a pan, stir in the flour, cook gently for 2–3 minutes, then blend in the strained liquid from cooking the scallops. Bring the sauce to the boil, stir over a low heat until thickened; add a little more milk if necessary. Put the potatoes into a piping bag with a ½ inch/1 cm. rose pipe, and pipe a border round the edge of the scallop shells, brown for a few minutes under a hot grill. Add the scallops to the sauce, heat for 2–3 minutes only, then spoon into shells. Garnish with lemon and parsley.

To serve:
Hot as an hors d'oeuvre or a main course; serve two scallops for a main dish.

To vary:
Coquilles St. Jacques Mornay: make the recipe as above, heat the scallops in the sauce, then add 2 oz./50 g. finely grated cheese and 2 oz./50 g. sliced fried mushrooms, heat gently, then put into the shells as above. This recipe is shown in the picture above.

Scallops and Bacon: wrap each well seasoned scallop in bacon, secure with wooden cocktail sticks and grill steadily.

Scallop Fritters: make the coating batter on page 44, using only the ¼ pint/1½ dl. milk. Coat about 8 medium-sized scallops in the batter and deep fry for 5–6 minutes. Serve with tartare sauce, page 55.

To freeze:
The basic recipe and variation with cheese freeze well; use within 1 month.

Secrets of Baking Fish

Remember when baking fish that it must not be spoiled by over-cooking, so that ingredients added, e.g. onions, must be grated or thinly sliced, so they do not prolong the cooking time.

To prepare

The simplest way to bake fish is to put it into a buttered dish, season and flavour it with lemon juice and top with melted butter and/or milk. For a golden top leave the dish uncovered, for a moist topping, cover the dish. Allow a few minutes longer cooking time when covering the dish. Cook for 12–20 minutes (depending upon the thickness of the fish) for fillets and place the dish just above the centre of a moderately hot oven, 400°F./200°C., Gas Mark 6. Thicker steaks need up to 20–25 minutes, and whole fish about 12 minutes per lb./500 g. in the centre of the oven; when you add a number of other ingredients, the temperature and cooking time will need to be adjusted.

Fish Pie

To make: 30 minutes **To cook:** 50 minutes **(Serves 4–6)**

1 lb./500 g. peeled potatoes
seasoning
1½ lb./750 g. white fish
¾ pint/4½ dl. white sauce
   (page 54)
1 oz./25 g. butter
little milk (see method)

Quick tip:
Use condensed cream of mushroom or other suitable soup instead of making the sauce. Keep all the ingredients hot and brown under the grill instead of in the oven.

To economize:
Use some fish stock in the sauce and the least expensive fish. Use more potatoes for topping.

Cook the potatoes in salted water and poach the fish in seasoned water, as page 48. Strain the fish, blend with the sauce. Put into an ovenproof dish. Strain and mash the potatoes with butter and a little milk. Spread thinly over the fish mixture and bake in the centre of a moderate oven, 375°F./190°C., Gas Mark 5, for 25–30 minutes.

To serve:
With baked tomatoes and other vegetables.

To vary:
The above is a very basic recipe that can be varied in many ways:
Cheese Fish Pie: Add grated cheese to the sauce and mashed potatoes. Add sliced fried mushrooms, parsley, sliced hard-boiled eggs to the sauce, or mix with diced cooked vegetables.
American Fish Pie: Fry chopped bacon and sliced tomatoes, put at the bottom of the dish, top with the fish and sauce and potatoes and heat as above.

To freeze:
A fish pie freezes well, except when hard-boiled eggs are added to the sauce. Use within 1 month, heat very gently from the frozen state or thaw out and then heat.

Psari Plaki

To make: 20–25 minutes **To cook:** 1¼ hours **(Serves 4)**

4 herrings
seasoning
juice of ½ a lemon
2 onions
1 lb./500 g. potatoes
2 carrots
2 sticks celery
8 oz./200 g. tomatoes
2–3 tablespoons olive oil
To garnish:
1 tablespoon chopped parsley

Quick tip:
Use canned fish and vegetables. Drain the latter, slice, season well and put into the casserole with the fish. Top with 2 teaspoons oil, cover and heat for 30 minutes.

This is an interesting way to make a main meal of oily fish. Prepare the fish, i.e. remove the backbones and cut into two fillets, see page 46. Place in a greased ovenproof dish, sprinkle with seasoning and the lemon juice. Prepare and slice the vegetables, toss in the hot oil separately in the following order, onions, potatoes, carrots, celery and tomatoes. Arrange the vegetables around the fish. Cover with greased foil and bake in the centre of a moderate oven, 350–375°F./180–190°C., Gas Mark 4–5, for 1 hour.

To serve:
Hot, sprinkled with parsley, with a green vegetable.

To vary:
Use mackerel, mullet or trout instead of herrings.

To freeze:
Cook as the recipe, but do *not* over-cook. Cool, cover and freeze. Use within 2–3 weeks. Thaw out, then reheat.

To economize:
Choose herrings, as the basic recipe, for these are one of the cheapest fish.

Psari pla

Pickled & Smoked Fish

While one can buy pickled herrings it is very easy to prepare your own pickled fish. White fish is excellent cooked in this way, see below.

There are home smoking outfits available now so if you are a keen fisherman and obtain large stocks of mackerel, herrings or salmon you could smoke this yourself, otherwise it means buying the fish ready-smoked. This method of preparing the various fish means they keep rather longer than fresh fish, but do not store for more than a few days except in the freezer. Smoked salmon and other smoked fish keep in good condition in the freezer for up to 6 weeks; separate the slices or portions with waxed paper. Smoked kippers or haddock should be packed in polythene cooking bags, with a knob of butter, and they can be cooked from the frozen state in the bag, so retaining their flavour.

Pickled Fish

To make: 15 minutes   **To cook:** 1 hour   (Serves 4–6)

4–6 portions white fish, or
   herrings, mackerel, etc.
2 onions
1–2 bay leaves
1 teaspoon pickling spice
seasoning
about $\frac{1}{2}$ pint/3 dl. vinegar
water (see method)
To garnish:
salad

Quick tip:
Cook for 20 minutes in a covered saucepan.
To economize:
Use cheaper fish, for the pickling improves the flavour of this.

Place the fish in a dish, add the sliced onions and the rest of the ingredients, except the salad. If the vinegar does not cover the fish, add more or dilute with a little water. Cover the dish and bake for 1 hour in the centre of a cool oven, 300°F./150°C., Gas Mark 2.
To serve:
Hot or cold with salad; allow to cool in the liquid. Strain the vinegar and use in a dressing for the salad.
To vary:
Pickled Herrings: Follow the recipe above, but add a peeled sliced apple, $\frac{1}{2}$–1 teaspoon mixed spice and $\frac{1}{2}$–1 teaspoon sugar to the vinegar liquid. Bone each herring, as page 46, cut into two fillets, then roll each fillet from the head to the tail. Some of the sliced onion can be spread over each fillet before rolling. Cook as above.
To freeze:
Although pickled fish can be frozen, some of the flavour tends to be lost. Use within 2–3 weeks.

Kedgeree

To make: 20 minutes   **To cook:** 30 minutes   (Serves 4)

1 medium-sized smoked haddock
   or 1 lb./500 g. haddock fillet
water
seasoning
2–3 oz./50–75 g. long grain rice
2 eggs
2 oz./50 g. butter
little milk or cream (see method)
To garnish:
1–2 tablespoons chopped parsley

Cut the haddock into portions, discard tail and fins from the whole fish. Poach in water with pepper to season for about 10 minutes; do not overcook. Put the rice into another pan with $2\frac{1}{2}$ times its weight in water, i.e. ($5–7\frac{1}{2}$ fl. oz./$1\frac{1}{2}$–$2\frac{1}{4}$ dl.) and a very little salt. Bring the water to the boil, stir briskly, cover the pan and simmer gently for 15 minutes. Meanwhile, hard-boil the eggs and shell. Strain the haddock, flake the fish and discard any bones. Heat the butter in a pan, add the cooked rice (all the liquid should have been absorbed by the end of the cooking time), the fish and enough milk or cream to make a creamy consistency. Heat gently for a few minutes, season well. Chop the egg whites and yolks separately; stir the whites into the fish mixture. Pile on to a hot dish and garnish with the chopped egg yolks and parsley.
To serve:
Hot as a supper or breakfast dish with crisp toast.
To vary:
To make a more savoury dish, top with fried onion rings.
To freeze:
This dish should be eaten when freshly made but frozen fish could be used.

For the flan case:
5 oz./125 g. plain flour
pinch of salt
3 oz./75 g. butter or margarine
1 egg yolk
water to bind
For the filling:
8 oz./200 g. smoked haddock
$\frac{1}{4}$ pint/1$\frac{1}{2}$ dl. water
juice of $\frac{1}{2}$ a lemon
1 oz./25 g. butter
1 small onion
2 oz./50 g. mushrooms
2 eggs
6 tablespoons single cream
4 oz./100 g. cottage cheese
1 tablespoon chopped parsley
seasoning

Quick tip:
Use frozen pastry or packet pastry
mix and canned tuna or salmon in
place of haddock.
To economize:
Use milk in place of cream and an
inexpensive white fish or flaked
cooked herrings or kippers in place
of smoked haddock. Use left-over
dry cheese in place of cottage
cheese; grate this finely.

Sieve the flour and the salt together. Rub the fat into the flour with your
fingertips, until the mixture looks like fine breadcrumbs. Add the egg yolk
and water to bind the dough. Knead lightly for a few seconds to give a firm,
smooth dough. Put in a cool place to 'rest' for 15 minutes. Roll out the pastry
to $\frac{1}{4}$-inch/$\frac{1}{2}$-cm. thick and use to line an 8-inch/20-cm. flan ring, on an
upturned baking tray. Prick the base of the case, line with foil or greaseproof paper and beans or crusts of bread and bake 'blind' in the centre of a
moderately hot oven, 400°F./200°C., Gas Mark 6, for 15 minutes. Remove
foil and continue cooking for a further 5–10 minutes until the pastry is
lightly browned. Cool. Poach the haddock in a pan with the water and half
the lemon juice. Drain, discard the skin and bones and flake the fish. Melt
the butter in a pan, cook the finely chopped onion for a few minutes then
add the chopped mushrooms and continue cooking for 3–4 minutes. Mix
the fish and vegetables and spread over the base of the flan case. Beat the
eggs, add the cream, cheese, remaining lemon juice and parsley. Season
lightly. Pour over the fish mixture. Bake in the centre of a moderate oven,
350–375°F./180–190°C., Gas Mark 4–5, for 30–35 minutes until set and
golden.
To serve:
Hot or cold with a salad or vegetables or by itself.
To freeze:
This freezes excellently. In this case it is better to cook, then freeze the
complete dish. Wrap after freezing. Use within 6 weeks. Reheat gently
from the frozen state.

Smoked haddock and cheese flan

Sauces for Fish

Many fish dishes are improved by the addition of a sauce and this can turn simple poached or grilled fish into unusual and interesting dishes.

White sauce

This is a basic sauce upon which so many other sauces are based. The proportions given here produce a coating sauce, ideal to serve over, or with fish. The version opposite gives a thick sauce, used to bind ingredients together.

To make a coating sauce

Heat 1 oz./25 g. butter or margarine in a pan, stir in either 1 oz./25 g. flour or ½ oz./15 g. cornflour. Cook for several minutes, stirring well. Gradually blend in ½ pint/3 dl. milk, bring to the boil and cook over a medium heat until thickened. Stir as the sauce thickens, and allow it to simmer gently for several minutes. Season to taste.
To freeze:
This sauce or dishes containing this and similar sauces, use cornflour, rather than flour, as it makes a sauce that is less likely to curdle. If the sauce does curdle (separate) slightly, whisk or emulsify in the blender before heating.

Anchovy sauce

Add a few drops of anchovy essence or several finely chopped anchovy fillets to the white sauce.

Béchamel sauce

Warm the milk with a piece of onion, carrot, celery and a bay leaf. Stand for a time then use (after straining) in the white sauce, above.

Cheese sauce

Make the sauce above, then add 2–4 oz./50–100 g. grated cheese; do not cook the sauce again after adding the cheese.

Curry sauce

A creamed curry sauce is delicious with white fish. Make the white sauce, adding ½–1 tablespoon curry powder with the flour. When the sauce has thickened, remove from the heat, whisk in 3–4 tablespoons single or double cream and serve.

A cold curry sauce

To serve with fish salads is made by adding a little curry powder and whipped cream to mayonnaise, page 111.

Fennel sauce

Fennel leaves give a delicious flavour to fish. Chop finely and add 2–3 teaspoons to the white sauce above. Fennel mayonnaise is made by adding the chopped fennel to mayonnaise, see page 111. More sauces are given on page 82.

Fish in a Jacket

To make: 35 minutes   To cook: 45 minutes   (Serves 4–6)

1 lb./500 g. frozen puff pastry or
   puff pastry made with 8 oz./
   200 g. flour, etc. (see page 97)
4 very large or 6 smaller fillets
   white fish
seasoning
For the sauce:
1 oz./25 g. butter
1 oz./25 g. flour
$\frac{1}{4}$ pint/1$\frac{1}{2}$ dl. milk
4 oz./100 g. mushrooms
seasoning
To glaze:
1 egg
1 tablespoon water
To garnish:
lemon
parsley

Quick tip:
Use frozen puff pastry and 4–5
tablespoons well seasoned double
cream in place of white sauce.
To economize:
See To vary

Prepare the pastry and roll out thinly, then cut into 4 or 6 squares, large enough to cover the fish. Lay the fillets flat on a board and season lightly. Make a thick sauce with the butter, flour and milk, see opposite. Add the chopped uncooked mushrooms and season well. Spread over half of each fillet. Fold the other half of the fish over the sauce. Lay on the squares of pastry, moisten the edges, fold over in triangles and seal the edges. Lift on to a baking sheet, brush with a little beaten egg, blended with water. Bake for 10 minutes just above the centre of a very hot oven, 475°F./240°C., Gas Mark 8, then lower the heat to moderate, 350–375°F./180–190°C., Gas Mark 4–5 and bake for a further 20–25 minutes until golden brown and well risen. Garnish with lemon and parsley.
To serve:
Hot or cold with a green salad.
To vary:
If preferred, blend flaked cooked fish with a thick sauce and chopped mushrooms and use as a filling for the pastry.
Fish Pancakes: The filling given in the variation above makes a good filling for pancakes. Make and cook pancakes, as page 169. Cook and flake the fish, mix with the thick sauce and sliced fried mushrooms. Spread over the pancakes, roll and serve. For a more moist dish make an additional pouring sauce, put some in an ovenproof dish, add the filled pancakes, top with sauce and heat in a moderate oven.
To freeze:
It is better to prepare the fish triangles, freeze then wrap. Use within 4–6 weeks. Allow to defrost then cook as recipe. If you cook the triangles and freeze after cooking, heat gently from the frozen state. The fish pancakes freeze well, use within 1 month.

Tartare Sauce

To make: 10 minutes   No cooking   (Serves 4)

$\frac{1}{4}$ pint/1$\frac{1}{2}$ dl. mayonnaise (see
   page 111)
$\frac{1}{2}$–1 tablespoon chopped gherkins
$\frac{1}{2}$–1 tablespoon chopped parsley
1–2 teaspoons capers

Mix all the ingredients together. This sauce is excellent with fried or grilled fish.
To vary:
Add other chopped herbs, including chopped fennel.
To freeze:
Do not freeze as this sauce tends to curdle.

Cod with Green Sauce

To make: 15 minutes   To cook: 15 minutes   (Serves 4)

1 medium-sized onion
2 tablespoons chopped parsley
2 teaspoons capers
2–3 gherkins
$\frac{1}{2}$ small can anchovy fillets
1 tablespoon soft breadcrumbs
1 tablespoon olive oil
juice of 1 lemon
seasoning
4 cutlets white fish (cod or haddock)

Quick tip:
Put all the ingredients for the sauce
into the blender goblet, switch on
for 30 seconds.
To economize:
Omit the anchovies.

Grate the onion and pound in a mortar together with the parsley, capers, chopped gherkins and anchovies. Continue pounding until a smooth paste is achieved, add the breadcrumbs and continue to pound. Pour in the oil and mix well, then add the lemon juice and season with pepper, and salt if necessary. Put the fish into an ovenproof dish, season well and cover each piece of fish with sauce. Cover the dish and bake for approximately 15 minutes just above the centre of a moderately hot oven, 400°F./200°C., Gas Mark 6.
To serve:
With boiled or jacket potatoes.
To vary:
Cod with red sauce: Omit anchovies and parsley and add skinned, chopped tomatoes.
To freeze:
Do not freeze this dish, but you can use frozen fish portions.

Meat

Cooking meat Meat is one of the more important foods in most family budgets, so buy wisely and learn to select the right cut for each cooking method. Store in the refrigerator, or cook soon after purchase. When buying look for the following points:

Beef: bright, moist-looking red lean with some fat, which should be firm and white.
Lamb: firm, pale pink lean, creamy-white fat; mutton is darker in colour with more fat.
Pork: pale pink lean, firm white fat.
Veal: very pale pink lean, very little fat.

Economical meat dishes: There are a number of inexpensive meat dishes in this section, see page 76 onwards.

Stuffings and pastry can play an important part in giving additional interest and flavour to meat dishes and they also help to economize by making meat go further. Do not be too conservative in your choice of stuffings. Recipes are given under various meat and poultry dishes, but these can be adapted in many ways. Use different herbs, add fruits and nuts for new flavours and textures.

Take the recipe on page 83 for a veal (parsley and thyme) stuffing as a basic recipe and enjoy changing this; for example you can add chopped mint in place of parsley as a stuffing with lamb; chives plus sage instead of parsley for a new stuffing with pork and duck; a little grated fresh horseradish or some horseradish cream and rather less parsley to serve with beef. Add chopped cooked apricots or prunes or chopped raw apples or sharp plums to the same basic stuffing; these blend particularly well with rich meats or game. Chopped walnuts, blanched almonds or salted peanuts may also be added for a firm texture.

To freeze: All meats freeze well, provided they are well wrapped, to retain the natural moisture and flavour of the meat. Always cut the meat into convenient-sized portions, or ask the butcher to do this for you, before wrapping. Bulk buying of meat is a sensible method of saving money, but always check that your family will enjoy all the cuts of meat if you buy half a lamb, etc.

Wrap meat thoroughly in thick polythene and/or foil and wrap as tightly as possible to exclude the maximum amount of air and so hasten freezing. Never try to freeze too much meat at one time; check with your manufacturer's instructions as to the maximum quantity recommended.

When freezing chops, steaks, home-made hamburgers, etc. separate these with squares of waxed paper, then wrap the pile all together or put them into a polythene container. In this way the meat does not stick but you can 'peel off' exactly the number of chops, steaks, etc. you desire.

Use uncooked beef, lamb and mutton within 8-9 months; pork within 6 months; veal within 4 months and salted meats within 3 months.

When the meat is cooked the storage times are roughly halved, but this does depend on the method of cooking and other ingredients added; details are given under the various recipes in this book.

To fry meat Choose the same cuts as for grilling, page 65. When frying lean meat (e.g. steak) heat a little fat in the pan; fat meat (e.g. bacon and pork) can be fried in its own fat.

Fry quickly on either side to 'seal-in' the flavour. Time as for grilling, page 65.

56

Crumbed chop

Crumbed Chops

To make: 5 minutes   **To cook:** 12–14 minutes   **(Serves 4)**

4 lamb chops
To coat:
seasoning
pinch dried rosemary
1–2 tablespoons flour
1 egg
2 oz./50 g. soft breadcrumbs
To fry:
2 oz./50 g. butter
2 tablespoons oil
To garnish:
4 oz./100 g. mushrooms
2–4 tomatoes

Quick tip:
Use packet stuffing instead of
making breadcrumbs.
To economize:
Coat with milk and breadcrumbs;
omit the egg.

Cut away the surplus fat from the chops. Mix the seasoning and rosemary with the flour, coat the chops in this, then in the beaten egg and crumbs. Heat the butter with the oil in a large frying pan; the oil prevents the butter over-heating. Fry the chops quickly on either side for 2 minutes until golden. Lower the heat for a further 6–8 minutes then add the mushrooms and halved seasoned tomatoes and cook for a further 2–4 minutes.
To serve:
As soon as cooked with a green salad.
To vary:
Chops Parmesan: Coat the chops with equal quantities of soft or crisp breadcrumbs and grated Parmesan cheese. Fry as above.
Chops in Sweet Sour Sauce: Season the chops, but coat only with the flour. Fry as above, remove from the pan and keep hot. Stir $\frac{1}{4}$ pint/1$\frac{1}{2}$ dl. stock, 1 tablespoon vinegar and 2 tablespoons redcurrant jelly into any butter remaining in the pan. Stir over a low heat until the jelly has melted then spoon over the meat.
To freeze:
Coat then freeze, or use frozen chops. Use within 6–8 months.

Swiss Steaks

To make: 15 minutes   **To cook:** 10–15 minutes   **(Serves 4)**

1 onion
1 oz./25 g. butter or margarine
1–1$\frac{1}{4}$ lb./500–600 g. minced topside
   of beef or best quality stewing
   steak
seasoning
pinch mixed herbs
1 egg
1–2 tablespoons flour
To fry:
2 oz./50 g. fat

Quick tip:
Grate the onion, or use dehydrated
onion.
To economize:
Use the cheaper stewing steak and
cook for a little longer.

Grate or chop the peeled onion finely and toss in the butter or margarine for a few minutes, then mix with the steak, seasoning, herbs and egg yolk. Form into 4 flat cakes, like a thin minute steak. Brush with the lightly beaten egg white, and coat with seasoned flour. Fry in the hot fat for 1–2 minutes on either side until firm and golden coloured. Lower the heat and continue cooking to personal taste.
To serve:
As fried steak with vegetables and/or salad.
To vary:
These steaks are rather like Hamburgers, but the thinner steaks look and taste not unlike ordinary fried steaks.
The Swiss Steaks can be topped with some of the traditional garnishes for fried steak, i.e. a little pâté, tomato purée, asparagus tips.
To freeze:
Prepare, but freeze before cooking. Use within 3 months. Separate each steak with waxed paper. Cook from the frozen state.

Stuffed Lamb Chops

To make: 20 minutes   **To cook:** 15–20 minutes   **(Serves 4)**

4 loin chops
2 rashers bacon
4 oz./100 g. mushrooms
2 oz./50 g. butter or fat
1 tablespoon chopped parsley
$\frac{1}{2}$ teaspoon chopped mint
3 tablespoons soft breadcrumbs
seasoning
1–2 tablespoons flour

To economize:
This is a good way to use up
'oddments' of bacon and to make
a more substantial meal from chops.

Remove the bones from the chops. These can be simmered in a little water to give stock to serve with the chops. Cut the rinds from the bacon and chop the bacon and mushrooms finely. Heat half the butter or fat and toss the bacon and mushrooms in this for several minutes. Add the herbs, breadcrumbs and seasoning. Press the stuffing together with a spoon and then spread against the sides of the chops, where the bones have been removed. Roll as the Noisettes on page 65, tie with fine string or secure with wooden cocktail sticks. Dust both sides of the meat with seasoned flour. Heat the remaining butter or fat and fry the stuffed chops until tender; turn very carefully, so the stuffing does not fall out.
To serve:
Hot with salad or cooked vegetables.
To freeze:
Prepare and freeze, ready to cook later. Use within 3 months.

Deep fried steak en croûte

Deep-fried Steak en Croûte

To make: 1 hour   **To cook:** 6–7 minutes   **(Serves 4)**

seasoning
4 'minute' steaks
1 oz./25 g. butter
4 oz./100 g. pâté (see page 24)
puff pastry made with 8 oz./200 g.
  flour, etc. (see page 97)
1 egg
To fry:
deep oil or fat
To garnish:
watercress

Quick tip:
Use bought pâté and frozen puff
pastry which will be very much
quicker
To economize:
Use rissoles, see page 94, wrap in
pastry and cook as above.

Season the meat and fry for 2–3 minutes in the hot butter, turning once. Lift from the pan, cool then spread with pâté on one side only. Roll out the pastry until only $\frac{1}{8}$-inch/$\frac{1}{4}$-cm. in thickness. Cut into 4 large rounds. Place the meat in the centre of each pastry round. Brush the edges with a little beaten egg and seal VERY FIRMLY. Cut any pastry trimmings into leaves for decoration. Brush the outside of each shape with the rest of the egg. Heat the oil, see page 44. Fry for 4 minutes only, drain on absorbent paper and serve at once garnished with watercress.

To vary:
Steak en croûte: This is a classic dish that can be baked, rather than fried. You can choose thicker steaks for baking. Cook to personal taste, prepare as above, then bake for 20 minutes in a very hot oven, 475°F./240°C., Gas Mark 8, reducing the heat after 10 minutes.

To freeze:
Prepare, freeze, but thaw out before cooking. Use within 6 weeks.

Steak in Pepper Sauce

To make: 8–10 minutes   **To cook:** 10–15 minutes   **(Serves 4)**

seasoning
4 fillet or rump steaks
2–3 oz./50–75 g. butter
1–2 canned red peppers
$\frac{1}{4}$ pint/1$\frac{1}{2}$ dl. single cream
few drops Tabasco sauce
2 teaspoons chopped parsley

Season the meat very well; be especially generous with the pepper. Heat the butter in a large, strong frying pan and cook the steaks on either side to taste. Lift out of the pan and keep warm. Add the diced peppers, cream, Tabasco sauce and parsley to the meat juices remaining in the pan. Stir over a low heat for 2–3 minutes, then spoon over the steaks.

To freeze:
Do not freeze this dish, but frozen steaks could be used.

Piquant veal escalopes

Piquant Veal Escalopes

To make: 10 minutes   **To cook:** 15 minutes   **(Serves 4)**

4 thin slices (escalopes) veal
seasoning
2 tablespoons flour
2 oz./50 g. butter, see method
6 spring onions
1 lemon
1–2 teaspoons chopped rosemary
$\frac{1}{4}$ teaspoon Tabasco sauce
$\frac{1}{4}$ pint/1$\frac{1}{2}$ dl. dry vermouth
To garnish:
1 tablespoon chopped parsley

Quick tip:
Simply season veal, do not coat
with flour.
To economize:
Use thin slices pork, if cheaper than
veal. Use dry cider instead of
vermouth.

Pound the meat until very thin, then cut each escalope in half. Coat with seasoned flour. Heat the butter, put in the meat and fry until golden, turning once. Remove from the pan and keep hot. Chop the spring onions, but keep the white and green parts separate. Add a little more butter to the pan if necessary and fry the white part of the onions until soft. Replace the veal, add the thinly sliced unpeeled lemon, rosemary, Tabasco sauce and vermouth. Simmer for 2–3 minutes. Check the seasoning and sprinkle with the chopped green part of the onions and chopped parsley.
To serve:
With mixed vegetables.
To vary:
Use soured cream in place of vermouth or cider.
Add chopped white fennel and a small amount of chopped fennel leaves to the mixture.
Escalopes Turin-style: Coat the slices of veal with seasoned flour, beaten egg and a mixture of soft breadcrumbs and grated Parmesan cheese. Fry in hot butter as the recipe above. Top with tomato slices and anchovy fillets and serve with lemon and a green salad (illustrated opposite).
To freeze:
Do not freeze this dish, but frozen veal could be used.

Sweet & Sour Pork

To make: 15 minutes   **To cook:** 25 minutes   **(Serves 4–6)**

1$\frac{1}{2}$ lb./750 g. pork fillet (cut from
the leg)
2 *level* tablespoons cornflour
seasoning
little oil or fat for frying
2–3 canned pineapple rings
4 tablespoons pineapple syrup
2–3 tablespoons cocktail onions
2 tablespoons vinegar
$\frac{1}{2}$ pint/3 dl. stock or water and $\frac{1}{2}$
chicken stock cube
1 tablespoon honey
2 tablespoons sherry
2 teaspoons soy sauce
1 tablespoon tomato ketchup

Cut the meat into neat 1-inch/2-cm. cubes. Dust with half the cornflour, blended with a little seasoning, and fry in the hot oil or fat until tender. Tip on to a dish and keep hot. Meanwhile chop the pineapple rings and put into a saucepan with the pineapple syrup, onions, vinegar, stock, or water and stock cube, blended with the remaining cornflour, and the rest of the ingredients. Stir over a low heat until a thickened and smooth sauce. Spoon over the pork.
To serve:
As soon as cooked, so the pork does not become too soft with the sauce. A green salad is a good accompaniment, or bamboo or bean shoots and boiled rice.
To vary:
Use diced steak or other meat, or diced chicken.
To freeze:
This dish does not freeze, but frozen meat could be used.

60

Fried Bacon & Egg

To make: 5 minutes **To cook:** 4–7 minutes (Serves 4)

4–8 rashers bacon, choose back, streaky or thin gammon
little extra fat if the bacon is very lean
4 eggs

Cut the rinds from the rashers, put these, and the bacon, into the unheated frying pan. Arrange the bacon rashers so that the fat of one rasher is under the lean of the next rasher; in this way the bacon will not dry. Fry until cooked, the time will depend upon the thickness of the bacon. Keep warm, add extra fat if needed, heat this and then fry the eggs.

Veal Chops with Tomato Sauce

To make: 15 minutes **To cook:** 20–25 minutes (Serves 4)

seasoning
4 veal chops
2 oz./50 g. butter
1 rasher bacon
1 onion
1 medium-sized can plum tomatoes
1 teaspoon cornflour
4 tablespoons stock or water

Season the veal, fry in the hot butter steadily until tender; veal, like pork, must be well cooked. Remove from the pan and keep hot. Cut the rind from the bacon, chop the bacon and the onion. Fry in any fat remaining in the pan for 2–3 minutes; do not allow the onion to brown or the bacon to become crisp. Add the tomatoes, then the cornflour, blended with the stock or water. Bring to the boil, lower the heat and stir until thickened. If the sauce is rather thick, add extra liquid. Serve over the chops.

To freeze:
Do not freeze this dish, but frozen veal could be used, see page 56.

Adding Flavours

Bacon and apple: Apple rings are delicious with fried bacon; cook the bacon rinds to give extra bacon fat. Put in thin slices cored cooking apples (peel if desired), cook for 2–3 minutes, turning once, then add bacon rashers and fry.

Bacon and cheese: Fry or grill bacon rashers, add thick slices Cheddar or Gruyère cheese towards the end of the cooking time.

Curried chops: Season pork, veal or lamb chops and add a sprinkling of curry powder. Fry or grill in the usual way.

Paprika chops: Season pork or veal chops well, then fry in the usual way. Lift out of the pan and keep hot. Blend 1–2 teaspoons paprika and 1–2 teaspoons chopped chives with $\frac{1}{4}$ pint/$1\frac{1}{2}$ dl. white wine. Pour into the pan and stir to absorb all the meat juices, heat thoroughly. Whisk in 3–4 tablespoons double cream, heat without boiling then spoon over the chops.

Steak Diane: Heat a generous amount of butter in a pan, fry 1–2 thinly sliced or chopped onions and thin slices seasoned steak until tender. Add 1 teaspoon Worcestershire sauce, a little brandy and 1 tablespoon chopped parsley. Heat for 1 minute and serve. Veal or pork fillets can be cooked in the same way.

Escalopes Turin-style

Sausagemeat Cakes

These are a great favourite with children. Buy sausagemeat or skin sausages and mix with a few raisins, some finely chopped apple and a few chopped nuts. Form into flat cakes, brush with egg and roll in crumbs or crushed potato crisps. Fry for 10–12 minutes in hot fat.

Pork with Spicy Orange Sauce

To make: 15 minutes **To cook:** 20 minutes **(Serves 4)**

1¼ lb./600 g. pork fillet (cut from the leg)
1 oz./25 g. flour
seasoning
3 oranges
1 small onion
1 green pepper
1 oz./25 g. butter
1 tablespoon Worcestershire sauce
¼ pint/1½ dl. beef stock or water and ¼ beef stock cube

Quick tip:
Use dehydrated onion, canned orange juice and canned mandarin oranges.

To economize:
Use cheaper belly of pork. Simmer for 15 minutes in stock, drain, coat in seasoned flour and proceed as recipe.

Trim the meat and cut into 1-inch/2-cm. cubes. Coat with flour mixed with seasoning. Grate the rind from one orange, then cut away peel and pith and cut into segments, squeeze out juice from the remaining two oranges. Chop the onion and pepper (discard core and seeds) and fry in the hot butter for 3 minutes. Add the meat and cook for 5 minutes, turning frequently. Pour in the orange juice and then stir in the grated orange rind, Worcestershire sauce and stock, or water and stock cube. Bring to boiling point and simmer for 10 minutes, stirring occasionally. Season to taste and add the orange segments just before serving.

To serve:
A green salad and boiled rice are good accompaniments.

To vary:
Use duck in place of pork; remove skin before dicing.

To freeze:
Do not freeze this dish if you want to retain the slightly firm texture of the onion and pepper, otherwise freeze and use within 3 months.

Pork with spicy orange sauce

Pork with Barbecue Sauce

To make: 15 minutes　**To cook:** 25 minutes　**(Serves 4–6)**

2 tablespoons oil
4–6 spare rib pork chops
2 medium-sized onions
2 tablespoons tomato purée
2 tablespoons water
2 tablespoons soft brown sugar
2 tablespoons vinegar
1 teaspoon Worcestershire sauce
1–2 teaspoons made mustard
pinch mixed dried herbs
seasoning

Quick tip:
Use dehydrated onion.
To economize:
Use diced belly of pork instead of chops.

Heat the oil in a pan and fry the meat on both sides until lightly browned. Remove from the pan and put on to a plate. Add the chopped onions to the pan, fry gently for 5 minutes; then stir in the remaining ingredients and bring to the boil. Replace the meat in the pan, cover and simmer for 15 minutes.
To serve:
With a green salad.
To vary:
Use lamb chops.
To freeze:
Do not freeze this dish, although frozen pork chops can be cooked from the frozen state.

Pork Normandy

To make: 10 minutes　**To cook:** 20–25 minutes　**(Serves 4)**

4 pork chops
2 medium-sized onions
2 medium-sized dessert apples
1 oz./25 g. butter
pinch dried sage
seasoning
$\frac{1}{4}$ pint/1$\frac{1}{2}$ dl. single cream
3–4 tablespoons Calvados

Fry the pork chops until tender, lift out of the pan and keep hot. Finely chop the onion and peel, core and thinly slice the apples. Heat the butter and fry the onions with the sage, seasoning and apples for 5 minutes. Add the cream and Calvados and heat, *without boiling*. Stir well to absorb the meat juices and pour over the chops and serve with green salad.
To freeze:
The dish does not freeze well, but you can use frozen pork chops.

Pork with barbecue sauce

Meats for Grilling

The meat you grill must be tender and of prime quality, as grilling is a quick method of cooking. Always pre-heat the grill except when cooking bacon, see page 66.

When grilling beef:

Choose thin (minute) steaks, fillet, rump, porterhouse, T-bone, entrecôte or sirloin.

When grilling pork or veal:

Choose loin or chump chops, cutlets or thin slices (fillets) from the leg.

When grilling lamb:

Choose loin, chump or best end of lamb, chops or cutlets or thin slices (fillets) from the leg.

Keep lean meat well basted with melted butter or oil during cooking; unless marinated as kebabs, page 66.

Do not over-cook the meat and do not keep it waiting before serving, otherwise it could become dry and less appetizing.

Cook the food quickly at the beginning, this 'seals-in' the meat juices. You can then lower the heat of the grill and/or lower the position of the grill pan so the meat cooks more slowly; this means it is cooked through to the centre without over-cooking the outside.

Timing for grilling and frying meats

Cook chops or cutlets quickly for 1–2 minutes on either side. Lower the heat, continue cooking for about 8 minutes, or a little longer for pork and veal. Time for steaks varies with personal taste. Seal the outside quickly, (thin 'minute' steaks would then be ready). For $\frac{1}{2}$–$\frac{3}{4}$-inch/1–$\frac{1}{2}$-cm. 'rare' steaks, lower the heat and cook for a further 2–3 minutes; for medium to well cooked steaks, cook for a further 4–8 minutes.

Noisettes of lamb

Noisettes of Lamb

To make: 15 minutes   **To cook:** 10–12 minutes   (Serves 4)

Maître d'hôtel butter:
2 oz. /50 g. butter
$\frac{1}{2}$–1 tablespoon chopped parsley
squeeze lemon juice
seasoning

8 best end or loin of lamb chops
seasoning
pinch dried rosemary

First make the *Maître d'hôtel butter*. Cream the butter with the parsley, lemon juice and seasoning. Form into a neat roll, chill and cut into portions before serving. Remove the bones from the chops, tie the meat into rounds. Flavour with seasoning and the rosemary. Grill as above; there is no need to brush with additional fat as the natural fat from the meat is sufficient. Top with the butter just before serving.
To serve:
On rounds of fried bread or toast with mixed vegetables and salad.
To freeze:
Prepare noisettes, freeze. Use within 6–8 months. Cook from the frozen state.

illed lamb chops

Grilled Gammon

To make: 5 minutes   **To cook:** 10–12 minutes   **(Serves 4)**

4 gammon steaks
1–2 oz./25–50 g. butter (see method)
tomatoes, mushrooms, fruit (see method)
seasoning and/or sugar

To economize:
Use thick rashers of back bacon (cheaper than gammon), often called bacon chops.

If you do not like a very salt flavour, soak the gammon for 1–2 hours, dry well. When cooking bacon under the grill, do not pre-heat this, as it makes the bacon curl badly and burn round the edges. Put the bacon under the grill, *then* switch on or light. As gammon is a lean bacon, you need to brush it with melted butter. Grill quickly for 1–2 minutes, turn, brush with more butter and cook on the second side. Bacon, like pork, must be well cooked, so lower the heat and continue cooking more slowly for 6–8 minutes or until tender. Tomatoes and mushrooms can be cooked with the gammon. Either cook in the grill pan, with seasoned butter, or add to the rack towards the end of the cooking time.

Fruits, peaches, pineapple, pears, orange rings, apple rings, etc. all blend well with gammon (or any fried or grilled bacon). Brush the fruit with butter, so it does not dry, and heat for a few minutes. To give an attractive glaze sprinkle the fruit and the edge of the gammon with a very little brown sugar.

Note: For crisp gammon fat, cut away the skin and snip the fat at regular intervals with kitchen scissors before cooking.
To serve:
Hot with creamed or fried potatoes, green vegetables or salad.
To freeze:
Do not freeze grilled gammon but you can use frozen gammon.

Roast

Sausages & Bacon with Mustard Sauce

To make: 10 minutes   **To cook:** 15–20 minutes   **(Serves 4)**

very little fat (see method)
1 lb./500 g. pork or beef sausages
4–8 rashers bacon
For the sauce:
1 oz./25 g. margarine (see method)
1 oz./25 g. flour
$\frac{1}{2}$–1 tablespoon dry mustard
$\frac{1}{4}$ pint/1$\frac{1}{2}$ dl. milk
$\frac{1}{4}$ pint/1$\frac{1}{2}$ dl. stock or water and $\frac{1}{4}$ beef stock cube

Heat a small amount of fat in a frying pan, use enough to give a greasy surface; this is not necessary in a non-stick pan. Fry the sausages and then the bacon until ready to serve. Put on to a hot dish while making the sauce in the frying pan; this is not only quicker, but gives the sauce more flavour. If you have plenty of fat left in the pan there is no need to use the amount of margarine given. Stir the flour and mustard into the fat, then blend in the milk and stock or water and stock cube. Bring slowly to the boil and cook, stirring well, until smooth and thickened, season to taste.
To serve:
Pour the sauce carefully over the sausages, but not the bacon. Serve at once with creamed potatoes and peas or beans.

Herbed Kebabs

To make: 10 minutes plus marinating   **To cook:** 20 minutes   **(Serves 4)**

1 lb./500 g. tender lean meat, lamb, pork or beef, or use a mixture of meats
For the marinade:
2 tablespoons oil
4 tablespoons wine vinegar
seasoning
1 tablespoon chopped mixed fresh herbs

4 oz./100 g. button mushrooms
1 green pepper
4 oz./100 g. long grain rice
$\frac{1}{2}$ pint/3 dl. water
seasoning

To economize:
Use sausages or meat balls, see page 78, in place of the diced meat; marinate sausages, but not meat balls.

Dice the meat and put into the marinade, made by mixing the oil, vinegar, seasoning and herbs; adapt the herbs according to the meats used, i.e. if choosing mainly pork, add plenty of sage, rosemary with lamb, chives and crushed garlic with beef. Leave for 1–2 hours. Wash, but do not peel the mushrooms, dice the pepper (discard core and seeds). Lift the meat from the marinade and put on to 4 long metal skewers with the mushrooms and green pepper. Put the rice with the cold water and salt or seasoning to taste into a saucepan. Bring the water to the boil, stir with a fork, lower the heat and cover the pan. Simmer gently for 15 minutes, by which time the rice should be cooked and the liquid absorbed. Grill the kebabs, turning once or twice and basting with any left-over marinade.
To serve:
Hot on the bed of hot rice and with a mixed or green salad.
To vary:
Use small par-boiled onions and tomatoes with the meat.
To freeze:
Dice then freeze meats for kebabs or freeze sausages. Diced meat should be used in half the time given on page 56 for joints.

To Roast Meat

Roasting is a simple method of cooking and can be done in the oven or under a rotisserie; the time for roasting in this manner is the same as for quick roasting, see page 87 and under 'Timing' for the individual meats.

Select the meat you roast most carefully, it must be of prime quality and the right cuts for successful cooking.

It is possible to roast meat in the same three ways as poultry, on page 87, although the ultra slow method is rarely used.

Frozen meat

If roasting frozen joints, either allow them to defrost thoroughly, this will take about 24 hours for a 4–5 lb./2–2½ kilo joint at room temperature, or almost twice as long in the refrigerator, *or* cook from the frozen state. If you use this method then do **not** attempt to roast by the quick method but the slower way (this does not mean the ultra slow method). Allow 50% longer cooking time than when roasting a fresh or defrosted joint, or use a meat thermometer, which will indicate the degree of cooking for you. Opinions vary as to which method is better, **a)** defrosting the meat first or **b)** cooking more slowly. Personally I am inclined to think the latter is more satisfactory as you seem to retain more of the natural meat juices. However, try both methods and decide for yourself.

To roast pork

One important rule when you cook pork by any method is to make absolutely certain the meat is thoroughly cooked. Under-cooked pork can cause food poisoning.

To give a crisp crackling to the skin of pork, score and rub with olive oil or melted lard. You can sprinkle it lightly with salt, but this is not essential. Use an open roasting tin.

Joints to choose

Bladebone, spare rib, leg or half leg or loin.

Timing

If using the quick roasting method on page 87 allow 25 minutes per lb./500 g. and 25 minutes over. If using the slower roasting method then 35 minutes per lb./500 g. and 35 minutes over. For the ultra slow roasting allow 2½ hours for the first 1 lb./500 g., then follow timing as for chicken. Serve with sage and onion stuffing and apple sauce or the cherry or orange sauces given for duckling on page 89, or a thickened gravy.

A new look to pork

Roast peeled onions, sprinkled with seasoning and sage, and whole peeled dessert apples, rolled in the pork fat and sprinkled with a little sugar, round the joint of pork, as shown in the picture.

67

To Roast Beef

Roast beef is one of the most delicious roast joints. When buying the beef see there is a good 'marbling' of fat, as this makes sure it will be moist when cooked. If you add fat to beef use very little, since an excess of fat is inclined to harden the meat. You can use an open roasting tin or cover with foil, put into a polythene cooking bag or into a covered tin. If using either of these last three methods allow about 15–20 minutes extra cooking time, see page 87 for details of this.

Joints to choose

Good quality aitch-bone, fillet, rib, rump, sirloin, topside.

Timing

If using the quick roasting method, see page 87, allow 15 minutes per lb./500 g. and 15 minutes over for under-done meat, 20 minutes per lb./500 g. and 20 minutes over for medium to well-done. If using the slower method then allow 25 minutes per lb./500 g. and 25 minutes over. For well-done beef add 15–20 minutes to the *total* time.

If you would like to follow the ultra slow method then allow just the same time as for chicken if you like your beef medium 'rare'.

Serve beef with mustard and horseradish cream or sauce, see page 82, Yorkshire pudding, below, and an unthickened gravy.

Yorkshire Pudding

One of the essentials of a good Yorkshire pudding is to cook it quickly, so you must choose the quick method of roasting on this occasion. In fact I prefer to raise the oven temperature by 25°F./10°C., or 1 Gas Mark, when I put the pudding into the oven; leave it at this high temperature for 10–15 minutes, then lower the heat for the rest of the cooking time.

To make the batter

Sieve 4 oz./100 g. plain flour and a pinch of salt. Gradually beat in 1 large egg and ½ pint/3 dl. milk or milk and water. Stand in a cool place until ready to cook.

If you prefer to cook the pudding under the meat, remove the meat tin from the oven and pour out all the fat except for 1 tablespoon. Heat this again, then pour in the batter. Put the beef on a trivet over the pudding and cook; the flavour is magnificent, but the pudding does not rise as when cooked by the more usual method below. To give a very well risen pudding heat about 1 oz./25 g. (no more) fat or dripping in a Yorkshire pudding tin. Pour in the batter and cook towards the top of a very hot oven, reduce the heat slightly after 10–15 minutes. Allow approximately 30 minutes until well-risen and brown. Individual puddings take about 15 minutes.

Stuffed Fillet of Beef

To make: 15 minutes   **To cook:** 1¼–1½ hours   **(Serves 4)**

1 lb./500 g. fillet of beef, in one piece
2 onions
1–2 oz./25–50 g. dripping (see method)
2 anchovy fillets
1 tablespoon chopped bacon
pinch of pepper
pinch of dried thyme
½ teaspoon finely chopped parsley
1 egg yolk
To garnish:
watercress

Quick tip:
Use a little sausagemeat flavoured with chopped anchovy fillets for the stuffing.

Trim the beef neatly. Chop or slice the onions. Fry the onions in 1 oz./25 g. dripping, until they are golden brown. Remove from the pan and place in a mixing bowl. Add the chopped anchovy fillets, bacon, pepper, thyme, parsley and the beaten egg yolk. Cut the fillet lengthways in about four places, but not right through. Put some of the stuffing into each cavity and tie the fillet up with string or secure with wooden cocktail sticks. Either wrap in greased foil, put into a polythene cooking bag or place in a roasting pan with the remaining dripping and cook in a low oven, 300°F./150°C., Gas Mark 2, for 1–1¼ hours, or until tender.
To serve:
Hot, cut into thick slices, with cooked vegetables and garnished with watercress.
To vary:
Use any other stuffing, see pages 82 and 83.
To freeze:
Prepare the fillet, wrap and freeze. Thaw out before cooking. Use within 4–5 months.
To economize:
Use a piece of topside of beef instead of fillet. As this is inclined to dry slightly, baste with a little stock during cooking, unless cooking in a bag, and allow 1½–1¾ hours in the slow oven.

Stuffed fillet of beef

To Roast Lamb or Mutton

Lamb should always be tender when roasted, provided you choose the correct joints, but take care to roast only tender young mutton. There should be no need to add extra fat with either lamb or mutton. You can use an open roasting tin, or cover with foil, put into a polythene cooking bag or into a covered tin. If using either of these last three methods allow about 15–20 minutes extra cooking time, see page 87 for details of this.

Joints to choose

Best end of neck (only of lamb, not mutton), breast, this is an economical but rather fat joint, it can be boned, covered with a stuffing, then rolled, leg, loin, saddle (this is a double loin and ideal for parties), shoulder. Another very impressive joint of lamb is a Crown Roast. This consists of a minimum of 12–14 best end of neck or loin chops, rolled into a 'crown'. The centre can be filled with a favourite stuffing.

Timing

Allow 20 minutes per lb./500 g. and 20 minutes over if using the quick roasting method on page 87. If you like very young lamb slightly 'pink' as in France, then reduce the total cooking time by about 15 minutes. If you prefer the slower roasting time then give 35 minutes per lb./500 g. and 35 minutes over; this is particularly suitable for mutton. The ultra slow method is also good for mutton, allow $2\frac{1}{4}$ hours for the first 1 lb./500 g., then follow timing as for chicken, page 87. Serve lamb with mint sauce, page 82, and mutton with redcurrant jelly.

To Roast Veal

Veal is an exceptionally lean meat and must be kept well basted with fat during cooking. It also needs adequate cooking. Either 'lard' the veal or cover with plenty of fat bacon or fat. To 'lard' veal, cut very thin strips of fat pork or bacon and thread through the raw meat with a 'larding' needle.

Joints to choose

Best end of neck, breast, fillet, chump end of loin or loin shoulder.

Timing

This is exactly the same as for pork on page 67.

To serve

Serve veal with bacon rolls, sausages, and bread sauce, see page 88, with veal stuffing, page 83, and thickened gravy.

A new look to veal

Although cranberry sauce is not a usual accompaniment to veal I find it blends very well indeed. I often flavour the gravy with port wine.

69

To Make Interesting Stews

A stew can be one of the most delicious, as well as economical dishes and basic methods of stewing are given in the recipes opposite. As you will see some stews do not have a thickened liquid, but in others the meat is first fried, to seal in the flavour, then cooked in a thickened sauce.

It is easy to change the flavour of a stew; simply use different vegetables, more herbs, add mixed spice or Worcestershire sauce or soy or soya sauce (although very similar, these two are not identical). Put in a pinch of curry powder and a few drops of Tabasco sauce or use some wine in the liquid, see also page 76.

Casseroles

Most stews can be cooked in a covered dish in a slow oven, rather than in a covered saucepan. If you adapt the recipe to cook in the oven, reduce the amount of liquid by 25%, as there is less evaporation in the oven than on top of the cooker.

Pork and bamboo shoots

Pork and Bamboo Shoots

To make: 15 minutes   **To cook:** 1 hour 20 minutes   **(Serves 6–8)**

2 lb./1 kilo. lean pork
2–3 tablespoons soya sauce
1–2 tablespoons sherry
1 teaspoon brown sugar
1 teaspoon ground ginger
seasoning
2 pints/1¼ litres water
4 oz./100 g. fresh or canned
   bamboo shoots
1 tablespoon cornflour

Quick tip:
Use diced fillet of pork, mix with the soya sauce, etc., then fry in hot oil until tender. Heat the bamboo shoots separately and serve round the pork.

Cut the pork into small cubes. Mix the soya sauce, sherry, sugar, ginger and seasoning together, add to the pork, toss well and leave for 10 minutes. Put the pork and flavourings into a large pan, add most of the water and bring gently to the boil, cover and simmer for 1 hour. Wash and drain fresh or canned bamboo shoots and shred finely. Add to the pan and simmer for another 10 minutes. Blend the cornflour with the remaining water, stir into the pan and continue cooking for 10 minutes, stirring from time to time.

To serve:
With extra soya sauce.

To vary:
Use diced raw chicken or other meat instead of pork.

To freeze:
This dish is better not frozen.

To economize:
Use diced belly of pork.

70

Goulash

1 lb./500 g. stewing steak
8 oz./200 g. stewing veal
2 oz./50 g. dripping or butter
2–3 medium-sized onions
1 clove garlic (optional)
1 lb./500 g. tomatoes
seasoning
½–1 level tablespoon paprika
1 pint/6 dl. stock or water and
    1 beef stock cube
1 lb./500 g. peeled potatoes
To garnish:
chopped parsley
¼–½ pint/1½–3 dl. yoghourt

Quick tip:
See Savoury Beef Stew (below).

Dice the meats then fry for a few minutes in the hot dripping or butter in a good-sized saucepan. Remove the meat, add the sliced onions, chopped garlic and fry for 2–3 minutes. Return the meat to the pan with the skinned tomatoes, seasoning and paprika, blended with the stock or water and stock cube. Cover the pan and simmer gently for 1¾ hours. Thickly slice the potatoes if large or leave whole if small. Add to the pan, cover and continue cooking gently for nearly 45 minutes.

To serve:
Spoon on to a hot dish and top with the parsley and yoghourt.

To vary:
Omit the potatoes in the stew and use a little less liquid; serve with noodles. Add 1–2 teaspoons caraway seeds.
Use all beef, all veal, or a mixture of veal and pork.

To freeze:
This freezes well, use within 2 months for the best flavour.

Savoury Beef Stew

1–1½ lb./500–750 g. stewing beef
seasoning
1 oz./25 g. flour
2 oz./50 g. dripping or fat
3–4 large onions
1 pint/6 dl. stock or water and
    1 beef stock cube
4–5 large carrots
2 small turnips
bouquet garni

Quick tip:
Use a pressure cooker for the Goulash and this stew. Allow 15 minutes at 15 lb./7 kilo. pressure. Reduce the pressure after 10 minutes with the Goulash, add potatoes then cook at the same pressure for 5 minutes.

Cut the meat into neat pieces. Mix the seasoning and flour, then coat the meat. Fry in the hot dripping or fat for several minutes, remove from the pan. Add the sliced onions and fry these gently until transparent. Gradually blend in the stock or water and stock cube and stir over a low heat until a thin sauce. Add the sliced or diced carrots and turnips, together with the herbs tied in muslin or with cotton. Cover the pan and simmer gently until the meat is tender.

To serve:
With dumplings, see page 75, creamed or boiled potatoes and a green vegetable. Remove *bouquet garni* before serving.

To vary:
Use other vegetables and flavourings, see opposite and page 76. Cook in a covered casserole in a slow oven, 300°F./150°C., Gas Mark 2 for the same amount of time.

To freeze:
This dish, like most stews, freezes well; use within 3 months.

To economize:
Use less meat and add protein vegetables – peas, beans, etc.

Spring Lamb

2½–3 lb./1¼–1½ kilo. middle neck
    of lamb
seasoning
12 small onions
1 lb./500 g. young carrots
1 lb./500 g. broad beans
1 lb./500 g. new potatoes
small bunch mint
To garnish:
cucumber sauce (see method)

Quick tip:
Use a pressure cooker, cook for 12 minutes at 15 lb./7 kilo pressure.

To economize:
Do not waste the stock, use in Mulligatawny soup, see page 36.

Put the lamb with water to cover and seasoning into a pan. Bring the water to the boil, remove any 'scum' from the surface, then add the onions and carrots. Cover the pan and simmer gently for almost 1 hour. Meanwhile shell the beans and scrape the potatoes; add to the lamb together with the mint, tied with cotton, and any extra seasoning desired. Simmer steadily for a further 30 minutes.

To serve:
Lift the meat and vegetables from the stock with a perforated spoon on to a hot dish. Top with the cucumber sauce, see below.

To vary:
Use vegetables in season, serve with a caper sauce. This is made by adding 2–3 teaspoons capers, plus a little vinegar from the bottle, instead of cucumber in the sauce below.

Cucumber sauce: Make a white sauce, as page 54, but using half milk and half lamb stock. When thickened add half a diced peeled cucumber, plus 1–2 teaspoons vinegar; heat gently, but do not boil.

To freeze:
Undercook slightly; use within 2 months.

Meat Pies & Puddings

A really light meat pudding is one of the most satisfying cold weather dishes. I have given the best known of all meat puddings on this page, but other meats and flavourings can be used, as you will see from the suggested variations.

When you make a meat pie you have a wide choice of pastries. There is the very light puff pastry, commercially frozen, as page 73, or home-made, page 97. The best known and easiest pastry to make, i.e. short crust, is given on page 122.

In the mutton pie opposite, the pastry is hot water crust, the speciality of raised pies.

Steak & Kidney Pudding

To make: 25–30 minutes   **To cook:** 4–5 hours   **(Serves 4–6)**

8 oz./200 g. self-raising or plain flour (see note under method)
pinch salt
2–4 oz./50–100 g. finely shredded suet
water to mix
For the filling:
1 lb./500 g. *good* quality chuck or flank steak
6–8 oz./150–200 g. ox-kidney
1 tablespoon flour
seasoning
2–3 tablespoons stock or water

To economize:
Use less meat and add onions and other vegetables.

Sieve the flour, or flour and baking powder, and salt. Add the suet. Mix to a rolling consistency with cold water. Roll out thinly as this pastry rises. Line a pudding basin with nearly three-quarters of the dough, leaving a good quarter for the lid. Dice the meat and roll in the flour mixed with the seasoning. Put into the pudding and add the stock or water. Roll out the remaining dough to a round. Press over the filling. Seal at the edges. Cover with greased greaseproof paper and foil. Steam or boil rapidly for 4–5 hours. For a good result make sure that the water is boiling rapidly when the pudding goes on, and always replenish with boiling water.

Note: If you like a light, well risen crust use self-raising flour or plain flour with 1–2 level teaspoons baking powder. If you prefer a thin, unrisen crust, use plain flour. For a thicker crust use 10 oz./250 g. flour, etc.
To vary:
Bacon and vegetable pudding: Use diced thick bacon rashers, a mixture of vegetables and tomato juice instead of the stock or water.
Chicken pudding: Use diced raw chicken and vegetables; flavour with a pinch of mixed herbs or add tiny balls of veal stuffing, see page 83.
Lamb pudding: Use diced lamb and lambs' kidneys in place of steak and kidney.

Old-fashioned Mutton Pie

To make: 35 minutes   **To cook:** 2¾ hours   **(Serves 5–6)**

1½–2 lb./750 g.–1 kilo. mutton, cut from the leg
seasoning
bouquet garni (see method)
1–2 onions
3 eggs
For the hot water crust pastry:
12 oz./340 g. flour,* preferably plain
pinch salt
5 oz./140 g. lard*
¼ pint/1½ dl. water
To glaze:
1 egg

Quick tip:
Make individual pies and bake for 1¼ hours.
To economize:
Use half mutton and half sausagemeat.
*use this metrication

Cut the meat into small 1-inch/2-cm. dice, put into a pan with a very little water, seasoning and the *bouquet garni*. (Use just one tiny sprig of mint as well as parsley, sage, chives.) Simmer gently in the covered pan for only 30 minutes. Meanwhile chop the onions finely, hard-boil and shell the eggs and make the pastry. Sieve the flour and salt, heat the lard and water until the lard has melted. Pour the lard mixture on to the flour and knead well. Roll out until about ¼-inch/½-cm. in thickness and cut a band for the sides of a 7-inch/18-cm. cake tin and two rounds for the top and bottom. Keep the pastry warm. Put one round into the lightly greased tin, moisten the edges, then put in the band of pastry and seal firmly. Drain the meat, pack half into the tin with half the onions and a little seasoning. Add the eggs, then the rest of the meat, onions and seasoning, press down firmly. Add 2 tablespoons only of the stock. Cover with the remaining round of pastry, sealing the edges firmly. Make a hole in the top of the pastry for the steam to escape. Cut leaves and make a rose shape from the left-over pastry, moisten and press on to the top, but not over the centre hole. Brush the pastry with beaten egg. Bake for 2¼ hours in the centre of a moderate oven, 350°F/ 180°C., Gas Mark 4, lowering the heat slightly after 1¼ hours. Cool in the tin.

To serve:
Serve this pie when freshly made, do not store.

Steak and kidney pie

Steak & Kidney Pie

To make: 25–30 minutes **To cook:** 3 hours **(Serves 4–6)**

2 oz./50 g. lard or dripping
1 large onion
1½ lb./750 g. mixed steak and
 kidney
1 oz./25 g. flour
¾ pint/4½ dl. water
seasoning
14 oz./400 g. frozen puff pastry
To glaze:
egg or milk

To vary:
Use other stewing meat with
vegetables to flavour.
Make short, flaky or puff pastry
with 7–8 oz./175–200 g. flour, see
page 72
To freeze:
Put the meat into the pie dish and
top with the pastry. Freeze, cover
and use within 3–4 months. Thaw
out before cooking. If preferred,
cook then freeze and reheat gently.

Heat the lard or dripping in a pan, put in the chopped onion and fry for
5 minutes. Add the steak and kidney and cook gently, stirring, for 5
minutes. Blend in the flour, lower the heat and cook, stirring two or three
times, for a further 10 minutes. Gradually stir in the water and add seasoning. Cover the pan and simmer gently, stirring from time to time, for about
2 hours or until the meat is tender. Remove the pan from the heat and allow
the meat to cool. When cold, turn the meat and gravy into a pie dish. Roll
out the pastry to an oval, just a little bigger than the pie dish. Cut a strip off
the pastry about ½-inch/1-cm. wide. Damp the rim of the pie dish and place
this strip all the way round. Damp the pastry strip and carefully place the
rolled-out pastry over the top of the pie dish. Trim off the edges of the
pastry with a sharp knife, knock up the edges and flute. Roll out the pastry
trimmings and cut out diamond shapes for leaves. Damp the leaves and
arrange in the centre of the pie. Brush with a little egg or milk before baking
to give it a golden shine. Bake the pie in the centre of a very hot oven,
450°F./230°C., Gas Mark 8, for 10 minutes, then lower the heat to 375–
400°F./190–200°C., Gas Mark 5–6, for a further 15–20 minutes.
To serve:
Hot with vegetables.
Quick tip:
Use canned stewing steak.
To economize:
Use a smaller quantity of meat with diced mixed vegetables.

Glazed bacon with apricots

To Boil Meat

The terms 'boiled bacon', 'boiled beef', etc. are widely used, but care must be taken that the liquid in which the meat is cooked does **not** boil, but just simmers steadily.

While all meats can be simmered in the same way as the recipes that follow, this method is most suitable for salted meats, i.e. bacon, tongue, brisket, etc.

In order to keep the meat moist, allow it to cool in the liquid in the pan. If you plan to serve some of the meat as a hot dish, carve the required amount for the hot meal, then return the joint to the liquid. The purpose of cooling the meat in this way is to prevent the outside hardening and to keep the meat very moist.

Make quite sure salted meats are covered with liquid when cooking, and read the comments about soaking in the recipes. When storing salted meats wrap well, as they have a tendency to harden.

To Freeze Meat

Wrap well when cold. It is a good idea to slice some of the joint, separating each slice with waxed paper, so you may 'peel off' slices as required. Salted meats do not store as well as fresh meats, so store uncooked salted meats for 3 months and cooked salted meats for 1 month.

Do not waste the stock from boiled meats; this is excellent in soups.

Glazed Bacon

The picture shown above is of glazed bacon. This is a delicious way to serve a bacon joint.

While you can roast a mild cure bacon in just the same way as pork, and for the same time, see page 67, it is better to par-boil the meat first and then to roast for a short time only in the oven.

Weigh the bacon first and boil for the time required, LESS 30 minutes, see opposite. When the bacon is ready to come out of the liquid, drain it well, score (cut) the fat and stud with cloves, if wished. Cover the fat with the selected glaze. Roast for 30 minutes in the centre of a moderately hot oven, 375–400°F./190–200°C., Gas Mark 5–6. Check that the glaze, which is generally fairly sweet, is not becoming too brown – if so, lower the heat slightly.

Simple Glazes for Bacon

Apricot and ginger
Blend brown sugar with a little apricot syrup (from canned or cooked apricots) and ground ginger to taste. Add the apricots to the pan for the last 5 minutes cooking.

Honey glaze
Blend honey and mixed spice to taste, spread over fat.

Orange glaze
Blend the finely grated rind of 2 oranges with the orange juice, $\frac{1}{2}$–1 tablespoon made mustard and 4–5 oz./100–125 g. brown sugar. Spread over the fat. Serve with orange slices.

Wine and Cherry glaze
Blend $\frac{1}{4}$ pint red wine, the syrup from a medium-sized can of cherries, 2 tablespoons of soy sauce and 1 teaspoon vinegar. Pour over the bacon. Baste once or twice during cooking. Add the cherries to the pan for the last few minutes cooking. Serve remaining basting liquid as a sauce.

Boiled Bacon & Vegetables

To make: 25 minutes plus soaking   **To cook:** see method   **(Serves: see below)**

collar, forehock or gammon of
   bacon*
pepper or peppercorns
mixed vegetables, e.g. carrots,
   onions, turnips
*Allow 6–8 oz./150–250 g.
uncooked meat per person

Quick tip:
Simmer rashers of back bacon or
gammon for 10–15 minutes only.
To economize:
Choose the cheaper forehock or
collar.

If buying cured bacon, soak in cold water to cover. If you like a very mild flavour soak overnight, otherwise for several hours. Green bacon, mild Danish bacon and 'sweet-cure' joints do not require soaking. Some joints can be cooked in their polythene wrapping, piercing a hole if directed to do so. Put the bacon joint in fresh cold water to cover, add pepper or peppercorns and mixed vegetables. Bring the liquid to boiling point only, remove any grey bubbles if they form on the surface. Lower the heat and simmer gently for 20 minutes per lb./500 g. and 20 minutes over for prime gammon, but up to 35 minutes per lb./500 g. and 35 minutes over for the less tender forehock.

To serve:
Hot with the vegetables and parsley sauce, see page 82; use some of the bacon stock in the sauce instead of all milk. Cold with salad. Cool the joint, or part of the joint (see opposite page), in the stock. Remove, drain and cut away the skin. Coat the fat with fine crisp breadcrumbs or brown sugar.

To vary:
Add dumplings towards the end of the cooking time, below.
Use cider, wine or ginger ale instead of all or some of the water.

Boiled Brisket with Dumplings

To make: 15 minutes plus soaking   **To cook:** see method   **(Serves: see below)**

salt brisket of beef*
mixed vegetables, e.g. onions,
   carrots, turnips
pepper or peppercorns
For the dumplings:
4 oz./100 g. self-raising flour or
   plain flour with 1 teaspoon
   baking powder
pinch salt
2 oz./50 g. shredded suet
water to mix
*Allow 6–8 oz./150–200 g.
uncooked meat per person.

To economize:
Allow less meat and add soaked
haricot beans to the liquid.

Quick tip:
A pressure cooker is an ideal way
of cooking brisket, silverside and
ox-tongue. Soak the salted meat
overnight as described in the method.
Put the meat with any vegetables
required to flavour the stock and
meat into the pressure cooker.
Bring up to 15 lb./7 kg. pressure
and allow 7 minutes per lb./500 g.
for prime meat or 10 minutes per
lb./500 g. for the less tender
brisket. Allow to drop at room
temperature.

Soak the meat overnight in cold water to cover. This is very important as the meat can be spoiled by being too salt. Put into a pan with fresh water to cover. If cooking a very large piece of beef, you may care to add the vegetables during the cooking period, so they remain a good shape and flavour; for a smaller joint put them in with the meat. Bring the liquid to the boil, then lower the heat and simmer steadily, adding pepper or peppercorns to taste. Allow nearly 35 minutes per lb./500 g. and 35 minutes over, as brisket is a firm-textured meat that needs plenty of cooking. To make the dumplings, sieve the flour or flour and baking powder with the salt, add the suet and enough water to make a slightly sticky dough. Form into about 8 small balls with floured fingers and put into the boiling liquid (always check there is plenty of liquid before cooking dumplings). Cook steadily for 15–20 minutes until well risen and light.

To serve:
Hot with the vegetables and dumplings; allow the remainder of the meat to cool in the liquid, see the top of the opposite page.

To vary:
Silverside: Salted silverside can be cooked in the same way, but as this is a slightly less tough piece of meat, 30 minutes per lb./500 g. and 30 minutes over cooking time should be sufficient.
Cook the meat in cider instead of water, this is particularly good with silverside.
Add chopped mixed herbs to the flour, in the dumplings.
Pressed ox-tongue: Soak an ox-tongue overnight in cold water to cover. Cook as the brisket above, allowing 30 minutes per lb./500 g. and 30 minutes over. Allow the tongue to cool sufficiently to handle, then remove from the liquid. Skin and remove all the tiny bones. Roll round and press into a cake tin or round mould; it should be a fairly tight fit. Boil the liquid until reduced to not much more than $\frac{1}{2}$ pint/3 dl. Blend 2 teaspoons powdered gelatine with 2 tablespoons cold water. Stir into the hot liquid and continue stirring until dissolved. Strain the liquid over the tongue, put a saucer and weight on top and leave to set. Turn out and serve with salad. This is sufficient for 12–18 good portions.
Calf's tongue and lambs' tongues can be cooked in the same way, but these are rarely sold pre-salted, so soaking overnight is unnecessary. Cook the tongues with seasoning to taste until tender, skin and proceed as under ox-tongue, pressing the meat into a neat shape. These smaller tongues are excellent served hot with some of the stock used to make a gravy.

Buying Economical Meat

Although there is a good selection of dishes for special occasions, you will also find plenty of practical and money-saving ideas using meat in this section.

When you want to save money, choose some of the less expensive meats, e.g. stewing steak, middle neck or even scrag end of lamb or mutton, or buy minced meat. A hotpot, in which both meat and vegetables are cooked together in the oven, is one of the most practical dishes.

To make a hotpot

Choose a strong, deep ovenproof dish with a lid. Put layers of well seasoned meat, sliced raw potatoes and onions into the dish. Add enough liquid to half cover the ingredients and always end with sliced, seasoned potatoes.

Try

Middle neck of lamb chops, flavoured with finely chopped mint and use cider as the liquid.

Diced rather fat belly of pork, mixed with diced lean stewing steak. Flavour with chopped mixed herbs and use beer as the liquid.

To cook a hotpot

Top the sliced potatoes with a little margarine or fat; make sure the lid does not press down on to this, as it would stick. Cover the casserole and cook for at least 2 hours in the centre of a slow to very moderate oven, 300–325°F./150–170°C., Gas Mark 2–3. Remove the lid for the last 30 minutes to encourage the potatoes to become crisp and brown.

Interesting New Stews

Italian Beef Stew

Follow the recipe for Savoury Beef Stew on page 71, but use half stock and half red wine. Add 1–2 teaspoons chopped fresh or $\frac{1}{4}$ teaspoon dried rosemary and 2 tablespoons tomato purée (from a tube or can).

Boeuf Flamande

Follow the recipe for Savoury Beef Stew on page 71, but use half stock and half beer. Do not use carrots or turnips in the stew, but add 2–4 oz./50–100 g. soaked dried prunes and/or apricots.

Lamb in Fruit Sauce

Follow the recipe for Spring Lamb on page 71, but omit the broad beans and add 2–3 peeled and thickly sliced dessert apples and several tablespoons seedless raisins for the last 30 minutes of the cooking time.

Curried Stuffed Peppers

To make: 20 minutes   To cook: 50 minutes   (Serves 4)

4 medium-sized green peppers
salt
For the filling:
1 onion
2 oz./50 g. fat
1 oz./25 g. flour
1 *level* tablespoon curry powder
$\frac{3}{4}$ pint/$4\frac{1}{2}$ dl. stock or water and
   1 beef stock cube
seasoning
10–12 oz./250–300 g. minced beef
bouquet garni

Quick tip:
Use canned stewing steak and flavour with a little curry powder.
To economize:
Use the stuffing above in or with cheaper vegetables, i.e. rings of cooked marrow.

Cut the tops off the peppers. Remove the centre cores and seeds and put the prepared peppers and tops on one side. Chop the onion and fry this in the hot fat for 2–3 minutes, then stir in the flour and curry powder and cook for several minutes. Blend in the stock or water and stock cube gradually, stir well, then bring to the boil and cook for 3 minutes, stirring continuously. Add the seasoning, mince and *bouquet garni*. Simmer gently for 40 minutes, stirring from time to time. Remove the *bouquet garni*. Meanwhile, blanch the peppers and tops, i.e. put into boiling salted water, bring the water to the boil again and simmer for 5 minutes only, then drain.
To serve:
Fill the hot peppers with the hot curried mixture, put the tops on and serve on a heated dish. The combination of the firm peppers and the curry mixture is delicious.
To vary:
To give a soft texture to the peppers, brush the stuffed vegetables with melted fat or butter and cook for 20–25 minutes in the centre of a moderately hot oven, 375–400°F./190–200°C., Gas Mark 5–6.
To freeze:
Freeze, then wrap and use within 6 weeks.

Hamburger

Hamburgers

To make: 10 minutes   **To cook:** 10 minutes   **(Serves 4)**

2 onions
1 lb./500 g. lean minced beef (fresh
    brisket or rump is ideal)
2 egg yolks or 1 egg
seasoned salt and pepper*
few drops Worcestershire sauce
    (optional)
little flour (see method)
To fry:
little fat
2 tomatoes
4 soft baps (rolls)
*or use ordinary salt and pepper

Quick tip:
Use dehydrated onion instead of
fresh.
To economize:
Use best quality stewing steak
instead of brisket or rump steak.
Omit egg and bind with a little milk
or grated raw potato.
Add a few breadcrumbs to make
the meat go further.

Cut the onions into rings, then finely chop two or three rings to give 2 table-spoons. Add to the beef with the egg yolks or egg, seasoning and Worcester-shire sauce, if using. Blend well then form into four flat cakes on a very lightly floured surface. Heat the fat in a fairly large frying pan and add the meat cakes to the pan with the onion rings. Fry the hamburgers for about 10 minutes, turning once. Turn the onions several times during cooking. Slice the tomatoes and add to the pan about 3 minutes before the ham-burgers are cooked. Split the baps and toast lightly, place on one half a layer of onion rings, the hamburger, and tomato slices. Top with the other half of the bun.

To serve:
Hot with chips or potato crisps and salad.
To vary:
See to economize. It is not essential to add the egg yolks or egg, but it helps to bind the meat together so that it does not break up during frying. This makes the mixture softer to handle so flour your hands.
To freeze:
These freeze better *before* cooking. Prepare, separate with waxed paper and freeze. Use within 3 months. Cook from the frozen state. It is also an excellent idea to keep rolls in the freezer, see page 148.

Sweet and sour meat balls

Sweet & Sour Meat Balls

To make: 25 minutes   **To cook:** 30 minutes   **(Serves 6)**

1½ lb./750 g. minced beef or pork
1 clove garlic
2 oz./50 g. flour
1 oz./25 g. soft breadcrumbs
seasoning
1 egg, beaten
To fry:
2–3 oz./50–75 g. lard
For the sauce:
3–4 oz./75–100 g. sugar
6 tablespoons vinegar
3–4 tablespoons soy sauce
2 level tablespoons cornflour
¾ pint/4½ dl. water
1 green pepper
12 oz./300 g. tomatoes
1 can crushed pineapple

Quick tip:
Use frozen hamburgers and fry
these, then heat in the sweet and
sour sauce.

Mix together the meat, crushed garlic, half the flour, the breadcrumbs and seasoning. Bind with the egg and form into balls (this quantity should make about 30 balls). Toss the meat balls in the remaining flour. Melt the lard and fry the balls in batches, allowing about 10 minutes for each batch; turn frequently during cooking. Keep each batch hot when cooked. Meanwhile prepare the sauce. Place the sugar, vinegar and soy sauce in a pan. Blend the cornflour with a little of the measured water and add to the pan with the remaining water. Bring to the boil, stirring, and simmer for 5 minutes. Dice the pepper (discard core and seeds), skin and chop the tomatoes and drain the pineapple well. Add to the sauce and simmer for 5–10 minutes. When the meat balls are cooked, divide between 2 large frying pans, pour the sauce over them and simmer gently for 3 minutes. Serve with noodles.
To vary:
Do not make meat balls, but dice tender fillet or other prime steak, pork, lamb or cooked lobster meat. Toss in hot butter then heat in the sauce.
To freeze:
The meat balls may be prepared then frozen. Fry from the frozen state. Use within 2–3 months. The sauce is better freshly made.
To economize:
Use inexpensive stewing steak.

Mince Stuffed Pancakes

To make: 25 minutes   **To cook:** 1 hour   **(Serves 4–6)**

For the filling:
1 onion
2 carrots
2 oz./50 g. dripping or fat
12 oz–1lb./300–500 g. minced beef
generous ½ pint/3 dl. stock or water
    and 1 stock cube
½–1 tablespoon tomato purée
seasoning
1 level tablespoon flour
For the pancakes:
4 oz./100 g. flour
¼ teaspoon salt
1 large egg
½ pint/3 dl. milk or milk and water
To fry:
fat or oil

Chop the peeled onion and grate the peeled carrots. Melt the dripping or fat in a pan and fry the minced meat and onion together, browning gently for 10 minutes. Add the grated carrots, most of the stock or water and stock cube, tomato purée and seasoning. Simmer for 30 minutes until tender. Skim off the surplus fat. Mix the flour with the remaining stock or water until smooth and add to the ingredients in the pan. Bring to the boil and simmer until it becomes a thick mixture. Make the pancake batter as page 169. Cook the pancakes until golden brown on either side and keep hot. Fill each pancake with a portion of the mixture and roll up. Arrange on an ovenproof dish, cover lightly and heat in a moderately hot oven, 375–400°F./190–200°C., Gas Mark 5–6, for 15–20 minutes.
To vary:
Chicken pancakes: Blend cooked minced or diced chicken with a white sauce, see page 54, or use minced uncooked chicken in the recipe above.
To freeze:
Add 2 teaspoons oil to the pancake batter. Freeze. Use within 6 weeks.

Speedy Moussaka

2 onions
3 oz./75 g. fat
1 oz./25 g. flour
½ pint/3 dl. stock or water and
    1 stock cube
1 lb./500 g. minced beef or lamb
seasoning
good pinch mixed herbs
12 oz./300 g. peeled potatoes
1 aubergine
½ pint/3 dl. full cream evaporated
    milk (or less if preferred)
6 oz./150 g. grated cheese

Quick tip:
Use canned stewing steak and omit
the first stage. Mix steak with 1–2
tablespoons dehydrated onion and
allow it to stand for 30 minutes to
improve the flavour.

To economize:
Use left-over cooked meat, mince
or dice finely. Make the sauce as
the recipe, stir in the cooked meat,
season and add herbs, then use.
Grate left-over pieces of rather dry
cheese.

Peel and chop the onions, toss in half the fat for a few minutes, then add the
flour and cook for 2 or 3 minutes. Gradually blend in the stock or water and
stock cube, bring to the boil and cook until thickened. Add the meat, stir
very well to break up the lumps that form. Season, add the herbs. then
bring the mixture to the boil, stir again. Lower the heat, cover the pan and
allow to simmer for 35–40 minutes. Stir once or twice during the cooking,
as the mixture is very thick. Meanwhile boil the potatoes in salted water,
drain and slice fairly thickly. Slice the unpeeled aubergine thinly and toss
in the remaining fat until tender. Put half the potatoes and half the sliced
aubergine into a casserole, top with a third of the evaporated milk and
cheese and seasoning. Add the meat mixture, another third of the milk and
cheese and seasoning, then the rest of the aubergine and potato slices. Pour
the remainder of the milk over the top very carefully and sprinkle with the
last of the cheese. Season the mixture and bake for 30 minutes in the centre
of a moderate oven, 350–375°F./180–190°C., Gas Mark 4–5.

To serve:
With salad or green vegetables. This makes an excellent dish for a buffet
supper.

To vary:
Make a cheese sauce with 1 oz./25 g. margarine, 1 oz./25 g. flour, ¾ pint/
4½ dl. milk, seasoning and 4–6 oz./100–150 g. grated cheese. Use instead of
the evaporated milk and cheese.
Add an egg to the evaporated milk or the cheese sauce.

To freeze:
Cook, freeze, then cover well. Use within 3 months.

Speedy moussaka

Cooking Offal

Offal, or variety meats as some people prefer to call them, embrace a wide range of very nutritious meats. Most of them are highly perishable, so store carefully after purchase and use as soon as possible, unless you plan to freeze them.

To freeze offal

Most offal should be eaten within 3 months.

Fried Sweetbreads

To make: 20 minutes plus soaking   **To cook:** 25 minutes   **(Serves 4)**

1 lb./500 g. lambs' or calves'
   sweetbreads
½ pint/3 dl. chicken stock or water
   and ½ chicken stock cube
juice of ½ a lemon
seasoning
To coat:
1 oz./25 g. flour
1 egg
2 tablespoons water
2–3 oz./50–75 g. crisp breadcrumbs
To fry:
oil, or butter and oil, see method
To garnish:
lemon slices

Quick tip:
Put crumbs into a bag, drop the sweetbreads into the bag. Shake vigorously.
To economize:
Sweetbreads are expensive, so serve small portions with plenty of vegetables.

Soak the sweetbreads in cold water for at least 1 hour. Drain, then put into a pan with fresh cold water to cover. Bring the water to the boil, throw this away. This is known as 'blanching' the sweetbreads and it whitens them. Return the sweetbreads to the pan with the stock or water and stock cube, lemon juice and seasoning. Simmer steadily for 10–15 minutes. Lift the sweetbreads from the liquid; this could be used as the basis for a brown sauce, see page 82, to serve with the sweetbreads. Allow the meat to cool and drain well, remove skin and gristle. Coat in flour mixed with seasoning. Beat the egg with the water, brush the sweetbreads with this, then coat in the crumbs. Either fry in hot deep oil for 5–6 minutes or shallow fry in a mixture of butter and oil (use about 2 oz./50 g. butter and 1 tablespoon oil). Turn the sweetbreads as they shallow fry. Drain on absorbent paper.
To serve:
Garnished with lemon slices and with brown sauce, as page 82, or tartare sauce, page 55.
To vary:
Coat the sweetbreads in dry packet stuffing in place of crumbs.
To freeze:
The sweetbreads can be prepared ready for frying, i.e. coated with egg and crumbs, then frozen on a flat tray and wrapped. Use within 6 weeks and fry from the frozen state.

Fried sweetbreads

Oxtail Ragoût

To make: 30 minutes plus soaking   **To cook:** 2½–3 hours   (Serves 4–6)

2–4 oz./50–100 g. haricot beans
seasoning
1 large or 2 smaller oxtail
1–2 oz./25–50 g. fat
1 lb./500 g. mixed vegetables, e.g.
    onions, celery, carrots
2 oz./50 g. flour
2 pints/1¼ litres water
bouquet garni

Quick tip:
Use canned beans.
To economize:
Increase the amount of beans.

Put the beans to soak overnight in cold water to cover. Next day simmer in fresh water, with seasoning to taste, for about 2 hours. Meanwhile joint the oxtail and fry in the hot fat for a few minutes, lift out of the pan. Prepare the vegetables and toss a small amount in any fat remaining in the pan. Stir in the flour, then blend in the water and bring to the boil. Cook until slightly thickened. Return the oxtail to the pan, season well and add the herbs. Cover the pan and simmer for about 1½ hours, add the rest of the vegetables and continue cooking until nearly tender. Add the cooked, well drained beans about 15–20 minutes before serving. Serve with potatoes and a green vegetable. If preferred cool, skim off the surplus fat, then reheat.
To freeze:
This dish can be frozen, but is slightly disappointing, as the oxtail loses its rich flavour. Use within 3–4 weeks.

Liver Risotto

To make: 15 minutes   **To cook:** 25 minutes   (Serves 4–6)

2–3 tablespoons oil
2 onions
2–4 oz./50–100 g. mushrooms
2–3 tomatoes
6 oz./150 g. long grain or Italian rice
¾ pint/4½ dl. stock or water and 1
    chicken stock cube
6–8 oz./150–200 g. chickens'
    calves' or lambs' liver
2 tablespoons sultanas
seasoning
1–2 tablespoons chopped parsley
grated cheese

Heat the oil in the pan and fry the chopped onions, skinned and chopped mushrooms and tomatoes. Add the rice and turn in the hot vegetable mixture (this prevents it becoming sticky). Add the stock or water and stock cube, and simmer for 10 minutes, stirring once or twice as the mixture thickens. Add the diced liver, sultanas, seasoning and parsley. Continue cooking for a further 10 minutes until the excess liquid has evaporated.
To serve:
Top with the grated cheese.
To freeze:
Although better eaten freshly made, this dish can be frozen for 1 month. See comments on page 96 about freezing rice mixtures.
To vary:
Seafood Risotto: Use shell fish instead of diced liver, add towards the end of the cooking time, omit the sultanas if wished.

Braised Kidneys

To make: 20 minutes   **To cook:** 20 minutes   (Serves 4)

12 lambs' kidneys
1–2 oz./25–50 g. fat
½ pint/3 dl. Espagnole sauce (see
    page 82)
Tabasco sauce
To garnish:
parsley
Quick tip:
Use canned kidneys and flavour with fried onion and Tabasco sauce.
To economize:
See To vary.

Skin the kidneys, then fry these in the hot fat. Pour over the Espagnole sauce and flavour with a few drops of Tabasco sauce. Cover and simmer for 15 minutes or until tender.
To serve:
As a substantial savoury on buttered toast, with mixed vegetables or as a filling for omelettes, see page 124. Garnish with parsley.
To vary:
Use economical diced ox kidney with double the amount of sauce, cook for 1½ hours. Serve with potatoes, rice or noodles.
To freeze:
Cook and cool, then cover and freeze. Use within 1 month.

Fried Liver & Bacon

To make: 5 minutes   **To cook:** 10 minutes   (Serves 4)

12 oz.–1lb./300–500 g. lambs' or
    calves' liver
1 tablespoon flour
seasoning
2 oz./50 g. fat, or butter, or mix
    butter and fat or dripping
4 rashers bacon
2–4 tomatoes

Coat the slices of liver with a little flour mixed with seasoning, do not use too much. Heat the fat or butter or mixture of fats and fry the liver for 1–2 minutes then turn and fry on the other side. Add the bacon rashers and halved seasoned tomatoes during cooking. DO NOT overcook the liver, otherwise it becomes tough. Serve as soon as possible.
To vary:
If you like gravy with liver make this in the frying pan so it absorbs the taste of the liver, bacon and tomatoes.

Accompaniments to Meat & Poultry

Many poultry and meat dishes depend upon a good sauce or stuffing to make them interesting. While there are certain basic, or traditional, stuffings and sauces that are served with certain meats or poultry, do not be too conservative. Be prepared to try new ideas to give a change of flavour to an old favourite.

Some Gravies for Meat & Poultry

Many of the most familiar sauces which are based upon a white sauce are found on page 54. Bread and cranberry sauces to serve with chicken and turkey are on page 88 as well as several sauces to blend with duckling or goose.

The most important sauce for meat is a gravy.

To make good gravy:

If roasting meat you can make the gravy in either the roasting tin, or in a saucepan. If making in a roasting tin, pour out all the fat except about 1 tablespoon. For a thin gravy: Blend a very little flour into the fat (use only 1 level tablespoon) and stir over a low heat. Gradually add up to $\frac{1}{2}$ pint/3 dl. meat stock, or strained water from cooking vegetables. Bring slowly to the boil and cook until clear. Flavour with gravy browning. Increase the amount of flour for a thicker gravy.

Brown sauce:

Try to use a good flavoured dripping for this sauce. Heat 2 oz./50 g. dripping (or fat) in a pan, add 1 chopped onion and a small piece of carrot and toss in the hot fat. Stir in 1 oz./25 g. flour, cook gently for 2–3 minutes then blend in $\frac{1}{2}$ pint/3 dl. stock or water and a beef or chicken stock cube. Bring to the boil, stir until thickened, strain or sieve, then season and reheat. This sauce can be flavoured with Madeira or port wine.

Mint sauce:

Mix finely chopped mint leaves with vinegar and sugar to taste.

Apple Sauce:

Many meats and poultry are improved with a fruit sauce and apple sauce blends particularly well with pork and duck. Simmer peeled sliced cooking apples in a little water with sugar or honey to sweeten. Sieve, emulsify or beat until smooth. This freezes well, see page 185.

Horseradish cream:

Grate a small horseradish and blend with lightly whipped cream. Season and flavour with a little made mustard, lemon juice or vinegar and a pinch of sugar.

Horseradish sauce:

Make a white sauce as page 54, remove from the heat and stir in a little grated fresh horseradish, made mustard and lemon juice or vinegar. Do not boil again.

Parsley sauce:

Although this is often served with vegetables or fish, it is also a good accompaniment to boiled bacon. Make a sauce with 1 oz./25 g. butter or margarine, 1 oz./25 g. flour and $\frac{1}{2}$ pint/3 dl. milk or half milk and half bacon stock (use fish stock or vegetable water when appropriate). Stir until thickened, as white sauce, page 54, then add seasoning and 1–2 tablespoons chopped parsley. Heat for 1–2 minutes only.

Some Stuffings for Meat & Poultry

An interesting stuffing adds flavour and a moist texture to all kinds of meat and poultry.

Apple and onion stuffing:

Peel and dice 4 large cooking apples and 4 large onions. Mix with 2 oz./50 g. melted butter or margarine, 1 tablespoon brown sugar, 4 oz./100 g. soft breadcrumbs or mashed potato and season well. Use for duck, goose and pork. If cooking in a separate dish cover well and allow 1 hour in the coolest part of a moderately hot oven, 375–400°F./190–200°C., Gas Mark 5–6. The recipe for Sage and Onion Stuffing is on page 89.

Roast beef

Chestnut Stuffing

To make: 15–30 minutes   **To cook:** see method   **(Serves 4–6)**

2 lb./1 kilo chestnuts or a 15 oz./
   425 g. can chestnut purée
little stock or water
seasoning
4 oz./100 g. chopped ham or
   bacon
2 oz./50 g. melted butter
2 tablespoons chopped parsley

To economize:
Mix with 4 oz./100 g. soft
breadcrumbs or 1 lb./500 g.
sausagemeat.

If using fresh chestnuts, split the skins, boil for 10 minutes, then remove the skins while warm. Return the nuts to the stock or seasoned water and simmer until tender then sieve or emulsify. Mix the fresh or canned purée with the remaining ingredients. Use as a stuffing for chicken, turkey or duck.
To vary:
If stuffing duck add 1–2 chopped fresh onions and a little sage.
To freeze:
This freezes well, use within 3 months.

Veal (Parsley & Thyme) Stuffing

To make: 15 minutes   **To cook:** see method   **(Serves 4–6)**

4 oz./100 g. soft breadcrumbs
2 oz./50 g. shredded suet or
   melted butter or magarine
grated rind and juice of $\frac{1}{2}$ a lemon
1–2 tablespoons chopped parsley
$\frac{1}{2}$–1 teaspoon chopped lemon
   thyme or $\frac{1}{4}$ teaspoon dried
   thyme
seasoning
1 egg, beaten

Mix all the ingredients together. This stuffing is excellent with chicken, turkey, veal, etc. You will need at least twice the quantity for a turkey. Put into the neck end of a bird. This stuffing can be rolled into small balls and baked for about 35 minutes in a moderately hot oven, 375–400°F/190–200°C., Gas Mark 5–6.
To vary:
Add a little finely chopped raw bacon, or the chopped cooked giblets of the bird or mix with 8 oz./200 g. sausagemeat.
To freeze:
Pack into a carton or polythene bag, use within 3 months.

Poultry and Game

Choose poultry carefully. Young birds have pliable wishbones and the legs and breast are plump and pliable, not sinewy. A boiling fowl is a creamy colour, but there should not be too much fat. Ducks and geese generally have little breast meat, but buy one with as much flesh on the breast and legs as possible. Avoid over-fat ducks and geese. Poultry should have bright-coloured, firm bills.

For frying or grilling buy a frying or 'broiler' bird, small-jointed and plump. For roasting buy a larger young chicken or capon. Boiling fowl can be cooked slowly in a casserole or steamed or boiled. If substituting an older boiling fowl for a chicken in casserole recipes, allow about twice the cooking time and increase the amount of liquid slightly.

Ducks and geese are less adaptable and are best roasted and used in casseroles, see page 94.

Economical poultry and game dishes: Use small pieces of cooked poultry as a filling in pancakes or in omelettes.

Heat fairly solid pieces of cooked poultry in a little hot fat, then pour over a Yorkshire pudding batter and make a poultry 'Toad in the Hole', see the recipe on page 99.

Really young tender jointed rabbit can be fried like young chicken. Coat the joints in seasoned flour, then in beaten egg and crumbs. Fry fairly quickly to brown the outside, then lower the heat and cook more steadily until tender. Drain the rabbit on absorbent kitchen paper and serve with Tartare sauce, as the recipe on page 55, and garnished with wedges of lemon.

The coating for the rabbit joints can be flavoured with a little grated lemon rind or chopped herbs.

To freeze: Poultry and game are successful foods to freeze, as indicated by the popularity of commercial products. When freezing poultry or game birds yourself, check they are well plucked, drawn and trussed. Wrap the giblets in a *separate* polythene bag, put this inside or near the birds. Cover the sharp leg bones with extra polythene or foil, so they do not pierce the wrapping. Wrap thick polythene or foil as tightly as possible round the birds. The tighter the wrapping, the more the air is excluded; this hastens freezing and gives the best result. Hang game to personal taste *before* freezing.

Frozen whole birds or large pieces of game meat should be defrosted *before* cooking. This takes a surprisingly long time. A good-sized chicken needs at least 24 hours in the refrigerator to thaw out properly; a large turkey takes from 48–82 hours. The reason it is important to allow the flesh to thaw out is that it is surprisingly easy to cook the outer flesh of poultry or game birds while still frozen, but the heat may not penetrate through to the inside of the carcass. Small portions of frozen chicken, such as breast and legs, can generally be cooked from the frozen state, if more convenient. There are exceptions to this, e.g. when coating the joints, or when they need to absorb extra flavour. This is indicated in the recipes in this book. Frozen jointed rabbit and hare can also be cooked without defrosting.

Store frozen chicken for up to a year, I prefer to use within 8 months. Duck, goose and turkey: use within 5–6 months. Game birds: freeze for up to 8 months, game meat for 6 months. When cooked, halve these times or store according to the dish.

Devilled chicken

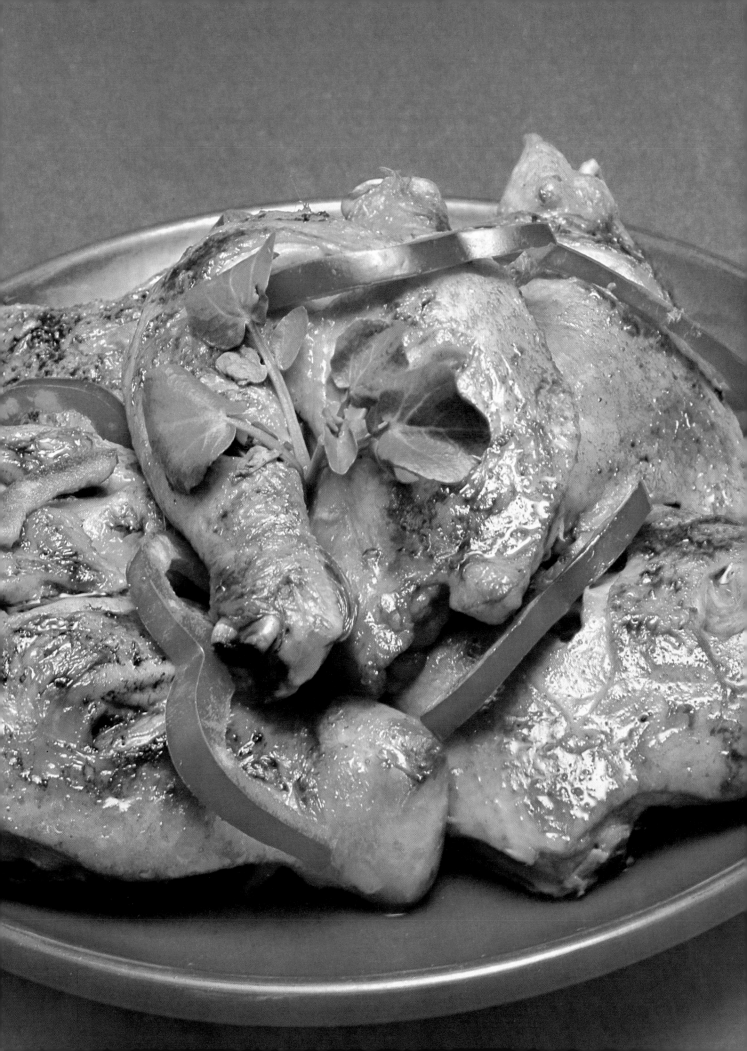

Devilled Chicken Legs

To make: 10 minutes   **To cook:** 16–20 minutes   **(Serves 4)**

For the devilled sauce:
3 tablespoons olive or corn oil
1 tablespoon Worcestershire
 sauce
1 tablespoon tarragon vinegar
1 tablespoon finely chopped
 onion or 1 teaspoon dehydrated
 onion
1 teaspoon French mustard
seasoning

4 chicken legs
4–8 oz./100–200 g. mushrooms
1 tablespoon olive or corn oil
To garnish:
parsley

Quick tip:
A good way to heat ready-cooked
chicken or turkey. Allow 2–3
minutes on either side.

Mix all the ingredients for the sauce together. If using frozen chicken joints, allow these to thaw out first. Score the chicken legs with a sharp knife and place in a grill pan. Brush with the Devilled sauce and place under a hot grill. Grill for 8–10 minutes, basting frequently with the sauce. Turn, brush with more sauce and continue grilling for a further 8–10 minutes, or until cooked. Brush the mushrooms with the oil, add to grill pan for the last 5 minutes cooking time.
To serve:
Hot, garnished with parsley and with salad.
To vary:
Add $\frac{1}{2}$–1 teaspoon curry powder to the sauce.
Cook lamb chops in the same way.
To freeze:
Do not freeze this dish, but you can use frozen chicken.
To economize:
Make chicken rissoles with $\frac{1}{4}$ pint/1$\frac{1}{2}$ dl. thick white sauce, see page 54, 8–12 oz./200–300 g. minced cooked chicken (mince skin and all the tiny pieces), 2 oz./50 g. soft breadcrumbs and seasoning. Make into flat cakes, heat in a *little fat*, pour over the Devilled sauce above and heat for 2–3 minutes only.

Chicken Cordon Bleu

To make: 10 minutes   **To cook:** 12–15 minutes   **(Serves 4)**

4 chicken breasts
4 slices ham
4 slices Gruyère cheese
seasoning
$\frac{1}{2}$ oz./15 g. flour
To coat:
1 egg
2 oz./50 g. soft breadcrumbs
To fry:
deep oil or fat

Quick tip:
Use ready-cooked chicken
breasts. Insert ham and cheese,
coat and heat for 2–3 minutes
only.
To economize:
Use snippets of fried bacon
pieces and grated cheese as the
filling.

If using frozen chicken breasts allow them to de-frost for this recipe. Dry well, then slit to make a pocket. Insert the slices of ham and cheese into the pockets. Mix a little seasoning with the flour and dust the chicken breasts with this. Coat in beaten egg and crumbs and fry steadily in the oil or fat until crisp, golden brown and tender. This takes about 12–15 minutes. Drain on absorbent paper. Serve at once with salad.
To vary:
Chicken Rossini: Fill the chicken breasts with pâté and finely diced uncooked mushrooms instead of the ham and cheese. Coat and fry as above.
Russian chicken: Blend a little made mustard with 2 oz./50 g. butter. Add 1 tablespoon finely chopped onion, 1 tablespoon finely diced green pepper and 2 tablespoons neatly sliced mushrooms. Press this mixture into the chicken breasts, then coat and fry as above.
Chicken in soured cream sauce: Do not coat or fill the chicken breasts. Simply fry until golden brown in a little butter. Lift out of the pan, add some finely diced onion and mushrooms and fry for 2–3 minutes. Pour in $\frac{1}{2}$ pint/3 dl. soured cream and season well. Replace the chicken breasts and heat gently until tender.
To freeze:
The completed dish is not suitable for freezing, but it is a good idea to prepare this, then freeze. Fry from the frozen state and use within 2 months.

To Grill Chicken

Joint chicken as below. Brush with melted butter or oil. Put on the oiled or greased grid of the grill pan and place under a hot grill until brown on either side. Lower the heat and cook more gently for 10 minutes. Some of the suggestions for adding flavour to grilled or fried meat on page 61 would also be suitable for chicken.

To Fry Chicken

Buy jointed frying 'broiler' chicken or cut a young chicken into halves or quarters. For shallow frying, heat fat, oil or butter and oil to give a depth of $\frac{1}{2}$-inch/1-cm. Fry quickly to brown the chicken on either side, lower the heat and fry gently for 10 minutes.
The chicken can be coated with seasoned flour, beaten egg and crumbs as recipe above or batter, page 44, then fried in shallow or deep fat. Drain on absorbent paper and serve hot or cold with vegetables or salad.

Chicken cordon bleu

To Roast Chicken & Turkey

Both chicken and turkey have the same tendency to dry during cooking, unless kept well covered with fat. Once we used bacon to cover the breast of the bird, but since this has become more costly I now use butter, margarine or chicken fat; meat dripping has too pronounced a flavour. Stuffings inside a bird give extra flavour and also help to keep it moist. If you want to roast a bird without stuffing, then place a good knob of butter inside to keep it from drying.

A covered roasting tin is ideal for these birds or put the bird into the tin, covered with butter or other fat, see above, then lay foil loosely over. I prefer this to wrapping the bird in foil. The modern polythene cooking-bags are also excellent for keeping the moist texture and allowing the bird to brown. When using a covered roasting tin, foil or bag allow 10–15 minutes extra cooking time, or use 25°F./10°C., 1 Gas Mark higher than when using an open roasting tin. If you choose to wrap the bird entirely in foil, then allow at least 15 minutes extra cooking time.
There are three ways of roasting poultry. These depend upon the weight of the bird, so weigh *after* trussing, but with the stuffing.

1) Fast roasting:

Allow 15 minutes per lb./500 g. and 15 minutes over up to 12 lb./6 kilo; after this add an extra 12 minutes only for each extra 1 lb./500 g. Use a hot oven, 425°F./220°C., Gas Mark 7, for the first 30–45 minutes, then lower the heat to moderately hot, 375–400°F./190–200°C., Gas Mark 5–6, for the rest of the time. This is suitable for prime birds, that have not been frozen.

2) Slower roasting:

Allow 25 minutes per lb./500 g. and 25 minutes over, plus an extra 20–22 minutes per lb./500 g. over 12 lb./6 kilo. The extra 2 minutes for large birds is good if the turkey has been frozen. Use a moderate oven, 325–350°F./170–180°C., Gas Mark 3–4. This method is far better for defrosted frozen birds, or if you feel the bird is not quite as perfect as you would wish.

3) Ultra slow roasting:

This appeals to many people who have bought a very large bird and want to roast it during the night. Allow 1½ hours for the first 1 lb./500 g. then 25 minutes for every extra 1 lb./500 g. up to 12 lb./6 kilo, then reduce the time to 20–22 minutes per extra 1 lb./500 g. Set the oven to 275–300°F./140–150°C., Gas Mark 1–2. The skin does not look very crisp and appetising with this method, so raise the temperature for the last 20–30 minutes.

To Roast Portions of Turkey

Make the stuffing in the usual way. Press this against the cut side of the bird and lay downwards in the roasting tin. It is quite a good idea to place a piece of foil under the stuffing as this makes it easier to remove from the tin. Cover if wished, see above. Time the roasting as for the whole bird, but tend to shorten the time by a few minutes, as it is easier for the heat to penetrate through part of a bird.

Using Frozen Poultry or Game

It is always rather surprising just how long it takes to defrost a frozen chicken, duck, goose or turkey. Allow at least 24 hours for a small bird and up to 72 hours for a very large turkey. Do not try to cook from the frozen state, but if you want to hurry defrosting put the bird into cold, *but not hot,* water.

After defrosting dry the bird very well, both inside and out. Remember that often the giblets are packed inside the bird, take these out and put into a pan. Cover with water, add seasoning and simmer to give you a really good stock for gravy.

To Serve with Chicken & Turkey

The traditional accompaniments to chicken and turkey are:

Bacon rolls: Stretch de-rinded rashers of bacon by stroking with a knife; this makes it easier to roll the bacon. Cut long rashers of bacon in half, roll firmly and secure with a skewer if wished. Either cook in the oven for the last 15–25 minutes of the roasting time, depending upon the heat of the oven, or grill. You can roll the bacon round sausages and cook these together.

Sausages: Cook round the bird or in a separate tin in the oven.

Bread sauce: Peel a small onion and press in 3–4 cloves (omit these if wished). Put the onion into a pan with ½ pint/3 dl. milk, 1–2 oz./25–50 g. butter or margarine, 2 oz./50 g. soft breadcrumbs and seasoning. Bring the milk to the boil, cover the pan and put on one side, in a warm place if possible. Leave until almost ready to serve the meal, then heat gently, stirring well. Remove the onion, beat hard, then serve. This is enough for 4–6.
It improves the flavour of bread sauce if you add 1–2 tablespoons cream before reheating. Bread sauce has a tendency to burn, so try cooking it in a basin over hot water, or the top of a double saucepan. Alternatively bring the sauce to the boil, transfer to a dish, cover, and stand in the warming drawer of your cooker.

Cranberry sauce: This is the traditional sauce for turkey. Simmer cranberries in a little sugar and water, flavouring this with orange juice, a little grated orange rind or port wine. When just tender remove from the heat and sieve or emulsify if preferred.
Another delicious sauce is made by putting the raw cranberries into the blender with tiny pieces of the orange rind (discard the pith), and the pulp of the oranges (remove all the skin and pips.) Allow 2 oranges to each 1 lb./500 g. cranberries. Add sugar to taste and emulsify.

To freeze: Both the bread sauce and the cranberry sauce freeze well. Use the bread sauce within about 6 weeks, but the cranberry sauce lasts up to 1 year.

Veal (parsley and thyme) and chestnut stuffing are excellent with chicken and turkey and these recipes are on page 83.

To Roast Duck & Goose

These birds have a generous amount of fat and it is important to encourage most of this to run out during cooking. Duck and goose are also much improved if the skin is crisp and brown. The way to achieve perfect roasting is to prick duckling once or twice during cooking and goose several times. Do this very lightly using a fine metal skewer so the fat 'spurts out' and does not soak through the flesh.

Use an open roasting tin and time as for roasting chicken or turkey, page 87. If you have a trivet stand the bird on this in the roasting tin; do not add extra fat. Follow the roasting times for chicken or turkey on page 87.

Roast goose

To Serve with Duck and Goose

These birds have a rich flavour and therefore all accompaniments should be well flavoured, preferably with fruit. Apple sauce, page 82, and sage and onion stuffing, below, are traditional, but there are other stuffings and sauces to serve with either bird.

Goose stuffed with prunes and apples:

Stuff the bird with stoned soaked prunes and quartered dessert apples sprinkled with a little sage.

Caneton aux cerises:

This is ideal for small young ducklings (allow half per person), rather than the larger duck (canard). Follow the roasting instructions opposite, but do not stuff. Simmer the giblets to give a good stock, then strain most carefully. To make a sauce for 6–8 people, pour ½ pint/3 dl. giblet stock, ½ pint/3 dl. cherry syrup, from canned or cooked Morello or black cherries, blended with 1 oz./25 g. cornflour into a pan. Stir over a low heat until thickened, add 2 tablespoons redcurrant jelly, 2 tablespoons cherry brandy and 8–12 oz./200–300 g. well drained cherries. Heat gently. This sauce does not need fat. Halve the ducklings and serve topped with sauce.

Caneton à l'orange:

To make enough sauce for 4 people, cut the rind from 2 oranges (bitter oranges are ideal) remove any pith, cut into matchstick pieces. Soak for 1–2 hours then simmer in ¾ pint/4½ dl. well strained giblet stock until the peel is tender. Do not cover the pan so the liquid evaporates a little. Blend ¼ pint/1½ dl. orange juice with ½ oz./15 g. cornflour, put into the pan with the stock, and simmer until thickened and clear. Add seasoning and a little sugar.

This sauce is varied in many ways; you can flavour a good gravy with orange juice and a little Curaçao (orange flavoured brandy). Another method is just to simmer large pieces of rind or even grated rind in the stock until it is reduced to about ½ pint/3 dl. then strain and use with the juice in the recipe above.

Sage and onion stuffing:

Peel and chop 4 large onions. Simmer in ½ pint/3 dl. seasoned water for 10 minutes. Strain (save some stock) and blend with 6 oz./150 g. breadcrumbs, ½–1 tablespoon chopped sage or 1 teaspoon dried sage and 4 oz./100 g. shredded suet or melted margarine. Bind with onion stock or 1–2 eggs and stock. Put into a duck or goose or cook separately in a covered dish. Serves 4–8.

To Roast Game

In order to judge whether game is sufficiently young to roast, rather than cook in a stew, check to see the legs are plump and not sinewy. While there may be some fat on a young bird, a thick layer of fat under the skin generally indicates an older bird, more suitable for cooking in a casserole dish.

If you like game with a strong flavour hang for more than a week before cooking, otherwise hang for a few days only; if cooked when freshly killed the meat tends to be tough.

All game tends to become dry when roasted unless you keep it well basted with fat.

While it is not traditional to stuff game birds, I always put in a generous piece of butter or cream cheese to make sure I moisten from the inside as well as the outside.

Roasting times:

Small birds: Partridge, pigeon, widgeon, woodcock need a total of about 25–30 minutes in a hot oven.
Larger birds: Grouse, pheasant, etc., roast as chicken, page 87.
Young hare: Roast the back joints (saddle) as pork, page 67, and casserole the legs.
Young rabbit or venison: Roast as pork, page 67.

To cook older game:

Simmer gently for the time given for 'boiled' chicken, page 91; then joint and put into the ragoût on page 94. 1–2 tablespoons redcurrant jelly would improve the flavour of the sauce. The Savoury Beef Stew on page 71 or variations on this, page 76 can also be used as a basis for stews using game.

To Serve with Roast Game

Serve game birds with bread sauce, page 88, or redcurrant jelly, fried crumbs, see below, and game chips; bacon rolls are often served as well. Roast rabbit, hare and venison are generally served with the same accompaniments as pork, page 67, although you could serve the same ones as for game birds.

To fry crumbs:

Make fairly coarse crumbs with your fingers (a blender makes them too fine), fry in hot butter or fat until golden brown and crisp. Drain on absorbent paper. It is worthwhile to fry a large quantity, freeze them, then pack into containers. Use within about 3 months.

Game chips:

Cut wafer thin slices of potato, fry quickly in hot fat or oil, see page 104 for details of frying potatoes and testing the temperature of the oil.

Chicken Curry

To make: 25 minutes   To cook: 1¼ hours   (Serves 4)

1 lb./500 g. chicken (weight without bone)
2 oz./50 g. butter
3 onions
1 clove garlic
2 sticks celery
1 apple
1–2 tablespoons curry powder
1 tablespoon flour
½ pint/3 dl. stock or water and ½ chicken stock cube
seasoning
¼ pint/1½ dl. yoghourt
1 banana
2 tablespoons chutney
To garnish:
1–2 bananas
few gherkins

Cut the chicken into cubes and fry these in the butter for a few minutes, then remove from the pan. Fry the sliced onions, crushed garlic, diced celery and peeled and diced apple in the remaining butter. Add the curry powder and flour, blend with the vegetable mixture. Stir in the stock or water and stock cube, add seasoning and replace the chicken. Lower the heat, cover the pan, then simmer for about 45 minutes. Add the yoghourt, sliced banana and chutney. Cook slowly for a further 15 minutes.

To serve:
In a border of cooked rice, see page 95, garnished with bananas and gherkins and accompanied by chutney, diced pineapple and diced preserved ginger.

Note: It is a good idea to make the curry, let it stand over-night then reheat.

To vary:
This particular recipe is delicious as a cold curry.
Use diced meat in place of chicken. If using stewing steak allow 2¼ hours cooking before adding the yoghourt and increase the liquid to 1 pint/6 dl. If using stewing lamb allow 1¼–1½ hours cooking and increase the liquid to ¾ pint/4½ dl.

To freeze:
This curry freezes well for 2 months or 3 months if the yoghourt etc., is not added until the dish is reheated.

Normandy Chicken

4–6 joints young chicken
1 oz./25 g. butter
1 tablespoon oil
1 onion
1 clove garlic
3 rashers streaky bacon
1 oz./25 g. flour
$\frac{3}{4}$ pint/4$\frac{1}{2}$ dl. dry cider
2 eating apples
$\frac{1}{4}$ pint/1$\frac{1}{2}$ dl. single cream
1 tablespoon chopped parsley

Quick tip:
Make the sauce, heat diced *cooked* chicken in this, then add the apple and cream.

To economize:
Use left-over cooked meat or chicken.

Dry the chicken joints. Heat the butter and oil in a large saucepan and fry the chicken on both sides until golden brown. Remove from the pan and put on a plate. Add the chopped onion, crushed garlic and chopped bacon to the fat in the pan and cook for 5 minutes, or until the onion is golden. Stir in the flour and cook for 1 minute. Gradually stir in the cider and bring to the boil; cook until a smooth sauce. Return the chicken to the pan, cover and simmer gently for 30 minutes. Core and dice the apples, but do not remove the peel. Stir into the chicken mixture with the cream. Heat for 2–3 minutes *without* boiling, turn into a heated serving dish and sprinkle with chopped parsley.

To serve:
With a green salad.

To vary:
Use a little less cider and add a small amount of Calvados.

To freeze:
This dish does not freeze well, but frozen chicken joints could be used; fry from the frozen state.

Normandy chicken

To Boil Chicken

The term 'boiling' is not correct in describing the way in which chicken is cooked in liquid as the liquid should only *simmer* gently; see comments under 'to boil meat', page 74. If 'boiling' a young chicken allow 20 minutes per lb./500 g. and 20 minutes over, from the time the liquid comes to simmering point. An older boiling fowl needs 35–40 minutes per 1 lb./500 g. and 35–40 minutes over.

To give extra flavour to the stock and chicken, add mixed vegetables, a little wine and a *bouquet garni*. Use the stock for soup and in making a sauce to serve with the bird, see parsley sauce, page 82 and sauce under Chicken Suprême page 95.

Pies & Puddings with Poultry

Chicken and turkey lend themselves to many varying recipes for pies and puddings. The recipe below could be adapted to use pieces of turkey instead of chicken which is particularly useful now it is possible to buy portions of turkey. The recipe below using turkey in a pudding is also suitable for chicken, or see the variation on page 72.

Chicken Pie

To make: 1 hour plus standing   **To cook:** $2\frac{1}{4}-2\frac{1}{2}$ hours   **(Serves 6–8)**

4 lb./2 kilo chicken
water
1 small onion
1 carrot
1 leek and/or 1 stick celery,
seasoning
For the sauce:
2 onions
1–2 red peppers
2 oz./50 g. green chilli peppers
2 oz./50 g. butter
2 oz./50 g. flour
1 pint/6 dl. chicken stock
   (see method)
4 oz./100 g. Cheddar cheese
seasoning
For the pastry:
6 oz./150 g. puff pastry (see
   page 97)
1 egg

Quick tip:
Use ready cooked chicken, a can of condensed cream of chicken soup and chopped canned red peppers. Use 12–13 oz./340–350 g. frozen puff pastry.
To economize:
Omit the rather expensive peppers and chillies and flavour the sauce with cooked peas and carrots.

Simmer the chicken in sufficient water to cover, with the vegetables and seasoning, for about $1-1\frac{1}{4}$ hours. Remove the chicken, reduce the liquor to 1 pint/6 dl. by rapid boiling and then strain. To make the sauce, chop the onions, red pepper(s) and chilli peppers (discard cores and seeds); if you wish to remove the chilli peppers after frying do not chop them but cut in half. Melt the butter in a pan, fry the onion, red peppers and chilli peppers for 10 minutes, then remove the chillies, if wished. Carve the chicken, cutting it into fork-size pieces, and discard the skin. Place the meat in a 3-pint/$1\frac{3}{4}$-litre pie dish with a funnel.
Blend in the flour and slowly add the stock, stirring continuously. Bring to the boil. When the liquid has thickened, add the grated cheese but do not cook again; adjust the seasoning. Spoon over the chicken and allow to cool. Roll out the puff pastry and use to cover the filled pie dish. Knock up and scallop the edge and score the top of the pastry into diamonds with a knife, glaze with beaten egg. Cook in the centre of a very hot oven, 450°F/230°C., Gas Mark 8, for 20–25 minutes. Reduce heat to very moderate, 325°F./170°C., Gas Mark 3, and cook for a further 30 minutes. Serve hot or cold.

To freeze:
Prepare the pie, freeze, wrap and use within 2–3 months. Thaw out before cooking. If more convenient to cook the pie first, reheat gently from the frozen state.
Chicken, mushroom and pepper pie: Follow the recipe above but cut the chicken into larger pieces. Omit the cheese from the sauce but add 4–6 oz./100–150 g. fried mushrooms. Turkey can be used instead of chicken and short crust pastry, see page 122, if preferred.
Game pie: Use jointed cooked grouse, pheasant or partridge in the chicken pie, omit the cheese and make the sauce with game stock.

Turkey Pudding

To make: 30 minutes   **To cook:** 2–3 hours   **(Serves 4–6)**

$1-1\frac{1}{4}$ lb./500–600 g. turkey meat
   (weight without bones)
2 onions
veal stuffing made with 4 oz./100 g.
   soft breadcrumbs (see page 83)
1–2 tablespoons flour
seasoning
suet crust pastry made with
   10 oz./250 g. flour, etc.
   (see page 72)
little turkey stock (see method)

This is an excellent dish to make if you buy part of a turkey; use some for roasting, see page 87 and some in this recipe. Dice the meat and chop the onions. Form the stuffing into little balls. Coat the meat, onions and the stuffing balls in the flour mixed with the seasoning. Make the pastry and line the basin as described under Steak and Kidney Pudding, page 72. Fill with the turkey mixture and stuffing balls. Add enough stock to come half way up the mixture. Cover and cook for 3 hours, see page 72.
To serve:
With mixed vegetables.
To vary:
Rabbit pudding: As above, but omit the stuffing balls. Mix a little freshly chopped or dried sage with the rabbit, etc., and add diced fat bacon and diced carrots.
To freeze:
Cook for $2\frac{1}{2}$ hours to make sure the pastry is light. Cool, wrap and freeze. Allow to thaw, then heat for 1 hour. Alternatively prepare, but do *not* cook, then freeze. Use within 2 months.

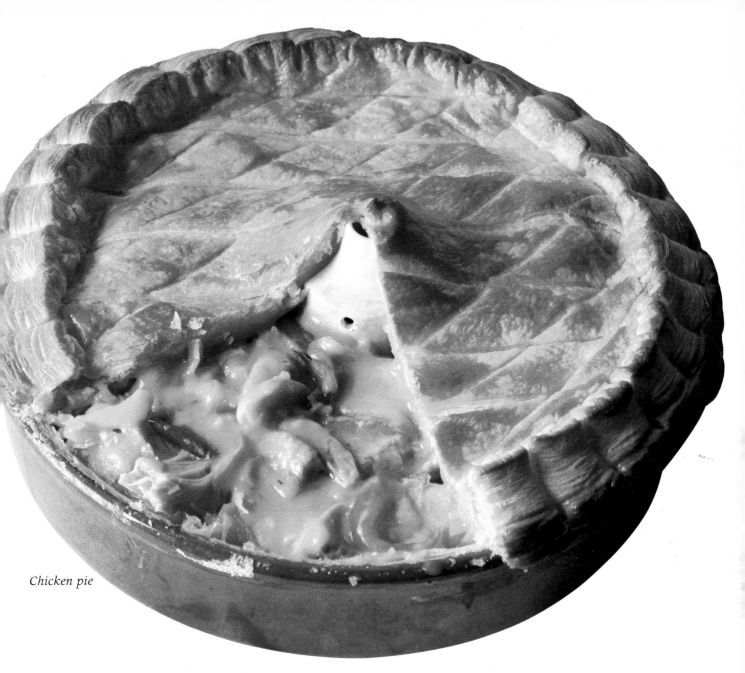

Chicken pie

Game Pasties

To make: 30 minutes **To cook:** 50 minutes plus making stock **(Serves 4)**

2–3 young pigeons, or
  1 small young pheasant
  or ½ large young rabbit
2–3 medium-sized onions
4 medium-sized potatoes
2 tablespoons stock (see method)
seasoning
pinch mixed herbs
short crust pastry made with
  12 oz./300 g. flour etc.
  (see page 122).
To glaze:
1 egg

Remove all the meat from the bones of the bird or rabbit; simmer the bones to give stock (any remaining stock can be used in a gravy to serve with the hot pasties or in soup). Cut the meat into ¼–½-inch/½–1-cm. dice. Peel the onions and potatoes, cut into the same-sized pieces. Mix with the stock, seasoning and herbs. Roll out the pastry to about ¼-inch/½-cm. in thickness. Cut into 4 large rounds. Put a quarter of the game mixture into the centre of each pastry round. Brush the edges of the pastry with water, seal firmly, then form into a pasty shape. Lift on to a greased baking tray. Brush with beaten egg. Cook for 20–25 minutes in the centre of a hot oven, 400–425°F/200–220°C., Gas Mark 6–7 to brown the pastry, then lower the heat to moderate, 350°F./180°C., Gas Mark 4 for a further 25–30 minutes.

To serve:
Hot or cold with vegetables or salad.
To vary:
Cornish Pasties: Use diced rump or topside of beef.
To freeze:
Do *not* freeze uncooked pasties as the potato will spoil; these are better eaten freshly made.

Using Cooked Meat & Poultry

I have grouped the recipes for using cooked meat and poultry together in this section as the recipes I have chosen are equally successful with either. You will notice however that I have adapted the herbs and flavouring according to the meat or poultry used. Remember cooked meat or poultry can be rather dry, so give flavour and an interesting texture to the food with good sauces.

Note: When reheating cooked poultry or meat it is essential that this is thoroughly heated and not just warmed for a few minutes. This rule applies also when reheating left-over stews. The liquid must come to the boil and be maintained at this temperature for some minutes.

Ragoût of Duckling

To make: 25 minutes   **To cook**: 1 hour   (Serves 4)

2 oz./50 g. fat
2 onions, chopped
1 oz./25 g. flour
¾ pint/4½ dl. duck stock or
    water and 1 chicken stock cube
seasoning
½–1 teaspoon freshly chopped or
    pinch dried sage
2 large carrots, diced
6–8 oz. cooked or canned
    chestnuts or diced Chinese
    water chestnuts
3 tablespoons port wine
enough cooked duckling for 4
To garnish:
1–2 oranges

Although this is a good way to use up pieces of cooked duckling, it is also a practical recipe when entertaining, as it can be prepared earlier and heated when required. If cooking a duckling specially do not over-cook, and joint.

Heat the fat and fry the onions, for 4–5 minutes. Blend in the flour, then stir over a low heat for 2–3 minutes. Add the stock or water and stock cube. Bring to the boil and cook until thickened. Add the seasoning, sage and carrots. Cover the pan, simmer for 40 minutes, then add the chestnuts, port wine and portions of duckling, heat gently, but thoroughly. Garnish with orange slices.
To serve:
With apple sauce, page 82, and an orange salad, page 110.
To vary:
Use game birds or rabbit, hare, goose, chicken, turkey, sliced cooked meat, cooked pork or lamb chops.
To freeze:
Cook, cool then freeze and use within 2 months. I prefer to add the chestnuts and port wine when reheating this dish.
Note: If you like the crisp skin on duckling or goose do not add the poultry to the sauce as described above. Prepare the sauce in the pan, then transfer to a large, heated shallow heatproof dish. Lay the portions of poultry on this, skin side uppermost. Cover the dish and heat thoroughly for about 30 minutes in a moderate oven, 350°F./180°C., Gas Mark 4. Remove the lid and crisp the skin for a few minutes under the grill.

Chicken Cutlets

To make: 25 minutes   **To cook**: 20 minutes   (Serves 4)

about 12 oz./300 g. cooked
    chicken (use the skin as well)
1 oz./25 g. chicken fat or
    margarine
1½ oz./40 g. flour
¼ pint/1½ dl. chicken
    stock or milk
seasoning
2 oz./50 g. soft breadcrumbs
1 tablespoon chopped parsley
1 egg
2 oz./50 g. crisp breadcrumbs
To fry:
little fat or oil
To freeze:
Either cook and freeze, or prepare and freeze. Use within 1 month. Do not cover the cutlets until frozen, otherwise the coating sticks to the wrapping.

Mince the chicken finely. Make a thick sauce with the chicken fat or margarine, 1 oz./25 g. of the flour and the stock or milk; stir well as the mixture thickens, see page 54. Add seasoning, the chicken, soft breadcrumbs and parsley. Make 8 small rounds on a plate and allow to cool. Form into cutlet shapes, coat in the remaining flour mixed with seasoning, then in beaten egg and crisp breadcrumbs. Fry for about 4–5 minutes in hot shallow fat or oil. Drain on absorbent paper.
To serve:
Hot with vegetables or cold with salad.
To vary:
Use any left-over cooked minced meat or poultry. Vary the binding sauce as required; use a brown stock with meat.
A little wine can be added to the sauce, if wished. If you have left-over stuffing mince or chop this and add to the mixture, in which case use slightly less breadcrumbs.
Double the amount of fat or margarine and fry 1–2 finely chopped onions in this, then make the sauce.
Rissoles: these are made in the same way as the cutlets, but the mixture is formed into flat round cakes.

Ragoût of duckling

Chicken Suprême

To make: 15 minutes   **To cook:** 30–40 minutes   **(Serves 4)**

few mushrooms
2 sprigs parsley
1 small onion
1 oz./25 g. butter
1 oz./25 g. flour
½ pint/3 dl. chicken stock or
    water and 1 chicken stock cube
2 teaspoons lemon juice
12 oz./300 g. cooked chicken
1 egg yolk
4 tablespoons double cream
seasoning
For the rice:
8 oz./200 g. long grain rice
1 pint/6 dl. water
½–1 level teaspoon salt
2 tablespoons chopped parsley

Quick tip:
Use canned mushrooms and dehydrated onion or heat the chicken in condensed cream of chicken soup. Flavour with sherry.

To economize:
If using a smaller amount of poultry, make a more satisfying meal by topping with sliced hard-boiled egg.

Chop the mushrooms, parsley and onion. Melt the butter in a saucepan and toss in this for 5 minutes. Stir in the flour and cook for 1 minute. Gradually stir in the stock or water and stock cube, bring to the boil, stirring all the time. Reduce the heat, cover the pan and simmer very gently for 20–30 minutes. Strain the sauce if wished and add the lemon juice. Slice the chicken; the skin can be left on for extra flavour and colour. Add to the sauce and heat the chicken through for about 5 minutes. Mix the egg yolk with the cream, season then stir in 3 tablespoons of the hot chicken sauce. Pour the cream mixture into the pan and heat *without boiling*. Put the rice, water, salt and parsley into a saucepan. Bring to the boil and stir once. Cover and simmer for 15 minutes or until the rice is tender and all the liquid is absorbed.

To serve:
Put the rice round the edge of the serving dish and spoon the chicken and sauce into the centre.

To vary:
Add 1–2 tablespoons sherry to the egg yolk and cream.

To freeze:
This dish can be frozen, but there is a possibility of the sauce curdling. It is better to make the sauce without the egg yolk and cream. Heat gently add the egg yolk and cream just before serving. Use within 2–3 months.

Note: This recipe is an ideal dish for an invalid. It may be a good idea to omit the mushrooms, parsley and onion and simply to serve the chicken coated with the plain sauce Suprême. To give extra food value make the sauce with half stock and half milk.

2 onions
1 clove garlic (optional)
2 tablespoons chicken fat or oil
8 oz./200 g. long grain rice
1 pint/6 dl. chicken stock made
    by simmering the chicken
    carcass or giblets
1–2 oz./25–50 g. sultanas
few pine or other nuts (optional)
12 oz./300 g. diced cooked
    chicken (weight without bone)
seasoning

To garnish:
few nuts or crisp breadcrumbs

Quick tip:
Use dehydrated onion and garlic
salt.

To economize:
Use only a small quantity of
chicken and add left-over cooked
vegetables.

Peel and chop the onions, crush the garlic. Fry in the hot chicken fat or oil for a few minutes, then add the rice, turning in the fat or oil. Add the stock, bring to the boil and stir. Simmer in an open pan for about 10 minutes. Add the rest of the ingredients, then cook for a further 10–15 minutes until the liquid has just been absorbed. Pile on to a hot dish and top with the nuts or crumbs.

To serve:
With salad or a green vegetable.

To vary:
Use diced cooked turkey or lean lamb instead of chicken.

Use uncooked chicken or turkey in the basic recipe. Allow at least 1 lb./ 500 g. boned diced chicken or turkey. Fry this in the hot oil with the onions and garlic, then add the rice and proceed as the basic recipe.

Use uncooked, diced lamb in the basic recipe. The ideal cut would be a thick slice, weighing 1¼ lb./750 g., from the top of the leg. Dice the lamb and fry with the onions and garlic. Add the rice, and proceed as the basic recipe, allow about 20 minutes cooking time and increase the amount of liquid slightly.

To freeze:
Do not freeze this dish, but frozen cooked chicken could be used. Thaw sufficiently to dice.

The reason for not recommending freezing is that much of the delicate flavour seems to be lost; lamb pilau is better. If you decide to freeze it use within 1 month. Freeze the mixture lightly, shake the container to break up the rice, then continue freezing.

Chicken pilau

Buying Cooked Meats & Poultry

The recipes on pages 94–96 and those that follow, could be made with either home-cooked meats and poultry or those you buy ready-cooked. Delicatessen counters in good food departments usually provide a wide variety of cooked meats. Most of these can be eaten with salad, and make a very easy meal but some are particularly suitable for using as the basis for hot dishes.

Diced cooked ham, tongue, turkey or chicken can be heated in a white sauce. It improves the flavour of the sauce if you let the meat stand in this for a while or if you add a little chicken stock cube. Use as a filling for omelettes, pancakes or a savoury topping on toast.

If preferred the meat or poultry can be chopped very finely and added to the beaten eggs before making an omelette. Salami and garlic sausage can also be used in this way.

A good way to use a little left-over cooked meat or poultry is to dice this, heat it in the margarine or butter used to scramble eggs, then add the beaten eggs and cook in the usual way.

Ham in cherry sauce:

Make half the quantity of cherry sauce as given on page 89, under Caneton aux cerises, but use water and $\frac{1}{2}$–1 chicken stock cube instead of giblet stock; be rather generous with the liquid. When the sauce has thickened add 8–12 oz./200–300 g. sliced cooked ham and heat. Serve with a salad. Serves 4.

Ham in Cumberland sauce:

Blend $\frac{1}{2}$ pint/3 dl. water with 2 level teaspoons cornflour. Put into a pan with $\frac{1}{2}$ chicken stock cube, the finely grated rind and juice of 2 oranges, 1 teaspoon made mustard and 3 tablespoons redcurrant jelly. Stir over a low heat until thickened and clear, then put in 8–12 oz./200–300 g. sliced cooked ham and heat. This sauce is also excellent with cold ham, but use only half the amount of water, stock and cornflour, then let the sauce cool. Serves 4.

Tongue in Madeira sauce:

Make a sauce with 1 oz./25 g. fat or margarine, 1 oz./25 g. flour and nearly $\frac{1}{2}$ pint/3 dl. brown stock or water and $\frac{1}{2}$ beef stock cube, see page 82. Add a wineglass of Madeira, season well and add a little chopped parsley. When the sauce is really hot put in 8–10 oz./200–250 g. sliced tongue and heat. Serve with diced carrots. Serves 4.

Turkey & Ham Medallions

To make: 40 minutes plus standing   **To cook:** 15 minutes   **(Makes about 20)**

For the puff pastry:
8 oz./200 g. plain flour
pinch salt
juice of $\frac{1}{2}$ a lemon
water to mix (see method)
8 oz./200 g. slightly softened
   butter, preferably unsalted
For the topping:
8 oz./200 g. cooked turkey
8 oz./200 g. cooked ham
2 oz./50 g. butter or turkey fat
2 oz./50 g. flour
$\frac{3}{4}$ pint/$4\frac{1}{2}$ dl. turkey stock or
   water and 1 chicken stock cube
   or half stock and half milk
seasoning

Quick tip:
Use 1 lb./500 g. frozen puff
pastry.

Sieve the flour with the salt, add the lemon juice and enough cold water to give an elastic dough, that is easily rolled out. Roll to an oblong shape Place all the butter in the centre of this shape, then bring up the bottom one third of the dough and fold over the butter. Bring down the top one-third until the butter is completely covered. It is rather like an open, then a closed envelope. Turn the pastry at right angles, seal the ends then 'rib' the pastry (this means depress it at regular intervals). Roll out again lightly but firmly, do not exert undue pressure at this stage, until an oblong shape again. Bring up the bottom third and bring down the top third again. Turn the pastry at right angles, seal the ends, 'rib' the pastry and continue as before. Altogether the pastry must have 7 foldings and 7 rollings before it is ready to use. You will need to put the pastry into the refrigerator once or twice between foldings and rollings so it does not get too sticky. Leave to rest for about 30 minutes before using. Roll out very thinly, cut into rounds, fingers or diamond shapes. Put on an ungreased baking tray and bake for 10–15 minutes just above the centre of a very hot oven, 475°F./240°C., Gas Mark 9. Lower the heat after 5–8 minutes. Mince the turkey and ham and make a fairly thick sauce with the butter or turkey fat, flour and stock, see page 54. Add the meat and season well.
To serve:
Top each medallion with the turkey and ham mixture and serve hot or allow both pastry and sauce mixture to cool then assemble. Serve with vegetables or salad.

Shepherd's Pie

To make: 25 minutes **To cook:** 55 minutes (Serves 4)

1–1½ lb./500–750 g. potatoes
seasoning
3 oz./75 g. margarine
2–3 tablespoons milk
12 oz.–1 lb./300–500 g. cooked
   meat or poultry
1–2 onions
2–3 tomatoes
1 tablespoon flour
¼–½ pint/1½–3 dl. stock or
   water and ½ beef or chicken
   stock cube
pinch mixed dried herbs

Quick tip:
Use canned steak or steak
and vegetables. Add fried onions
to this and top with dehydrated
potatoes.

Peel the potatoes, cook in boiling salted water until tender, then strain and mash with 1 oz./25 g. margarine and the milk, season well. Mince or dice the meat or poultry, peel and chop the onions, skin and chop the tomatoes and toss the onions and tomatoes in 1½ oz./40 g. margarine for about 8–10 minutes; take care the onions do not discolour. Stir in the flour then add the stock or water and stock cube. The varying amounts of liquid are dependent upon whether you like a moist or relatively dry mixture. Blend in the meat or poultry, herbs and seasoning. Put into a pie or ovenproof dish. Top with the potato and remaining margarine. Bake for about 25–30 minutes in the centre of a moderate oven, 375°F./190°C., Gas Mark 5.
To serve:
Hot with green or mixed vegetables.
To vary:
Top the meat or poultry mixture with halved or thickly sliced hard-boiled eggs.
Flavour the meat or poultry mixture with a little curry powder.
To freeze:
This freezes well; do not add eggs. Use within 6 weeks.

Savoury Meat Slice

To make: 20 minutes **To cook:** 45–50 minutes (Serves 4)

1 large onion
2 large tomatoes
1 oz./25 g. dripping or fat
8 oz./200g. cooked meat,
   chicken or corned beef
pinch mixed herbs
seasoning
suet crust pastry made with
   8 oz./200 g. flour (see page
   72)
To glaze:
1 egg or a little milk

Peel and chop the onion and skin and chop the tomatoes. Fry in the hot dripping or fat. Add the minced or flaked meat, herbs and seasoning, blend well and allow to cool. Roll out the suet crust pastry until just over ¼-inch/½-cm. in thickness, cut into two oblongs. Lift one oblong on to a greased baking tray and cover with the filling then the second oblong of pastry. Seal the edges, score the top and brush with beaten egg or milk. Bake for approximately 35–40 minutes in the centre of a hot oven, 425–450°F./220–230°C., Gas Mark 6–7, lowering the heat slightly after 20 minutes.
To serve:
Hot with mixed vegetables.
To freeze:
This is better eaten fresh, or prepared but not cooked and frozen. Use within 1 month.

Beef Fritters

To make: 10 minutes **To cook:** 3–6 minutes (Serves 4–6)

batter made with 4 oz./100 g.
   flour, etc. (see coating fish, page
   44)
12 oz./300 g. corned beef
To fry:
deep fat or oil

Make the batter as page 44, but for a very light result use self-raising flour or plain flour with 1 level teaspoon baking powder. Cut the corned beef into thin slices, or, if it shows signs of breaking, dice it neatly. Coat the slices with the batter or mix the diced beef into the batter. Fry for about 3 minutes until golden brown, see page 44.
To serve:
Hot as a light snack or main dish.
To freeze:
Do not freeze.

Speedy Chicken Curry

To make: 10 minutes **No cooking** (Serves 4)

4 portions cooked chicken
½ pint/3 dl. yoghourt
½–1 tablespoon curry powder
1 tablespoon tomato ketchup
seasoning
few spring onions
1–2 tablespoons sultanas

Skin the portions of chicken, so they absorb the dressing more readily. Mix the yoghourt, curry powder, tomato ketchup, seasoning, chopped spring onions (use grated onion when these are not available), and sultanas. Put the chicken in a dish, pour over the dressing and leave for a short time.
To serve:
In a border of the Rice and Vegetable salad, see page 107.
To freeze:
Do not freeze this dish, but defrosted frozen cooked chicken could be used.

Toad-in-the-hole

Toad in the Hole

To vary:
Instead of sausages you can use canned Frankfurter sausages as in the picture, lambs' kidneys, tomatoes, mushrooms, fingers of steak or chops, or a selection of these.

To freeze:
Do not freeze this dish, but frozen sausages could be used.

Make a pancake batter with 4 oz./100 g. flour, see page 169. Heat a small knob of fat or dripping, then put 1 lb./500 g. sausages into a Yorkshire pudding tin or oven-proof dish. Cook for about 10 minutes in a hot oven, 425°F./220°C., Gas Mark 7. Pour in the batter and return to a hot to very hot oven, 425–450°F./220–230°C., Gas Mark 7–8 for approximately 25–30 minutes. If using a very hot oven, which is ideal to give a light batter, lower the heat slightly after 10–15 minutes so the batter does not get too brown before being cooked. Serve with vegetables.

Sweet & Sour Medley

To make: 20 minutes   **To cook:** 20 minutes   **(Serves 6–8)**

For the sauce:
2 large cooking apples
2–3 tablespoons honey or brown sugar
1 tablespoon cornflour
$\frac{1}{4}$ pint/1$\frac{1}{2}$ dl. beef stock or water and $\frac{1}{2}$ beef stock cube
1 tablespoon vinegar
2 tablespoons mustard pickle
For the medley:
about 8 oz./200 g. cooked or raw chicken
about 4 oz./100 g. cooked ham, cut into a thick slice
about 8 oz./200 g. cooked beef or raw steak
about 8 oz./200 g. cooked pork
1 small cauliflower
3–4 medium-sized onions
little milk
little cornflour (see method)
To fry:
little oil or fat

Peel and slice the apples, simmer with the honey or sugar until soft, then beat hard or sieve or emulsify for a very smooth mixture. Blend the cornflour with the stock, or water and stock cube. Add this to the apple purée, stir over a low heat until thickened and smooth. Add the vinegar and chopped pickle; keep hot while cooking the meat and vegetables. Cut the chicken and meat into small dice. Divide the cauliflower into small sprigs; there is no need to pre-cook these as they are very good as a crisp contrast to the meat but if you like you can boil them for 2–3 minutes only. Peel the onions, cut into rings, then divide into separate pieces. Dip the chicken, meat and vegetables into milk, then coat in cornflour. Fry in the hot oil or fat for 2–3 minutes only. When using raw chicken or steak lower the heat and cook more slowly for a few more minutes. Drain on absorbent paper.

To serve:
Arrange the fried meat and vegetables on a large hot dish, put cocktail sticks through them and put the bowl of hot sauce in the centre. This can also be served for a main dish with rice or crispy fried noodles, see page 131.

To freeze:
Although defrosted chicken and meat could be diced and used the fried meat and vegetables must be served freshly cooked. The sauce can be frozen, but tends to lose flavour.

Vegetables and Salads

We are very fortunate in having a good selection of fresh, frozen, canned and dried vegetables from which to choose. Serve vegetables often, for they are an important food as they supply many of the minerals, vitamins and roughage we need for good health.

Shop wisely for fresh vegetables; good stores have daily deliveries, so they are in prime condition when you buy them. Store in a cool, airy place or put salads into a covered container in the refrigerator.

To cook vegetables: Follow the directions on packets or cans and *do not* over-cook. Prepare fresh vegetables just before cooking, if possible, as long soaking destroys some of their food value; this applies particularly to green vegetables. If boiling, put into boiling salted water; the old adage used to be 'anything that grows above the ground goes into boiling water, anything that grows below the ground goes into cold water'. We have now learned that all vegetables are better placed into boiling water if we are to retain maximum flavour, colour and vitamins. Serve as soon as possible after cooking.

Economical vegetable dishes: Treat vegetables as a dish in themselves, as well as an accompaniment to meat, fish, etc. Platters of mixed cooked vegetables can be served with a cheese sauce. If you include cooked peas, beans and/or lentils you will have more than an adequate amount of protein for the family's needs.

Cooked vegetables can be used as a filling in pancakes, omelettes (see the Spanish type omelette on page 126) or can be added to a batter to make a vegetable 'Toad in the Hole' as page 99.

To freeze: You will find information on freezing foods throughout this book and also on pages 10, 184 and 185. If you grow, or can obtain, stocks of *really* fresh young vegetables, it is worth feezing these yourself. However, if you cannot, then I would suggest you are better to buy commercially frozen ones. Firms who freeze vegetables have become experts at knowing which varieties to freeze, and they also pick and freeze the vegetables within a matter of hours, so the young fresh taste is retained.

If you do freeze your own vegetables, you will find detailed instructions in freezer books. Here, however, are the basic steps you need to take, after selecting the right vegetables.
a) Prepare the vegetables as for cooking.
b) 'Blanch' them as shown in the picture.
This means immersing in boiling water for a recommended time, to destroy harmful enzymes that might be present and so retain the colour, texture and flavour. It is important to follow instructions on 'blanching' time and the quantity of vegetables to handle at one time.
c) Cool rapidly, to prevent over-softening.
d) Pack carefully to exclude the air, seal and freeze.
e) Label so you know what is in the packet.
Frozen vegetables can be stored for 1 year.

It is also worthwhile freezing small containers of cooked vegetables to use in salads, see page 107 and omelettes, see page 126. Do not over-cook these so they retain the maximum flavour and use within 3–4 months.
Note: Some vegetables cannot be frozen, see page 10. The keeping times for cooked vegetable dishes will vary according to the particular recipe, and these are given in this section.

Vegetable risotto

Vegetable Risotto

To make: 25 minutes   **To cook:** 30 minutes   **(Serves 4–6)**

2 large onions
2 cloves garlic (optional)
2 tablespoons oil
1 lb./500 g. tomatoes
6 oz./150 g. long grain rice
1 pint/6 dl. water or water with
   a little yeast extract
2–3 large carrots
2–4 oz./50–100 g. peas (fresh,
   frozen or canned)
seasoning
1–2 oz./25–50 g. mushrooms
2–3 tablespoons chopped parsley
6–8 oz./150–200 g. grated Gruyère
   or Cheddar cheese

Quick tip:
Choose canned peas, canned
tomatoes (use liquid from can
in place of some of the water),
canned mushrooms and dehydrated onions.

To economize:
This is an inexpensive recipe,
but use left-over pieces of cheese.

Slice the peeled onions, separate into rings and crush the cloves of garlic, if used. Fry for a few minutes in the hot oil, then remove some of the onion rings. Skin and slice the tomatoes. Stir a few slices into the onion mixture, together with the rice, mix thoroughly. Add the water or water and yeast extract, bring to the boil. Finely dice or coarsely grate the peeled carrots and add to the pan with the peas if fresh or frozen. Cook steadily for about 10 minutes until the rice and vegetables are beginning to become more tender, season. Slice the mushrooms and add with the remaining tomato slices and onion rings and canned peas, if using these. Cook gently, stirring a few times until the rice is tender and most of the liquid is absorbed. Blend in half the parsley and half the cheese. Pile on to a hot dish, top with the remainder of the parsley and cheese.

To serve:
As a light supper dish with a salad.

To vary:
Add pieces of diced cooked chicken or meat during cooking; it is then important to use within 2–3 months if freezing the risotto.

To freeze:
Rice does lose some texture when frozen but if you want to prepare in advance or freeze any left-over, cook then cool. Pack into a container, freeze *lightly*, then break up by handling the container and continue freezing. Use within 4–5 months.

Some Basic Ways to Cook Vegetables

To bake:

Certain vegetables are delicious baked in the oven, the most usual, and popular, being potatoes. Scrub the potatoes; if you want a really crisp skin rub this with melted fat, margarine or oil. A medium- to large-sized potato, in a moderately hot oven, 375–400°F./190–200°C., Gas Mark 5–6. bakes in about 1 hour, but can be baked for a longer period at a lower temperature. It is not advisable to bake it any quicker. Cut a cross in the top of the cooked potato, put a knob of butter, cream cheese, cottage cheese mixed with chopped parsley or chives, on top, then serve.

When the potato is baked it can be filled in many ways. Halve the potato, scoop out the pulp, mash with seasoning and butter, then add:

a Grated cheese.
b Chopped fried bacon and tomatoes.
c Cooked sliced mushrooms.
d Beaten egg and cheese.
e Cubes of blue cheese, a little yoghourt and chopped parsley. Top with a rasher of grilled bacon and garnish with parsley as in the picture.
Return the pulp to the potato skin and heat again in the oven.

Onions are also delicious baked. Peel the onions and bake in a little butter and milk, basting once or twice during cooking.

To boil:

The most usual way to cook vegetables is that of boiling and this is introduced on page 100. The vegetables are put into boiling salted water, using just the minimum amount, then cooked quickly in a covered pan for the shortest possible time. One exception to the rule of quick cooking is potatoes. If you boil these too quickly they become broken on the outside, before they are cooked in the centre, so cook these *steadily,* and not too quickly. Strain the vegetables, toss in hot margarine or butter and chopped parsley or chives, then serve or use in the recipes on page 107. In order to shorten the cooking time it is a good idea to shred green vegetables finely just before cooking, and to sprig cauliflower.

Carrots and other root vegetables are delicious if cooked in a good white or brown stock. Use the minimum amount and lift the lid as the vegetables come to the end of the cooking time, so excess liquid evaporates, top with chopped parsley. Shredded cabbage and sprouts can be cooked in tomato juice or a mixture of tomato juice and water or chicken stock. Strain the cooked vegetables and thicken the remaining liquid with a little flour or cornflour, serve as a sauce.

To braise:

This is an interesting way of cooking onions, leeks and quartered hearts of celery. Prepare the vegetables, then toss in a little hot margarine, butter or dripping. Remove from the pan, make a brown sauce, see page 82 and when this has thickened replace the vegetables in the sauce, cover the pan and simmer steadily until tender. Serve in the sauce.

To grill:

Tomatoes and mushrooms can be cooked under the grill, and this is a particularly good way of cooking, when fish, meat, or poultry are being grilled. Prepare the vegetables and brush with plenty of seasoned butter or oil. Either put into the grill pan itself, heat for 1–2 minutes then put the rest of the food on to the grid and continue cooking together or, if preferred, start to cook the meat or fish then add the vegetables towards the end of the cooking time.
Vegetables can be put on to skewers, as in the Herbed Kebabs on page 66, or mixed with diced cheese, see page 160.

103

To fry vegetables:	Not all vegetables are suitable for frying; the best vegetables to use are aubergines, courgettes, mushrooms, onions, potatoes, tomatoes.
To fry aubergines and courgettes:	Slice, coat in seasoned flour or egg and crumbs or batter, see page 44, then fry in shallow or deep fat as above.
To fry onions:	Cut into rings, coat with seasoned flour, or milk and flour, or batter, see page 44 and fry in shallow or deep oil as above.
To fry tomatoes and mushrooms:	Fry in a little shallow fat or margarine for a few minutes.
To fry potatoes:	Cut the potatoes into the desired shape, i.e. fingers (chips), slices, ribbons (long strips of potato). Dry well. To shallow fry, heat enough oil or fat to give a $\frac{1}{2}$-inch/1-cm. in the pan. Fry the potatoes until golden brown and crisp, turn once; or fry twice, as for deep frying below.
To deep fry:	Half-fill a pan with oil or use enough fat to half-fill the pan when melted. *Do not over-fill.* Heat the frying basket in the pan, so the potatoes will not stick to this. Test the oil or fat before adding the potatoes; at the right temperature, a cube of day-old bread should turn golden brown within 1 minute (it is a little quicker with oil than fat). Put some of the potatoes into the frying basket, do not over-fill. Fry steadily until soft, remove from the pan, fry the next batch in the same way. Before serving, reheat the oil or fat and fry the potatoes quickly for 2 minutes until crisp and brown. Drain on absorbent paper. Frozen potato chips do not need the double frying.
To roast vegetables:	Potatoes, parsnips and onions are the most popular vegetables to roast. Peel the vegetables, cut potatoes and parsnips into halves or quarters, depending on size and leave onions whole. Parsnips do not roast well unless they are first boiled for 15–20 minutes in boiling salted water. Opinions vary about the advisability of par-boiling potatoes for part of the cooking time. If you like them to be 'floury' in the centre then boil steadily for 10–15 minutes, depending upon the size, then drain. Dry the raw or cooked vegetables well, then turn in very hot fat in the roasting tin, so they are evenly coated. Cook parsnips and raw potatoes for about 1 hour, par-boiled potatoes for about 45 minutes and medium-sized onions for $1-1\frac{1}{4}$ hours in a moderately hot to hot oven, 400–425°F./200–220°C., Gas Mark 6–7.

Courgettes à la Grecque   **To make:** 15 minutes plus standing   **To cook:** 30 minutes   (Serves 4–6)

1 lb./500 g. small courgettes
seasoning
4 tablespoons olive oil
juice of 1 lemon
$\frac{1}{2}$ pint/3 dl. water
1 bay leaf
$\frac{1}{4}-\frac{1}{2}$ teaspoon chopped lemon
   thyme
6 crushed peppercorns
$\frac{1}{4}$ teaspoon coriander seeds
2 large tomatoes
1 clove garlic

Quick tip:
Use well drained canned
tomatoes and garlic salt.
To economize:
Use peeled diced marrow.

Wash and dry the courgettes and cut off any damaged skin. Remove both ends and slice into $\frac{1}{2}$–1-inch/1–2-cm. pieces. Spread on a flat dish and sprinkle *very lightly* with salt, leave for 30–45 minutes; this extracts the surplus liquid which should be poured away. This stage is not essential but saves having to drain off liquid later. If more convenient, stand in a colander and leave for 1 hour, then drain well. Bring the oil, lemon juice, water, bay leaf, thyme, peppercorns and coriander seeds to the boil in a saucepan. Add the skinned and chopped tomatoes and well drained and dried courgettes. Cook quite quickly for 20 minutes in an uncovered saucepan. Drain off any excess water if necessary. Add the crushed garlic, season and chill before serving.
To serve:
As a vegetable hors d'oeuvre or with a main dish.
To vary:
Mix sliced green and red peppers with the courgettes.
To freeze:
This freezes excellently. Use within 8–9 months.

Some Ways to Serve Vegetables

You will find some ideas for vegetable dishes in the pages that follow, but here are some very quick and easy ways of turning cooked vegetables into interesting dishes.

Vegetables mornay:

Make a cheese sauce as the recipe on page 54 while the vegetables are cooking. You can make the sauce with all milk, but I find the flavour is better if I use just a little of the vegetable water (which contains a great deal of flavour as well as mineral salts and vitamins) and a little less milk. Strain the vegetables, pour the sauce over and garnish with chopped parsley, sliced tomatoes or chopped chives.

Vegetable pancakes:

Make and cook pancakes as the recipe on page 169. Cook the vegetables and blend with a white, cheese or parsley sauce, pages 54 and 82. Fill the pancakes with the vegetable mixture and serve. A more interesting dish is made by topping the filled pancakes with extra sauce and browning this lightly under the grill.

Vegetable pie:

Prepare the vegetables and put into a pie dish. Cover with a white, cheese or parsley sauce pages 54 and 82, then with creamy mashed potatoes. Bake in the oven until crisp and brown, or, if all the ingredients are hot, brown under the grill.

Vegetables Niçoise:

Make a good tomato sauce, see below, and mix the vegetables with this; serve topped with grated cheese.

To make a tomato sauce:

Heat 1 oz./25 g. margarine in a pan and gently fry a chopped onion, a chopped rasher of bacon (optional), and a crushed clove garlic (optional) for 2–3 minutes. Add 1 lb./500 g. skinned chopped tomatoes, $\frac{1}{4}$ pint/ 1$\frac{1}{2}$ dl. water, seasoning and a good pinch sugar. Simmer gently in a covered pan for 15 minutes, then sieve or emulsify and use.

See also vegetable soufflé, page 121 and Spanish omelette, page 126.

Rice and vegetable salad:

Although left-over vegetables can be used for this salad, it is nicer if you cook them specially and mix them with hot cooked rice. It can be served hot instead of the risotto on page 102, or mix with mayonnaise, see page 111 and chopped herbs and allow to cool. This is excellent with fish.

Sweet Corn Scallops

To make: 20 minutes **To cook:** 30 minutes **(Serves 6–8)**

10 oz./250 g. packet frozen
    sweet corn
$\frac{3}{4}$ pint/4$\frac{1}{2}$ dl. white sauce (see
    page 55)
2 tablespoons double cream
pinch cayenne pepper
pinch ground nutmeg
seasoning
1 oz./25 g. butter
2 oz./50 g. breadcrumbs
To garnish:
3 rashers bacon
parsley sprigs

Quick tip:
Use canned sweet corn, drain and use the liquid in the white sauce.
To economize:
Use left-over diced cooked vegetables in place of sweet corn.

Cook the sweet corn according to the directions on the packet, drain well. Make the white sauce as page 54, then add the cream, cayenne pepper, nutmeg and seasoning to taste. Stir in the sweet corn and divide between 6–8 scallop dishes or shells. Heat the butter in a shallow frying pan then toss the breadcrumbs in this. Sprinkle over the scallops. Stand on a baking tray and place above the centre of a moderate oven, 350–375°F./180–190°C., Gas Mark 4–5, for 15–20 minutes or until heated through. Remove the rinds from the bacon rashers and stretch to equal thickness by stroking with the back of a knife. Cut each rasher into three pieces, roll up tightly and thread on to a metal skewer. Either cook the bacon rolls in the oven with the scallops or under a hot grill (turning occasionally if using the grill) until cooked and crisp.
To serve:
Stand the scallops on small plates and garnish with the bacon rolls and parsley sprigs.
To freeze:
Do not freeze this dish.

Preparing Salads

A salad depends not only upon using really fresh ingredients, but in preparing and serving these well.

Green salad vegetables should be washed thoroughly, but carefully, in cold water, then shaken dry in a salad shaker or patted in a clean tea cloth. Do this very carefully, otherwise you can bruise the delicate leaves, this is particularly important with forced lettuce. Tomatoes can be skinned if desired, just lower into boiling water, leave for 30 seconds, lift out, then lower into cold water. This prevents the tomato becoming too soft. The skin comes away immediately.

Red and green peppers can be diced or cut into rings. Discard the core and seeds. If you like pepper flesh slightly soft, 'blanch' by putting into boiling salted water and heating for a few minutes, drain and use.

Radishes should be washed, then sliced or served whole or cut into fancy shapes.

Cucumber can be peeled or the peel can be left on. To give a serrated edge run the prongs of a fork down the cucumber, then slice.

Apples can be added to salads; remember the flesh discolours so dip in lemon juice or coat in mayonnaise. Most other fruits blend well in a salad, they add flavour and colour, see page 110.

Simple Salads

Use these salads as the basis for other more imaginative ideas.

Green salad:

This blends with most ingredients and is the salad generally served with hot, as well as cold, dishes. Choose lettuce or other green salad ingredient, wash as above, dry, then shred – it is better not to cut lettuce, but to shred it with your fingers. Mix with watercress, diced green pepper, sliced or diced cucumber, celery or chicory, but do not add tomatoes or hard-boiled eggs. Toss in French dressing, see page 110, just before serving and top with chopped parsley or other green herbs.

Mixed salad:

This term covers almost every selection of salad ingredients, but generally does not mean you have a protein food among the ingredients. It is usually served with meat and fish.

Main dish salads:

These are outlined in the pages that follow, but can be very simple as the anchovy and egg salad picture opposite shows. Simply mix sections of crisp prepared lettuce with hard-boiled eggs, anchovy fillets and other salad ingredients and add dressing to taste, see pages 110 and 111.

Ratatouille

To make: 20 minutes   **To cook:** 40–50 minutes   **(Serves 4–6)**

2 onions
1 lb./500 g. tomatoes
1 medium-sized marrow or 1 lb./
    500 g. courgettes
4 small aubergines
seasoning
1 red or green pepper
1–2 cloves garlic
3 tablespoons oil
To garnish:
1–2 tablespoons chopped parsley

Quick tip:
Use canned tomatoes, but not all the liquid from the can, and de-hydrated onion.
To economize:
Make the dish when the vegetables are at their cheapest, then freeze.

Chop the peeled onions. Skin the tomatoes and halve or quarter. Peel the marrow, cut in large chunks and discard the seeds, or slice unpeeled courgettes, discard just the hard ends. Remove the stalks from the aubergines and cut into small chunks. If you dislike the rather bitter taste of the skin, score the vegetables with a knife, sprinkle lightly with salt and leave for 15 minutes then cut into pieces. Slice the pepper (discard core and seeds) and crush the garlic. Heat the oil in a strong pan and gently fry the onions and garlic. Add the aubergines, marrow or courgettes, tomatoes and pepper. Season well and simmer slowly, with a well-fitting lid on the pan, until the vegetables are tender. Stir once or twice during cooking.
To serve:
Hot or cold, sprinkled with parsley. This makes an excellent hors d'oeuvre.
To vary:
Add sliced mushrooms.
To freeze:
Excellent when frozen; use within 1 year.

Anchovy and egg sa

Fruit in Salads

Add seasonal fruits to salads, as most fruits blend well with the vegetables and other ingredients and they add colour, as well as a refreshing flavour. Soft berry fruits are particularly good with cottage or cream cheese salads as are apples and pears. These also blend with ham, pork or fish salads, but remember the flesh discolours, so dip in lemon juice or coat in mayonnaise to prevent this. Cooked dried fruits, such as apricots and prunes are excellent with cold meat salads.

Orange salad:

This is one of the best accompaniments to roast duckling or goose. Mix segments of orange, free from pips and pith, with a green salad and French dressing, see below.

A salad dressing provides both a moist texture and additional flavour to a salad. The two classic dressings, i.e. mayonnaise and French or vinaigrette dressing are given here together with other suggestions for a variety of dressings.

Avocado pear dressing:

Halve a ripe avocado pear as described in the recipe below. Mash the pulp with at least 1 tablespoon lemon juice, then add seasoning, a little olive oil and enough yoghourt or soured cream to give the consistency of a mayonnaise. Flavour with a few drops Worcestershire sauce or extra lemon juice. This is particularly good with chicken or cheese salads.

Blue cheese dressing:

Mash blue cheese with a little oil, lemon juice or vinegar, then add mayonnaise, soured cream or top of the milk to make a soft consistency. Excellent over vegetable salads.

French or vinaigrette dressing:

Most people like twice the amount of oil to vinegar (wine vinegar is ideal) or lemon juice. Blend the oil into a little made mustard and seasoning, then add the lemon juice or vinegar or a mixture of vinegar and lemon juice. Crushed garlic, a little sugar and chopped fresh herbs can be added for extra flavour. This dressing is used over most salads.

Hard-boiled egg mayonnaise:

Rub the yolks of 2 hard-boiled eggs through a sieve or mash with a fork, then beat in seasoning, a little oil, lemon juice and soured cream or extra oil to give the consistency of a thick mayonnaise. Fresh whipped cream can be added for a richer flavour. This blends with fish, meat or chicken salads.

Slimmer's dressing:

Either use lemon juice on salads or season natural yoghourt and flavour with herbs.

Walnut & Avocado Salad

To make: 15 minutes **No cooking** (Serves 4)

1–2 tablespoons lemon juice
2 ripe avocado pears
2 crisp, sweet apples
2 oz./50 g. walnuts
3–4 tablespoons French dressing
  (see above)
1 clove garlic (optional)
seasoning

To garnish:
few lettuce leaves

Quick tip:
Make a larger supply of French dressing and store in a screw-topped jar. Shake before serving.
To economize:
Use peanuts instead of the more expensive walnuts.

Put the lemon juice into a basin. Cut the avocado pears carefully in half and remove the stones. Scrape the flesh gently into the basin without damaging the skins. Mash with the lemon juice; this stops it turning brown. Peel and core the apples, chop them and the walnuts into small pieces and mix with the avocado pulp, the French dressing, crushed garlic, if wished, and a little seasoning. Blend well and refill the avocado skins. Garnish with lettuce leaves.
To serve:
With thin slices of wholemeal bread and butter.
To vary:
Instead of serving in the avocado skins, pile the mixture on to a bed of crisp lettuce and surround with sliced cucumber, strips of green pepper and celery sticks. Garnish with extra walnut pieces or hard-boiled eggs.
To freeze:
Do not freeze this dish. Frozen avocado pears can be used, see page 12.

110

Mayonnaise

2 egg yolks (or you can use
    whole eggs when making this
    in a blender, see method)
½–1 teaspoon French or English
    mustard
salt
pepper (this can include a little
    paprika)
pinch sugar
up to ½ pint/3 dl. olive or other
    first class oil
1–2 tablespoons vinegar
    or lemon juice
1–2 tablespoons boiling water
    (optional)

To economize:
Use only up to ¼ pint/1½ dl.
oil to the egg yolks.
To freeze:
Mayonnaise is one of the foods
that does not freeze well.
If you are likely to waste food
blended with mayonnaise freeze
for a short time only.

Walnut and avocado salad

If making by hand or with a mixer, put the egg yolks only into a clean dry bowl. Add the mustard, salt, pepper and sugar, then add ¼ pint/1½ dl. of the oil gradually, drop by drop, beating as you do so. If the oil is added too quickly the mayonnaise could curdle. If by any chance this should happen, put another egg yolk into a second basin and gradually beat in the curdled mayonnaise. When the first half of the oil is blended in you can increase the speed with which you add the rest. There is no need to add the whole ½ pint/3 dl., but the more oil used the thicker and richer the dressing. Finally beat in 1–2 tablespoons vinegar (distilled white or white wine vinegar is ideal) or lemon juice. I also like to add 1–2 tablespoons boiling water.

Quick tip:
Use the blender method or an electric mixer to make it.

If making with a blender, use the same recipe, but, because of the speed of emulsifying, you can use whole eggs which give a very light almost 'fluffy' mayonnaise. Put the eggs or yolks, seasoning, sugar and vinegar or lemon juice into the blender. Switch on for a few seconds, then add the oil gradually, but not drop by drop, through the hole left by removing the cap in the lid or make a foil cover with a hole in the centre or a foil funnel, see page 11. Lastly add the boiling water.

To vary:
Tartare sauce: Add chopped gherkins, chopped parsley and capers to the mayonnaise. Serve with fish salads and hot fish dishes.
Marie Rose dressing: Add tomato purée or ketchup to taste and a little whipped cream and sherry with a few drops Worcestershire sauce.
Piquant dressing: This is rather like Tartare sauce but also add a little chopped vinegar pickles, chopped canned red pepper and crushed garlic.

Vegetables in Salads

Most left-over cooked vegetables can be added to salads, mixed with mayonnaise and chopped herbs. Grated raw vegetables add a crisp texture as well as being extremely colourful and good to eat: try grated carrot, cabbage (see below), swede or finely shredded raw leek, as well as the more familiar salad vegetables.

One of the most popular vegetable salads is **Coleslaw**: ideally this should be made with a white cabbage, but when these are not available use any crisp young cabbage heart (or even Brussel sprouts). Wash, dry and shred the cabbage finely and mix with mayonnaise. This is the basic recipe only, you can add grated carrot, chopped celery or dessert apple, chopped nuts, sultanas or other dried fruit, chopped gherkins or grated cucumber.

A tomato and green pepper salad is very good. Cut rings of tomatoes and peppers (discard the cores and seeds), arrange on a flat dish and top with French dressing, chopped parsley and chives.

Mix rings of raw onion and fresh orange and top with French dressing.

While left-over cooked potatoes can be used in a potato salad, the flavour is 100% better if freshly cooked, diced, hot potatoes are blended with grated onion or chopped chives and the mayonnaise. Allow to cool.

Mushrooms Vinaigrette

To make: 10 minutes   **No cooking**   (Serves 4)

4 oz./100 g. mushrooms
3 tablespoons olive oil
1 tablespoon lemon juice
1 clove garlic
seasoning
1 teaspoon finely chopped parsley

Quick tip:
Use well drained canned mushrooms and garlic salt.
To economize:
Use less expensive salad oil and vinegar for the dressing.

Wipe the mushrooms with a clean, damp cloth and leave whole or slice thinly; do not remove the stalks or peel. Combine the oil, lemon juice, crushed garlic, seasoning and parsley. Pour the dressing over the mushrooms and make sure they are coated on all sides. Chill, covered, for several hours before serving. The raw mushrooms are extremely absorbent so you may have to pour over more of the dressing.
To serve:
Chilled, as part of an hors d'oeuvre or with cold meat.
To vary:
Blend 2 tablespoons Vinaigrette dressing (see page 110) with 2 tablespoons mayonnaise and coat the mushrooms.
To freeze:
Do not freeze this dish, although frozen mushrooms could be used.

Mushrooms vinaigrette

Main Dish Salads

If you plan a salad for a main course make certain it has plenty of protein, as well as the salad ingredients, so it is sustaining as well as being pleasant to eat.

Most cheese can be served in a salad, either grated, sliced or spooned on to a bed of lettuce, etc., as in the case of cottage or cream cheese. Fruit and nuts blend well with all kinds of cheese and children will enjoy this mixture, see the recipes on page 114.

If you are tired of hard-boiled eggs in a salad try rather soft scrambled eggs. Cook the eggs in the usual way, adding chopped parsley and/or chives, then blend in a little mayonnaise as the mixture cools. In Spain the tortilla (Spanish omelette, page 126) is often eaten cold and this is very good with a mixed salad.

White fish may not appear as colourful as shell or oily fish in a salad, but the recipes on page 114 give two ways of making white fish look, as well as taste, interesting.

All salads should be kept covered until ready to serve, but be particularly careful that sliced meat is covered, as it has a tendency to dry, which spoils both the flavour and appearance. The beef and tomato mould, below, is a very simple way of using part of a cooked joint in an economical way, and gives a pleasantly moist texture to the cooked beef.

Beef & Tomato Mould

To make: 15 minutes plus setting   **To cook:** 10 minutes   **(Serves 4–6)**

2 eggs
1 pint/6 dl. tomato juice
½ oz./15 g. powdered gelatine
1 lb./500 g. cooked or corned beef
½–1 teaspoon made mustard
seasoning
To garnish:
lettuce
tomatoes
cucumber

To economize:
Mince other left-over meat or poultry and use instead of beef, (see To vary:)

Hard-boil the eggs, crack the shells and plunge into cold water. Remove the shells, but do not chop the eggs until later, as they would become dry. Heat most of the tomato juice, soften the gelatine in the remaining cold tomato juice, then stir into the hot liquid and continue stirring until thoroughly dissolved. Allow this to cool and just begin to stiffen slightly. Meanwhile mince or chop the meat very finely and chop the hard-boiled eggs. Stir into the lightly set tomato mixture, then add mustard and seasoning. Spoon into an oiled mould or basin and allow to set.
To serve:
Wrap a warm teacloth round the mould or basin and leave for a few seconds, then invert the mould on to a damp serving dish (this enables you to slide it into position if it is not in the centre of the dish). Garnish with lettuce, tomatoes and sliced cucumber.
To vary:
Use good stock instead of tomato juice or other meat or poultry; or use half tomato juice and half stock.
Aspic jelly could be used instead of plain gelatine.
To freeze:
Do not freeze this but defrosted cooked meat could be used.

Stuffed Eggs

To make: 10 minutes   **To cook:** 10 minutes   **(Serves 4–6)**

6 eggs
little mayonnaise or softened
   butter
sardines, ham, anchovy fillets,
   chicken or prawns (see method)
seasoning
To garnish:
lettuce
tomatoes
cucumber

To economize:
An ideal way of using small amounts of left-over food.

Hard-boil the eggs, crack the shells and plunge into cold water. Remove the shells and allow the eggs to cool slightly. Halve each egg, removing the yolks and blend with a little mayonnaise or butter. You can then choose which flavouring you wish, mashed sardines, finely chopped ham, chopped anchovy fillets, minced or diced chicken, chopped prawns, etc. Taste the mixture, add seasoning as necessary and spoon the yolks back into the egg whites.
To serve:
On a bed of lettuce, garnished with tomatoes and cucumber. This is good either as a main dish or hors d'oeuvre.
To freeze:
Hard-boiled eggs do not freeze.

Fish Cream

To make: 25 minutes plus setting   **To cook:** 10 minutes   **(Serves 4)**

1 lb./500 g. white fish (weight without skin and bone)
½ pint/3 dl. water
seasoning
1 bay leaf
½ oz./15 g. powdered gelatine
2 tablespoons sherry
3 tablespoons mayonnaise
¼ pint/1½ dl. double cream
2 teaspoons chopped parsley

Quick tip:
Use canned salmon or tuna, measure liquid from can and add water to make up to ½ pint/3 dl.

Put the fish into the cold water with seasoning and the bay leaf. Bring the water to boiling point, lower the heat and simmer gently for a few minutes only, until the fish is cooked; do not over-cook, see page 48. Lift the fish from the liquid, drain carefully. Measure the liquid and add a little extra water if necessary to make it up to ½ pint/3 dl. again. Soften the gelatine in the sherry, stir into the hot fish liquid, stir until dissolved, then strain into a basin. Leave until cold and just beginning to stiffen slightly, then add the mayonnaise, flaked fish, and lightly whipped cream and chopped parsley. Taste and season well. Put into an oiled basin or mould, leave until set.
To serve:
Turn out on to a bed of mixed salad.
To vary:
Use aspic jelly powder instead of plain gelatine.
To freeze:
Do not freeze this dish, but frozen fish could be used.

Paella Salad

To make: 25 minutes   **To cook:** 20 minutes   **(Serves 6–8)**

1–2 cloves garlic
2 medium-sized onions
½ small chicken
2 tablespoons olive oil
4–6 oz./100–150 g. long grain rice
¾ pint/4½ dl. chicken stock or water and 1 chicken stock cube
pinch saffron
3–4 tablespoons mayonnaise
½–1 tablespoon lemon juice
8–12 oz./200–300 g. cooked white fish
2 teaspoons chopped parsley
½–1 teaspoon chopped fennel (optional)
1 canned red pepper
2–4 oz./50–100 g. cooked peas
2–4 oz./50–100 g. prawns or other shell fish

To economize:
This is a good way to use small quantities of chicken and fish to produce a satisfying dish.

Peel and chop the garlic and onions. Cut the chicken into small pieces and toss in the hot oil for a few minutes. Add the garlic, onions and rice and turn in the oil for 2–3 minutes. Blend the stock, or water and stock cube, with the saffron, pour into the pan and stir well. Lower the heat, but do not cover the pan and cook steadily for about 15 minutes, until the rice is tender and has absorbed the liquid; stir once or twice during this period. Remove from the heat and add the mayonnaise and lemon juice while the mixture is hot. Cool, then add the flaked fish, herbs, chopped red pepper, peas and shell fish.
To serve:
On a bed of green salad.
To vary:
Paella: Proceed as the recipe above, but omit the mayonnaise and the lemon juice. Heat the fish, vegetables and herbs in the pan with the rice, and serve this as a hot dish. A greater selection of shell fish can be added, together with thinly sliced garlic sausage, and you can omit the white fish if desired. There are many recipes for this famous dish, varying with the region of Spain, but the rather unusual mixture of chicken, fish etc. is a great success.
To freeze:
This is better served soon after cooking.

Blue Cheese & Pear Salad

To make: 6–8 minutes   **No cooking**   **(Serves 4)**

6–8 oz./150–200 g. blue cheese
little mayonnaise (see method)
8 canned pear halves
1 lettuce heart
To garnish:
few grapes, de-seeded

Quick tip:
Use canned cherries in place of grapes.
To economize:
Use left-over grated cheese (see To vary:)

Crumble the cheese and blend with enough mayonnaise to make a creamy consistency. Arrange the pear halves on a bed of lettuce. Top with the cheese mixture and garnish with the grapes.
To serve:
As a light main dish.
To vary:
Add chopped nuts to the cheese mixture.
Use grated Cheddar cheese, mixed with seedless raisins, in place of blue cheese.
Use halved fresh pears, sprinkle with lemon juice or French dressing, see page 110, to prevent their discolouring.
To freeze:
Do not freeze this dish.

Blue cheese and pear s

Light Dishes

There are many occasions when a light quick dish is all that one requires for a meal. In the next pages you will find suggestions that are suitable for lunches, suppers or high tea for the children. In most cases these are 'one dish meals', which can be served with vegetables, but they can also be served simply accompanied by a salad, with toast or rolls and butter.

Economical light dishes: There are so many foods that can be served for a light luncheon or supper or a T.V. snack later at night, or for children's high tea dishes.

Soups can form a complete meal if followed by cheese and fruit or some of the ideas given in the chapter on Appetizers, starting on page 12, are equally as good for a light complete meal as for an hors d'oeuvre. Some of the most economical foods upon which to base your light dishes are eggs and cheese. Both these foods are high in protein value. Remember it is important that light meals should be well balanced so check to see that the family are having essential vitamins in the form of fresh fruit and vegetables too. There are many economical ways in which you can add extra food value to the popular convenience foods, such as frozen fish fingers and hamburgers. Serve them with baked beans for extra protein and fresh tomatoes or salad for vitamins.

Serve a cheese sauce, as the recipe on page 54, with fish fingers; this adds protein and a lot more flavour too. A crisp green salad turns this into a complete light meal.

Top cooked hamburgers or other meat cakes with a slice of cheese, heat under the grill or in the oven until the cheese bubbles and browns lightly. Serve with fresh or cooked tomatoes.

Toasted snacks: Poached or scrambled eggs, see page 122, Welsh rarebit, page 118, fried or grilled mushrooms, sardines, baked beans are all savouries that can be served on hot buttered toast. To make a complete meal serve raw or grilled tomatoes and green salad with the toasted dish or follow this with fresh fruit.

Most cheese and egg dishes are quick to prepare, easily made and sustaining and there are a number in this chapter, and throughout the book that would be a good choice for a light meal. Encourage children to enjoy cheese, as it contains calcium which is so important for the formation of strong teeth and bones.

Savoury rice or pasta dishes are an ideal choice for a quick meal, there are a number in this book, see pages 81, 102, 114 and 128–131 in particular.

Growing children often feel no meal is complete without potatoes; so make these ahead of time:

Duchesse potatoes: Blend a generous amount of butter or margarine with mashed potatoes, together with 1–2 egg yolks (use the whites in meringues). Spoon or pipe into fancy shapes on a heatproof dish; brown and heat under the grill or in the oven when required. These freeze well, so are also ideal for special occasions.

Scalloped potatoes: Slice peeled old or new potatoes thinly, put into an ovenproof dish with seasoned milk to cover. Top with a little butter or margarine and bake slowly in the coolest part of a very moderate oven, 325°F/170°C., Gas Mark, 3, rather like a milk pudding, for about $1\frac{1}{4}$–$1\frac{1}{2}$ hours. The creamy potato mixture blends with hot or cold dishes and the potatoes can be prepared earlier in the day.

Cheese and tomato me

Cheese & Tomato Medley

To make: 15 minutes **To cook:** 20–25 minutes (**Serves 4–6**)

2 onions
8 oz./200 g. bacon
4 oz./100 g. mushrooms
4–6 large cooked potatoes
1 clove garlic
2 oz./50 g. butter
1 lb./500 g. tomatoes
4 tablespoons water
seasoning
6 oz./150 g. Gouda or Edam
  cheese

Quick tip:
Use canned tomatoes, plus liquid
from can; omit the water. You can
also use canned potatoes and
mushrooms.
To economize:
Use any left-over vegetables
and left-over pieces of cheese.

Chop the peeled onions and de-rinded bacon, slice the mushrooms and potatoes and crush the garlic. Cook the onions and garlic in half the butter until quite soft (you will need a good-sized pan), then heat the remaining butter. Add the bacon and mushrooms and stir over the heat for 5–10 minutes. Stir in the halved or quartered tomatoes and water, then the potatoes and seasoning. Stir well and cook for a further 3 minutes. Blend in most of the grated cheese and as soon as it melts the medley is ready to serve.
To serve:
Sprinkle the rest of the cheese on top.
To vary:
Use other vegetables that are in season.
This is an excellent dish to make in a fondue pan or table cooker.
To freeze:
This dish does not freeze, but it is a good way of making a quick meal from frozen vegetables.

Welsh Rarebit

To make: 10 minutes **To cook:** 12 minutes (**Serves 4–8**)

2 oz./50 g. butter or margarine
1 oz./25 g. flour
2 tablespoons milk
2–3 tablespoons beer or more
  milk (use the larger amount for
  a softer mixture)
$\frac{1}{2}$–1 teaspoon made mustard
seasoning
few drops Worcestershire sauce
6–8 oz./150–200 g. grated
  cheese (see opposite)
4 large slices toast

Heat half the butter or margarine in a pan, stir in the flour and cook for 2–3 minutes, stirring well. Gradually blend in the milk and beer, if using; as this is a very stiff mixture, keep the heat very low and stir until well blended. Add the mustard, seasoning and Worcestershire sauce. Do not add the cheese over the heat, but take the pan off the cooker and stir in the cheese. Good cooking cheeses are suggested opposite. Meanwhile toast the bread and spread with the rest of the butter or margarine. Spread the Welsh rarebit mixture over the top. Heat for 2–3 minutes under the grill until golden.
To serve:
As a light lunch or supper dish with grilled tomatoes and/or salad or cut each slice in half and serve as an after-dinner savoury.

Cheese Pudding

To make: 10 minutes plus standing **To cook:** 30–35 minutes (**Serves 4**)

4 oz./100g. soft breadcrumbs
$\frac{3}{4}$ pint/4$\frac{1}{2}$ dl. milk
1 oz./25 g. butter or margarine
2–3 eggs
6–8 oz./150–200 g. grated cheese,
  choose Cheddar, Gruyère or
  Emmenthal
seasoning
To garnish:
parsley
2 tomatoes

To economize:
This is a good way of using
up left-over bread and rather dry
cheese.

Put the breadcrumbs into a basin. Warm the milk with the butter or margarine, pour over the crumbs and allow to stand for about 10 minutes; this is not essential but softens the breadcrumbs and produces a smoother mixture. Add beaten eggs, the third egg would give a lighter result, and grated cheese. Season well. Pour into a 2-pint/1$\frac{1}{4}$-litre pie dish or shallow casserole and bake for 30–35 minutes in the centre of a moderately hot oven, 400°F./200°C., Gas Mark 6.
To serve:
As soon as baked, topped with parsley and sliced tomato and with a green vegetable or salad.
To vary:
If baking in a rather deeper soufflé dish, use a slightly lower oven temperature and allow about 40 minutes cooking time.
Add finely diced cooked ham or flaked fish to the mixture; do not add more than about 4 oz./100 g. otherwise the pudding will not rise.
To freeze:
Do not freeze this dish, but it is a good idea to have a container of soft breadcrumbs in the freezer to use when required.

Cooking with Cheese

There are a great variety of cheeses on sale, but best to use for grating and cooking are Cheddar or Cheshire or the stronger Parmesan. Gruyère, Emmenthal, Dutch Gouda or Edam or processed cheeses are also excellent either chopped, grated or sliced.

Do not over-cook cheese, as this makes it tough and rather stringy. When making a cheese sauce, cook the white sauce, see page 54, add the cheese, then stir off the heat until the cheese has melted or reheat for a *very short time* only.

Cheese Dreams

To make: 5 minutes   **To cook:** 5 minutes   (Serves 2)

4–6 large slices bread
little butter
2–3 slices processed or Cheddar
    cheese
1 egg
2 tablespoons milk
seasoning
To fry:
1–2 oz./25–50 g. fat, butter or
    margarine
To garnish:
tomatoes (see method)

To economize:
Even very stale bread and dry cheese becomes appetizing when cooked like this.

Make sandwiches with the bread, butter and cheese. Cut into fingers. Break the egg on to a plate, add the milk and seasoning. Heat the fat, butter or margarine in a frying pan; make sure it is not too hot. Dip each sandwich into the egg and milk for a few seconds only, if left too long they will become soft and break. Fry for 1–2 minutes on either side, until crisp and brown.
To serve:
As soon as cooked with raw or fried, halved tomatoes.
To vary:
Spread the bread and butter with mustard, chutney or pickle.
Put slices of ham as well as cheese into the sandwiches.
To freeze:
The cooked dish cannot be frozen, but frozen sandwiches could be coated like this then fried. If you are planning a picnic or other occasion where you need to prepare a lot of sandwiches, make these, then wrap and freeze. Use within 1 month; do not use hard-boiled egg or crisp salad ingredients in the filling.

Cheese & Bacon

To make: 5 minutes   **To cook:** 8–10 minutes   (Serves 4)

4 slices bread
a little butter
4–8 rashers bacon
8 slices Cheddar or Samsoe cheese
To garnish:
4–8 tomatoes
seasoning
few gherkins (optional)
Quick tip:
Cut off bacon rinds with kitchen scissors. Cover grill pan with foil to ease washing-up.

Toast the bread and spread with butter. Cut off the bacon rinds and grill the rashers. Cover the toast with the cheese and grill until it bubbles. Grill the halved and seasoned tomatoes. Top the toast with the bacon and garnish with the tomatoes and gherkins, if wished.
To serve:
As a light main dish; also good for breakfast.
To vary:
Top with a poached egg instead of bacon.
To freeze:
Do not freeze this dish, but sliced bread may be toasted straight from the freezer.
To economize:
Use left-over grated cheese instead of sliced cheese.

Grilled cheese and bacon

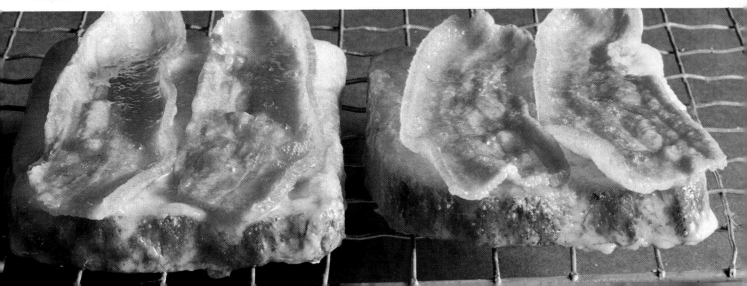

Cauliflower basket

Cauliflower Basket

To make: 20 minutes   **To cook:** 20–25 minutes   **(Serves 4–6)**

1 medium-sized cauliflower
salt
For the cheese sauce:
1 oz./25 g. butter or margarine
1 oz./25 g. flour
$\frac{1}{4}$ pint/1$\frac{1}{2}$ dl. milk
$\frac{1}{4}$ pint/1$\frac{1}{2}$ dl. liquid from cooking
   the cauliflower (see method)
seasoning
4 oz./100 g. grated Cheddar
   cheese
2 eggs
1 tablespoon chopped gherkins
1 teaspoon capers
1 tablespoon chopped parsley
1 tablespoon chopped chives

Quick tip:
Sprig cauliflower and cook for 7–8
minutes only. Put into a heated
serving dish, top with the sauce
mixture and brown under the grill.
To economize:
Use left-over cheese for the sauce.
Dry cheese grates well and is quite
suitable for cooking, providing it
is the type that does melt easily.

Prepare the cauliflower, keeping it whole. Cook in boiling salted water until just tender, drain, reserving $\frac{1}{4}$ pint/1$\frac{1}{2}$ dl. of the liquid. While the cauliflower is cooking, prepare the sauce. Heat the butter or margarine in a pan, stir in the flour and cook over a gentle heat for 2–3 minutes, stirring well. Gradually add the milk, bring to the boil, then add the cauliflower liquid and stir as the sauce thickens over a medium heat. Remove from the heat and add seasoning and nearly all the cheese. Hard-boil the eggs, shell and chop, blend with the hot cheese sauce, together with the gherkins, capers and herbs. Scoop out the centre part of the cauliflower. Put this on to a plate, chop coarsely and add to the sauce. Stand the cauliflower in a heated serving dish. Pile the cheese sauce mixture into the centre. Top with the remainder of the cheese and brown for 1–2 minutes under a very hot grill.
To serve:
Hot as a light main course with tomato salad or with meat, fish or poultry.
To vary:
Omit the eggs and use shelled prawns or diced cooked ham instead.
This dish can be adapted as a cold salad dish.
Cook the cauliflower as described in the method above, but be extra careful when cooking the vegetable that it does not become too soft, for it should have a firm texture when cold. Blend grated cheese into mayonnaise instead of a white sauce, add the chopped hard-boiled eggs, gherkins, capers and herbs. Spoon over the hot cauliflower, then allow to cool.
To freeze:
Do not freeze this dish if possible, see page 184, although frozen cauliflower sprigs could be used.

Creamed Fish with Anchovies

To make: 15 minutes   **To cook:** 15–20 minutes   **(Serves 4)**

1½ lb./750 g. haddock or cod
  fillet
seasoning
3 oz./75 g. butter or margarine
6 canned anchovy fillets
2–3 small onions
3 tomatoes
1½ tablespoons chopped parsley
¼ pint/1½ dl. double or single cream
  or evaporated milk

Quick tip:
Use well drained canned tomatoes
and dehydrated onion.
To economize:
Single cream can be used in the
recipe above or top of the milk.

Cut the skinned fish into pieces, season well. Melt 2 oz./50 g. of the butter
or margarine in a saucepan, add the chopped anchovies and cook gently
for 2 minutes. Put in the coarsely chopped onions and quartered tomatoes
and cook gently for a further 5 minutes. Stir in the parsley and spoon the
hot mixture into a *heated* fireproof dish. Place the fish portions on top, dot
with the rest of the butter or margarine and cook under the grill until
brown, about 7–10 minutes, turning the fish during cooking. Spoon the
cream over the fish during the last few minutes cooking.
To serve:
With cooked rice, pasta or Duchesse potatoes above; this is particularly
good with the Crispy Fried Noodles on page 131.
To freeze:
While you can freeze the cooked dish, it is better to serve it when freshly
cooked. Frozen fish can be used.

Cheese Soufflé

To make: 15 minutes   **To cook:** 30 minutes   **(Serves 4)**

3–4 oz./75–100 g. Cheddar,
  Gruyère, Parmesan or Gouda
  cheese*
1 oz./25 g. butter or margarine
1 oz./25 g. flour
generous ¼ pint/1½ dl. milk
seasoning
4 eggs or 3 egg yolks and 4
  egg whites
*Do not exceed this amount.

Quick tip:
Make up nearly ½ pint/3 dl.
dehydrated potato mixture,
add the cheese then the eggs as the
recipe
To economize:
This is a fairly inexpensive, but
a very nutritious and substantial
dish.
To vary:
Chicken soufflés: Use minced
chicken and chicken stock instead of
cheese and milk.

Fish soufflés: Use finely chopped
or flaked cooked or canned fish
(white fish, shell fish or oily fish
such as salmon) instead of cheese.

Meat soufflés: Use finely chopped
or minced cooked ham, uncooked
liver or cooked tongue and stock
or stock mixed with milk instead
of cheese and milk.

Vegetable soufflés: Use vegetable
purée, tomato or spinach are
particularly good, instead of milk.
A little cheese can be added to the
mixture.

Grate the cheese finely. Heat the butter or margarine in a large pan, stir
in the flour and cook over a low heat for several minutes. Gradually add
the milk, stirring well, over a medium heat until the sauce becomes
really thick. Remove from the heat, add seasoning and cheese. Separate
the eggs and beat the yolks into the cheese mixture. Whisk the whites
until they are almost as stiff as a meringue; if they are beaten until they
are very stiff the soufflé rises dramatically, but may be a little dry. Put
into a buttered 6-inch/15-cm. soufflé dish. Bake in the centre of a
moderate to moderately hot oven. 375–400°F./190–200°C., Gas Mark 5–6.
Serve at once.

Cheese soufflé

Cooking with Eggs

Eggs are an essential ingredient in many recipes, but they also form the basis for many quick and easy dishes on their own.

Remember practically all hot egg dishes should be served as soon as they are cooked, waiting will spoil them. The basic ways of cooking eggs are given below, for many seemingly elaborate dishes are based upon these methods.

To freeze:

Many dishes containing eggs freeze well, but cooked whole eggs cannot be frozen as they become tough.

Basic Ways to Cook Eggs

Baked eggs:

Butter small ovenproof dishes, break eggs into these and top with a little milk or single or double cream and seasoning. Bake for about 10 minutes towards the top of a moderately hot oven, 375–400°F./190–200°C., Gas Mark 5–6. Eat with a teaspoon. This is only the beginning of an interesting dish, you can add grated cheese, chopped ham, asparagus tips, prawns, etc.

Boiled eggs:

Lower the eggs into boiling water, allow 3½–4 minutes for soft-boiled eggs or up to 10 minutes for hard-boiled eggs.

Fried eggs:

Make sure the bacon or other fat is hot before adding the eggs to the frying pan. Break the eggs on to a saucer (then slide into the fat), or break straight into the hot fat. Lower the heat slightly and fry until set.

Poached eggs:

Either heat small knobs of butter or margarine in metal egg poacher cups, then add the eggs and poach for about 3 minutes over boiling water or heat seasoned water in a pan; add a few drops of vinegar to keep the eggs a good shape (this is not essential). Break the eggs into a cup (then slide into the water), or break straight into the water and cook steadily for 2–3 minutes. A potato masher is ideal to slide under the egg and lift it out of the liquid.

Scrambled eggs:

Beat the eggs very lightly with seasoning and add 1 teaspoon milk or single cream for each egg. Heat a good knob of butter or margarine in a pan, add the eggs and stir gently over a low heat until *just* set. Do not over-cook, as the eggs continue to set in the heat of the pan.

Quiche Lorraine

To make: 25 minutes   **To cook:** 1 hour 20 minutes   **(Serves 4–6)**

For the shortcrust pastry:
6 oz./150 g. flour, preferably plain
pinch salt
3 oz./75 g. butter, margarine or
   cooking fat
water to mix
For the filling:
4–5 oz./100–125 g. bacon rashers
4–6 oz./100–150 g. Cheddar or
   Gruyère cheese
3 eggs
½ pint/3 dl. milk
5 tablespoons single cream or
   top of the milk
seasoning
To garnish:
lettuce
tomato

Sieve the flour and salt, rub in the butter, margarine or cooking fat, until the mixture resembles fine breadcrumbs. Bind with the water to a firm dough. Roll out and line a 7½–8-inch/19–20-cm. sandwich tin or oven-proof flan dish (at least 1½-inches/3-cm. in depth). Fill with greaseproof paper and beans or crusts of bread and bake 'blind' for about 18–20 minutes in the centre of a hot oven, 400–425°F/200–220°C., Gas Mark 6–7, until golden coloured and set; *do not overcook*. The paper and beans or bread should be removed after 15 minutes.

To prepare the filling, fry or grill the bacon lightly, do not overcook. Chop finely. Put at the bottom of the flan case. Grate the cheese and beat the eggs. Blend the cheese, eggs, milk, cream or top of the milk and seasoning and pour over the bacon. Set for approximately 50 minutes – 1 hour in the centre of a cool to very cool oven, 300–325°F./150–170°C., Gas Mark 2–3, until firm to the touch.

To serve:
Hot or cold, garnished with lettuce and tomato slices.

To freeze:
This freezes well for some weeks, but you must use nearly all single cream instead of milk and cream.

Oeufs Florentine

Oeufs Florentine

To make: 20 minutes   **To cook:** 30 minutes   **(Serves 4)**

1 lb./500 g. spinach
seasoning
1½ oz./40 g. butter
1 oz./25 g. flour
½ pint/3 dl. milk
2½ oz./65 g. grated Parmesan or
   Cheddar cheese
4 eggs
2–3 tablespoons single cream
To garnish:
tomato slices

Quick tip:
Use canned or frozen chopped
spinach.
To economize:
If spinach is expensive, use
kale or other cheaper green
vegetable.

Wash the spinach well, put it into a pan with a little salt and just the water
that clings to the leaves. Cook for 10–15 minutes, until tender, then drain
well. Chop roughly and mix with ½ oz./15 g. of the butter and seasoning.
Put into an ovenproof dish. Meanwhile make a cheese sauce, melt the
remaining butter in a pan, blend in the flour and cook over a gentle heat
for 1 minute. Remove pan from heat, stir in milk and bring to the boil,
stirring. Cook for 2 minutes. Stir in 2 oz./50 g. of the cheese; do not cook
again. Poach the eggs lightly, see opposite, and place side by side on the
spinach. Add cream to the cheese sauce and pour over the spinach and
eggs, sprinkle with the remaining cheese. Put the dish in the centre of a
moderate oven, 375°F./190°C., Gas Mark 5 and bake for 10–15 minutes,
until golden. Alternatively, brown under the grill. Garnish with tomato
slices.
To serve:
As a light main dish.
To vary:
Boil the eggs instead of poaching them. You can have soft or hard-boiled
according to personal taste.
To freeze:
Do not freeze this dish, but you can use frozen spinach.

Egg & Tomato Pie

To make: 20 minutes   **To cook:** 1 hour   (Serves 4)

2 large onions
2 oz./50 g. butter
1 lb./500 g. tomatoes
3–4 oz./75–100 g. soft
    breadcrumbs
seasoning
4 eggs
To garnish:
parsley

Peel the onions then slice them and fry lightly in most of the butter. Skin and slice the tomatoes. Butter an ovenproof dish and fill it with alternate layers of the fried onions and tomatoes, sprinkling each layer with a few of the breadcrumbs and seasoning. Finish with a good layer of the crumbs, dot with flakes of the remaining butter and bake in the centre of a moderate oven, 350–375°F./180–190°C., Gas Mark 4–5, for 45 minutes. Poach the eggs just before the pie is cooked.

To serve:
Top with the eggs and garnish with parsley.

To freeze:
The vegetable mixture can be frozen, but not the poached eggs. Use within 3 months.

French Omelette

To make: few minutes   **To cook:** 4–5 minutes   (Serves 2)

4 eggs
seasoning
1 tablespoon water
1–1½ oz./25–40 g. butter

To economize:
See To vary: and Spanish omelette page 126.

Beat the eggs with seasoning and the water very lightly; there is no need to do more than blend the yolks and whites. Heat the butter in a 6–7-inch/ 15–18-cm. omelette pan (do not use a larger pan otherwise the mixture will be too thinly spread over the base). Pour in the eggs and leave for about ½–1 minute, until set at the bottom, then loosen the eggs away from the side of the pan, tilting this at the same time. Continue 'working' the omelette until just set, or even a little liquid in the centre. Fold away from the handle. Tip on to a hot plate and serve at once.

To vary:
Fry diced bread or cooked potatoes in the butter, add the eggs and continue as above. The omelette will then serve 3–4 people.
Fill with grated cheese, cooked fish, braised kidneys or canned kidneys, see page 81, before folding.
Flavour the eggs with chopped herbs, sliced fried mushrooms, or finely chopped ham before cooking.

Kidney Omelette

Soufflé Omelette

This type of omelette is made differently from the French or plain omelette opposite. Separate the egg yolks from the whites and put the yolks into a basin. Although soufflé omelettes are often served as a dessert, you can also use this lighter type of mixture with a savoury filling. Add seasoning or 1 tablespoon sugar to each 3–4 egg yolks plus 1 tablespoon milk or cream (double or single). Beat together. Whisk the egg whites until they stand up in peaks then fold into the yolks. Heat 1–1½ oz./25–40 g. butter in a 6–7-inch/15–18-cm. omelette pan. Pour in the egg mixture and cook over a low to moderate heat until just set at the bottom. Meanwhile heat the grill. Place the omelette pan under the grill, with the heat set to medium. When the omelette is just set, mark across the centre with a knife (this makes the omelette easier to fold). Spread with the filling, fold and tip on to a hot dish. The picture shows a sweet omelette filled and topped with halved strawberries and hot strawberry jam, or you could use redcurrant jelly.

Soufflé omelette

Oven Baked Omelette

To make: 10 minutes   **To cook:** 20 minutes   **(Serves 3–4)**

few cooked vegetables
little cheese, or cooked ham or
    chicken
2 oz./50 g. butter
4–6 eggs
seasoning

Quick tip:
Use left-over vegetables and meat, or open a small can; baby food cans are quite useful for omelette fillings.

Mix the diced vegetables with the grated cheese, diced ham or chicken. Put the butter into an ovenproof serving dish and heat this for 2–3 minutes in the oven. Spoon a little butter into the vegetables and mix with the eggs and seasoning (this helps to keep the egg mixture moist). Pour the eggs and vegetables into the hot dish and bake just above the centre of a moderate to moderately hot oven, 375–400°F./190–200°C., Gas Mark 5–6, for a little over 15 minutes until just set.

To serve:
As soon as it is cooked.

To vary:
Any fillings used for omelettes can be adapted for this type of cooking. If you prefer a soufflé type omelette, prepare as the recipe above, warm the fruit or savoury filling in the dish, add the egg mixture and bake as above. Do not over-cook, as this would spoil the texture of the eggs.

Spanish omelette

Spanish Omelette

To make: 15 minutes **To cook:** 10 minutes **(Serves 2)**

1 small onion
3 small cooked potatoes
1 canned red pepper
1 large tomato
1 clove garlic
2 tablespoons oil
2–3 tablespoons cooked peas
3 eggs
$\frac{1}{2}$ teaspoon Tabasco sauce
seasoning
pinch mixed herbs

Quick tip:
Prepare all the vegetables earlier, keep in a covered container until ready to cook the omelette.
To economize:
Use up an left-over vegetables or meat in this dish.

Chop the peeled onion finely, dice the potatoes, pepper and skinned tomato (discard seeds if possible.) Crush the garlic. Heat 1 tablespoon oil in the pan and fry the onion and garlic until soft. Add the remaining oil, heat, then stir in the rest of the vegetables and heat thoroughly. Meanwhile, beat the eggs lightly, add Tabasco sauce and seasoning and pour into the pan over the vegetables. Stir lightly, then leave until the eggs are just set. Sprinkle with herbs just before serving.
To serve:
Immediately after cooking. Do not fold like most omelettes. This makes an excellent main dish with salad or green vegetables.
To vary:
Add small pieces of left-over ham, fish, poultry or other meat, etc.
To freeze:
One cannot freeze an omelette, but I find it useful to freeze small containers of mixed cooked vegetables.

Savoury Egg Custard

To make: 10 minutes **To cook:** 1 hour **(Serves 3–4)**

3–4 eggs
seasoning
1 pint/6 dl. milk or half milk and half stock
4–6 oz./100–150 g. cheese or cooked ham or skinned raw fish

Beat the eggs with seasoning, add the warmed milk or milk and stock, then stir in the grated cheese, diced ham or fish. Spoon into an ovenproof dish and stand in cold water, as described on page 145. Bake for 1 hour or until set in the coolest part of a slow oven, 275–300°F./140–150°C., Gas Mark 2–3. If more convenient steam for the same time.
To serve:
Hot or cold with thin bread and butter; this is a good invalid dish.

Piperade

To make: 10 minutes   **To cook:** 10–15 minutes   (Serves 2–4)

1–2 onions
1–2 cloves garlic (optional)
2–3 tomatoes
1 green pepper
2 oz./50 g. butter
   or 1 oz./25 g. butter and
   1 tablespoon oil
4–6 eggs
seasoning
To garnish:
toast

Peel and chop the onions, chop or crush the garlic, if using, skin and chop the tomatoes and chop the green pepper (discard core and seeds). Heat the butter or butter and oil in a pan, add the vegetables and fry steadily until tender. Add the eggs with the seasoning, lower the heat and stir gently until just set, see page 122 for comments about scrambling eggs.
To serve:
Although this can be served cold as an hors d'oeuvre or main dish, I think it is better hot; serve immediately it is cooked garnished with toast.
To freeze:
Although scrambled egg is spoilt by freezing, it is a good idea to freeze small packages of cooked vegetables, reheat, then continue as above.

Egg & Cheese Pie

To make: 15 minutes   **To cook:** 20–25 minutes   (Serves 4–6)

6–8 eggs
seasoning
½ pint/3 dl. cheese sauce
   (see page 54)
1 lb./500 g. mashed potatoes
2 oz./50 g. grated cheese

Hard-boil then halve the eggs, put them into an ovenproof dish, cover with the well seasoned cheese sauce and pipe a border of mashed potato round the dish. Top with grated cheese and brown under the grill or in a moderately hot oven 375–400°F./190–200°C., Gas Mark 5–6 for about 10–15 minutes.
To serve:
With green salad, cooked cauliflower or mixed vegetables.
To vary:
Mix diced cooked vegetables or crisply fried bacon rashers, chopped into small pieces, with the cheese sauce.
To freeze:
This dish cannot be frozen.

Surprise Scotch Eggs

To make: 20 minutes   **To cook:** 20–25 minutes   (Serves 4)

4 eggs
1 oz./25 g. butter
1–2 oz./25–50 g. Parmesan cheese,
   grated
½–1 teaspoon made mustard
seasoning
1–2 tablespoons flour
12 oz./340 g.* sausagemeat
1 egg
2 oz./50 g. crisp breadcrumbs
To fry:
deep fat or oil
*use this more accurate
metrication

To economize:
Use well seasoned mashed potato
instead of sausagemeat.

Hard-boil the eggs for just 10 minutes, crack the shells and plunge into cold water; this prevents a dark line forming round the yolks. Remove the shells, halve the eggs lengthways and take out the yolks. Mash with the butter, then add the cheese, mustard and seasoning. Spoon back into the white cases. Press the two halves together again and coat in a little of the flour, mixed with seasoning. Divide the sausagemeat into 4 portions, press out each portion on a floured board and wrap around the eggs, moulding this carefully. Coat in seasoned flour, then in beaten egg and crumbs. Fry steadily for 10–12 minutes in the hot fat or oil, see page 44 for details of testing the fat or oil. Drain on absorbent paper.
To serve:
Hot or cold with salads or vegetables.
To vary:
Scotch eggs: Do not flavour the eggs, simply hard-boil and coat as above, then fry.
To freeze:
Never try to freeze this dish, the eggs will be tough.

Stuffed Tomatoes

To make: 10 minutes   **To cook:** 10–15 minutes   (Serves 4)

4 large or 8 medium-sized
   tomatoes
2 eggs
2 oz./50 g. grated cheese
seasoning
2 teaspoons chopped gherkins
1 oz./25 g. butter
To garnish:
chicory or watercress

Cut a slice off each tomato, do this at the end opposite from the stalk then the tomatoes tend to stand more securely. Scoop out the centre pulp, chop this, and add the beaten eggs, cheese, seasoning and gherkins. Spoon this mixture into the tomato cases, replace the 'lids', and put into a buttered dish, top each tomato with a little butter. Bake for 10–15 minutes in the centre of a moderate oven, 375°F./190°C., Gas Mark 5.
To serve:
As soon as cooked with a border of chicory or watercress.

Pasta

Pasta, i.e. spaghetti, macaroni, noodles, etc. have become very popular today. They are inexpensive and easy to store and can be combined with many different foods.

Secrets of Cooking pasta:

There are two golden rules, the first is never to over-cook the pasta, particularly if it is being reheated with other ingredients, as the macaroni cheese on page 130 or the fried noodles on page 131.

The second point to remember is to allow sufficient water in which to cook the pasta as if you use too little it becomes sticky. Allow about 2 pints/1¼ litres water to each 4 oz./100g. pasta; make certain the water is boiling BEFORE the pasta is added, and keep the water boiling steadily throughout the cooking period. With long pasta, such as spaghetti, it is advisable to keep it moving in the boiling water, by lifting it with two spoons to prevent it from sticking. Test the pasta by pressing gently, but firmly, against the side of a pan; the pasta is cooked when it breaks with light pressure. The Italians call it 'al dente' which means it is just firm to bite, but not over-soft. Strain the pasta, you may like to rinse it in boiling water to get rid of any sticky coating, but this is not essential if you have cooked it correctly.

Cooked pasta can just be tossed in melted butter and chopped parsley or grated cheese and melted butter and served instead of potatoes with main dishes.

To freeze:

While you can cook a large amount of pasta, use what you want and freeze the rest, this does seem pointless as it is so quick and easy to prepare. It is, however, worth preparing and freezing dishes such as Spaghetti Bolognese and Spaghetti à la Napolitaine below.

Some interesting pasta shapes:

In addition to the more familiar macaroni and spaghetti look for cannelloni (like very large macaroni). Cook, fill with a meat mixture, such as the filling for Mince Stuffed pancakes, page 78. Top with white or cheese sauce, page 55 and heat.

Buy pasta shells, cook, then toss in butter and parsley, and serve instead of potatoes, or mix with mayonnaise and diced cheese for a salad. Fine noodles make an excellent accompaniment to dishes, especially when fried, see page 131.

Spaghetti à la Napolitaine

To make: 15 minutes **To cook:** 15 minutes (Serves 4–5)

6–8 oz./150–200 g. spaghetti
seasoning
little grated Parmesan cheese
　(see method)
little butter (see method)
1 medium-sized can tomatoes
　(preferably plum type)
1 tablespoon tomato purée
8 oz./200 g. cooked ham
little chopped parsley

Quick tip:
Use quick-cooking pasta
To economize:
Use small pieces of left-over
cooked meat instead of ham.

Cook the spaghetti in boiling salted water (allow at least 3 pints/1¾ litres water to the smaller quantity of pasta) until tender. Strain then toss with the Parmesan cheese and butter. Meanwhile heat the canned tomatoes with the tomato purée, add the diced ham, parsley and seasoning. Spoon the spaghetti on to a hot dish and top with the tomato sauce.

To serve:
Hot with plenty of grated cheese or a green salad. This also makes a good hors d'oeuvre.

To vary:
Spaghetti à la Reine: Cook the spaghetti as above, strain, tip back into the pan, add a little butter, diced cooked chicken, enough beef stock to moisten and grated cheese. Heat for a few minutes then serve with more grated cheese.

To freeze:
Pasta tends to lose some of its texture when frozen, so use within 4–6 weeks. Cook, drain, then rinse in cold water; mix with the cheese and butter, pack and freeze. Freeze the tomato mixture separately.

Spaghetti à la Napoli

Macaroni Cheese

To make: 15–20 minutes   **To cook:** 40 minutes   **(Serves 4)**

3 oz./75 g. macaroni
salt
½ pint/3 dl. cheese sauce (see page 54)
2 oz./50 g. grated cheese
1 tablespoon crisp breadcrumbs
1 oz./25 g. margarine or butter
To garnish:
tomato

To economize:
Use partly milk and partly the water in which the macaroni was cooked.

Put the macaroni into about 1½ pints/9 dl. boiling water, with a level teaspoon salt. Cook steadily until the macaroni is just tender. Do not over-cook; quick-cooking elbow macaroni takes only 7 minutes. Drain well, mix with the sauce. Sprinkle the cheese and breadcrumbs on top and dot with the margarine or butter. Either bake for about 25 minutes near the top of a moderately hot oven, 400°F./200°C., Gas Mark 6, until crisp and brown, or put under a hot grill. Garnish with tomato slices.

To vary:
If the dish is to stand or if you prefer a more moist mixture, use sauce made with ¾ pint/4½ dl. milk, etc.

Spaghetti with Anchovies

To make: 20 minutes   **To cook:** 20 minutes   **(Serves 4)**

4 oz./100 g. spaghetti
seasoning
3 tablespoons olive oil
8 oz./200 g. mushrooms
2 onions
2 cloves garlic
5 anchovy fillets
3 rashers lean bacon
6 black olives
little roughly chopped parsley
2–3 tablespoons grated Parmesan cheese

Cook the spaghetti in boiling salted water (allow 2 pints/1¼ litres water) until tender, strain. Meanwhile, heat the oil in a heavy-based pan. Add the sliced mushrooms and onions, crushed garlic, chopped anchovy fillets and bacon, olives and parsley, and cook gently for about 15 minutes.

To serve:
Top the spaghetti with the anchovy mixture and grated Parmesan cheese.

To vary:
Spaghetti Marinara: Omit the bacon and add flaked tuna fish and prawns.

To freeze:
This dish is better eaten when freshly made.

Spaghetti with anchovies

Fried Crispy Noodles

To make: 5–6 minutes   To cook: 10 minutes   (Serves 4)

4 oz./100 g. noodles
salt
To fry:
deep fat or oil

To economize:
Cook and fry a good quantity of noodles for these are an inexpensive and interesting food. Freeze excess as given right.

Cook the noodles in boiling salted water (allow 3 pints/1¾ litres) for 5 minutes only. Drain, rinse in cold water and drain again until *really dry*. Place in a heated frying basket in hot fat or oil, see page 44 for the way to test the temperature of oil. Cook for 5 minutes or until crisp and golden brown. Drain well on absorbent paper and keep hot until required.
To serve:
With most savoury dishes instead of potatoes.
To vary:
Fried rice: Choose long grain rice, boil until *nearly* soft, see page 66, then rinse as above. Fry in a little oil or butter and oil in a frying pan until golden.
To freeze:
Spread out on a flat tray, this prevents the fried noodles sticking to the wrapping. Pack when frozen. Use within 2 months. To reheat spread out on a *heated* flat baking tray, do not cover, and warm through in a hot oven for a few minutes only. Drain on absorbent paper.

Spaghetti with Ham & Mushrooms

To make: 15 minutes   To cook: 15–20 minutes   (Serves 4)

6 oz./150 g. spaghetti
seasoning
8 oz./200 g. mushrooms
2 oz./50 g. butter
4 oz./100 g. cooked ham
   or tongue
1 small onion
To garnish:
olives

Cook the spaghetti in boiling salted water (allow 3 pints/1¾ litres water) until tender, strain. Meanwhile fry the sliced mushrooms in the hot butter until tender, add the diced ham or tongue and the finely chopped or grated onion and continue to cook until slightly brown. Blend with the spaghetti and add seasoning to taste.
To serve:
On a hot dish, garnished with olives.
To freeze:
This dish is better eaten when freshly made.

Spaghetti Bolognese

To make: 25 minutes   To cook: 1 hour   (Serves 4–6)

Ingredients as the filling for the
   Mince Stuffed Pancakes
   (see page 78)
1–2 cloves garlic
2–3 large tomatoes
8–10 oz./200–250 g. spaghetti
salt
grated Parmesan cheese
   (see method)

Prepare the meat mixture as the filling for the pancakes on page 78, but fry the finely chopped garlic and skinned, chopped tomatoes with the chopped onion. Leave the sauce to simmer until the meat is tender. About 15–20 minutes before the end of the cooking time put the spaghetti into boiling salted water (allow 4–5 pints/2½–3 litres water) and cook until tender, strain.
To serve:
Top the spaghetti with the meat sauce and serve with the cheese.
To freeze:
See the comments under Spaghetti à la Napolitaine, page 128.

Tagliatelle with Tomato Sauce

To make: 20 minutes   To cook: 25 minutes   (Serves 4–5)

For the tomato sauce:
1 lb./500 g. tomatoes
2 onions
1 clove garlic
2 oz./50 g. butter or margarine
½ pint/3 dl. water
2 tablespoons tomato purée
seasoning

8 oz./200 g. tagliatelle

Skin and chop the tomatoes, peel and chop the onions and garlic. Toss the vegetables in the hot butter or margarine. Add the water, cover the pan and simmer for 15 minutes. Sieve or emulsify in the blender, then return to the saucepan with the purée and seasoning. Meanwhile cook the tagliatelle (ribbon type noodles) in boiling salted water (allow 4 pints/2½ litres water) until tender, strain.
To serve:
Top the pasta with the tomato sauce and serve with grated cheese or savoury dishes.
To freeze:
See comments under Spaghetti à la Napolitaine, page 128. Use tomato sauce within 6 months.

Puddings and Desserts

The selection of foods served as a pudding or dessert has become much more versatile during the last years, as we enjoy more gâteaux as a change from the familiar heavy puddings. You will find most kinds of recipes covered in this section, together with advice on freezing that particular type of dish. The rather more special occasion desserts are at the beginning of this chapter, commencing with a traditional syllabub.

Economical Puddings: One of the best ways to make economical puddings is to utilize fresh fruit when in season. I like to fill pancakes with a hot fruit purée or make a delicious *Danish fruit cake:* Make about 6 oz./150g. coarse breadcrumbs. Fry until crisp in 2 oz./50g. butter. Cool, then mix with 2–3 oz./50–75g. sugar. Put on top of a thick fruit purée, press neatly until flat on top. Chill and serve with cream. If preferred, put half the crumbs into the serving dish, top with the fruit purée, then the rest of the crumbs.

To freeze: The method of freezing puddings will vary with the particular dish and you will find information given under the various recipes in this section.

It is helpful to have a selection of puddings and desserts in your freezer, and often it is so easy to make double, treble or even larger quantities of a pudding, pie or ice cream, enjoy some when freshly cooked and freeze the rest.

Freeze raw and cooked fruit to use throughout the year. Purées of fruit are particularly useful, for they can be used for sauces over ice cream, as well as the basis for other hot or cold puddings.

I like a selection of fruit pies in the freezer. The pastry may be pre-cooked or just made then cooked when desired.

Steamed sponge puddings freeze very well indeed. If you cook the puddings, freeze, then turn out of the basins and wrap firmly. Put back into the basins when you want to serve these, allow to thaw out to room temperature then heat thoroughly. The pudding is just as light as when freshly cooked. If more convenient you can mix the pudding, put into the basin, freeze and store. Thaw out thoroughly and steam in the usual way.

Jellied desserts can be frozen; I am always slightly disappointed in the texture, but that is being super-critical.

Pancakes are a wonderful 'stand-by' in the freezer for they can be used as the basis for both savoury and sweet dishes. Separate each pancake with greaseproof or waxed paper, oiled on both sides, the pancakes can be 'peeled off' easily. Wrap in thick foil and freeze. Just take the number of pancakes desired, heat then fill.

Decorated gateaux have become a most popular form of dessert. These take a considerable time to prepare and yet they freeze wonderfully. Always freeze the gateaux *before* covering, then wrap carefully, but thoroughly. Unwrap while still frozen, put on to the serving dish and allow to thaw out for several hours at room temperature. In this way you do not spoil the appearance.

One would expect ice cream to freeze well and home-made ice cream is both a nutritious and delicious dessert. The recipe on page 136 is a good basic one and you can easily adapt it in a variety of ways.

Berry Me

Berry Mould

To make: 30 minutes plus chilling   **To cook:** 15 minutes   **(Serves 4–6)**

8 oz./200 g. strawberries
8 oz./200 g. black cherries, stoned
1 cooking apple, peeled, cored and sliced
approx. 4 oz./100 g. sugar
sliced white or fruit loaf (see method)
To decorate:
extra fruit (optional)

Quick tip:
Use ready sliced bread or cut loaf lengthways.
To economize:
Use the most inexpensive fruit available.

Put the fruit in a pan with sugar to taste. Cover and heat gently until the juice leaves the fruit, stirring constantly to prevent the fruit from sticking. Crush the fruit slightly with a wooden spoon. Grease the inside of a small pudding bowl and line with thin slices of crustless bread or fruit loaf. Fill with the fruit and top with more bread or fruit loaf. Grease the bottom of a small plate or saucer that will fit into the top of the bowl. Place it on top of the pudding and put a weight on top of this. Chill overnight.
To serve:
Turn out and decorate with whole fruit if wished. Serve with cream.
To vary:
Try rhubarb or other fruit. This makes a more attractive dessert if some red or dark fruit is used. If the fruit is very firm add a *little* water when cooking.
To freeze:
This freezes well. Chill before freezing. Use within 6 months.

Cherry Compôte

To make: 10 minutes   **To cook:** 15 minutes   **(Serves 6–8)**

1½ lb./750 g. black, red or Morello cherries
¼ pint/1½ dl. red wine or dry sherry
3 tablespoons redcurrant or apple jelly
1 tablespoon sugar
grated rind and juice of 1 orange
pinch ground cinnamon
1 tablespoon arrowroot or cornflour
2 tablespoons cold water

Quick tip:
Use canned fruit and add a little wine, jelly and orange rind and juice.

Stone the cherries with a cherry stoner, the bent end of a fine clean hair pin or the point of a vegetable peeler. Place the red wine or sherry, jelly, sugar, orange rind, juice and cinnamon into a pan. Cover and heat gently until the jelly is melted. Add the cherries, cover and simmer for 5 minutes. Blend arrowroot or cornflour to a smooth paste with cold water. Stir into the cherries and bring to the boil, stirring continuously. Cool and serve at room temperature.
To vary:
Use apricots, pears, plums or greengages instead of cherries, but simmer for 15 minutes instead of 5 minutes.
To freeze:
Although this dish can be frozen, the flavour of the wine tends to be 'lost', so freeze cherries in a plain syrup then add the wine etc, when serving, see page 185.
To economize:
Mix apple slices or diced rhubarb with the cherries.

Crêpes aux Pommes

To make: 15 minutes   **To cook:** 20 minutes   **(Serves 4–6)**

½ pint/3 dl. water
2 oz./50 g. sugar
3 medium-sized cooking apples
pancake batter made with 4 oz./100 g. flour (see page 169).
For the sauce:
2 oz./50 g. butter
juice of 1 orange
2 oz./50 g. sugar
3 tablespoons Cointreau or brandy
To decorate:
grated orange rind

Quick tip:
Use canned apple pie filling.
To economize:
Serve as fruit-filled pancakes, top with hot marmalade and omit the sauce.

Heat the water and sugar in a large pan. Peel, core and slice the apples and poach in the sugar syrup until tender. Make the pancakes as page 169 and fold each pancake round several drained apple slices. Use any leftover syrup in a fruit salad. Melt the butter in a chaffing dish, add the orange juice and sugar and simmer for 4–5 minutes. Put in the pancakes, pour over the liqueur and heat through. Sprinkle with orange rind and serve at once.
To vary:
Use other fruits to fill the pancakes, e.g. apricots, pears or peaches and flavour the sauce with lemon, cherries, strawberries or other fruit, which can be heated in diluted redcurrant jelly.
Flavour the sauce with cherry brandy.
To freeze:
Page 185 gives details on freezing pancakes. The entire dish can be frozen then reheated gently just before serving. Freeze in a flame-proof dish and heat in a slow oven. Use within 2 months.

Lemon Syllabub

To make: 15 minutes   No cooking   (Serves 4–6)

2 oz./50 g. loaf sugar (see method)
2 large lemons
½ pint/3 dl. double cream
½ pint/3 dl. single cream
about 4 tablespoons sweet white
   wine

Rub the loaf sugar over one of the lemons to absorb the flavour from the rind; if you have no loaf sugar and have to use caster sugar, then grate just the very top 'zest' so there are no bitter pieces of pith. Cut 4–6 thin slices from the remaining lemon. Squeeze the juice from the whole lemon and any pieces remaining from the second lemon. Dissolve the sugar in these. Whip the double cream, then gradually whip in the single cream, lemon juice and wine. Serve chilled with lemon twists, but do not freeze.

Choux Pastry

To make: 20 minutes   To cook: see method   (Serves 6–8)

¼ pint/1½ dl. water
1 oz./25 g. margarine or butter
pinch sugar or seasoning
3 oz./75 g. flour, plain or self-
   raising
2 whole eggs and yolk of 1 egg
   or 3 small eggs

Put the water, margarine or butter and sugar (or seasoning if making savoury choux pastry) into a saucepan. Heat gently until the margarine or butter has melted. Remove from the heat and stir in the flour. Return the pan to a low heat and cook very gently but thoroughly, stirring all the time, until the mixture is dry enough to form a ball and leave the pan clean. Once again remove the pan from the heat and gradually add the well beaten eggs. Do this slowly to produce a perfectly smooth mixture. Allow to cool then use as required.

Cream Buns: Grease and flour individual patty tins and put in a spoonful of the mixture, or put in spoonfuls on greased and floured flat baking trays or force through a ¼–½-inch/½–1-cm. plain pipe on to the trays. To bake the buns, allow about 10–15 minutes for large buns in a hot oven, 425°F./220°C., Gas Mark 7, then lower the heat to 350–375°F./ 180–190°C., Gas Mark 4–5, for a further 20 minutes. Split, remove any uncooked mixture, then return to a cool oven for a few minutes to dry out. Cool, and fill with whipped cream. Top with sieved icing sugar.

Eclairs: Pipe into finger shapes or put into greased sponge finger tins. Bake as Cream buns, above, but allow only 20 minutes baking time. Split when cooked, remove any uncooked mixture and 'dry out' in a cool oven. Fill with whipped cream and top with chocolate icing, see below.

Profiteroles: Put small teaspoonfuls of the mixture on to baking trays. Bake for only 15 minutes. Cool after baking, split and fill with whipped cream. Pile on to a dish and top with the richer chocolate sauce on page 136.

Chocolate icing: Melt 4 oz./100 g. plain chocolate with ½ oz./15 g. butter or a teaspoon of olive oil in a basin over hot water. Cool slightly then spread over the éclairs.

To freeze:
Cooked choux pastry freezes well, but do not put on the chocolate icing before freezing. Use within 6–8 weeks.

Profiteroles

Apricot Meringue Gâteau

To make: 35 minutes   **To cook:** 1 hour 20 minutes   (Serves 8–10)

Victoria sandwich with 3 eggs, etc.
   (see page 151)
1 large can apricots or 1 lb./500 g.
   cooked apricots
2 tablespoons apricot brandy
2–3 oz./50–75 g. blanched almonds
For the meringue:
3 egg whites
6 oz./150 g. caster sugar

Quick tip:
See tips for making sponges
(page 151).

Make the sponge, bake in two tins as page 151 then split each half to give 4 layers. Drain the syrup from the canned or cooked apricots and blend a little with the apricot brandy, slice the apricots and chop the almonds. Put the first layer of sponge on an ovenproof serving dish and moisten with a little apricot syrup, cover with sliced apricots and chopped almonds, then with the second layer of sponge. Continue like this until the cake is complete. Make the meringue as page 137, pipe over the top and sides of the gâteau. Put into the coolest part of a very slow oven, 225–250°F./ 110–130°C., Gas Mark $\frac{1}{4}$–$\frac{1}{2}$, and leave for 1 hour. Allow to cool.
To serve:
With cream or ice cream.
To freeze:
This gâteau is better frozen before topping with the meringue. Use within 3 months. Defrost then top with the meringue and continue as the recipe.

Lemon & Apricot Cheesecake

To make: 30 minutes   **No cooking**   (Serves 8–10)

For the crust:
8 oz./200 g. digestive biscuits
2 oz./50 g. butter
8 oz./200 g. cooked or canned
   apricot halves
For the filling:
2 eggs
3 tablespoons milk
2 oz./50 g. caster sugar
12 oz./300 g. cottage cheese
3 tablespoons lemon juice
2 tablespoons whipped cream
$\frac{1}{2}$ oz./15 g. gelatine
2 tablespoons water
To decorate:
8–9 glacé cherries

Crush the biscuits with a rolling pin, melt the butter and stir into the biscuits. Mix well, then press out into a loose-bottomed 8–9-inch/ 20–23-cm. cake tin so that the bottom and sides are coated. Cover the base with a layer of apricots, saving a few for decoration. Separate the egg yolks from the whites. Place the yolks, milk and sugar in a basin over hot, but *not boiling* water, and heat gently, stirring all the time until the mixture thickens enough to coat the back of the spoon. Cool, then stir into the sieved cottage cheese and add the lemon juice and cream. Soften then dissolve the gelatine in the water (see note below). Stir into the cheese mixture and finally fold in the stiffly beaten egg whites. Pour the mixture into the biscuit-lined cake tin, leave to set. Decorate with apricots and glacé cherries.
To serve:
Remove from the tin.
To vary:
Use fresh strawberries or other fruit instead of apricots.
To freeze:
This freezes perfectly. Use within 6–8 weeks.

Note: It is easier to dissolve gelatine if it is first softened in cold liquid. Either stir into hot liquid or purée, as in Apple Lemon Mould, page 142, or place the basin over a pan of hot water and heat until the gelatine has dissolved.

Ice Cream

To make: 15 minutes plus freezing   **To cook:** 10–15 minutes   (Serves 6)

2 eggs
2 oz./50 g. sieved icing or caster
   sugar
$\frac{1}{4}$–$\frac{1}{2}$ teaspoon vanilla essence
$\frac{1}{2}$ pint/3 dl. milk
$\frac{1}{4}$ pint/1$\frac{1}{2}$ dl. double cream
$\frac{1}{4}$ pint/1$\frac{1}{2}$ dl. single cream

Quick tip:
Simply whisk the double and single cream, add a little less sugar and flavouring and freeze.
To economize:
Use whipped evaporated milk instead of cream

Separate the egg yolks from the whites. Make a custard with the yolks, sugar, vanilla essence and milk as page 143. Allow this to cool. Whip the double cream until it stands up in peaks, gradually whisk in the single cream, then blend with the custard. Pour into a freezing tray.
To freeze:
If using a modern refrigerator, with star markings, or a home freezer, there is no need to alter the setting. If using an older refrigerator turn to the coldest setting 30 minutes before freezing. Leave until lightly frozen, remove from the tray into a bowl, whip lightly, then fold in the stiffly whisked egg whites and return to the freezer until firm. Return setting to normal (in the older tye of refrigerator). Use within 3 months.
To vary:
Flavour the custard with 1 oz./25 g. sieved cocoa powder or 2 oz./50 g. chocolate powder or 1–2 teaspoons instant coffee powder. Add up to $\frac{1}{2}$ pint/3 dl. thick fruit purée. In this case, use all double cream.

Easy Sweets with Ice Cream

Make the ice cream as the recipe opposite, the marshmallow ice cream, below, or use bought ice cream. These recipes serve 4–6.

Baked Alaska:
Put a round of sponge on to an ovenproof dish. Moisten with syrup from canned fruit, or with sherry or white wine, top with fruit and a firm block of ice cream. Make a meringue with 4 eggs as page 137, but use only half the sugar. Spread the meringue completely over the sponge and ice cream. Brown for only 3 minutes in a very hot oven, 475°F./240°C., Gas Mark.9. Serve at once or within 25 minutes. Serves 6.

Banana splits:
Put scoops of strawberry and vanilla ice cream on long dishes with bananas. Coat at once with Melba sauce and decorate with whipped cream and fresh strawberries.

Chocolate walnut sundaes:
Put scoops of vanilla or coffee ice cream into sundae glasses, top with chocolate sauce, page 138, whipped cream and chopped walnuts.

Coupe Jacques:
Top fruit salad and ice cream with Melba sauce and whipped cream.
Melba sauce: Heat 8 oz./200 g. raspberries, $\frac{1}{4}$ pint/$1\frac{1}{2}$ dl. water, blended with 1 level teaspoon arrowroot or cornflour, 3 tablespoons redcurrant jelly and sugar to taste. When clear and smooth, sieve or emulsify and cool.

Jelly whip:
Make a 1 pint/6 dl. fruit flavoured jelly and leave until set. Whisk sharply with several spoonfuls of ice cream, pile into glasses and serve with small meringues.

Marshmallow ice cream:
Heat 4 oz./100 g. marshmallows with $\frac{1}{4}$ pint/$1\frac{1}{2}$ dl. milk until the sweets are almost melted, leave in the pan until cool, then fold in $\frac{1}{4}$ pint/$1\frac{1}{2}$ dl. whipped double cream. This is a delicious basic ice cream that can be flavoured as the recipe opposite. Add a little extra sugar if wished, then flavour with chopped glacé cherries, canned pineapple, chopped nuts, etc.

Chocolate nut sundae

Meringues

To make: 10–15 minutes   To cook: 2–3 hours   (Makes: see method)

2 egg whites
4 oz./110 g.* caster sugar or use
   half caster sugar and half sieved
   icing sugar
* use this metrication

Quick tip:
Use an electric mixer.
To economize:
Use the egg yolks in an egg custard (see page 145) or for mayonnaise (see page 111)

Put the egg whites into a clean dry bowl. Whisk until they stand up in peaks; do not over-whip. Gradually beat in half the sugar then fold in the remaining sugar. Brush baking trays, or greaseproof paper on baking trays, with a little oil or butter, or use the modern silicone (non-stick) cooking paper as directed on the pack. Form into 8–10 large rounds with two tablespoons or 30 small rounds with two teaspoons. If preferred use a $\frac{1}{4}$–$\frac{1}{2}$-inch/$\frac{1}{2}$–1-cm. pipe in a large piping bag and pipe the desired shapes. Bake in the coolest part of a very slow oven, 225°F/110°C, Gas Mark 0 or the lowest setting. Allow nearly 2 hours for the tiny meringues, and up to 3 hours for the larger meringues. Lift from the trays with a warmed palette knife. Cool, store in airtight tins.
To serve:
Sandwich with whipped cream or ice cream.
To vary:
Pavlova cake: Make as the meringues above, but use 4 egg whites and 8 oz./225 g. sugar. Whisk a teaspoon of cornflour in with half the sugar and fold a teaspoonful of vinegar in with the second half. Form the mixture into three 9-inch/23-cm. rounds and bake as above for 2–$2\frac{1}{2}$ hours. Sandwich together and top with whipped cream and fruit.
To freeze:
Meringues do not freeze due to high sugar content, and it is pointless to try to freeze them (unless part of a dish) as they store perfectly in the tin until ready to fill and serve.

Steamed Puddings

These puddings are ideal for chilly days, and are very easy to make. Remember to put a sponge or suet pudding in a steamer over *boiling* water and to cook fairly quickly for the first hour: this makes sure the pudding rises well and is light in texture. The cabinet pudding however is based upon an egg custard and must be cooked slowly.

Sponge pudding:

Make the Victoria sandwich as page 151 (you can economize by using only 2 oz./50 g. margarine and sugar and mixing with 1 egg and milk). Put into a well-greased pudding basin, cover with greased greaseproof paper and foil and steam for 1¼ hours. Serve a plain sponge with hot jam; an orange sponge with hot marmalade; a chocolate sponge with chocolate sauce, below; or put a good layer of golden syrup in the basin, top with the sponge, then cook. Serve with golden syrup diluted with a little water and flavoured with lemon juice.
Freeze as Cherry Layer Pudding, opposite.

Chocolate Sauce

To make: 5 minutes   To cook: 10 minutes   (Serves 4)

½ level tablespoon cornflour
½ level tablespoon cocoa
½ pint/3 dl. milk
1 tablespoon sugar
few drops vanilla essence
½–1 oz./15–25 g. butter

Blend the cornflour and cocoa with a little cold milk. Heat the remainder of the milk and when boiling pour on to the blended mixture. Return to the heat and cook for 2–3 minutes, stirring continuously. Add the sugar, vanilla essence and the butter, serve hot.
To vary:
If serving this sauce cold, use slightly more milk, stir as the sauce cools or put into the blender and emulsify until smooth.
A richer chocolate sauce is made by heating 4 oz./100 g. plain chocolate with 4 tablespoons water, a small knob butter and ½ level tablespoon golden syrup in a basin over hot water.

Cabinet Pudding

To make: 20 minutes   To cook: 1½ hours   (Serves 4–6)

4 oz./100 g. sponge cake, sweet
    biscuits or macaroons
3 eggs or 3 egg yolks
1–2 oz./25–50 g. sugar
1 pint/6 dl. milk
2–4 oz./50–100 g. glacé cherries
small piece angelica
1–2 oz./25–50 g. blanched
    almonds

To economize:
Use the egg whites for meringues.

Make crumbs from the sponge, biscuits or macaroons. Beat the eggs or egg yolks with the sugar. Add the warmed milk, pour over the crumbs, then add the quartered cherries, finely diced angelica and chopped nuts. Put into a well greased basin, cover with greased greaseproof paper and foil. Steam over hot, but not boiling water, until firm.
To serve:
Turn out and serve with cream or custard sauce, page 145.
To freeze:
This pudding does not freeze well.

Fruit Pudding

To make: 25 minutes   To cook: 3 hours   (Serves 6)

suet crust pastry made with
    10 oz./280 g.* flour
about 1½ lb./750 g. plums,
    damsons, sliced apples or fruit
    in season
sugar to taste (see method)
little water (see method)

*use this metrication

Make the suet crust pastry, and line a greased basin, as the method on page 72. Add the fruit with sugar to taste and enough water to come half way up the fruit. Roll out the remaining pastry and make a 'lid', then cover with greased greaseproof paper and foil. Steam rapidly for about 3 hours.
To serve:
Turn out and serve with cream or custard sauce, page 145.
To freeze:
As Cherry Layer Pudding, see opposite.

Cherry layer pudding

Cherry Layer Pudding

To make: 20 minutes **To cook:** 3 hours or 1 hour **(Serves 4–6)**

½ oz./15 g. butter
2 oz./50 g. demerara sugar
6 oz./150 g. self-raising flour or
    plain flour and 1½ teaspoons
    baking powder
pinch salt
3 oz./75 g. shredded suet
2x14 oz./350 g. cans cherry
    pie filling

Quick tip:
Use a pressure cooker (see method) or make 4–6 individual puddings and steam for 45 minutes.
To economize:
Use more economical fruit with a little water and sugar to taste.
To freeze:
Cook, cool, freeze and use within 3 months. Or prepare, freeze and store for 2 months. Thaw out before cooking.

Butter a 2-pint/1¼-litre pudding basin and sprinkle round 1½ oz./40 g. of the sugar. Mix the flour and baking powder, if using, with the remaining sugar, salt and suet and add enough cold water to make a soft dough. Divide into 4 pieces of graduating sizes. Roll out the pieces individually. the smallest to fit the base of the basin, the largest to fit the top. Place the smallest piece in the base. Drain off most of the sauce from the cherries and reserve. Put the cherries and pastry in layers in the basin, finishing with the largest piece of pastry. Cover with greased greaseproof paper and/or foil. Steam over boiling water. Allow 1 hour with the water boiling briskly then lower the heat so the water bubbles steadily and cook for a further 2 hours. To cook in a pressure cooker: Bring 1¾ pints/1 litre water to the boil. Place the basin on the trivet in the cooker, fit on the lid. Turn the heat to high, wait until the steam escapes freely from the vent. Lower the heat and cook gently with the vent open and steaming gently, for 15 minutes. Raise the heat and bring to 5 lb./2½ kilo. pressure for 40 minutes. Reduce pressure at room temperature.
To serve:
Hot with custard or with reserved cherry sauce.
To vary:
Use any other fruit pie filling.

Making Pastry

There are many recipes in this book for pastry of various kinds. Learn to handle pastry gently but firmly so you do not stretch it in rolling.

Quantity of pastry: When a recipe states 8 oz./200 g. pastry it means pastry made with 8 oz./200 g. flour, etc., *not* the total weight.

Fruit Flans:
The flan may be filled with cooked, canned, frozen or raw fruit. If using cooked or canned fruit, strain carefully. If using frozen fruit, allow to defrost lightly and strain. If using raw fruit make a syrup of ½ pint/3 dl. water boiled with approximately 4 oz./100 g. sugar (more or less as required) and simply put the raw strawberries, cherries or other fruit in the warm syrup for 2–3 minutes then strain. In this way the fruit absorbs the flavour of the syrup but does not become too soft. To fill an 8–9-inch/20–23-cm. flan allow 1–1¼ lb./500–600 g. fruit. Make the fleur pastry as the recipe below, or use short crust pastry, see page 122, made with 6 oz./150 g. flour etc. Roll out and line the flan case, or flan ring on an upturned baking tray or shallow baking tin.

Baking 'blind':
Fill the pastry with greased greaseproof paper and beans or crusts of bread or with foil to keep the pastry a good shape.

Bake in the centre of the oven until golden brown (approximately 20–25 minutes); use a moderately hot oven, 400°F./200°C., Gas Mark 6, for fleur pastry and a hot oven, 425°F./220°C., Gas Mark 7, for short crust. Remove the flan ring, paper and beans or foil after 15 minutes and lower the heat slightly. Allow the pastry to cool, then arrange the cold fruit in this. Measure the syrup and to each ¼ pint/1½ dl. allow 1 teaspoon arrowroot or cornflour. Blend with the liquid and boil until thickened and clear. Cool slightly then brush over the fruit.

Fleur Pastry

To make: 15 minutes   **To cook:** 20–25 minutes   (Serves 6–8)

3–4 oz./75–100 g. butter or best
   quality margarine
2 oz./50 g. caster sugar
1 egg yolk
6 oz./150 g. flour, preferably plain
little cold water

Cream the butter or margarine and sugar until soft and light. Beat in the egg yolk, add the sieved flour, and blend with a palette knife. Gradually stir in enough water to bind to a firm dough. Use as required.
To vary:
Omit 1 oz./25 g. flour and add 1 oz./25 g. chopped nuts. Use the smaller amount of butter or margarine.

Treacle Tart

To make: 25 minutes   **To cook:** 30–35 minutes   (Serves 4–6)

short crust pastry made with
   6 oz./150 g. flour (see page 122).
grated rind of ½ a lemon
1 tablespoon lemon juice
4 good tablespoons golden syrup
soft breadcrumbs or crushed
   cornflakes (see method)
To decorate:
icing sugar (optional)

Quick tip:
Use 9 oz./225 g. frozen pastry or pastry mix
To economize:
Use up stale bread

Roll out the pastry and line an 8–9-inch/20–23-cm. pie plate. Prick the pastry and bake 'blind' towards the top of a moderately hot oven, 400°F./200°C., Gas Mark 6, until set. Meanwhile, mix the grated lemon rind with the lemon juice, golden syrup and enough breadcrumbs or cornflakes to give a soft consistency. Cover the pastry with this. Move to a cooler part of the oven, or lower the heat slightly, and continue cooking for a further 15–20 minutes until the pastry is crisp.
To serve:
Hot or cold with cream. Dust with sieved icing sugar, if wished.
To vary:
Add twisted strips of pastry over the syrup mixture for decoration. Bake as above, then fill with the syrup mixture and return to the oven for a few minutes until heated through.
To freeze:
See comments on page 184.

Biscuit crumb crust:

Cream 4 oz./100 g. butter and 2 oz./50 g. caster sugar. Add 8 oz./200 g. crushed biscuits. Form into a flan case and chill, then fill as instructions for 'baking blind', opposite. Crushed cornflakes or other breakfast cereals could be used instead of biscuits.

Fruit Pies

The recipe below is given as a pie, but many people may well consider it a tart, as it has pastry both above and below the fruit. When you want to make a pie in a pie dish with one crust use 6 oz./150 g. pastry. Put the fruit with sugar to taste and a very little water into a pie-dish. Roll out the pastry, cut a narrow strip and press this on to the rim of the dish. Roll out the remaining pastry to a piece large enough to cover the fruit. Damp the pastry rim, lay the rolled-out pastry over the top, trim, seal and flute the edges. Bake as below.

Blackberry & Apple Pie

To make: 25 minutes   **To cook:** 30–40 minutes   **(Serves 4–6)**

short crust pastry made with
   8 oz./200 g. flour (see page 122)
little flour or cornflour (see
   method)
2–3 tablespoons sugar
1 lb./500 g. cooking apples
8 oz./200 g. blackberries
¼ teaspoon ground cinnamon
   (optional)
To decorate:
caster sugar (optional – see method)

Quick tip:
Use frozen or packet pastry
mix and canned pie filling.
To economize:
Choose inexpensive fruit when in
season.
To freeze:
This freezes well, see page 184.

Roll out half the pastry into a round and line an 8–9-inch/20–23-cm. pie plate. Sprinkle with a light dusting of flour or cornflour and sugar; this absorbs the juice from the fruit and helps to keep the bottom pastry crisp. Peel, core and slice the apples. Wash and dry the blackberries. Place the apple and blackberries in the pie plate and sprinkle with the remaining sugar and the cinnamon, if wished. Brush the edge of the pastry with water. Roll out the remaining pastry to a round to fit the pie plate. Place on top of the fruit. Seal the edges, trim neatly, and decorate the edge. Make a hole in the centre of the pastry with a skewer to allow the steam to escape. You can sprinkle the pastry with a little caster sugar before baking to give a glaze, if wished. Cook in the centre of a moderately hot to hot oven, 400–425°F./200–220°C., Gas Mark 6–7, for 30–40 minutes, until the pastry is cooked and golden brown, lower the heat slightly after 20–30 minutes if the pastry is becoming too brown.
To serve:
Hot or cold with custard or cream.
To vary:
Use 1½ lb./750 g. apples, gooseberries, raspberries, cherries or apricots in the pie.
Sprinkle the bottom pastry with semolina instead of flour.

Lemon Meringue Pie

To make: 30 minutes   **To cook:** see method   **(Serves 6–8)**

fleur pastry made with 6 oz./150 g.
   flour (see opposite)
For the filling:
1 oz./25 g. cornflour
½ pint/3 dl. cold water
1 oz./25 g. butter or margarine
grated rind and juice of 2 lemons
5–8 oz./125–200 g. caster sugar
2 eggs

Quick tip:
Use pastry mix plus a little sugar,
or frozen short crust pastry.
To economize:
Use packet lemon meringue pie
filling.

To freeze:
This freezes well, use within
6 weeks. Serve or heat gently as
soon as defrosted.

Make the pastry and line a 7–8-inch/18–20-cm. flan ring or an ovenproof dish. Bake 'blind', see opposite, until firm and golden; *do not over-bake*. Blend the cornflour to a smooth paste with a little of the water. Bring the butter or margarine and rest of the water to the boil, pour over the blended cornflour and stir well. Pour back into the saucepan and cook for 3 minutes, stirring all the time. Remove from the heat, stir in the lemon rind and juice and 3–4 oz./75–100 g. of the sugar. Allow to cool. Separate the yolks from the whites of the eggs. Stir the yolks into the cooled mixture and pour into the flan case. Whisk the egg whites very stiffly, beat in 2 oz./50 g. caster sugar and fold in the remaining 2 oz./50 g. sugar, or see below. Pile on top of the lemon mixture, making sure the meringue touches the edge of the pastry all round. Place in the centre of a slow oven, 275–300°F./140–150°C., Gas Mark 1–2, for 20–30 minutes or until the meringue is firm.
To serve:
Hot or cold. When serving cold, bake for 1 hour in a very slow oven, 225–250°F./110–130°C., Gas Mark 0–½. This makes sure the meringue will not 'shrivel' as it cools. If serving the meringue hot, then 2 oz./50 g. sugar only can be used.
To vary:
Use orange rind and juice.

Apple pan dowdy

Apple Pan Dowdy

To make: 25 minutes **To cook:** 45–50 minutes (Serves 4)

3 good-sized cooking apples
1–2 tablespoons brown sugar
1–2 tablespoons golden syrup
grated nutmeg (see method)
ground cinnamon (see method)
4 oz./100 g. self-raising flour
   or plain flour and 1 *level*
   teaspoon baking powder
pinch salt
2 oz./50 g. sugar
1 egg
4 tablespoons milk
2 oz./50 g. butter or margarine
little extra sugar

Quick tip:
Use canned apple pie filling plus
the spices.

To economize:
Use windfall apples and only half
the butter or margarine.

Peel and slice the apples. Put into a greased 1½-pint/9 dl. pie or ovenproof
dish with the brown sugar, syrup and a sprinkling of grated nutmeg and
ground cinnamon. Do not add any water. Cover the dish with foil and bake
in the centre of a moderate oven, 350°F./180°C., Gas Mark 4, for about
15–20 minutes until the apples are nearly soft. Meanwhile make a thick
batter mixture by blending the flour or flour and baking powder, salt,
caster sugar, egg, milk and melted butter or margarine. Spoon the mixture
over the apples, sprinkle lightly with sugar and bake in the centre of the
oven for 30–35 minutes. (If you use a deeper dish, allow about 45–50
minutes, lowering the heat after 25 minutes.)

To serve:
Turn the pudding upside-down on to a dish, serve with cream, brandy
butter or vanilla flavoured sauce (made as the rum sauce on page 177 but
using ½–1 teaspoon vanilla essence instead of rum.)

To vary:
Use sharp plums in place of apples.

To freeze:
Cook, cool, freeze then wrap. Use within 2 months. Reheat gently from the
frozen state.

Milk Puddings

The secret of a good milk pudding is in slow cooking.
Allow 2 oz./50 g. round grain rice (or sago or tapioca) to each 1 pint/6 dl. milk with 1–2 oz./25–50 g. sugar. Put these into a buttered pie dish and add ½–1 oz./15–25 g. butter or pure suet for a creamier pudding. Cook in the coolest part of a slow oven, 275–300°F./140–150°C., Gas Mark 1–2 for 1½–2 hours. Semolina should be sprinkled on to boiling milk in a pan, stirred over a low heat until thickened and smooth, then transferred to a dish, with sugar to taste and baked for about 45 minutes.

To freeze:

Milk puddings are better eaten freshly made. If you want to use up a surplus of liquid milk though you can freeze this dish. Allow at least 24 hours to defrost and use within 3 months.

Apples with Calvados

To make: 10 minutes   **To cook:** 10 minutes   (Serves 4)

4 large Granny Smith apples*
1½ oz./40 g. butter
2 tablespoons vanilla sugar or
    sugar with vanilla essence
2 tablespoons Calvados
*or use any other dessert apple that can be cooked.

Quick tip:
This is a very quick recipe.
To economize:
Omit Calvados and flavour with orange juice.

Peel the apples, remove the cores and slice thinly. Melt the butter in a large frying pan, stir in the sugar, then add the apple slices. Turn in the butter mixture until pale golden and transparent; when turning the apple slices, do so gently to avoid breaking them.
To serve:
When the apples are tender warm the Calvados over a flame in a soup ladle or spoon, ignite and pour over apples. Serve the apples as soon as the flames go out.
Note: Vanilla sugar is caster sugar which is flavoured with a vanilla bean. You can make it yourself by placing a cut vanilla bean in a jar of caster sugar or you can buy it from leading grocery stores.
To vary:
Use sliced firm pears instead of apples.
To freeze:
Do not freeze this dish, but frozen apple slices could be used.

Apples with Calvados

Caramelled Oranges

To make: 20 minutes   **To cook:** 15 –20 minutes   **(Serves 4)**

4 large oranges
½ pint/3 dl. water
3 oz./75 g. caster sugar

Quick tip:
Prepare oranges as recipe then coat in warmed marmalade, diluted with a little water. Allow to cool.

Cut away the orange 'zest' and white pith, but leave the fruit whole. Place in a serving dish. Slice some of the 'zest' into matchstick pieces. Simmer these in the water for 10 minutes. Take 3 tablespoons of this liquid and add to the sugar in a strong pan. Stir until the sugar has dissolved, then boil until a golden caramel. Add the softened orange 'zest' and 6 tablespoons of the liquid in which this was cooked. Pour over the oranges.
To serve:
Chill and serve with cream or ice cream.
To freeze:
Oranges can be frozen, but not caramel, so this is essentially a dessert to serve when freshly made.

Apple Lemon Mould

To make: 20 minutes plus setting   **No cooking**   **(Serves 4)**

grated rind and juice of 2 lemons
1 pint/6 dl. hot *thick* apple
   purée
½ oz./15 g. powdered gelatine
2 tablespoons golden syrup
To decorate:
lemon

Quick tip:
Use canned apple sauce or frozen purée.
To economize:
Buy apples when cheap and freeze. Use lemon squash when lemons are expensive. Omit decoration.

Stir the grated rind of the lemons into the hot apple purée. Blend the powdered gelatine with the juice from the lemons. Stir into the hot apple purée with the golden syrup. Turn into a rinsed mould and allow to set.
To serve:
Turn out and decorate with lemon slices.
To vary:
Use other fruit purée.
To freeze:
Either freeze the dish, and use within 2–3 weeks, or use frozen purée, see page 185.

Apple lemon mould

Egg Custards

An egg custard needs careful cooking, as excessive heat or cooking for too long a period means that the temperature of the milk and eggs will reach boiling point. The custard will then 'curdle', i.e. separate, so it has an unpleasant layer of water.

To give a pouring custard sauce:

Whisk together 2 eggs or 2 egg yolks and 1–2 tablespoons sugar and add 1 pint/6 dl. warm milk. Flavour with a few drops of vanilla essence or a strip of lemon rind (but no lemon juice). Cook in the top of a double sauce-pan or basin over hot, but *not boiling* water, stirring all the time, until the mixture is sufficiently thick to coat the back of a wooden spoon; or use a thick pan over a *very low* heat. If serving cold cover with damp greaseproof paper to prevent a skin forming, or stir several times as the mixture cools.

To give a stiffer custard:

Use 4 eggs or egg yolks, 1–2 tablespoons sugar and 1 pint/6 dl. warm milk. If you intend to turn out the custard you can increase the yolks to 5. Strain into an ovenproof dish and either steam over hot water or bake in the coolest part of a slow oven, 275–300°F./140–150°C., Gas Mark 1–2. Allow about 1 hour, depending upon the depth of the custard. To prevent the sides of the custard becoming hard and to assist in lowering the temperature, stand the dish containing the egg custard in a tin of cold water (a bain marie).

To freeze:

A cooked egg custard does not freeze well unless using half double cream and half milk, but an uncooked egg custard can be frozen, so if you have made the custard and then find it will not be eaten, freeze rather than waste it. Use within 2 months and cook from the frozen state.

Puddings Based on Egg Custard

These puddings are made and cooked as egg custards, although, since the proportion of milk, etc., varies the cooking times may not be exactly the same. See also Cabinet pudding, page 138. All recipes serve 4.

Bread and butter pudding:

Cut thin slices of bread and butter, divide into squares or triangles and put into a pie dish with 1–2 oz./25–50 g. dried fruit. Prepare a custard with 2 eggs or yolks, ¾ pint/4½ dl. milk, and 1–2 tablespoons sugar. Pour over the bread and butter. Sprinkle a little extra sugar on top together with grated nutmeg. Cook as the baked custard above, although you can raise the oven temperature slightly to crisp the bread on top.

Caramel custard:

Make a caramel sauce. Stir 3 oz./75 g. caster, granulated or loaf sugar and 3 tablespoons water over a low heat until the sugar has dissolved. Continue cooking without stirring, until a golden brown caramel. Add 1–3 extra tablespoons water and stir until blended. Cool slightly then pour the caramel into an ovenproof dish, turning this round, so the sauce coats the sides and bottom. Cool. Prepare the custard with 4 eggs or 4–5 yolks, etc. Strain into the dish and cook as the baked custard. Leave until nearly cold then turn out on to a serving dish.

Queen of puddings:

Spread a little jam or lemon curd at the bottom of a pie dish. Put 2 oz./50 g. fine plain cake or sweet biscuit crumbs into a basin. Beat 2 egg yolks with 1–2 tablespoons sugar. Add ½–¾ pint/3–4½ dl. milk and strain over the crumbs. Mix thoroughly, pour into the pie dish. Bake as the egg custard. Remove from the oven, spread the pudding with more jam or curd. Whisk the egg whites until stiff, add 2 oz./50 g. caster sugar, see instructions under meringues, page 137. Spoon over the top of the pudding and bake for 15 minutes. Serve hot.

Swiss roll pudding:

As Queen of Puddings above, but omit jam or curd. Put slices of jam filled Swiss roll into the dish, add the custard. Bake as Queen of Puddings then remove from the oven, top with meringue and continue cooking as Queen of Puddings.

Baking for the Family

Home made bread and cakes enable you to add your own individual touch to the tea-table. *When baking, remember:* Check on oven temperatures with your manufacturers' instructions, for cookers vary quite a lot in their temperature setting and careful baking is part of the secret of successful results.

Follow the recommended method of blending the ingredients, in a Victoria sandwich (page 151), for example, you are advised to 'fold' in the flour, this retains the light texture.

Careful weighing and measuring are important, see the comments about metrication on page 6.

To freeze: Many cakes and breads freeze well, see under the individual recipes for details. When a cake is iced or decorated, freeze without covering, then wrap when frozen.

Economical Baking

Yeast cookery is one of the most economical methods of providing bread etc. for the family, recipes and suggestions are on the right and pages 148 and 149.

Yeast cookery: Cooking with yeast is not only very simple, but very economical too, as you can produce a whole batch of bread and buns at little expense. The quantity of dough given in the bread recipe on page 148 will make three out of the four loaves suggested below or some of the other recipes on page 149.

Plain flour is used for making bread, but if you can obtain strong flour (sometimes called bread flour) you will have an even better result.

To make loaves

You will find the recipe for a white bread dough, together with variations on this basic recipe, on page 148.

The quantity given in this recipe is sufficient to enable you to make three loaves of bread, either all the same shape, or choose three different shapes from the four suggestions given below. The same basic bread recipe can be used to make rolls or baps and you will find the instructions for shaping and cooking these on page 149. Make the bread dough, allow this to 'prove' then knead well, cut the dough into three parts and proceed as below.

Cob loaf: Shape the dough into a round. Either put on to a warmed greased baking tray or into a 6-inch/15-cm. round cake tin. Cover the tin lightly and allow to 'prove' for about 1 hour in a warm place. Bake for 35–40 minutes in the centre of the oven; allow about 20 minutes in a moderately hot to hot oven, 400–425°F./200–220°C., Gas Mark 6–7, then reduce temperature to moderate, 350°F./180°C., Gas Mark 4. To test if the bread is cooked, knock the loaf firmly on the bottom; if it sounds hollow the bread is cooked.

Cottage loaf: Shape as cottage rolls. Prove and bake as cob loaf.

Fruit loaf: Knead 2–4 oz./50–100 g. dried fruit into one batch of dough. Roll lightly into an oblong shape the length and three times the width of a 2-lb./1-kilo loaf tin. Fold in three then put into the warmed greased tin, brush with egg, diluted with water; 'prove' and bake as cob loaf.

Poppy seed loaf: Make a long strip, fold and twist the two ends loosely, brush with egg diluted with water and top with poppy seeds. 'Prove' as cob loaf, but bake for about 30 minutes.

8 oz./200 g. plain flour
½ teaspoon salt
½ teaspoon bicarbonate of soda
1 teaspoon cream of tartar
1–1½ oz./25–40 g. butter or
　　margarine
1 oz./25 g. sugar
about ¼ pint/1½ dl. milk

Quick tip:
All scones are quick to make and
cook.
To economize:
Halve the butter or margarine.

Sieve the flour, salt, bicarbonate of soda and cream of tartar into a bowl. Rub the butter or margarine into the flour with the tips of your fingers; add the sugar. Bind the mixture with the milk to give a soft, but not too wet, consistency, using a round-bladed knife. Lightly flour a working surface and pat or roll out the dough until it is ½-inch/1-cm. thick. Either cut into squares or cut into 2-inch/5-cm. rounds, using a pastry cutter or top of a small glass. Place the scones on a baking tray and bake towards the top of a hot oven, 425°F./220°C., Gas Mark 7, for 10 minutes or until risen and golden brown.
To serve:
When fresh, with butter and jam.
To vary:
Use self-raising flour and omit the bicarbonate of soda and cream of tartar or add only half the quantities for a very light scone.
Brown scones: Use half white and half wholemeal flour.
Cheese scones: Omit sugar, season flour well, use only 1 oz./25 g. butter or margarine and 1–2 oz./25–50 g. grated cheese.
Fruit scones: Add 1–2 oz./25–50 g. dried fruit.
Oatmeal scones: Use half rolled oats or oatmeal and half flour.
Potato scones: Use half flour and half mashed potatoes.
Treacle scones: Omit sugar and add 1 level tablespoon black treacle to the dough before binding with milk.
To freeze:
Scones freeze perfectly. Bake, cool and freeze then use within 6 months. Heat gently for a short time from the frozen state. If preferred, freeze on trays before baking, then pack, use within 2 months. Thaw out before baking.

White Bread　　　To make: 30 minutes plus 'proving'　To cook: see method　(Makes 3 loaves)

1 oz./25 g. fresh yeast or
　　1 tablespoon dried yeast
1½ pints/ 9 dl. warm water, milk
　　or milk and water
2 teaspoons sugar (see method)
3 lb./scant 1½ kilo plain flour
1 level tablespoon salt
2–4 oz./50–100 g. lard or
　　margarine

Quick tip:
Make the dough into rolls
(see opposite)
To economize:
Use water to mix the dough.
Never waste left-over bread, the
crumbs can be used in cooking. If
you moisten the outside of the
loaf with water or milk, so it
does not harden with heating, you
can crisp up quite stale bread by
heating it in a moderate oven for
about 20 minutes.
If you dislike a too crisp outside
wrap the moistened bread in foil
before warming through.

If using fresh yeast simply blend this with the warm liquid, although you may prefer to cream it with the sugar, then add the liquid. If using dried yeast blend the sugar with the warm liquid, sprinkle the dried yeast on top, then wait for about 10 minutes; after this continue as though using fresh yeast. Mix the flour and salt, rub in the lard or margarine, add the yeast liquid. Mix together until you have a firm dough and the bowl is clean. Turn out on to a floured board and knead until a smooth elastic dough. To tell if the dough is sufficiently kneaded, press with a lightly floured finger; if the impression comes out, the dough has been handled enough. Either return to the bowl and cover with a cloth or put into a large, lightly oiled polythene bag and tie loosely at the top. Allow the dough to 'prove', i.e. rise until double its original size. You can control the time quite appreciably; if you are in a hurry, leave in a warm, *but not too hot*, place for 1–1½ hours (this means the airing cupboard or similar conditions); or about 2 hours at room temperature; or 12–24 hours in a refrigerator (the nearer the freezer compartment the longer the dough will take to 'prove'). Allow to return to room temperature then shape as below.
To vary:
Brown bread: Use half white and half stoneground (wholemeal) flour.
Wholemeal bread: Use stoneground flour and rather more liquid.
To freeze:
Use 50% more yeast, 'prove' as above, then form into a neat shape. Return to a large, lightly oiled polythene bag and seal. Freeze, but use within 8 weeks. Always allow to return to room temperature before shaping. Cooked bread can be kept for 6 weeks. Wrap and warm in the oven or thaw out at room temperature.

Swedish Tea Ring

Take about 12 oz./generous 300 g. of the 'proven' dough. Roll out to a 12 x 9-inch/30 x 23-cm. rectangle. Brush with 1 oz./25 g. melted butter, sprinkle with 2 oz./50 g. brown sugar, a little cinnamon and 1–2 oz./25–50 g. finely chopped blanched almonds. Roll up like a Swiss roll, form into a round and seal the ends. Put on to a warmed greased baking tray. Make cuts with scissors about 1-inch/2-cm. apart. Allow to 'prove' and bake as the cob loaf. When cold top with icing made with 2–3 oz./50–75 g. icing sugar, blended with a little warm water. Decorate with blanched almonds and halved glacé cherries.

To Make Rolls

Bridge rolls:
Cottage rolls:

Knot rolls:

Take off pieces of dough about 2–3 oz./50–75 g. in weight.
Form into finger shapes.
Use three-quarters of the dough to make the round base. Make a smaller round and press this on top of the larger one, then make an impression with a floured finger. Brush with a little egg diluted with water.
Roll the dough into a long strip. Tie in a loose knot and sprinkle with poppy seeds. Brush with a little egg, diluted with water.
Place the rolls on to warmed greased baking trays, allow to 'prove' in a warm place then bake for 12–15 minutes above the centre of a moderately hot to hot oven, 400–425°F./200–220°C., Gas Mark 6–7.

Baps: These are large, fairly flat, rolls served in Scotland for breakfast, but they are also ideal for serving topped with Hamburgers, see page 77. Make the dough a little softer than usual, form into rounds then flatten slightly before 'proving'. 'Prove' and cook as opposite.

Making Cakes

There are several ways of mixing cakes. Melting some of the ingredients is both quick and simple, see opposite and page 152. Another easy method is to rub the fat into the flour, see page 153 but do not over-handle the mixture when blending by this method. The creaming method of mixing is described below and on page 151, and whisked sponges on page 154.

Always choose the type of flour recommended in the recipe, as this is very important.

Test a cake thoroughly before turning it out of the tin. Most cakes are cooked when they are firm to pressure, but see the individual recipes.

Secrets of Light Cakes

Most light cakes are made by creaming; this method is used in the well known recipes below and on other pages in this section. Always cream (i.e. beat), the fat and sugar well. This is important whether you use an electric mixer or beat with a wooden spoon. The reason for creaming is to incorporate as much air as possible and so lighten the cake; modern soft margarines cream easily. Use caster sugar for light cakes as this has a finer texture than granulated. Do not add the eggs too quickly, as the mixture could 'curdle' (separate) and this spoils the smooth texture. If the mixture shows any signs of 'curdling' add a little flour at once and stir gently and carefully into the mixture to retain the lightness of the cake.

Cider crumble cake

Cider Crumble Cake

To make: 15 minutes   **To cook:** 50 minutes   **(Serves 8–10)**

1 lb. 2 oz./525 g. self-raising flour
   or plain flour and 4½ *level*
   teaspoons baking powder
4 oz./100 g. moist brown sugar
2½ oz./65 g. dates
3 tablespoons black treacle
½ pint/3 dl. cider
2 eggs
For the topping:
1½ oz./40 g. caster sugar
1½ oz./40 g. plain or self-raising
   flour
1½ oz./40 g. butter
1½ oz./40 g. walnuts
½ teaspoon ground cinnamon
3 tablespoons apricot or plum jam

Sieve the flour or flour and baking powder. Add the sugar and chopped dates. Heat the treacle and cider until the treacle has melted, then stir into the flour mixture. Lastly add the eggs and mix thoroughly. Line a 9-inch/23-cm. square cake tin with greased greaseproof paper, and pour in the mixture. Bake in the centre of a very moderate oven, 325°F./170°C., Gas Mark 3 for 30 minutes. Meanwhile prepare the topping, mix the sugar and flour, rub in the butter, add the chopped walnuts and cinnamon. Bring the cake from the oven, spread with the jam and press the crumble over the top. Return to the oven for a further 20 minutes. As one cannot press this cake to see it if is firm to the touch, test to see if it is cooked by inserting a fine wooden cocktail stick, if it comes out clean the cake is cooked. Cool in the tin for 10–15 minutes, then turn out carefully.

To serve:
Although the cake itself has no fat in it, it is better if matured for 2 days before cutting.

Victoria Sandwich or Butter Sponge

To make: 10–15 minutes   **To cook:** 15–20 minutes   **(Serves 4–5)**

4 oz./100 g. margarine, butter
   or cooking fat
4 oz./100 g. caster sugar
2 eggs
4 oz./100 g. self-raising flour or plain
   flour and 1 teaspoon baking
   powder.
Quick tip:
Use your mixer for creaming the fat and sugar and adding the eggs. Fold in the flour by hand.
Use quick creaming margarine, put all the ingredients into the bowl and cream. This sponge is not as light, but is very acceptable.
To economize:
Use only 2 oz./50 g. fat and 2 oz./50 g. sugar, one egg and milk to mix to the correct consistency.

Cream the margarine, butter or fat with the sugar until soft and light in colour, using a wooden spoon. If using the mixer warm the bowl, *but not the fat,* to ease mixing. Gradually beat in the eggs, then fold in the sieved flour or flour and baking powder with a metal spoon. Divide the mixture between two 6–7-inch/15–18-cm. greased and floured sandwich tins. Bake above the centre of a moderate oven, 350–375°F./180–190°C., Gas Mark 4–5, for 15–20 minutes until just firm to the touch. Cool for 2–3 minutes in the tins then turn out carefully.

To serve:
Fill with jam or jam and whipped cream and top with sieved icing sugar or caster sugar and serve with coffee, or for tea. Or fill with fruit and cream and serve as a dessert.

To vary:
Chocolate sponge: Omit ½ oz./15 g. flour and use cocoa instead.
Orange sponge: Add finely grated 'zest' of 1–2 oranges to margarine and sugar. Use small eggs and add orange juice to give the correct consistency. Lemon rind and juice could also be used.

To freeze:
Use within 10 weeks, and allow 3–4 hours to defrost.

Dundee Cake

To make: 15–20 minutes   **To cook:** 2–2¼ hours   **(Serves 8–10)**

6 oz./150 g. margarine or butter
6 oz./150 g. caster sugar
3 large eggs
8 oz./200 g. flour*
1 lb./500 g. mixed dried fruit
2 oz./50 g. glacé cherries
2 oz./50 g. chopped candied peel
little milk
To decorate:
1–2 oz./25–50 g. blanched almonds
*either half self-raising and half plain flour or all plain flour with 1½ *level* teaspoons baking powder

Quick tip:
Use your mixer for creaming the fat and sugar and adding the eggs or use a quick creaming margarine (see Victoria Sandwich above).

Cream the margarine or butter and sugar together and gradually add the eggs. Fold in the sieved flours or flour and baking powder gently, then the fruit, cherries and peel and just enough milk to make a soft, consistency. Put into a 7–8-inch/18–20-cm. greased and floured, or lined and greased tin and cover with the almonds. Brush these with a little egg white, (there is enough left in the egg shells after making the cake). Bake for 2–2¼ hours in the centre of a very moderate oven, 325°F./170°C., Gas Mark 3, reducing the heat to slow after about 1–1½ hours. Cool slightly, then turn out carefully.

To vary:
Spiced Dundee Cake: Sieve 1–2 teaspoons mixed spice with the flour.
To freeze:
It is generally pointless to freeze a rich Dundee cake, as this matures and keeps well in a tin for up to two months. If you want to keep it longer, freeze and use within 2–3 months.
To economize:
Use only 5 oz./125 g. fat, 5 oz./125 g. sugar and 2 eggs. Increase the amount of baking powder to 2 teaspoons with plain flour or use self-raising flour and increase the milk to give a soft, dropping consistency.

151

Golden Ginger Loaf

To make: 15 minutes   **To cook:** 1–1¼ hours   (Serves 10–12)

10 oz./250 g. plain flour
1 *level* teaspoon bicarbonate of
    soda
½ teaspoon ground ginger
6 oz./150 g. clear honey
4 oz./100 g. fat
6 oz./150 g. sugar
2 tablespoons syrup from a jar of
    preserved ginger
1½ tablespoons milk
2 eggs

To decorate:
1 tablespoon honey
few leaves angelica
2–3 tablespoons preserved
    ginger, cut in neat pieces

Quick tip:
The melting method is one of the
speediest ways of producing a
cake. You cannot hasten this
particular recipe.

To economize:
Omit preserved ginger and increase
the milk to 4 tablespoons and the
ground ginger to 1½ teaspoons.

Sieve the dry ingredients into the mixing bowl. To weigh the honey, put
an empty saucepan on the scales, note the weight, then add 6 oz./150 g.
honey. Add the fat and sugar. Heat gently until the fat melts, then pour
over the flour and beat well. Warm the syrup and milk in the pan, add to
the flour mixture with the eggs and beat until smooth. Line a 2½–3-lb./
1¼–1½-kilo loaf tin with greased greaseproof paper. Pour in the mixture.
Bake in the centre of a slow to very moderate oven, 300–325°F./150–
170°C., Gas Mark 2–3, for 1–1¼ hours until *just firm* to the touch, do not
over-cook. Remove from the oven and cool in the tin for about 15 minutes.
Remove from the tin, take off the paper, then brush the top with the
honey and press the pieces of angelica and ginger into position.

To serve:
As a cake with coffee or tea, or spread with butter as a tea-bread. This is
also delicious sliced and topped with apple purée.

To vary:
To make a darker, stronger flavoured loaf use golden syrup or black
treacle, or a mixture of these, in place of honey. The amount of ground
ginger may be increased to 2 teaspoons as this recipe gives a very mild
flavour.

To freeze:
This freezes excellently. Use within 3 months.

Golden ginger loaf

Grasmere cake

Grasmere Cake

To make: 15 minutes (see method) **To cook:** 1¾–2 hours (Serves 10–12)

12 oz./300 g. plain flour
1 teaspoon mixed spice
1½ *level* teaspoons bicarbonate of
soda
6 oz./150 g. butter or margarine
1 tablespoon lemon juice
½ pint/3 dl. milk plus 1 tablespoon
6 oz./150 g. demerara sugar
6 oz./150 g. currants
3 oz./75 g. sultanas

Quick tip:
This is a quick cake to prepare.
To economize:
This is an economical cake, but
use vinegar in place of lemon juice.

Line a 9–10 x 5–6 inch/23–25 x 13–15 cm. loaf tin with greased greaseproof paper. Sieve the flour, spice and bicarbonate of soda into a bowl. Rub the butter or margarine into the flour until the mixture resembles fine breadcrumbs. Add the lemon juice to the milk (the milk will clot and turn sour). Mix the sugar, currants and sultanas with the dry ingredients. Gradually add the soured milk, stirring with a wooden spoon, until a dropping consistency is reached. Leave the mixture covered for several hours or overnight. Spoon the mixture into the prepared tin. Bake in the centre of a very moderate oven, 325°F./170°C., Gas Mark 3, for 1¾–2 hours, or until firm to the touch. Leave for a few minutes in the tin before turning it out on to a wire rack to cool. Remove the paper. Grasmere cake can be stored satisfactorily for about 1 week. Wrap in foil or in greaseproof paper when cold and store in an airtight tin.
To freeze:
This is the type of fruit cake to bake then freeze, as the storage life is limited in a tin. Use within 2 months.

Rock Buns

To make: 10 minutes **To cook:** 10–12 minutes (Makes 10–12)

8 oz./200 g. self-raising flour
or plain flour and 2 *level*
teaspoons baking powder
4 oz./100 g. margarine
4–6 oz./100–150 g. sugar
4–6 oz./100–150 g. dried fruit
1 egg
milk to mix

Sieve the flour, or flour and baking powder. Rub in the margarine, add most of the sugar, the fruit, then the beaten egg and enough milk to make a stiff mixture. Put small heaps of the mixture into greased patty tins or on to flat baking trays, allowing room for them to spread. Sprinkle lightly with the remaining sugar and bake for 10 minutes near the top of a hot to very hot oven, 425–450°F./220–230°C., Gas Mark 7–8. Lower the heat, if necessary, after the first 5 minutes.
To vary:
Flavour the buns with grated lemon or orange rind and mix with fruit juice instead of milk.
Coconut and fruit buns: Use 6 oz./150 g. flour and 2 oz./50 g. desiccated coconut.
To freeze:
These economical cakes will not become stale if you freeze them the day they are baked. Use within 3 months.

Madeira Cake

To make: 10–15 minutes **To cook:** 1¼–1½ hours (Serves 10)

4–6 oz./100–150 g. butter or
margarine
4–6 oz./100–150 g. sugar
8 oz./200 g. self-raising flour or
plain flour and 2 *level* teaspoons
baking powder
2–3 eggs
1 teaspoon grated lemon rind
milk to mix
little extra sugar
piece candied lemon peel

Quick tip:
Use the mixer to cream the butter
and sugar and add the eggs, or
use quick creaming margarine
(see Victoria Sandwich page 151).

Cream the butter or margarine and sugar together until soft and light. Sieve the flour or flour and baking powder. Beat the eggs. Add the eggs and flour alternately to the margarine mixture, with the lemon rind and enough milk to make a soft consistency. Put into a greased and floured 7-inch/18-cm. cake tin. Bake the richer mixture for a good 1½ hours in the centre of a very moderate oven, 325°F./170°C., Gas Mark 3, the plainer version for about 1¼ hours at 350°F./180°C., Gas Mark 4, lowering heat after about 50–60 minutes. Sprinkle with a little sugar and top with the peel after about 45 minutes cooking time.
To vary:
Cherry cake: Ingredients and method of mixing as above. If making the richer version use 1 *level* teaspoon baking powder and plain flour if possible, 3 eggs and no milk. Add 6–8 oz./150–200 g. halved glacé cherries which should be rinsed in cold water, dried and floured before adding to the mixture.
Seed cake: Add 2–3 teaspoons caraway seeds to the mixture.
To freeze:
These freeze well; use within 10 weeks. Allow 4–5 hours to defrost.

153

Honey Cheesecake

For the crust:
8 oz./200 g. wheatmeal biscuits
2 oz./50 g. butter or margarine
For the filling:
12 oz./300 g. cottage cheese
4 oz./100 g. honey
2 teaspoons sugar
2 eggs
pinch salt
ground cinnamon (see method)

Quick tip:
Crush biscuits in a blender
To economize:
Use finely grated stale Cheddar
cheese plus 2 tablespoons milk.

To serve:
Cold with cream or ice cream.

To vary:
Flavour with grated lemon rind.
Sieve cottage cheese.

To freeze:
This, like most cheesecakes,
freezes well. Use within 2–3
months.

Crush the biscuits and mix with the melted butter or margarine. Press around the inside edge and over the bottom of an 8-inch/20-cm. sandwich or flan tin. Chill until ready for use. Beat the cheese, honey, sugar, eggs and salt together until smooth. Spoon into the biscuit crumb shell, sprinkle liberally with cinnamon and cook for 35–45 minutes in the centre of a slow oven, 275–300°F./140–150°C., Gas Mark 1–2. Allow to cool in the oven with the heat turned off. As an electric oven holds the heat, allow only 35–40 minutes.

Honey cheesecake

Sponge Sandwich

3 large eggs
4 oz./100 g. caster sugar
3 oz./75 g. plain or self-raising
   flour*
1 tablespoon hot water
*air is incorporated into this
mixture by whisking, so raising
agent is really unnecessary.

Quick tip:
Use the mixer to whisk the eggs
and sugar.

Whisk the eggs and sugar until thick; you should see the trail of the whisk in the mixture. Sieve the flour, then fold into the egg mixture with a metal spoon. Add enough hot water to give a flowing consistency. Pour into two 7-inch/18-cm. greased and floured sandwich tins. Bake above the centre of a moderately hot oven, 375–400°F./190–200°C., Gas Mark 5–6 until firm to the touch. Cool for 2–3 minutes then turn out.
To serve:
Sandwich together with jam or fruit and whipped cream, top with sugar.
To freeze:
Freeze, then wrap and use within 10 weeks. Allow 3–4 hours to defrost.

Swiss Roll

Ingredients as sponge sandwich
   above
4–6 tablespoons jam
2 tablespoons caster sugar

Make the sponge as the recipe above, using up to 1 tablespoon hot water. Pour into a large Swiss roll tin, lined with greased greaseproof paper. Bake towards the top of a moderately hot to hot oven, 400–425°F./200–220°C., Gas Mark 6–7, until firm to the touch. Meanwhile warm the jam, and sprinkle the sugar over a sheet of greaseproof paper. Turn the sponge on to the sugared paper, remove the greased paper and cut off the crisp edges. Spread with the warm, but not too hot, jam then roll firmly.
To freeze:
Freeze, then wrap and use within 10 weeks. Allow 3–4 hours to defrost.

Golden Cake

1 small packet instant mashed
   potato
1½ *level* teaspoons baking powder
3 oz./75 g. margarine
1 *level* tablespoon golden syrup
3 oz./75 g. caster sugar
finely grated rind 1 orange
2½ tablespoons orange juice
2 eggs
To decorate:
piece candied peel

Quick tip:
Use a mixer.
To economize:
Use grated rind only from
2 oranges and mix with water.

Line a 6-inch/15-cm. cake tin with greased greaseproof paper. Mix the potato powder and baking powder in a large bowl. Put the margarine, syrup, sugar, grated orange rind and orange juice in a saucepan. Heat gently until the sugar has dissolved, stirring occasionally. Remove from the heat and pour on to the potato mixture. Beat well. Separate the egg yolks and whites, add the egg yolks to the potato mixture. Whisk the egg whites to a stiff snow and gently fold into the potato mixture with a metal spoon. Put into the prepared tin and bake in the centre of a moderate oven, 350°F/180°C., Gas Mark 4, for about 45 minutes until well risen, golden and firm to the touch. Halfway through the cooking time, place the peel on top of the cake and cover with paper to avoid over-browning, or lower the heat slightly. Leave the cake in the tin for 5 minutes before turning out on to a wire rack.
To vary:
Use lemon rind and juice instead of orange juice.
To freeze:
This cake can be frozen; use within 6–8 weeks.

Golden cake

Secrets of Making Biscuits

Most biscuit doughs should contain little liquid as it is the right proportion of fat or syrup and fat that binds the ingredients. Store biscuits in tins away from other foods. The Date Crunchies are not a true biscuit and should be stored separately. Knead biscuit dough vigorously. Bake most biscuits steadily rather than quickly. See pages 174–175 for using a basic recipe.

To freeze:

It seems pointless to freeze biscuits since they keep so well in an airtight tin.

Scotch Shortbread

To make: 10 minutes   **To cook:** 40–45 minutes   **(Serves 8)**

6 oz./150 g. plain flour
2 oz./50 g. ground rice
pinch salt
2 oz./50 g. caster sugar
5 oz./125 g. butter

Sieve the flour, ground rice and salt. Add half the sugar then the butter and knead this into the dry ingredients. Finally add the rest of the sugar. Form into a 7-inch/18-cm. round and put into an ungreased sandwich tin. Prick the shortbread and mark into triangles. Bake for 40–45 minutes in the centre of a cool to very moderate oven, 300–325°F./150–170°C., Gas Mark 2–3. Lower the heat after 20 minutes if the shortbread is browning. Cool for a time in the tin, then lift out carefully.

Flapjacks

To make: 10 minutes   **To cook:** 20–25 minutes   **(Makes 18–24)**

4 oz./100 g. butter or margarine
1 oz./25 g. brown sugar
4 *level* tablespoons golden syrup
8 oz./200 g. rolled oats

Melt the butter or margarine with the sugar and syrup in a large pan. Add the oats and mix well. Spread the mixture smoothly over an 8 x 12-inch/ 20 x 30-cm. tin and bake in the centre of a moderate oven, 350°F./180°C., Gas Mark 4, for 15–20 minutes, or until golden brown and firm to the touch. Mark into squares or fingers while warm, but cool in the tin then remove carefully. Store in an airtight tin.

Date Crunchies

To make: 15 minutes   **To cook:** 30 minutes   **(Makes 12–14)**

4 oz./100 g. wholemeal plain flour
6 oz./150 g. rolled oats
8 oz./200 g. butter or margarine
8 oz./200 g. dates
2 tablespoons water
1 tablespoon lemon juice
1 tablespoon honey
pinch of ground cinnamon

Put the flour and oats into a mixing bowl. Add the butter or margarine and rub in well. Knead until a smooth dough. Divide the mixture into two and press half over the bottom of a greased 7-inch/18-cm. square cake tin. Simmer the chopped dates with the water until soft. Cool and stir in the lemon juice, honey and cinnamon. Spread the date mixture over the oat dough and cover with the remaining oat dough. Smooth flat with a palette knife. Bake in the centre of a moderate oven, 350°F./180°C., Gas Mark 4, for 25 minutes. Cut into fingers while still warm. Cool in the tin and remove carefully. Store away from cakes and biscuits.

Ginger Nuts

To make: 15 minutes   **To cook:** 15 minutes   **(Makes 12–16)**

4 oz./100 g. plain flour*
¾ *level* teaspoon bicarbonate of soda*
½–1 *level* teaspoon ground ginger
½–1 *level* teaspoon ground cinnamon
½–1 *level* teaspoon mixed spice
1–2 oz./25–50 g. sugar
2 oz./50 g. lard or butter
2 *level* tablespoons golden syrup

*if using self-raising flour use ¼ teaspoon bicarbonate of soda.

Sieve the flour with the bicarbonate of soda and the spices. Add the sugar (this can be granulated, caster or brown sugar). Heat the lard or butter with the golden syrup in a fairly large saucepan until the fat has melted. Stir the dry ingredients into the saucepan with a wooden spoon. Cool slightly then knead hard with your fingers. Roll into balls and put these on to two well greased baking trays, allowing plenty of room for the biscuits to spread. Bake just above the centre and in the middle of a moderately hot oven, 400°F./200°C., Gas Mark 6 for 5 minutes only, then lower the heat to very moderate, 325°F./170°C., Gas Mark 3 for a further 10 minutes. This quick start makes the ginger nuts spread and crack but they would burn before they were cooked if you continued to bake so quickly. Cool for about 15 minutes on the tins, but remove when just warm.

Celebrations

Most of us like to entertain, but sometimes worry about the amount of cooking or the expense it will entail. I wish people would worry less about the food they serve; perhaps that sounds odd from a cookery writer, but if you appreciate that the guests come to see *you*, rather than check upon your cooking ability, perhaps that will make you a little less worried.

However, having decided that we are going to plan some kind of a party, most of us then give thought to the organising of the food etc., and it *is* wise to think ahead and save last-minute panic or work.

Decide upon just what form your party will take, there are various suggestions in the pages that follow. Sit down quietly and work out the menu, write your shopping list or lists and buy as much as possible beforehand. Of course, if you have a freezer you can not only buy ahead but prepare much of the food in advance.

Make a time-table then as to what you must do first thing on the day of the party, etc. If you stick fairly closely to your time-table nothing will be forgotten. Always allow adequate time to 'dress up' for the party and have a few minutes' relaxation before your guests arrive.

One important point to consider is just how to dish up everything and keep it hot. If you have an electric hotplate, dish up as many of the foods as possible and keep them warm. If you have no hotplate put the food on to hot dishes, cover with foil and turn the oven heat as low as possible. If there is not sufficient room in the oven, keep sauces etc. warm over pans of hot, but not boiling water.

A dinner party for friends, or even business acquaintances, need not be a worrying affair. Plan 'eye-catching' and delicious dishes, but base these upon more simple family meals, with additional garnishes and flavourings. Choose your wines carefully and plan the dishes, so you have no last-minute panic.

The easiest way for most of us to entertain is to give an informal buffet party where our friends can help themselves to the food. This form of entertaining also means one can accommodate rather more people in a restricted space. On the next few pages you will find ideas for buffets, including suggestions for simple, but very popular, cheese and wine parties, and the more sophisticated fondue party.

Planning a buffet party

If space is limited and people will have to stand up to eat, make sure everything is easy to handle with a fork or fingers. Kebabs (see opposite and pages 66, 160 and 161) are fun for an informal party; learn the trick of slipping them off the skewer with a fork. Further suggestions for food for buffets are on pages 160–163.

If you are entertaining without a lot of help it is simpler to have a few outstanding dishes, and the choice of two wines, rather than a great variety of food and drinks. Some suggestions for wines are on pages 161 and 166 and some unusual drink recipes are given on page 183.

To freeze: If you have a freezer you can prepare, or even cook many dishes ahead and freeze these. Hints on freezing are given under most recipes in this book. See also pages 10, 184 and 185.

If you pack everything for the party in one part of your freezing cabinet and mark it clearly it is easy to find on the important day.

Cheese ke

Cheese Kebabs

6–8 oz./150–200 g. cheese (see
  method)
1–2 green peppers
8 small mushrooms
8 small firm tomatoes
8 small onions, par-boiled
1–2 oz./25–50 g. butter
seasoning

Quick tip:
Use cocktail onions (instead of
softening onions by boiling until
almost tender).
To economize:
Omit peppers and use more onions.

Dutch cheeses, Edam or Gouda, are ideal for these, as they cook well
and do not crumble when put on to the metal skewers. Cut the cheese
into $\frac{3}{4}$–1-inch/$1\frac{1}{2}$–2-cm. cubes and cut the pepper(s) into pieces (discard
core and seeds). Put on to metal skewers with the mushrooms, tomatoes,
and onions. Brush with the melted butter, season and cook for a few
minutes under a hot grill, turn once or twice.
To serve:
With cooked rice or hot rolls and butter.
To vary:
Soften green pepper by 'blanching' in boiling salted water for 5 minutes,
then drain and dice.
Cheese and bacon kebabs: Put diced cheese and small bacon rolls on to
the skewers. Cook as above.
Cheese and fruit kebabs: Put diced cheese, segments of orange, rings of
banana and segments of apple (both dipped in lemon juice) on to the
skewers. Cook as above.

Easy Canapés

Canapés can be served for buffet
and cocktail parties and can be
varied in many ways.
Bases for Canapés:
Use buttered bread, crisp toast,
buttered biscuits or crispbreads as
the base. If you are putting a fairly
soft topping such as pâté, on a
crisp base, then do this at the last
minute as otherwise the topping
would soften and spoil the toast or
biscuit.

Top cold canapés with:
Cream cheese and pieces of melon.
Cream cheese and pieces of
pineapple.
Less expensive Danish caviar
and chopped hard-boiled egg.
Ham and a piping of soft cream
or demi-sel cheese.
Pâté and sliced gherkin.
Prawns with a piping of thick
mayonnaise.
Scrambled egg and anchovies.
Smoked salmon and asparagus
tips.

Some ideas for hot canapés:
Fried button mushrooms on fried
bread.
Grilled bacon rolls on toast
spread with pâté
Mashed sardines on toast,
topped with grated Parmesan
cheese
Miniature Welsh Rarebit
(see page 118).

Piroshki

160

For the batter:
4 oz./100 g. flour, preferably plain
pinch salt
1 egg
½ pint/3 dl. milk
To fry:
oil (see method)
For the filling:
8 oz./200 g. cream or cottage
   cheese
1 oz./25 g. butter
1 egg yolk
seasoning
For part of the batter:
2 egg whites

Quick tip:
Use all the batter to make the
pancakes, fill and serve at once.
To economize:
Use grated dry Cheddar or
other cheese, moistened with milk
instead of cream or cottage cheese.

Sieve the flour and salt, add the whole egg and milk to make a smooth, thin batter. Use two-thirds of the batter to make 6 medium-sized or 8 smaller pancakes (see page 169). Blend the cheese, butter and egg yolk together and season well. Whisk the egg whites and fold into the remaining one-third of the batter. Put the filling into the pancakes, tuck in the ends to make very secure 'parcels'. Dip each 'parcel' into the remaining batter and fry in hot oil. Although shallow oil could be used, a pan of deep oil is better. Drain on absorbent paper.
To serve:
Hot as a light main dish or an hors d'oeuvre.
To vary:
Omit the seasoning, spread the pancakes with strawberry jam then with the cheese filling.
The method of coating the pancakes with batter is rather complicated, so instead use all the batter for pancakes, fill and roll in the usual way. Put the rolled pancakes into a hot ovenproof dish and spread a little melted butter on top. Sprinkle with grated cheese and heat for a short time.
To freeze:
Add 1 teaspoon oil to the pancake batter (this prevents the batter from being 'leathery'). Cook, fill then freeze. It is better to coat and fry after freezing. Wrap and use within 6–8 weeks.

Menus for Buffets

Have a selection of canapés, see opposite. You may care to make these cocktail size, so they can be eaten in your fingers, or slightly larger if you are having a buffet party where people can sit down and eat.

Piroshki:

The Piroshki, above and left, can be prepared beforehand and would make a good main dish with interesting salads.

Quiches:

Quiches are ideal, especially as these may be prepared and frozen. The Quiche Lorraine on page 122 is the best known, but I often make a selection of these savoury custard tarts.
Instead of the bacon filling, add flaked cooked fish or cooked vegetables (mushrooms are very good) to the eggs, cheese, etc. If you intend to freeze these tarts, read the comments on page 122.

Meat, fish and salads:

Cold meats, cooked cold fish and interesting salads can be served, but make certain the ingredients are cut into small pieces for a 'stand-up' buffet, for nothing is worse than trying to cope with large slices of meat, halved tomato, etc. with a fork.

Kebabs:

Kebabs would be appreciated by the young. Choose cheese as opposite or meat as the recipe on page 66 or serve fish kebabs with shell fish and diced raw white fish.

Desserts:

There are a number of desserts that would be suitable for a buffet throughout this book, but look on pages 134–135 and 162 and 169 which are planned for special occasions.

Cheese:

Serve a good selection of cheese with small biscuits (again these are easier to deal with than large biscuits or rolls.)

Drinks to offer:

When your guests arrive you may care to have a complete range of drinks, i.e. sherry, vermouth, whisky, gin, etc., but it is simpler to offer a choice of dry, medium and sweet sherry with perhaps vermouth too. Some people will prefer to drink spirits throughout the party, but most people today enjoy wine with the food. There are some suggestions on page 166, but in addition consider: *White wines:* Chablis; white Mâcon; Montrachet *Red wines:* Médoc, Nuits St. Georges, Beaujolais *Rosé wines:* Mateus, Tavel rosé.

Sherry Trifle

4–6 trifle sponge cakes
little apricot jam
small can apricots
¼ pint/1½ dl. sherry
2 oz./50 g. blanched almonds
1 pint/6 dl. egg custard
　(see page 145)

To decorate:
¼–½ pint/1½–3 dl. double cream
few glacé cherries
leaves of angelica

Split the sponge cakes through the centre and spread with the jam. Put together again and arrange in the serving dish. Drain the apricots and heat the fruit syrup for a few minutes. Add the sherry, then spoon over the sponge cakes. Add half the almonds and the fruit. Make the custard (if you do not want an egg custard use custard powder with milk and sugar, as directed on the packet). Pour the custard over the sponge cakes and leave until cold; if you cover the dish with greaseproof paper it helps to prevent the custard forming a skin. When cold top with whipped cream, and decorate with glacé cherries, angelica and the rest of the nuts.

To serve:
Serve the custard as chilled as possible; it improves with standing in the refrigerator for a few hours after cooling.

To freeze:
Due to the high water content in the custard it is advisable not to freeze this.

Sherry Savarin

For the savarin:
¾ oz./20 g. fresh yeast or
　3 *level* teaspoons dried yeast
1–2 oz./25–50 g. sugar
generous ¼ pint/1½ dl. warm milk
8 oz./200 g. plain flour
good pinch salt
2 oz./50 g. butter
4 oz./100 g. currants or mixed
　dried fruit
2 eggs
1 oz./25 g. blanched flaked
　almonds

For the syrup:
½ pint/3 dl. water
1 lemon (see method)
3 oz./75 g. sugar
1–2 tablespoons golden syrup
2–3 tablespoons sweet sherry

To decorate:
little whipped cream
glacé cherries

To economize:
Omit dried fruit and whipped cream.

If using fresh yeast, cream with 1 teaspoon sugar in a good-sized bowl, add the milk and a sprinkling of flour. If using dried yeast, dissolve the teaspoon of sugar in the milk. Sprinkle yeast on top, wait for 10 minutes, mix well, then add a sprinkling of flour and proceed as fresh yeast. Wait for 10–15 minutes until the mixture looks frothy. Add the remaining flour, salt, sugar, melted butter, fruit and eggs to the yeast mixture and, using a wooden spoon, beat thoroughly. Grease an 8–9-inch/20–23-cm. oven-proof tin or mould and sprinkle with almonds. Spoon the mixture into the mould and cover with foil or polythene. Leave to rise in a warm place for about 45 minutes–1 hour, until the mixture almost reaches the top of the mould. Cook for about 25 minutes in the centre of a moderately hot oven, 400°F./200°C., Gas Mark 6, until firm to the touch and golden brown. Remove from oven but leave in the mould for 5 minutes before turning out on to a cooling rack. Meanwhile prepare syrup, heat the water with ¼ teaspoon finely grated lemon rind, sugar and syrup for 3–4 minutes. Add a little lemon juice and the sherry and heat for 1 minute. Replace the savarin in the mould. Prick the surface with a skewer, then spoon over half the syrup. Leave for about 30 minutes, then spoon over a little more. Repeat at intervals of 1 hour until all the syrup has been absorbed.

To serve:
Invert the mould on to serving dish and top the savarin with whipped cream and glacé cherries.

To vary:
Flavour savarin dough with grated lemon rind and use lemon juice and water instead of milk to mix the dough. Fill the centre with fresh fruit salad.

To freeze:
It is better to freeze the savarin then warm it slightly to thaw out and add syrup as recipe. Use within 2 months.

Baba au Rhum

Ingredients as savarin above with alterations as given right, plus glaze.

For the glaze:
3 tablespoons sieved apricot jam
2 tablespoons water

Follow the recipe above but omit the almonds. To give a richer dough use 4 eggs and only 6 tablespoons milk. Put the soft mixture into 8–12 (depending upon size) warmed, greased, individual ring or flan tins. Allow to 'prove' for about 20 minutes then bake as the temperature above for 15 minutes. Soak with syrup, made with rum instead of sherry. Make a glaze by heating the sieved apricot jam and water. Brush over the rum-soaked babas, cool, then decorate with whipped cream.

A Fondue Party

This is one of the easiest parties to organize and is ideal for young people. In order to do this successfully you need a fondue heater and pan. Ideally one needs an earthenware pot for cheese fondues and a metal pan for heating oil.

Check the heater is in a safe place, away from curtains or other inflammable items and that it will not harm the table.

Serve the fondue with French bread and have bowls of salad as well.

Classic Cheese Fondue

To make: 15 minutes   **To cook:** 15 minutes   **(Serves 4–6)**

1 lb./500 g. Emmenthal or
  Gruyère cheese or use half of
  one cheese and half of the
  other or rather more than half
  Emmenthal
1 clove garlic (optional)
½ pint/3 dl. dry white wine,
  a Graves ideal
juice of ½ a lemon (optional)
1–2 tablespoons kirsch or brandy
  (optional)
1 teaspoon cornflour (optional)
little grated nutmeg (optional)
pepper to taste

Quick tip:
See To vary:

Shred or grate the cheese. For a delicate garlic taste, halve the clove and rub the cut surfaces round the fondue pot. Pour all the wine, or nearly all the wine, if using the cornflour, into the fondue pot, with the lemon juice and/or kirsch or brandy. Add the cheese, stir over the heater until melted and an occasional bubble appears; *on no account should the mixture boil*. Do not cover the pan as the cheese heats. If using the cornflour (this is an added precaution against the fondue 'curdling', i.e. separating) blend with the remainder of the wine and stir into the cheese mixture. Add the grated nutmeg and pepper. Turn the fondue heater low and keep the cheese mixture warm. If it becomes a little too thick, dilute with warmed wine.

To serve:
Arrange cubes of bread, toast, steak or cooked prawns on dishes and dip into the fondue.

To vary:
If more convenient make the fondue in a saucepan over a *low* heat in the kitchen. When the cheese melts transfer to the fondue pot over the fondue heater. If you do not possess a fondue heater it is better to make large quantities of white sauce, page 54, then add plenty of grated cheese just before serving.

Fondue with Herbs

To make: 15 minutes   **To cook:** 10–15 minutes   **(Serves 4–6)**

1 clove garlic
¼ pint/1½ dl. dry white wine
1 lb./500 g. Gouda cheese, grated
3 teaspoons cornflour
2 tablespoons kirsch
1 teaspoon finely chopped parsley
½ teaspoon finely chopped
  tarragon
pinch black pepper
pinch grated nutmeg

Rub the inside of the fondue pan with the cut clove of garlic. Put in the wine, heat a little then add the cheese gradually and stir until it has melted and the mixture begins to bubble. Add the cornflour, blended smoothly with the kirsch, the parsley, tarragon, black pepper and nutmeg. Allow it to bubble for 1–2 minutes. Keep warm (see above).

To serve:
As suggested above.

Fondue Bourguignonne

To make: few minutes   **To cook:** 2–3 minutes   **(Serves 4–6)**

1–1½ lb./500–750 g. fillet or
  other good quality steak
oil
1 bay leaf
1 clove garlic

To economize:
Make tiny rissoles or meat balls
(see pages 94 and 78) and cook
instead of steak.

This dish is often also called Beef Bourguignonne, which is a little confusing, as there is a stew of that name, see page 170.

Dice the meat neatly. Heat the oil until a cube of day-old bread turns golden in under 1 minute. Flavour with the bay leaf and cut garlic. Spear the beef with fondue forks and cook in the hot oil. Remove from the fondue forks and dip into a sauce before serving.

To serve:
With tomato sauce, page 107, tartare sauce, page 111, or any of the variations of mayonnaise on page 111.

To freeze:
Frozen diced meat could be used.

A Cheese & Wine Party

This is one of the easiest ways to entertain. Plan a good selection of cheese, and allow 6–8 oz./150–200 g. per person, half a bottle of wine, several slices of French bread and/or crispbread with salad and fruit. A cheese-flavoured dish, such as the Pizza Pie below, would be a good addition to the menu.

Cheeses to choose:

A traditional Cheddar or Cheshire; a less well-known cheese such as Sage Derby or Tôme au Raisin (creamy cheese coated with grape pips); choose one of the veined cheeses, such as Stilton, Danish Blue, Roquefort or Gorgonzola; have a creamy Brie or Camembert; a mild cheese such as Demi-sel or a processed cheese and general favourties like Edam and St. Paulin.

Do not overlook the 'slimmers'; have bowls of cottage cheese.

Arrange the cheeses on trays with salad and fruit to decorate.

Wines to choose:

One or more well-chilled white wines such as a medium-dry Gravès, a Pouilly-Fuissé or the less well known Pouilly-Fumée or you may prefer a hock such as Niersteiner.

A red wine is ideal with the more strongly-flavoured cheeses, a Margaux is a good claret or have one of the popular Burgundies, such as Mâcon or Pommard. Remember many people would enjoy beer or cider as well.

Pizza Pie

To make: 25 minutes plus 'proving'   **To cook:** 35–40 minutes   (Serves 5–6)

For the base:
12 oz./300 g. plain flour
pinch salt
1 tablespoon olive oil
scant ½ oz./12 g. fresh yeast or
   1½ teaspoons dried yeast and
   ½ teaspoon sugar
scant ¼ pint/1½ dl. water

For the topping:
2 large onions
1–2 cloves garlic
1½ lb./ 750 g. tomatoes
1 tablespoon olive oil
1–2 tablespoons concentrated
   tomato purée
seasoning
¼ teaspoon dried or 1 teaspoon
   fresh chopped oregano or
   marjoram
4–6 oz./100–150 g. Cheddar,
   Mozzarella or Gruyère cheese,
few anchovy fillets
few black olives
grated Parmesan cheese
   (see method)

Quick tip:
Make a scone dough with 12 oz./ 300 g. self-raising flour, pinch salt, 2 oz./50 g. margarine and milk to mix. Roll out as the recipe and top with the tomato mixture. Bake as recipe.
Use 2 tablespoons dehydrated onion and 1 large can well drained tomatoes in place of fresh vegetables.

Sieve the flour and salt into a mixing bowl. Make a well in the centre and add the oil. Cream the fresh yeast and add the tepid water, or dissolve the sugar in the water and sprinkle on the dried yeast. Pour the yeast liquid over the oil in the bowl. Sprinkle a little of the flour on top of the yeast liquid. Cover the bowl with a cloth and leave in a warm place for about 15–20 minutes until the yeast liquid begins to bubble. Blend all the in-gredients together and knead until smooth. Return to the bowl and cover. Leave in a warm place for 1¼–1½ hours or until the dough has doubled its bulk. Knead again. Roll out to a 9–10-inch/23–25-cm. round then put on to a warmed, greased baking tray. While the yeast dough is rising for the first time, prepare the topping. Peel and chop the onions and garlic and skin and chop the tomatoes. Toss the onions and garlic in the hot oil, then add the tomatoes, the purée and seasoning. Simmer in an uncovered pan until the mixture is thick. Stir in the oregano or marjoram. Spread the tomato mixture over the yeast round. Top with the sliced or grated cheese, the anchovy fillets, olives and a sprinkling of Parmesan cheese. Allow to 'prove' for about 20 minutes (although this stage is not essential). Cook in the centre of a hot oven, 425–450°F./220–230°C., Gas Mark 7–8, for about 15–20 minutes. If the yeast mixture is not quite cooked, put some foil over the topping to protect it, lower the heat to moderate and leave for a little longer.

To serve:
Hot or cold as a light main dish with salad or as an hors d'oeuvre.

To vary:
Use thin strips of streaky bacon or strips of uncooked kipper fillet in place of anchovies.

To freeze:
This freezes well. Either prepare the dough, top with the filling, freeze then wrap; or cook, freeze then wrap. Use within 2 months.

To economize:
Use less cheese on the topping and omit the anchovy fillets and olives, see also To vary: above.

Pizz

Planning a Dinner Party

This is one of the most pleasant and leisurely ways to entertain. Try to plan to avoid a last minute rush; I would choose the menu so that at least one course can be prepared ahead. Work out how you will keep food hot without it spoiling and to help with this I have put suggestions under the recipes in this section. Toss cooked vegetables in plenty of butter, cover and keep hot in a low oven, over a pan of hot water, or on a hot plate. If you dislike carving, do this before the meal, arrange meat or poultry on a dish and cover with foil.

To start the meal:

The first course could consist of one of the appetizers from pages 12–27, a Quiche Lorraine, page 122, or the salmon recipe on page 170, or serve smoked salmon, trout or eel; the last two with horseradish cream, page 82, and lemon. A pâté with smoked salmon is given below, and an interesting adaptation of a fish cocktail.

Salmon pâté:

Put 2 oz./50 g. softened butter, a crushed clove garlic, 4 oz./100 g. minced smoked salmon, 4–6 tablespoons single cream, the juice of 1 lemon and pepper to taste into a bowl and beat until smooth and creamy. Serve with lettuce, lemon and hot toast and butter. If more convenient, emulsify all the ingredients in a blender.

Melon and shellfish cocktail:

Follow the directions for making shellfish cocktails on page 17, but make the dish more original by adding melon balls or diced melon and/or de-seeded grapes to the mixture.

Pasta:

The younger generation enjoy pasta dishes and half portions would be enjoyed. Serve spaghetti with anchovies if meat or poultry follow, or with ham and mushrooms if fish is the main course, see pages 130 and 131.

Soup:

A soup could follow, or replace, an hors d'oeuvre, see pages 28–41, below and page 170.

Meat and fish:

This book has many fish, meat or poultry dishes sufficiently interesting for a dinner party, see page 42–99 but one of the classic stews, together with a speedy chicken dish, is on page 170.

Desserts:

One of the desserts to consider is given on the opposite page, together with hints on freezing pancakes, so the dish can be cooked ahead of time, see also pages 137 and 171.

To finish:

End the meal with an interesting cheese board and excellent coffee and your dinner party menu must be a success.

Speedy Gazpacho

To make: 15 minutes   **No cooking**   (Serves 4)

1 pint/6 dl. tomato juice
1 tablespoon lemon juice
2 tablespoons olive oil
1–2 cloves garlic
1 medium-sized onion
seasoning
To garnish:
cucumber
green pepper
onion
bread

Mix together the tomato juice, lemon juice, oil, crushed garlic and finely chopped onion. Taste and season well. Chill thoroughly.
To serve:
In individual soup bowls or a larger bowl with some garnish in separate dishes, so everyone can take their own. Dice the cucumber (peel if preferred); dice the pepper (discard core and seeds), chop the onion very finely; take the crusts from the bread and cut the crumb into tiny cubes.
To vary:
Make fresh tomato purée, skin tomatoes, sieve or emulsify WITH the rest of the soup ingredients, or sieve tomatoes THEN add other ingredients.
To freeze:
It is not worth freezing the quick version of this soup, but freeze tomato purée, see page 185; do not freeze the garnishes.

Crêpes Suzette

To make: 30 minutes   **To cook:** 20 minutes   (Serves 6)

For the pancake batter:
4 oz./100 g. plain flour
pinch salt
2 eggs
scant ½ pint/3 dl. milk
1 tablespoon oil or melted butter
To fry:
oil or butter
For the sauce:
4 oz./100 g. caster sugar
finely grated rind of 1 orange
juice of 2 oranges
1 tablespoon Grand Marnier or
    Curaçao
3 tablespoons brandy
To decorate:
orange slice

Quick tip:
Make batter in a blender.
To economize:
Omit liqueur and brandy.

Sieve the flour and salt into a basin. Add the eggs, then gradually beat in the milk to make a smooth batter. Finally, stir in the oil or butter. Pour into a jug, whisk before using. Pour a little oil into a 6-inch/15-cm. frying pan and heat until really hot, or melt a knob of butter. Pour off excess. Pour in enough batter, about 2 tablespoons, to thinly coat the base of the pan, tilting the pan so that the base is evenly covered. Cook until the underside is golden brown, turn and cook the other side. Slip the pancake on to oiled greaseproof paper to cool. Repeat this method using the rest of the batter to make 12 pancakes; grease and heat the pan between each pancake. Separate cooked pancakes with squares of greaseproof paper. Fold the pancakes into 4 and heat in the sauce. To make the sauce, stir the sugar in the frying pan until pale golden, then stir in the orange rind and juice. When all the pancakes have been heated, lift on to hot serving plates and keep warm. Stir the liqueur and brandy into the sauce remaining in the pan. Heat for 1 minute, ignite if wished and pour over the pancakes.
To serve:
Immediately after cooking. This is a good dish to complete at the table. Decorate with a slice of orange, if wished.
To vary:
Fill the pancakes with redcurrant jelly before heating in the sauce.
Use tangerine rind and juice instead of orange.
To freeze:
Prepare pancakes and freeze as page 185, or prepare complete dish except for adding liqueur and brandy. Freeze and use within 3 months. Reheat in a pan over a very low heat, then add the liqueur or heat in a slow oven then add the liqueur.

Lobster & Salmon Bisque

To make: 10 minutes **To cook:** 15 minutes (Serves 6–8)

1 small cooked lobster
4–6 oz./100–150 g. cooked salmon*
½ pint/3 dl. single cream
½ pint/3 dl. dry white wine
2 egg yolks
seasoning
*the salmon must not be
over-cooked

Remove the flesh from the lobster and save a few of the small claws. Flake the cooked salmon and cover the fish to prevent drying. Put the cream, the white wine, blended with the egg yolks, and seasoning into a basin over a pan of hot, but not boiling water. Whisk until just thickened; it is a good idea to do this earlier in the day, even if serving hot, then just reheat for a short time. If serving hot, add the fish just before the meal and warm through.
To serve:
Hot or cold, garnished with lobster claws, but *freshly made.*

Salmon with Cream Topping

To make: 10 minutes **To cook:** see method (Serves 4)

4 salmon steaks
¼ pint/1½ dl. soured cream
2 oz./50 g. grated cheese
To garnish:
mixed salad

Poach the salmon as page 48. If serving hot, top with the cream mixed with the cheese, then serve at once with salad. If serving cold, open the 'parcels' or bags when the fish is cold, drain and put the fish on to a plate. Top with the cream mixed with the cheese, then lift on to the salad.
To freeze:
Frozen salmon could be used; do not freeze the topping or salad.

Chicken with Orange & Almond Sauce

To make: 10 minutes **To cook:** 15–20 minutes (Serves 4)

seasoning
paprika
4 joints frying chicken
2 oz./50 g. butter
1 tablespoon oil
3 oranges
2 teaspoons caster sugar
1½ oz./40 g. almonds, shredded
  and browned

Mix the seasoning and paprika and sprinkle over the chicken. Heat the butter and oil in a large pan and fry the joints until golden brown, see page 86. Meanwhile, squeeze the juice from two of the oranges, cut the skin and pith from the third and cut into segments. Remove the chicken joints from the pan and arrange on a hot serving dish. Drain the excess butter from the pan and add the orange juice, segments and sugar to the pan. Bring slowly to the boil, stirring, and allow to boil rapidly for 2–3 minutes. Adjust the seasoning, pour the orange mixture over the joints, sprinkle with the almonds and serve.
To freeze:
Do not freeze this dish, but frozen chicken could be used.
Note: If preparing for a party cook the chicken for a few minutes less than usual, put on a heated dish, add the sauce, cover and keep hot in a low oven.

Boeuf à la Bourguignonne

To make: 20 minutes **To cook:** 35 minutes (Serves 4–6)

2 large onions
1 clove garlic
2–3 rashers streaky bacon
2 tablespoons olive oil
1 oz./25 g. flour
generous ½ pint/3 dl. beef stock
2 oz./50 g. button mushrooms
2 large tomatoes
bouquet garni
¼ bottle red Burgundy
seasoning
1¼–1½ lb./600–750 g. fillet steak
To garnish:
parsley
lemon
canned red pepper

Peel and chop the onions and garlic, remove rinds and chop bacon. Heat the oil, add the onions, garlic and bacon and cook gently for a few minutes. Stir in the flour, cook for 2–3 minutes then blend in the stock. Bring to the boil and cook until thickened, stirring well. Slice the mushrooms and skin and chop the tomatoes, add to the pan with the *bouquet garni* and wine. Season, cover the pan and simmer for 10–15 minutes, remove *bouquet garni*. Cut the meat into fingers, cook for JUST 10 minutes in the sauce or add the beef to the warm, but not hot sauce just before serving the first course. Tip into a warmed dish, cover with foil and cook in a low oven.
To serve:
Garnished with parsley, rings of lemon and canned red pepper.
To freeze:
Do not freeze the cooked dish but you can freeze the sauce without the wine.

Citus Water Ice

To make: 15 minutes plus freezing   **To cook:** 5 minutes   **(Serves 6–8)**

1 pint/6 dl. water
4–8 oz./100–200 g. sugar (to taste)
2 teaspoons powdered gelatine*
½ pint/3 dl. lemon or orange juice
2 egg whites
*the gelatine is not essential if serving within 1–2 days. If storing longer it prevents the mixture having splinters of ice and helps to retain a smooth texture.

Quick tip:
Use canned fruit juice.
To economize:
Use any fruit in season (see To vary).
To vary:
Sprinkle water ice with a little liqueur before serving. Simmer thin strips orange or lemon 'zest' in the sugar and water.

Fruit purée water ice: Use ½ pint/3 dl. water, 4 oz./100 g. sugar and 1 pint/6 dl. fresh fruit purée such as crushed or sieved strawberries, raspberries, blackberries, apricots or mangoes and 2 egg whites.

Coffee water ice: Use same proportions as for fruit purée water ice but substitute 1 pint/6 dl. strong black coffee for crushed fruit.
To freeze:
There is no need to alter setting of freezer to freeze water or other ices. Use within 4 months.

Iced pudding: Make the ice cream as page 136 and make the citrus water ice above. Freeze both mixtures until the consistency of a thick cream. Pack the ice cream round the inside edge of a metal mould and the water ice in the centre. Freeze together then turn out when required.
Cassata: This famous dessert is made as described above. Choose three different ice creams, e.g. chocolate, strawberry and vanilla. Chopped glacé cherries, sultanas and nuts can be added. Pack one flavour round the inside edge of the mould or basin, add the second flavour, fill the middle with the third flavour. Freeze and turn out.

Place most of the water and sugar in a pan and heat until the sugar dissolves. Blend the gelatine with the remaining water, stir into the hot sugar and water and continue stirring until dissolved. Allow to cool. Stir in the lemon or orange juice, pour into an ice tray and freeze until soft and mushy, about 1–2 hours. Fold in the whisked egg whites until the texture is smooth Return to the ice tray and freeze for 2–3 hours or overnight.
To serve:
The water ice should be a soft mushy texture. If it is frozen hard, allow to stand at room temperature until it softens a little. Serve in glass dishes or in hollowed-out oranges or lemons.

Citrus water ice

Celebration cake

Cakes for Parties

The cake shown above is based upon a simple sponge and would be ideal for children's parties. You will see it iced differently in the picture opposite and again on pages 174–175. For adults use the rich cake given for Christmas as the basic recipe and ice suitably, see page 180.

Simple Celebration Cake

To make: 1 hour   **To cook:** 25–30 minutes   **(Serves 16)**

8 oz./200 g. margarine or butter
8 oz./200 g. caster sugar
4 eggs, beaten
8 oz./200 g. self-raising flour or
  plain flour and 2 teaspoons
  baking powder
For the icing:
12 oz./300 g. butter or margarine
1½ lb./750 g. icing sugar
finely grated rind 1 orange
about 3 tablespoons orange juice
few drops yellow or pink colouring
To decorate:
ribbon, candles and/or flowers

Quick tip:
Use quick creaming margarine or cream fat and sugar and add eggs with a mixer (see page 151).

Make the Victoria sandwich mixture as page 151. Divide between 2 greased and floured 8–9-inch/20–23-cm. sandwich tins and bake for approximately 25–30 minutes above the centre of a moderate oven, 350–375°F./180–190°C., Gas Mark 4–5. Turn out carefully and cool. Prepare the icing by creaming the butter or margarine, sieved icing sugar, orange rind and juice and colouring. Sandwich the cakes together with one quarter of the icing. Coat the sides and top with some of the icing, then tint the remaining icing a slightly deeper colour and pipe over the top of the cake. Decorate with a ribbon, candles and/or a few flowers.

To vary:
Use lemon instead of orange rind and juice.

To freeze:
See under general information on freezing cakes, page 151.

To economize:
See Victoria sandwich.

172

Sandwiches are Fun

Before giving toppings for sandwiches I would suggest you think also of new ways of presenting ordinary sandwiches.

Ribbon sandwiches:

These look pretty, all you do is butter slices of brown and white bread, then use one of each kind for a narrow ribbon effect. Alternatively use white bread, then filling, brown bread, filling, white bread, filling, then more brown bread. When the sandwiches are made, cut into narrow fingers.

Pinwheel sandwiches:

Cut a loaf lengthways if you have many of these to make. Spread with butter and then filling. Cut off the crusts and roll just like a Swiss Roll. Cut into slices.

Fillings children enjoy:

Most children like Marmite, potted meats and fish, they generally like cheese, scrambled egg, ham and chicken too. Sweet fillings are also popular, choose jam, honey, chocolate spread, mashed banana.

Toppings for open sandwiches:

Although these toppings are primarily chosen with children in mind, they can be adapted for adults by using more sophisticated garnishes. Suggestions for adults are given in brackets after the main topping.
Before planning the toppings make sure the bread has a good spread of butter. Crisp lettuce is the usual base for toppings but many children do not enjoy 'green stuff', so I would avoid this in some cases.
Egg: Top with scrambled eggs, made pretty with twists of tomato (adults could have strips of anchovy or smoked salmon).
Ham: Rolled round cream cheese or cheese spread (add chopped gherkins and capers).
Crisp bacon rolls: With tiny cooked sausages and prunes (fill bacon rolls with pâté).
Cheese slices: Decorated with orange segments or rings of apple, dipped in lemon juice and cherries (choose blue or Stilton cheese as well).

Jumbo the clown

Children's Party Menu

Various sandwiches
Hot sausages with potato crisps
Hamburgers, page 77
Assorted biscuits, page 174
Meringues, page 133
Cream buns, page 133
Birthday cake
Orange Clowns, page 175
Ice cream
Orange squash or milk

Jumbo the Clown

You need for this cake a sponge, see below, soft frosting, an ice cream cone, a table-tennis ball, a length of ribbon and coloured vermicelli.
Make a Victoria sandwich mixture as page 151, using 8 oz./200 g. butter or margarine, etc. Bake in two 8–9-inch/ 20–23-cm. fairly deep sandwich tins for about 25 minutes (temperature as Victoria sandwich). Turn out and cool.

Make some American frosting:
Put 3 egg whites, 1 lb. 2 oz./510 g. caster sugar, pinch salt, 6 tablespoons water and a pinch cream of tartar into a large mixing bowl. Stand over a pan of hot water and whisk briskly (use an electric hand whisk if possible) for about 7 minutes until the mixture stands up in peaks. Sandwich the cakes together with a little icing, and spread most of the remainder over the cake; swirl this into a design. Cut the base off the cone, then place on the cake

as the clown's collar. Paint a clown's face on the ball, stick it to the collar with frosting and decorate with a ribbon bow. Cover the top of the ice cream cone with the remaining frosting, peaking it up and sprinkling with vermicelli. Attach it carefully to the 'face' with the remaining frosting, to make a tall clown's hat. Sprinkle vermicelli on the cake round the base of the collar to make a ruff. Serves 12.
To serve: On a flat plate or cake board.

173

Meringues

The recipe is on page 137. Make rather tiny ones for little children and colour them pretty colours with vegetable colourings. I would not fill them with cream, but pile them up in a gay and colourful pyramid. You could have whipped cream or ice cream to serve with them. Home-made ice cream recipes are on pages 136 and 137, but these could be rather rich for little children, so it might be wiser to buy the ice cream.

Biscuits

There are many different shapes you can make with the Shrewsbury biscuits, opposite, some of which are shown in the picture below.

Traffic light biscuits:

Cut out the rounds as given in the basic recipe or cut into strips, then cut out three little 'holes' for half the rounds or strips; do this with a thimble if you have no special cutter. Bake the biscuits as the basic recipe, sandwich together, then fill the 'traffic lights' with raspberry, sieved apricot and greengage jams.

Jam rounds:

Cut out the rounds and cut a smaller round from half of these to turn the biscuit into a ring. Bake the biscuits as the basic recipe. When cold shake sieved icing sugar over the rings. Spread the whole rounds with different coloured jams and place the rings into position.

Animal biscuits:

Cut out animal shapes and bake as the basic recipe. When cooked and cooled, cover with glacé (water) icing made by blending 4 oz./100 g. sieved icing sugar with a few drops of water. When this has set, pipe with coloured icing (use a little cocoa or vegetable colouring). For plainer biscuits press currants into the uncooked dough for 'eyes' before baking.

Name biscuits:

Cut fingers, hearts or diamond shapes, then pipe the children's names on these in different coloured icings.

Children's Birthday Cake

The cake shown in the picture below was made exactly as the Celebration cake on page 172, but decorated with animals and men to look like a circus ring.

Orange Clowns

There are several ways of making these clowns; an easy method is as follows: Cut a slice from a large orange and remove the pulp carefully. Cut a slit (use a sharp knife or kitchen scissors) from the empty case for the clown's mouth and rounds for the eyes and nose. Put back the orange segments after removing the skin and pips and top with chopped orange jelly.

Stick smarties or glacé cherries into the holes for the eyes and nose. Replace the orange slice and decorate this with a cherry on a cocktail stick. If preferred top the orange pulp with ice cream and place an ice cream cone on top as the clown's traditional hat.

Shrewsbury Biscuits

To make: 20–40 minutes   **To cook:** 12–15 minutes   **(Makes about 60)**

6 oz./170 g.* butter or margarine
6 oz./170 g.* caster sugar
few drops vanilla essence
12 oz./340 g.* plain flour
little egg

*use this metrication

Cream the butter or margarine and sugar with the vanilla essence. Gradually stir in the flour, then enough egg to bind and knead well with your fingers. You should not need any liquid at all, but if the dough is very hard to handle and you have used all the egg add only a few drops of milk. Roll out the dough to about ¼-inch/½-cm. in thickness; roll biscuit dough quite firmly. Cut into the desired shapes, see suggestions opposite. Put on to ungreased baking trays and bake in the centre of a very moderate to moderate oven, 325–350°F./170–180°C., Gas Mark 3–4 for 12–15 minutes. These biscuits should not become too dark in colour. Cool for a few minutes on the baking trays, then remove.

from the left: Open sandwiches, Children's Birthday Cake, Meringues, Name biscuits, Traffic light biscuits and Jam rounds

Planning for Christmas

To many people Christmas catering is a 'nightmare' of feverish planning and cooking but this is not really necessary. Most of the traditional Christmas dishes, the pudding, the cake and mincemeat can be prepared ahead and if you have a freezer you can:

Make and freeze both stuffings and sauces for the turkey or other bird, see pages 83, 88 and 89. Make the mince pies; cook these if more convenient, although many people find they prefer to make and freeze, then cook on Christmas Eve or Christmas morning and reheat.
Prepare additional desserts and savouries and freeze these.
Prepare some vegetable dishes, e.g. Ratatouille, page 108, Duchesse potatoes page 116. Make brandy or rum butter, cover and freeze, or see recipe opposite.

All this means a leisurely Christmas Day and time to enjoy the festivities with your friends and family.
I have selected Christmas catering especially, but obviously you can apply these principles to New Year or any other celebrations.

Christmas Menu

Melon or shellfish cocktail, page 17

Roast turkey with bacon rolls, sausage, chestnut and veal stuffing, cranberry and bread sauces, page 88

Christmas pudding, page 178

Mince pies with brandy butter, rum sauce or cream, page 177

Have jellies or other light desserts for children
or a Jellied Christmas pudding, see page 178

Cheese

Fruit and nuts

Mince Pies

Make the mincemeat as the recipe below. Make short crust, fleur or puff pastry, see pages 122, 138 and 97.

Roll out the pastry. Cut into rounds for the base of the mince pies. Fit into patty tins, put in the mincemeat and top with smaller rounds of pastry. Make two slits on top with kitchen scissors to allow the steam to escape. Bake for about 20 minutes in the centre of the oven. Use a moderately hot oven for fleur or short crust pastry, but start in a very hot oven with puff pastry, then lower the heat after 10 minutes. For temperatures see page numbers above. Serve with rum sauce or brandy butter, see below.

Mincemeat:

Mix together 1 lb./500 g. mixed dried fruit, 4 oz./100 g. shredded suet or melted butter, 4 oz./100 g. moist brown sugar, 4 oz./100 g. chopped candied peel, 4 oz./100 g. grated apple, 4 oz./100g. chopped blanched almonds, 1 teaspoon mixed spice, $\frac{1}{2}$–1 teaspoon ground cinnamon, grated rind and juice of 1 lemon and 2–3 tablespoons whisky. Put into jars, cover tightly and store in a cool, dry place.

Rum sauce:

Blend 1 oz./25 g. cornflour with just under 1 pint/6 dl. milk. Put into a saucepan with 2 oz./50 g. sugar and 1 oz./25 g. butter. Stir over a moderate heat until thickened. Remove from the heat and whisk in 3–4 tablespoons rum.

Brandy or Rum Butter

To make: 10 minutes   **No cooking**   (Serves 12–14)

6 oz./150 g. butter
9 oz./225 g. sieved icing sugar
4 tablespoons brandy or rum
To decorate:
blanched almonds
glacé cherries

Quick tip:
Use a mixer.

Cream the butter and sugar until soft and light. Add the brandy or rum very gradually; if added too quickly the mixture will curdle.
To serve:
Spoon or pipe into a serving dish. Decorate with blanched almonds and/or glacé cherries for added colour.
To freeze:
It is not ideal to freeze this, for some of the flavour is lost. Chill in a refrigerator.

Christmas Pudding

½–1 teaspoon ground cinnamon
1 teaspoon mixed spice
6 oz./150 g. soft breadcrumbs
3 oz./75 g. flour
2 oz./50 g. ground almonds
6 oz./150 g. shredded suet or
   melted margarine
6 oz./150 g. moist brown sugar
4 oz./100 g. grated cooking apple
4 oz./100 g. grated carrot
4 oz./100 g. diced prunes
8–12 oz./200–300 g. seedless
   or chopped large raisins
8 oz./200 g. currants
8 oz./200 g. sultanas
4 oz./100 g. chopped glacé cherries
3 oz./75 g. chopped blanched almonds
4 oz./100 g. chopped candied peel
grated rind and juice
   1 large lemon
3 large eggs
¼ pint/1½ dl. beer
3–6 tablespoons brandy, rum or
   extra beer (see method)

Mix all the ingredients together; use the small quantity of brandy, rum or extra beer if you like a firm textured pudding. Leave overnight if possible, then stir again and divide between two 3-lb./1½-kilo greased basins, press down firmly. Cover with greased greaseproof paper and foil and steam each pudding for 4–5 hours. Take off the damp papers and cover with fresh dry paper and foil. Store in a cool dry place. Steam each pudding again on Christmas Day for about 2 hours. Turn on to a hot dish.

To serve:
Pour over a little warmed brandy, ignite and serve.
Note: Always store the pudding in a cool, dry place.
To freeze:
There is really no need to freeze Christmas Pudding unless your storing conditions are very bad, i.e. damp and warm as it keeps well for months. Indeed, many people like to make a pudding a year ahead as they feel it matures. I have however experimented with freezing a cooked pudding for 6 months and it does not spoil the texture or flavour.
To economize:
Reduce the amount of fruit and omit the ground almonds. Naturally this give a less rich pudding which will not keep as long, but which many people prefer.
It is not necessarily an economy, but an interesting variation of a Christmas pudding to use white instead of brown sugar, rather more sultanas and less currants and raisins. This give a pleasantly golden coloured pudding. If you have rather a lot of bread use 9 oz./225 g. breadcrumbs and omit the flour; this gives a very light, rather 'crumbly' texture.

More Festive Dishes

Christmas is a long holiday and one needs more than just the Christmas menu itself, and I am sure you will find ideas for other meals in the pages of this book; here are a few more suggestions and recipes, for the Christmas lunch or evening buffet:

Jellied Christmas pudding:

Make a blackcurrant jelly, but use slightly less water than usual, add a little mixed dried fruit to the hot mixture and when it is cold, but not quite set put in chopped nuts or a very little grated dessert apple. Put into a basin, leave to set, turn out and serve with lightly whipped cream.

Mincemeat apples:

Recipe below, would be another way of serving mincemeat. To give a true Christmas look the cooked apples could be coated with meringue, as in Baked Alaska, page 137, browned for a few minutes in the oven, then decorated with sprigs of holly.

There are two more desserts on the opposite page to serve at Christmas time.

The Christmas cake is on pages 180–181.

Mincemeat Apples

4–6 large cooking apples
2 tablespoons lemon juice
2 tablespoons water
2–3 tablespoons mincemeat
1–2 tablespoons brown sugar
1 oz./25 g. butter

Wipe the apples, then cut through the skin around the centre. Remove the cores with an apple corer and stand the apples in an ovenproof dish or baking tin. Pour the lemon juice and water round and fill the centre of each apple with mincemeat, adding a sprinkling of sugar and a knob of butter. Bake in the centre of a moderate oven, 350–375°F./180–190°C., Gas Mark 4–5, for 1 hour. Serve hot or cold.

Chocolate Coffee Mousse

To make: 10 minutes   No cooking   (Serves 6–8)

4 oz./100 g. plain chocolate
4 eggs
1 tablespoon strong black coffee
1 tablespoon rum (optional)
¼ pint/1½ dl. double cream
To decorate:
grated chocolate or chopped nuts

Break up the chocolate and place it in a basin over hot but not boiling water to melt. When melted, add the beaten egg yolks, coffee and rum, if using. Beat well until thick and creamy. Remove from the heat and continue whisking as the mixture cools. Fold in the lightly whipped cream and stiffly whipped egg whites.
To serve:
Pour into individual glasses and sprinkle with grated chocolate or chopped nuts.
Chocolate finger biscuits: These are a good accompaniment to this dessert. Top baked Shrewsbury biscuits, page 175 with melted chocolate and leave to set.

Fresh Fruit Salad

To make: 15 minutes   To cook: 5 minutes   (Serves 8–10)

½ pint/3 dl. water
2 oranges
1 lemon
3–4 oz./75–100 g. sugar
2 lb./1 kilo mixed prepared
   fresh fruit

Quick tip:
Use some canned fruit and syrup from the can, mix with some fresh fruit.
To economize:
Use fruit in season.

Put the water, with *thin* strips of orange and lemon rind, into the saucepan; take just the top 'zest' from the fruit, as the white pith would make the sauce bitter. Simmer for 5 minutes. Add the sugar, stir until dissolved then add the orange and lemon juice. Strain over the prepared fruit, and allow to become cold.
To vary:
Add a little sherry, kirsch, Cointreau or Maraschino to the syrup. Use all fresh orange and lemon juice and omit the water and sugar.
To freeze:
See page 185.

Fruit salad

Making the Christmas Cake

Rich Fruit Cake

Amounts of ingredients for different sized tins:
In view of the large quantity involved in making a Christmas cake, I have not used the 25 g. = 1 oz., but a rather more accurate measure.

Size of cake tin:	6-inch/15-cm. square 7-inch/18-cm. round	8-inch/20-cm. square 9-inch/23-cm. round	10-inch/25-cm. square 11-inch/28-cm. round
Butter	6 oz./170 g.	12 oz./340 g.	1 lb. 2 oz./510 g.
Soft brown sugar	6 oz./170 g.	12 oz./340 g.	1 lb. 2 oz./510 g.
Lemon rind	$\frac{1}{2}$ lemon	1 lemon	$1\frac{1}{2}$ lemons
Eggs – large	3	6	9
Brandy, sweet sherry, rum or milk	1 tablespoon	2 tablespoons	3 tablespoons
Plain flour	6 oz./170 g.	12 oz./340 g.	1 lb. 2 oz./510 g.
Ground cinnamon	$\frac{1}{4}$ teaspoon	$\frac{1}{2}$ teaspoon	1 teaspoon
Ground mace	$\frac{1}{4}$ teaspoon	$\frac{1}{2}$ teaspoon	1 teaspoon
Currants	10 oz./280 g.	1 lb. 4 oz./570 g.	1 lb. 14 oz./850 g.
Sultanas	8 oz./225 g.	1 lb./450 g.	1 lb. 8 oz./675 g.
Raisins	6 oz./170 g.	12 oz./340 g.	1 lb. 2 oz./510 g.
Glacé cherries	4 oz./110 g.	8 oz./225 g.	12 oz./340 g.
Blanched almonds	4 oz./110 g.	8 oz./225 g.	12 oz./340 g.
Mixed peel	4 oz./110 g.	8 oz./225 g.	12 oz./340 g.
Cooking time	$2\frac{3}{4}$–3 hours	4–$4\frac{1}{2}$ hours	$6\frac{1}{2}$–7 hours
Test after	$2\frac{1}{2}$ hours	$3\frac{3}{4}$ hours	5 hours

Additional ingredients you may add: Grated orange rind – as lemon. Allspice or mixed spice – as mace or reduce cinnamon slightly and use more spice. Ground almonds—add 1 oz./28 g. to small, 2 oz./56 g. to medium-sized and 3 oz./85 g. to large cake.

Black treacle – helps to make the cake very moist and slice well. Use 1 tablespoon in small, 2 tablespoons in medium-sized, and 3 tablespoons in large cake; cream with the butter and sugar.

Cream the butter and sugar with the grated lemon rind and black treacle if used. Gradually beat in the eggs, plus the liquid given in the recipe. If the mixture shows signs of curdling, stir in a little extra flour. Add the sieved flour and spices to the egg mixture. Stir in the dried fruit, halved or quartered cherries, chopped nuts and ground almonds, if you are using these, together with the chopped peel. Put into the prepared tin, see below, and bake in the centre of a cool to very moderate oven, 300–325°F./150–170°C., Gas Mark 2–3. Allow just about 1 hour at this temperature then lower the heat to 275–300°F./140–

150°C., Gas Mark 1–2, for the remainder of the cooking time. If it is the first time you have baked a cake as rich as this in your oven do remember that you can open the door and look inside to see that the cake is not getting too brown. At the end of 1 hour it should hardly have changed colour. At the end of two hours the small cake should be a pleasant brown, but still slightly soft, the larger ones should be still very pale and will not darken until after half the cooking time. To test the cake, see that it is firm to the touch and silent. An uncooked rich fruit cake makes a distinct humming sound. Allow the cake to cool in the tin. If desired you can prick the cooked cake at intervals of a week to 10 days and spoon sherry, brandy or rum over it to keep it moist.
To store: In an airtight tin or wrapped in foil.

Note: To prepare the cake tin: Always line the tin with double greased greaseproof paper and have rounds of brown paper under the greaseproof paper at the base. I tie a deep band of brown paper round the outside of the tin to prevent the mixture darkening too much.

To Decorate the Christmas Cake

This is an art, at which you will improve as you become more experienced. One of the easiest cakes to decorate is the Christmas cake, as the icing can be 'roughed up', which looks quite suitable and very festive.

To coat the cake
First brush away any surplus crumbs·from the cake, then coat with sieved apricot jam or egg white then with marzipan, see below. If you are fairly experienced and handle the marzipan quickly and deftly you can put on the icing at once, but if you are fairly new to icing and need to handle it quite a lot, this will have caused the oil from the ground almonds to 'seep out' and could spoil the colour of the Royal icing. In this case it is better to allow the marzipan to dry out for 48 hours, then ice the cake.
After putting on the marzipan coat with the Royal icing. The quantity given is enough for one very thick coat, plus a little over for piping.

Marzipan
To coat a 6–7-inch/15–18-cm. cake use: 8 oz./225 g. ground almonds, 4 oz./110 g. caster sugar, 4 oz./110 g. sieved icing sugar, a few drops almond essence and 2 large egg yolks. To coat an 8–9-inch/20–23-cm. cake use: 50% more of all the ingredients, i.e. 12 oz./340 g. ground almonds, etc.
To coat a 10–11-inch/25–28-cm. cake use: 1 lb. 4 oz./570 g. ground almonds, etc.

To make the marzipan, mix all the ingredients together, knead very lightly, then roll out on a sugared board to a round sufficiently large to cover the cake. Support over the sugared rolling pin and lower over the cake. Press against the cake and neaten the bottom edges. Brush with a little egg white, as an added precaution against the almond oil soaking into the icing. Lift the cake on to a cake board.

Royal icing
To coat a 6–7-inch/15–18-cm. cake use: 1 lb. 4 oz./570 g. sieved icing sugar, $2\frac{1}{2}$ egg whites, $1\frac{1}{2}$ tablespoons lemon juice. To coat an 8–9-inch/20–23-cm. cake use: 2 lb./scant kilo sieved icing sugar, 4 egg whites and 2 tablespoons lemon juice. To coat a 10–11-inch/25–28-cm. cake use: 3 lb./scant $1\frac{1}{2}$ kilo sieved icing sugar, 6 egg whites and 3 tablespoons lemon juice.

To make the icing beat the egg whites lightly, then gradually beat in the sieved icing sugar and lemon juice. Beat until white and shiny. Spread over the cake with a broad bladed knife until evenly covered. Cover any icing left over for piping with a damp cloth so it does not dry out.
To give the snow effect of the Christmas cake, sweep up the icing with the tip of the knife. Decorate with tiny figures and put the remaining icing into a piping bag or syringe with a shell pipe and pipe a neat border around.

181

Interesting Drinks

There are many interesting drinks that can be made; both alcoholic and non-alcoholic.

Iced Irish coffee

Milk Shakes

Very often children who are disinclined to drink milk will enjoy it when blended with flavouring and served as a milk shake.

The recipe below is a good luxury milk shake and you can substitute flavoured fruit syrups for the chocolate syrup or use blackcurrant syrup or rose hip syrup, both of which are excellent sources of Vitamin C.

Obviously one would not use ice cream all the time as in the recipe below, but just whisk the cold or hot milk with the flavouring. Be careful when trying to blend hot milk with very acid fruit flavours, such as blackcurrant as it could curdle unless emulsified in a blender.

You will find luxury milk shakes with different flavoured ice creams and syrups a great success at a children's party.

Summer Sauterne

Negus

To make: 10 minutes   **To cook:** 5–10 minutes   **(Serves 10 –12)**

2 lemons
¾ pint/4½ dl. water
3–4 oz./75–100 g. sugar
little grated nutmeg (see method)
1 bottle port wine

Cut the lemon rind from the fruit, avoid any bitter white pith and use just the top yellow 'zest'. Put the lemon rind, water and sugar into a pan, stir until the sugar has dissolved. Add the lemon juice, grated nutmeg to taste and port wine. Heat thoroughly then pour into hot glasses, or a hot bowl. Top with a little more nutmeg.

Chocolate Mint Shake

2 pints/1¼ litres milk
½ pint/3 dl. ice cream
4 tablespoons chocolate syrup
    or melted chocolate
2 tablespoons peppermint syrup
To decorate:
grated chocolate

Put the milk, ice cream and syrup into a tall jug and whisk, or into a cocktail shaker and shake well or into a electric blender and switch on for a few seconds. Pour into glasses and decorate with grated chocolate.
To vary:
Use 2–3 oz./50–75 g. chocolate powder. Omit peppermint.

Fresh Lemon Drink

3 large lemons
4 oz./100 g. sugar
2 pints/1¼ litres boiling water
To decorate:
sprigs of mint
· sliced lemon
crushed ice

Wash the whole lemons, then cut into ½-inch/1-cm. cubes, taking care not to lose the juice. Put into a strong jug, add the sugar and pour on the boiling water. Leave approximately 20 minutes, then strain. Add the mint, slices of fresh lemon and ice. Leave time for the ice to cool the drink, then serve.

Summer Sauterne

1 bottle Sauterne (or other
    white dessert wine)
2 liqueur glasses Cointreau
2 liqueur glasses brandy
juice of 1 lemon
crushed ice (see method)
1 pint/6 dl. tonic water
To garnish:
mint
orange and lemon slices

Mix the wine, Cointreau, brandy and lemon juice in a punch bowl. Add several handfuls of crushed ice and pour in the tonic water. Serve in tall glasses garnished with a sprig of mint and a slice each of orange and lemon.

Iced Irish Coffee

½ pint/3 dl. strong sweetened
    black coffee
2–3 tablespoons Irish whiskey
crushed ice
whipped cream

Chill the coffee well. Mix whiskey and coffee in a tall glass and add ice. Decorate with whipped cream.
To serve:
At once.

Gluwein

about 8 cloves
1 orange
1½ bottles dry red wine
¼ bottle brandy
¼ pint/1½ dl. water
¼ pint/1½ dl. orange juice
1–2 tablespoons lemon juice
2–3 sticks cinnamon

To economize:
See To vary:

Stick the cloves into the orange. Combine all the ingredients in a large saucepan and simmer over a low heat. Do not boil. Serve in mugs.
To vary:
Mulled ale: Use ale instead of red wine; 1–2 tablespoons sugar can be added, if wished.

Your Store Cupboard & Freezer

Most of us would sympathize with Old Mother Hubbard of nursery rhyme fame, who found her cupboard bare, but I doubt if we would applaud her method of housekeeping.

Nowadays with the great variety of excellent canned and dried foods and the ability of many housewives to store perishable foods in a refrigerator, and frozen foods in the refrigerator or home freezer, most of us can produce a meal without rushing out to shop.

In addition to all the basic requirements, you are wise to ensure you have:

Soups: Either canned or home-frozen, which can be heated and served in minutes. Remember some varieties of canned soup make excellent speedy sauces. See Quick Tips, under several recipes.
Fish and meat: Canned or frozen so you can produce main dishes.
Vegetables: To serve with main dishes or make into interesting salads.
Fruit: For desserts and puddings.

Perfection in Freezing

Most of us want the very best results when we freeze foods, but there are occasions when to save time at a particular period or to save wastage of food we are prepared to compromise a little. Here are some of the examples I would give:

Sauces:

I sometimes prepare filled pancakes and other dishes, top them with a cheese sauce or other variation of a white sauce and freeze them. The sauce is NOT as perfect as when freshly made, but the difference in texture is so slight that I overlook this because it enables me to plan ahead when I am busy.

Pastry:

I do believe that uncooked pastry is better frozen than cooked pastry in many cases, but there are occasions when it is more suitable for my plans to cook, cool then freeze pastry dishes, and I do this quite happily.

Cheese:

If you have had a cheese and wine party or entertained and have a lavish cheese board left-over, I would freeze these cheeses rather than risk wasting them, but use as quickly as possible.

184

Make Use of Seasonal Foods

To freeze fruits:

Some foods, vegetables and fruit in particular are not available throughout the year, and they also fluctuate in price, so it is wise economy to freeze them when they are at their best and cheapest.

There are several ways in which fruit can be frozen, so select the most useful method for each kind of fruit.

Fruit purée: Simmer the fruit with the minimum of water and sugar to taste. Sieve or emulsify in a blender, cool then pack into containers, leaving about $\frac{1}{4}$–$\frac{1}{2}$-inch/$\frac{1}{2}$–1-cm. space at the top of the container for expansion as the mixture freezes. Apples are splendid for sauces, soft fruit for ice cream.

As raw fruit for desserts: This is ideal for fruits such as raspberries and loganberries. Pack in containers with or without sugar. Strawberries (a disappointing fruit anyway to freeze) are better if frozen individually on flat trays, then packed when hard.

Freezing in a syrup: Some fruits such as plums and apricots are best frozen in a syrup. Poach the fruit lightly in the sugar and water, cool, pack and freeze.

Packing Your Freezer Wisely

When you buy a freezer obviously you will listen to as much advice as possible, for one can learn so much from other people's experiences. On the other hand, remember that no two families are exactly the same, and plan the foods you freeze and store to fit in with your own way of life.

Underneath most of the recipes in this book you will find a note about freezing, but you cannot do this in an ordinary refrigerator, you must have a home freezer, as it is essential that the food is frozen quickly. The only exceptions to this are ice cream and iced desserts, such as water ice.

This does not mean you cannot carry a supply of frozen foods in your own home. If you have a good space in the freezing compartment of your refrigerator then keep this well filled. The refrigerators with 3-star markings mean food can be stored for up to three months, but always read storage instructions from the food manufacturer, as it may be that they do not recommend quite so long a period for a particular food.

To Store & Pack in Your Freezer

The specialist freezer books will give detailed help on packaging etc., but here are some of the important points I have found helpful. Some of these will apply whether you freeze the food yourself or buy it ready frozen.

Length of storage time:

You will notice that in most cases I indicate the length of time the food should be kept in the freezer before using it. This means that even at the end of the time suggested you should find the food compares favourably with the flavour of the freshly prepared dish or the fresh food. I must stress that this assumes you have frozen the food quickly and packed it correctly. If you leave the food in the freezer or freezing compartment longer than recommended you will be disappointed in the result. This is why it is sensible to date packages and use them in the order they have been prepared or purchased.

Packing the freezer:

I find it helpful to store all meats in one place, fish in another etc., and I keep a record of just where they are kept in a note-book, so that when I am in a hurry I can find the package at once. Never pack in such large quantities that you find it difficult to separate the food. Put squares of waxed paper or greaseproof paper (although the former is better) between individual chops, steaks, fillets of fish etc. This means you can take off just the number required.

While it is better to pack stuffing in a separate container from the poultry or meat, pack it near the food it 'goes with'. It takes time to cook a number of pancakes so freeze any left. Add oil or melted butter to the batter, separate each pancake with a piece of oiled paper, then wrap well.

Index

Introduction

We all know about healthy eating and healthy lifestyles, and we all do our best to include wholesome food in our daily diets, but every now and then we deserve a treat, don't we?

In this book I've put together 100 delicious – and sometimes, admittedly quite decadent – recipes for sweet treats, from indulgent puddings, cooling ice creams and classic cakes to healthy sweet snacks and cookies for the kids.

The joy of baking and making your own treats is that you know exactly what has gone into them – so sometimes even the sweetest treat can be packed with nutritious and often healthy ingredients, such as fruit, seeds, nuts and yoghurt. I've tested all of these recipes and ensured that in lots of them the fresh and flavourful ingredients mean you can cut down on the sugar if you want to without sacrificing the taste.

In all the chapters I've tried to provide treats for every situation. The Quick treats chapter will give you just that – superfast steps to a sweet fix just when you need one. Fluffy blueberry pancakes or Yoghurt, toffee figs and honey are perfect breakfast bites to set you up for the day ahead or Quick cinnamon crumble cake or Superfast lemon ice cream will restore your senses after a long day. There's also a chapter of sweet things for children that you can whip up to reward the kids for great work – Crunchy, chewy ginger cookies with a glass of milk, Real fruit sugar popsicles on a hot summer's day, or Honey, cranberry and sesame oat bars for healthy but delicious lunch-box treats. Some of the recipes are so easy you can make them together with your children.

Sometimes I think fresh and fruity treats make me feel less guilty when I need to indulge my sweet tooth, simply by mixing sugary treats with healthy ingredients – Sweet labneh with honey, pistachios and orange blossom water brings a taste of the exotic, and refreshing and naughty Watermelon ginita always helps to cool down and unwind at the end of a hot day. And some days, when I'm rushed off my feet, I love a mini treat to keep me going, or something simple I can pack up for a picnic or pick at after dinner – Cinnamon cigars, Baklava and Pistachio, apricot and cardamom biscotti are all perfect restorative bites.

Of course, afternoon tea just calls out for sweet treats – what's tea without cake? Lavender sponge cake with rhubarb curd is perfect for a summer's day, or you could curl up in front of the fire with a piping hot cup of tea on a wet winter afternoon, munching on a delicious Pear and nutmeg cake.

When you're feeling really decadent or you want to impress, there are ridiculously rich and gooey recipes that will comfort and satisfy. When you're craving winter comfort food in summer, try a scoop of Apple crumble ice cream, or if you need a serious chocolate fix, bake an American chocolate fudge pie or a Double chocolate mousse cake. Showstoppers such as Layered mocha mousse coffee meringue, Chocolate coconut cake and Gooey date and stem ginger pudding will hit the spot and provide the wow factor for any dinner for friends.

And sometimes you just want the comfort of something you know well, so there's a whole chapter of classic recipes that have a little twist; favourite desserts get a fruity makeover in Blueberry bread and butter pudding and Apple and cinnamon baked cheesecake, and crème brulee gets a special salted caramel hit.

Personally I don't think you need a special occasion for a treat, but if you need an excuse, there is a chapter of puddings that will become festive favourites: Spiced plum tarte tatin or Nectarine and sloe gin jelly trifle for Christmas and New Year, or a Chocolate meringue cake for Easter.

So get over the guilt and make more of those 'me' moments, pick a treat and enjoy. With simple techniques, and lots of clever tips, there's something here for every mood and every situation. Make every day a special occasion.

Contents

QUICK

Roasted plums with white chocolate sauce

Quick cinnamon crumble cake

Fluffy blueberry pancakes with maple syrup

Really French toast!

Ivan's coconut and lime ice cream
with mango in mint syrup

Strawberry and rhubarb cobbler

Zesty fluffy orange pudding

Yoghurt, toffee figs and honey

Apricot and almond crumble

Superfast lemon ice cream

Strawberry, peach and vanilla fool
with orange sablé biscuits

Gooseberry clafoutis

A great little recipe this: simple, delicious and superfast, too. The white chocolate sauce will also feel very at home with fresh raspberries, blueberries, strawberries and blackberries.

Roasted plums with white chocolate sauce

SERVES 6

6 plums

6 tsp brown sugar

For the white chocolate sauce

100ml (3½fl oz) double or regular cream

25g (1oz) butter

100g (3½oz) white chocolate, chopped or in drops

Preheat the oven to 200°C (400°F), Gas mark 6.

Cut the plums in half, remove and discard the stones and lay the plums cut side up on a roasting tray. Scatter each half with ½ teaspoon of brown sugar and place in the oven to cook for 20–25 minutes or until the plums are tender and juicy.

To make the white chocolate sauce, place the cream and the butter in a saucepan and bring up to the boil to melt the butter. Take off the heat and add in the white chocolate, stirring to melt. Reheat the chocolate sauce just before serving.

To serve, drizzle warm plates generously with the warm white chocolate sauce and place the plums on top.

This cake, which has been inspired by German and Austrian baking, has become one of my go-to recipes for when I want something delicious to enjoy with a cup of coffee or tea.

Quick cinnamon crumble cake

SERVES 4-6

For the crumble

60g (2½oz) butter

100g (3½oz) brown sugar

1½ tsp ground cinnamon

50g (2oz) rolled (porridge) oats

For the cake

175g (6oz) plain flour

1 tsp baking powder

75g (3oz) caster sugar

½ tsp salt

75g (3oz) butter

1 egg

100ml (3½fl oz) milk

1 tsp vanilla extract

Equipment

20cm (8in) square tin

Preheat the oven to 180°C (350°F), Gas mark 4. Line the base and butter the sides of the tin.

Start by making the crumble top. Melt the butter and mix it in a bowl with the sugar, cinnamon and oats, then set aside.

Put all the dry ingredients for the cake mixture into the bowl of a food processor with the butter and buzz to make a crumbly texture. Mix together the egg, milk and vanilla extract and beat lightly, then pour into the flour and mix in the food processor, pulsing a couple of times until it forms a soft dough. Alternatively, place the flour, baking powder, sugar and salt in a bowl and rub in the butter, then mix in the beaten egg, milk and vanilla extract.

Pour the cake mixture into the lined tin and sprinkle the crumble topping over the top.

Place in the oven and bake for 25–30 minutes until set in the centre.

For a breakfast, brunch or mid-afternoon treat, these pancakes take just minutes to knock up and even less time to be demolished by your hungry ones!

Fluffy blueberry pancakes with maple syrup

MAKES ABOUT
12 PANCAKES

100g (3½oz) plain flour

25g (1oz) caster sugar

1 tsp baking powder

Pinch of salt

2 eggs, separated

125ml (4½fl oz) milk

2 tbsp sunflower oil

15g (½oz) butter

125g (4½oz) blueberries, fresh or frozen

To serve

Icing sugar

Maple syrup

Sift the flour, sugar, baking powder and salt into a bowl. In a separate bowl, mix together the egg yolks with the milk and whisk into the dry ingredients to form a thick batter. In another bowl, whisk the egg whites until stiff, then fold into the batter.

Place a frying pan on a medium–high heat. When the pan has heated up, drizzle over a few drops of sunflower oil and add a knob of butter to the pan. Allow to melt, then drop in three or four generous tablespoonfuls of batter at a time, leaving plenty of space in between.

Reduce the heat to medium–low, then place about seven blueberries on each pancake. After about 2 minutes, the pancakes should be turning golden underneath and holes should be forming on the top. At this stage, flip them over and cook for another 1–2 minutes until golden on both sides.

Serve the pancakes on a warm plate dusted with icing sugar and drizzled with maple syrup.

As if your average French toast weren't luxurious enough! When made with buttery croissants, this definitely has a certain *je ne sais quoi* about it. A great way of using up slightly stale croissants.

Really French toast!

SERVES 4

1 egg

2 tsp caster sugar

30ml (1¼fl oz) milk

½–1 tsp ground ginger

4 croissants, split in half lengthways

20g (¾oz) butter, for frying

Whisk together the egg, sugar, milk and ginger. Pour into a large, flat dish, place the croissants cut side down in the eggy mixture and allow to soak for a few minutes. Then turn to soak the other side.

Melt the butter in a frying pan over a medium heat. You will probably need to do this in two batches, so use half of the butter at a time. Fry the croissants cut side down first until golden brown, then flip over to cook the crusty side. Serve with a good drizzle of honey and maybe a dollop of softly whipped cream.

When my husband's cousin Ivan Whelan described this ice cream to me, I was instantly intrigued. Just three ingredients and, to top that, three of my very favourite ingredients. This ice cream delivers a rich, but extremely refreshing, punch of flavour. The mango in mint syrup, while not essential, does bring it all together to make a lovely way to end a meal.

Ivan's coconut and lime ice cream with mango in mint syrup

SERVES 6

For the ice cream

1 x 400g (14oz) tin of coconut milk

1 x 400g (14oz) tin of condensed milk

Juice and finely grated zest of 3 limes

For the mango in mint syrup

50g (2oz) caster or granulated sugar

20 mint leaves, finely chopped

Juice of ½ lime

1 large ripe mango, sliced

To make the ice cream, mix together all the ingredients well with a whisk, then pour into a container and place in the freezer for 3–4 hours until frozen.

In a small pan over a medium heat, dissolve the sugar in 50ml (2fl oz) water. Allow to cool slightly, then add the mint leaves and lime juice and mix the syrup with the mango slices.

Serve the ice cream with the slices of mango in the lime and mint syrup.

Strawberry and rhubarb has to be my favourite early-summer flavour combination and in this recipe, the two juicy fruits lie underneath a thick blanket of crunchy, buttery deliciousness.

Strawberry and rhubarb cobbler

SERVES 6

300g (11oz) rhubarb, cut into 2cm (¾in) pieces

300g (11oz) strawberries, sliced

100g (3½oz) caster sugar

For the batter

50g (2oz) butter, plus extra for greasing

225g (8oz) plain flour

2 tsp baking powder

75g (3oz) caster sugar

75ml (3fl oz) milk

1 egg

50g (2oz) almonds, chopped

25g (2oz) caster sugar

Equipment

1 litre (1¾ pint) capacity pie dish

Preheat the oven to 170°C (325°F), Gas mark 3.

Grease the pie dish with butter, then pour in the chopped rhubarb and strawberries and scatter over the caster sugar.

To make the batter, sift the flour and baking powder together into a bowl. Rub in the butter, then mix in 75g (3oz) of the sugar. Beat the milk and egg together and mix in to form a soft dough. Place in 'blobs' over the top of the fruit.

Mix the almonds together with the remaining sugar, then sprinkle over the top of the cobbler.

Place in the oven and bake for 45–50 minutes until the centre is cooked through. Stick a skewer into the batter – the cobbler is ready if it comes out clean.

A firm family favourite in our house. This is the kind of pudding I love after something cosy like roast chicken, mashed potatoes and lashings of gravy.

Zesty fluffy orange pudding

SERVES 4

25g (1oz) butter

250g (9oz) caster or granulated sugar

2 eggs, separated

25g (1oz) plain flour

Zest and juice of 1 orange

Juice of ½ lemon

150ml (5fl oz) milk

Equipment

1 litre (1¾ pint) capacity ovenproof dish

Preheat the oven to 180°C (350°F), Gas mark 4.

Place the butter, sugar and egg yolks in a bowl and cream together, using a wooden spoon or the paddle attachment of an electric food mixer, until light and fluffy.

Sift in the flour, then fold into the mixture along with the orange zest, orange and lemon juice, and milk.

In a separate, clean dry bowl, whisk together the egg whites until they form stiff peaks. Fold the egg whites into the orange mixture.

Pour the mixture into the dish, then place in the oven and bake for about 40 minutes. The top should be set, with a layer of orange curd on the bottom. Remove from the oven and serve with softly whipped cream or ice cream.

Something magical happens when figs are cooked with brown sugar. As the sugar caramelises, the figs take on a flavour like that of a sweet, dark, toffee-like sherry. The tangy Greek yoghurt is the perfect foil for the figs – and when toasted pine nuts and a drizzle of honey are added into the mix, this makes for a delightful Middle-Eastern-inspired treat.

Yoghurt, toffee figs and honey

SERVES 4

20g (¾oz) soft light brown sugar

4–8 ripe figs, depending on size

300g (11oz) Greek yoghurt

4 tsp honey

25g (1oz) pine nuts, toasted (see tip below)

Spread the sugar out on a plate, then cut the figs in half.

Place a frying pan on a medium–high heat. Place the figs cut side down in the sugar, then place in the frying pan. Cook for a few minutes until the sugar darkens and caramelises.

As the figs cook, divide the yoghurt among the plates, drizzle over the honey and sprinkle with the toasted pine nuts. Arrange the figs on the plate next to the yoghurt, then serve.

Rachel's Tip: To toast the pine nuts, place in a non-stick pan over a medium–high heat and cook for a minute or so, tossing once or twice, until slightly darker in colour and toasted.

Have you ever split open an apricot stone and eaten the little almond-like kernel inside? I did when I was really young and I still remember its bitter but very almondy flavour. This is why apricot kernels feature in many almond-flavoured delicacies, such as amaretto and amaretti biscuits. Anything made with apricots goes with almonds – and vice versa. This crumble is a lovely take on an age-old pairing of ingredients.

Apricot and almond crumble

SERVES 6

10 ripe apricots (650g/1lb 7oz in weight, with stones)

75g (3oz) caster sugar

For the crumble

150g (5oz) plain flour

100g (3½oz) caster sugar

75g (3oz) butter, cubed

50g (2oz) whole almonds with their skins on, roughly chopped

Equipment

1 litre (1¾ pint) capacity pie dish

Preheat the oven to 180°C (350°F), Gas mark 4.

Cut the apricots in half, then remove the stones and cut each half in half again. Place these apricot quarters in the pie dish and sprinkle with the caster sugar, then set aside while you make the crumble.

Place the flour and the sugar in a bowl and rub in the butter to resemble coarse breadcrumbs. Stir in the almonds, then scatter the crumble over the fruit to cover.

Bake in the oven for 20–30 minutes until the crumble is golden, bubbling and the fruit is deliciously tender.

Serve with softly whipped cream or ice cream.

We've always known that opposites attract. Here's a perfect example: smooth, rich, velvety cream and sharp, refreshing, tangy lemon couldn't be more different, but with just some sugar to bring them together, they're a match made in heaven.

Superfast lemon ice cream

SERVES 4

2 lemons

150g (5oz) caster sugar

300ml (½ pint) double or regular cream

First, finely grate the zest from one of the lemons, then squeeze the juice from both. Strain the juice into the zest and add the sugar, stirring and gradually adding the cream. It will thicken slightly as you add it. Pour it into a container and place in the freezer.

Freeze until solid around the outside and mushy in the centre. Mix with a fork and place back in the freezer again to freeze until firm.

I used to assume that a fruit fool was called a fool because any fool could make it (try to say that really quickly ten times!), but the term actually comes from the French verb *fouler*, which means 'to crush'. This is a gorgeous way to end a summer feast.

Strawberry, peach and vanilla fool with orange sablé biscuits

SERVES 6-8

For the orange sablé biscuits

Makes 40–45

150g (5oz) butter, softened

110g (4oz) caster sugar

1 egg

Finely grated zest of 1 orange

275g (10oz) plain flour

½ tsp baking powder

For the fool

225g (8oz) strawberries

2 ripe peaches, halved and stones removed

125g (4½oz) caster sugar

2 tsp vanilla extract

Juice of 1 lemon

2 egg whites

150ml (5fl oz) double or regular cream

First make the biscuits. Place the butter in a bowl and beat until soft. Add in the sugar and beat again until light and creamy. Add in the egg and the orange zest, then sift in the flour and the baking powder and mix to bring together.

Place the dough on a sheet of baking parchment and roll into a log about 35cm (14in) long and 5cm (2in) in diameter. Cover with the baking parchment and twist at the ends to close. This can sit in the fridge for 2 weeks or it can be frozen for up to 3 months.

When ready to cook, preheat the oven to 180°C (350°F), Gas mark 4.

Cut the dough into slices 5–7.5mm (about ¼in) thick. Place on a baking tray lined with baking parchment and bake for 8–12 minutes until light golden. Take out of the oven and let sit for 2–3 minutes before transferring to a wire rack to cool.

Place the strawberries, peaches, 75g (3oz) of the sugar, vanilla extract and lemon juice in a blender and whiz up, then push through a sieve into a bowl.

In another bowl, whisk the egg whites with the remaining sugar until stiff peaks appear. Then whisk the cream until almost, but not quite, stiffly whipped. Fold the egg-white mixture into the fruit, then gently fold in the whipped cream until light and fluffy.

Serve with the orange sablé biscuits.

Rachel's Tip: This mixture freezes well to make an ice cream.

While most traditional clafoutis recipes contain cherries, I find that gooseberries make a delicious alternative. The sharp, tangy flavour of the berries is perfectly complemented by the sweet vanilla custard. I adore eating this still a little warm from the oven, with cold, softly whipped cream.

Gooseberry clafoutis

SERVES 4–6

25g (1oz) butter

350g (12oz) gooseberries (fresh or frozen), topped, tailed and cut in half

125g (4½oz) brown sugar

2 tbsp brown sugar, for sprinkling

For the batter

125ml (4½fl oz) milk

125ml (4½fl oz) double or regular cream

4 eggs

60g (2½oz) plain flour

100g (3½oz) caster sugar

1 tsp vanilla extract

Equipment

1 litre (1¾ pint) capacity pie dish

Preheat the oven to 180°C (350°F), Gas mark 4 and place the pie dish in the oven to heat up.

Place a frying pan on a high heat. Tip in the butter, gooseberries and the brown sugar. Cook, uncovered, for about 5–8 minutes, until the gooseberries have softened and sweetened.

While this cooks, place all the ingredients for the batter in a blender or food processor (or just a bowl using a hand whisk) and whiz/whisk until completely blended.

Take the dish out of the oven, pour the gooseberries and all their juices into the dish, then pour the batter over the gooseberries carefully so as not to disturb the fruits. Scatter the 2 tablespoons of brown sugar over the top and cook in the oven for 40 minutes or until a skewer inserted into the centre comes out clean.

SWEET THINGS
FOR CHILDREN

Banoffee ice cream

Milk chocolate mousse, caramel sauce,
toffee popcorn

Chocolate peanut brittle butter cookies

Crunchy, chewy ginger cookies

Rocky Road bites

Tropical fruit sorbet

Choux nuts with cinnamon sugar and
pastry cream

Deep-fried honey puffs

Melon popsicles

Warm chocolate spoon cake

Cinnamon and maple oat cookies

Dulce de leche brownies

Peanut butter and chocolate ripple ice cream

Honey, cranberry and sesame oat bars

Taking its name from the ubiquitous Banoffee Pie, which has a biscuit base topped with banana slices, toffee (or boiled condensed milk) and heaps of whipped cream, this ice cream is always a winner with children. Delicious vanilla ice cream with ripples of boiled condensed milk, crunchy biscuits and caramelised bananas; too good not to be shared with the adults!

Banoffee ice cream

SERVES 8–10

For the banoffee

1 x 400g (14oz) tin of full-fat condensed milk

75g (3oz) butter

75g (3oz) caster or granulated sugar

4 bananas, cut in quarters lengthways, then sliced

12 digestive biscuits, broken into pieces

For the ice cream

4 egg yolks

100g (3½oz) caster or granulated sugar

1 tsp vanilla extract

1.2 litres (2 pints) softly whipped cream (measured when whisked)

Boil the unopened tin of condensed milk in a large saucepan for 2½ hours, topping up the water from time to time, then remove from the heat and allow the tin to cool in the water.

To make the ice cream, place the egg yolks in a bowl and whisk until light and fluffy. Combine the sugar and 250ml (9fl oz) water in a small saucepan, then stir over a medium heat until the sugar is completely dissolved. Remove the spoon and boil the syrup until it reaches the 'thread' stage, 106–113°C (223–235°F). It will look thick and syrupy and when a metal spoon is dipped in, the last drops of syrup will form thin threads. Pour this boiling syrup in a steady stream onto the egg yolks, whisking all the time. Add the vanilla extract and continue to whisk until it becomes a thick, creamy white mousse. Fold in the softly whipped cream, place in a container, cover and place in the freezer for an hour.

Place the butter and sugar in a pan on a medium heat. When the butter has melted, add the bananas and continue to bubble for a few minutes until the sugar browns and caramelises. Then remove from the heat and allow to cool.

Remove the ice cream from the freezer, fold in the broken biscuits and toffee bananas, then add the boiled condensed milk in ½ teaspoon amounts, continuing to mix and fold.

Return to the freezer and allow to freeze for about 3–4 hours until frozen all through.

Rachel's Tip: Do not use 'light' condensed milk, as it will not set on boiling.

Popcorn never fails to add a playful, Willy Wonka-like note to a dish. But it's more than just a bit of fun here, as it adds a welcome crunch with the slightest hint of salt to the sweet chocolate mousse and caramel sauce. This is a great assemble-it-yourself recipe for children.

Milk chocolate mousse, caramel sauce, toffee popcorn

Serves 4–6

For the chocolate mousse

125g (4½oz) milk chocolate

75ml (3fl oz) double or regular cream

2 eggs, separated

For the toffee popcorn

1 tbsp sunflower oil

25g (1oz) popcorn kernels

20g (¾oz) butter

Pinch of salt

20g (¾oz) brown sugar

1 tbsp golden syrup

Cont. opposite

Finely chop the chocolate. In a saucepan, bring the cream up to the boil, turn off the heat, add the chocolate to the cream and stir it around until the chocolate melts. Allow to cool slightly, then whisk in the egg yolks.

In a separate clean, dry bowl, whisk the egg whites until just stiff, then stir a quarter of the egg white into the cream mixture. Gently fold the chocolate mixture into the rest of the egg whites.

Spoon into little bowls, glasses or cups or one serving bowl and leave in the fridge for 2–3 hours to set.

Next make the toffee popcorn. Place the oil in a saucepan with a lid on a medium–low heat. Add the popcorn kernels and swirl the pan to coat the popcorn in the oil. Put the lid on, then turn the heat down to low and listen for the popping! As soon as the popping stops, turn off the heat and tip into a bowl.

Melt the butter in a separate saucepan with the pinch of salt, add the brown sugar and golden syrup and stir over a high heat for 1–2 minutes. Pour the toffee over the popcorn, and toss to mix in the toffee sauce. Allow to cool.

As it cools, the toffee surrounding the popcorn will harden – break it up with your hands so that it doesn't set into one great big lump.

For the caramel sauce

225g (8oz) caster or granulated sugar

110g (4oz) butter

175ml (6fl oz) double or regular cream

To make the caramel sauce, dissolve the sugar in 75ml (3fl oz) water in a pan over a medium heat. Stir in the butter, raise the heat a little and bubble, stirring occasionally, until it turns a light toffee colour. This may take about 15–20 minutes. Turn off the heat and stir in half the cream. When the bubbles die down, stir in the rest of the cream.

The sauce can be stored in the fridge for up to 2 weeks and reheated when necessary.

To serve, drizzle the caramel sauce over the chocolate mousse, then scatter with the toffee popcorn.

Simple shortbread biscuits dipped in melted milk chocolate, then scattered with salted peanut brittle; this could be the perfect cookie.

Chocolate peanut brittle butter cookies

MAKES 20 COOKIES

For the peanut brittle

40g (1½oz) caster or granulated sugar

40g (1½oz) salted peanuts

For the cookies

150g (5oz) plain flour

50g (2oz) caster or granulated sugar

100g (3½oz) butter, softened

To finish

100g (3½oz) milk chocolate, in drops or broken into pieces

To make the peanut brittle, first line a baking tray with baking parchment and set aside. Place the sugar in a frying pan and scatter the peanuts over the sugar. Place on a medium heat, not stirring but swirling the pan every so often to caramelise the sugar evenly. Cook until the sugar has completely melted and is a deep golden colour. Swirl the pan again so that the peanuts are coated in the caramel. Transfer the coated nuts to the prepared baking tray. Once cool and completely set (it will be hard), break up the brittle using your hands, then place in a food processor and whiz until just slightly coarse or chop coarsely by hand.

Preheat the oven to 180°C (350°F), Gas mark 4. Put the flour and sugar into a mixing bowl. Rub in the soft butter and bring the whole mixture together to form a stiff dough. Alternatively, you can whiz everything up briefly in a food processor. Roll the dough into a log approximately 30cm (12in) long and 4cm (1½in) in diameter (the log of cookie dough can be covered and kept in the fridge like this for up to a week). Now cut into 7mm (¼in) slices.

Place on baking trays (no need to butter or line) and cook in the oven for 8–10 minutes until light golden brown. Allow to cool for 1 minute before placing on a wire rack to cool completely.

Alternatively, you could roll out the dough to about 7mm (¼in) thick and cut it into shapes to bake.

Once the cookies have cooled, place the chocolate in a bowl sitting over a saucepan with a few centimetres of water. Bring the water up to the boil, then take off the heat and allow the chocolate to melt slowly. Once melted, dip the top of each cookie into the chocolate, then scatter the peanut brittle over the chocolate and place somewhere cool to set.

I love how, when cookies have golden syrup in them, they manage to be both crunchy and chewy at the same time. Packed with ground ginger and cinnamon, these cookies are great for a snack with a glass of cold milk.

Crunchy, chewy ginger cookies

MAKES 18–20 COOKIES

125g (4½oz) butter

75g (3oz) brown sugar

75g (3oz) golden syrup

1 egg, beaten

150g (5oz) plain flour

1 tsp bicarbonate of soda

3 tsp ground ginger

1½ tsp ground cinnamon

1½ tsp mixed spice

50g (2oz) caster or granulated sugar

Beat the butter, then add in the brown sugar, the golden syrup and then the egg. Use a whisk for a few seconds to bring the mixture together. Take out the whisk, then sift in the remaining ingredients, but not the sugar.

The mixture can be used straight away or it can placed in the fridge for 1 week.

Preheat the oven to 180°C (350°F), Gas mark 4. Line a baking tray with baking parchment.

Place the sugar in a bowl. Take dessertspoonfuls of the cookie dough, roll into balls, toss in the sugar, flatten and place spaced apart on the lined tray.

Bake for 12–15 minutes until just set, but still slightly soft in the centre. Take out of the oven and let sit for 4 minutes before removing to a wire rack to cool.

This particular Rocky Road recipe is a bit of a homage to the Daim bar. Originally known as Dajm in Swedish, we in Ireland and the UK first knew of it as a Dime bar. I remember when they first came out in Ireland; I immediately adored the brittle toffee with bits of almond, all covered in milky chocolate. Anyway, when chopped up with marshmallows and biscuits before being stirred into melted chocolate and golden syrup and allowed to set, this is a Rocky Road that I love to take.

Rocky Road bites

MAKES ABOUT
25 SQUARES

450g (1lb) milk or dark chocolate (55–70% cocoa solids) or ½ of each

75g (3oz) golden syrup

4 x 28g (1¼oz) Daim bars, broken into chunks

150g (5oz) marshmallows, chopped

200g (7oz) biscuits, such as shortbread, leftover cookies or digestives, broken into chunks

Equipment

20cm (8in) square tin

Line the tin with baking parchment on the base and up the sides.

Melt the chocolate with the golden syrup, then remove from the heat. Add in the remaining ingredients, then press into the tin. Place somewhere cool for a couple of hours to set.

Cut into squares to serve.

The day that I tested this recipe at home I happened to have half a dozen or so children at our house. This sorbet disappeared in front of my very eyes. The banana adds a smooth sweetness to the pineapple, giving you that totally tropical taste.

Tropical fruit sorbet

SERVES 6

1 medium banana

½ pineapple, peeled and cored (about 200g/7oz)

Juice of 1 large orange (about 150ml/5fl oz)

Juice of 1 large lime (about 50ml/½fl oz)

100g (3½oz) caster or granulated sugar

Equipment

Ice-cream machine (optional)

Place all the ingredients in a food processor and whiz together until smooth. Taste for sweetness – you're looking for a balance between sweet and sharp. Add more lime juice or sugar to get the right balance if necessary.

Freeze in an ice-cream machine according to the manufacturer's instructions. Alternatively, put in a container in the freezer and leave for an hour. Remove from the freezer and whisk, then return to the freezer. Repeat this process two or three more times.

OK, these are most definitely not an everyday treat, but it has to be said they are completely divine. Like doughnuts, but made with the faster-to-put-together choux pastry, these will disappear as soon as they're made.

Choux nuts with cinnamon sugar and pastry cream

SERVES 8–10

For the choux pastry

100g (3½oz) strong white or plain flour

Pinch of salt

75g (3oz) butter

3 eggs, beaten

Sunflower or vegetable oil, for deep-frying

For the pastry cream

4 egg yolks

100g (3½oz) caster sugar

25g (1oz) plain flour, sifted

1 vanilla pod, with a line scored down the side, or ½ tsp vanilla extract

350ml (12fl oz) milk

For the cinnamon sugar

50g (2oz) caster or granulated sugar

1 tsp ground cinnamon

First, make the choux pastry. Sift the flour and salt into a large bowl and set aside.

Place 150ml (5fl oz) water and the butter in a medium-sized saucepan with high sides, set over a medium–high heat and stir until the butter melts. Allow the mixture to come to a rolling boil, then immediately remove the pan from the heat. Add the flour and salt and beat in very well with a wooden spoon until the mixture comes together.

Reduce the heat to medium and return the saucepan to the heat, stirring for 1 minute until the mixture starts to 'fur' (slightly stick to the base of the pan). Remove from the heat and allow to cool for 1 minute.

Pour about a quarter of the beaten egg into the pan and, using the wooden spoon, beat very well. Add a little more egg and beat well again until the mixture comes back together. Continue to add the egg, beating vigorously all the time, until the mixture has softened, is nice and shiny and has a dropping consistency. You may not need to add all the egg or you may need a little extra. If the mixture is too stiff (not enough egg), then the choux pastries will be too heavy, but if the mixture is too wet (too much egg), they will not hold their shape when spooned onto greaseproof paper.

Although the pastry is best used right away, it can be placed in a bowl, covered and chilled for up to 24 hours, until ready to use.

Cont. overleaf

Next, make the pastry cream. In a bowl, whisk the egg yolks with the sugar until light and thick, then stir in the flour.

Place the vanilla pod, if using, in a saucepan with the milk and bring it slowly just up to the boil. Remove the vanilla pod and pour the milk onto the egg yolk mixture, whisking all the time. Return the mixture to the pan and stir over a low–medium heat until it comes up to a gentle boil (it must boil for it to thicken). Continue to cook, stirring all the time (or use a whisk if it looks lumpy), for 2 minutes or until it has thickened. The mixture is thick enough when it falls off the spoon in large blobs rather than pouring off it. If the mixture goes a little lumpy while cooking, remove the saucepan from the heat and whisk well.

After 2 minutes, remove the saucepan from the heat, add the vanilla extract, if using, and pour into a bowl. If it is still lumpy now cooked, push it through a sieve.

Cover with cling film and allow to cool. It must be covered or the surface must be rubbed with a tiny knob of butter to prevent a skin from forming.

To make the cinnamon sugar, combine the sugar and cinnamon and set aside.

When you're ready to cook the choux nuts, turn on a deep fryer to 180°C (350°F), or place the oil in a saucepan on a medium–high heat. The oil is ready to cook with when a small piece of bread dropped into it bubbles and rises quickly back up to the surface.

Scoop up little blobs of the choux pastry with a kitchen teaspoon, round and scoop off with a second teaspoon, drop into the deep-fat fryer and fry for 5–6 minutes, turning over a few times, until they are four times the size and golden brown.

Remove, drain briefly on kitchen paper, and then, using a skewer or the tip of a small sharp knife, make a hole in the side or the base of each puff. Toss the puffs in the cinnamon sugar, then, using a small piping bag and small nozzle, pipe pastry cream into the centre through the hole you have just made. Serve while warm.

Little puffs of honey deliciousness, these are best eaten while still warm. That won't be a problem at all, but make sure to save some for yourself.

Deep-fried honey puffs

**MAKES ABOUT
20 PUFFS**

350ml (12fl oz) water, at blood temperature

2 tbsp honey

10g (⅜oz) dried yeast or 20g (¾oz) fresh yeast

300g (11oz) plain flour

25g (1oz) cornflour

½ tsp salt

Sunflower or vegetable oil, for deep-frying

To serve

100ml (3½fl oz) honey

Icing sugar, for dusting

Place the water in a bowl or jug and stir in the honey to mix. Add in the yeast and leave to stand on your worktop for 5 minutes. Meanwhile, mix together in a bowl the flour, cornflour and salt.

Pour the yeast and honey water into the dry ingredients and stir well to mix. Cover with cling film and leave to stand at room temperature for 30 minutes until bubbles start to appear on the surface. The puff batter can also be placed in the fridge, where it will sit perfectly for up to 24 hours.

When you are ready to cook the puffs, turn on a deep fryer to 180°C (350°F), or place the oil (a tasteless oil such as sunflower or vegetable oil) in a saucepan on a medium–high heat. The oil is ready to cook with when a small piece of bread dropped into it bubbles and rises quickly back up to the surface. While you're waiting for the oil to heat up, place some kitchen towel on a baking tray or a wide bowl.

Using a dessertspoon, scoop out a spoonful of the batter and, using another dessertspoon, scrape it off into the oil. Put a few more spoonfuls into the oil, but don't overcrowd it or the temperature will drop, resulting in oily, heavy puffs. I like to cook about six at a time. Allow them to cook for about 2 minutes until golden on the bottom, then tip over and cook on the other side for about 2 minutes or until golden again.

When cooked, the puffs will be golden all over and cooked through in the centre. Using a slotted spoon, lift the puffs out of the oil and onto the kitchen towel to drain.

Serve warm with a dusting of icing sugar, a drizzle of honey over the top and a scoop of ice cream on the side, if you wish.

Rachel's Tip: I sometimes scatter chopped toasted nuts such as walnuts, pistachios or hazelnuts over the honey when serving these.

A popsicle is a great refreshing treat to serve after a meal or just any time on a sunny day, and when made with sweet, ripe melons, hardly any sugar is needed. The children might not want to share these with you.

Melon popsicles

MAKES 8 X 50ML
(2FL OZ) POPSICLES

400g (14oz) honeydew, cantaloupe or Galia melon flesh (about ¼ melon with the seeds and skin removed)

40ml (1½fl oz) lemon juice (about ½ lemon)

40g (1½oz) caster sugar (if you use a Galia melon, you might need more sugar)

Equipment

Ice lolly/popsicle moulds

Put the melon flesh, lemon juice and sugar in a blender and whiz until completely smooth. Pour into the popsicle moulds and place in the freezer for 4–6 hours until frozen.

Rachel's Tip: Other summer fruits also work well in these popsicles. Try using peaches, raspberries or strawberries.

Not quite a cake, not quite a pudding, this gluten-free recipe has lots of ground almonds in it to keep it deliciously nutty and fudgy.

Warm chocolate spoon cake

SERVES 4–6

150g (5oz) dark chocolate (55–70% cocoa solids)

150g (5oz) butter

125g (4½oz) caster sugar

1 tsp vanilla extract

75g (3oz) ground almonds

4 eggs, separated

Pinch of salt

Equipment

1 litre (1¾ pint) capacity pie dish

Preheat the oven to 190°C (375°F), Gas mark 5.

Place the chocolate, butter and sugar in a bowl sitting over a saucepan of simmering water and allow to melt. Take the bowl off the heat and stir in the vanilla extract, the ground almonds and the four egg yolks, one by one.

Put the egg whites in a bowl with the pinch of salt and whisk just until stiff, but still creamy rather than grainy.

Fold in the chocolate mixture and tip into the pie dish.

Bake in the oven for 22–25 minutes until the outsides are set and the centre just has a thick wobble. If you take this out of the oven before it has completely cooked, it will stay nutty and fudgy, even when it cools down.

Allow to sit for a few minutes before serving. Wonderful with cold, softly whipped cream or ice cream.

One taste of cinnamon mixed with maple syrup never fails to take me back to family holidays visiting our relatives in Canada. I was so enthralled with this classic North American flavour that I find myself using it time and time again in baking.

Cinnamon and maple oat cookies

MAKES 24 COOKIES

100g (3½oz) butter

100ml (3½fl oz) maple syrup

125g (4½oz) plain flour

¼ tsp bicarbonate of soda

125g (4½oz) caster sugar

1½ tsp ground cinnamon

150g (5oz) rolled (porridge) oats

1 egg

Preheat the oven to 180°C (350°F), Gas mark 4.

Place the butter and maple syrup in a saucepan on a medium heat and stir together until the butter has melted. Then set aside and allow to cool slightly.

Sift the flour and bicarbonate of soda into a mixing bowl, then stir in the sugar, cinnamon and oats. Mix the egg with the butter and maple syrup and then mix with the dry ingredients to form a soft, sticky dough.

Spoon out the mixture onto a lined baking tray using two dessertspoons, forming balls of dough spaced at least 2–3cm (1in) apart.

Bake in the oven for about 15 minutes until spread out and just dry to the touch. Once out of the oven, allow the cookies to sit on the tray for a few minutes to set before transferring to a wire rack to cool.

As if brownies aren't good enough already, these are outrageously divine, with ripples of boiled condensed milk swirling through dense chocolate heaven.

Dulce de leche brownies

MAKES 16 SQUARES

½ x 400g (14oz) tin of full-fat condensed milk or ½ x 400g (14oz) tin of dulce de leche (also labelled 'caramel')

175g (6oz) dark chocolate (55–70% cocoa solids)

175g (6oz) butter, cubed

25g (1oz) good-quality cocoa powder, sifted

3 eggs

225g (8oz) caster or soft light brown sugar

1 tsp vanilla extract

100g (3½oz) plain flour

Equipment

20cm (8in) square cake tin

Boil the unopened tin of condensed milk in a large saucepan for 2½ hours, topping up the water from time to time, then remove from the heat and allow the tin to cool in the water.

Preheat the oven to 180°C (350°F), Gas mark 4. Line the base and sides of the cake tin with baking parchment.

Melt the chocolate, butter and cocoa powder together in a bowl set over a saucepan with a few centimetres of simmering water. Do not let the base of the bowl touch the water. Remove from the heat.

In a separate large bowl, whisk the eggs, sugar and vanilla extract for 2 minutes until a little light and creamy. Continuing to whisk, add the chocolate mixture until well combined. Sift in the flour and fold through with a spatula or metal spoon.

Spoon the mixture into the prepared tin. Use a teaspoon to add blobs of the boiled condensed milk/dulce de leche/caramel all over the surface of the brownies. Then using a small sharp knife or skewer, run it around in swirls for a marbled effect.

Bake in the oven for 20–25 minutes. When cooked it should be dry on top, but still slightly 'gooey' and 'fudgy' inside. Don't be tempted to leave it in the oven any longer than this or you will have cake and not brownies. Allow to cool in the tin, then cut into squares.

Rachel's Tip: Do not use 'light' condensed milk, as it will not set on boiling.

No wonder so many different chocolate bars contain both peanut butter and chocolate; it's a winning combination, and particularly so in this ice cream. All you need now is a good movie and a spoon.

Peanut butter and chocolate ripple ice cream

SERVES 6–8

30ml (1fl oz) water

30ml (1oz) caster sugar

50g (2oz) dark chocolate

75g (3oz) crunchy peanut butter

2 eggs

100g (3½oz) caster or granulated sugar

1 tsp vanilla extract

250ml (9fl oz) double or regular cream (measured before whisking)

Equipment

This can be frozen in a bowl or tub or it can be made into an ice-cream 'cake' if you freeze it in a 20cm (8in) spring-form cake tin that you've lined with a double layer of cling film

Place the water and sugar in a small saucepan and heat gently until the sugar has dissolved. Remove from the heat and add the chocolate, stirring until smooth. Then stir in the peanut butter. Set aside to cool.

Place a saucepan with a few centimetres of water on a medium heat. Put the eggs and sugar into a bowl and sit it over the saucepan so that the water is not touching the bottom of the bowl. I use a heatproof glass bowl for this – a stainless-steel one is not a good idea, as it will get too hot and scramble the eggs.

Using either a hand whisk or a hand-held electric beater, whisk the eggs and sugar over the simmering water for about 5–10 minutes until the mixture is pale, light and will hold a figure of eight. Believe it or not, this is not difficult to do by hand, and will be necessary if your hand-held electric beater cannot reach your hob. Once it's holding a figure of eight, take the water off the heat and continue to whisk for about 8–10 minutes until the mixture has cooled down to room temperature.

Whip the cream in a mixing bowl until just holding stiff peaks. Too stiff and it will go grainy, too soft and it won't be able to hold the sugar mousse mixture.

Tip one quarter of the sugar mousse mixture in and fold to combine, then tip this mixture into the cream along with the vanilla extract and gently fold until it has mixed completely, but is still light and airy.

Tip into the bowl, tub or prepared tin, then pour in the peanut butter chocolate sauce and swirl through the mixture, keeping it marbled by not mixing together too thoroughly. Place in the freezer for about 6 hours or overnight, until frozen.

I love a really good oat bar, and this one ticks all the boxes for me – dense, chewy, and oh-so-packed with goodness. The tahini paste really packs a sesame punch, while the dried cranberries add their own distinctive rich sweetness.

Honey, cranberry and sesame oat bars

MAKES ABOUT 24 BARS

300g (11oz) rolled (porridge) oats

100g (3½oz) sesame seeds

50g (2oz) plain flour

200g (7oz) butter

300g (11oz) honey

150g (5oz) soft dark brown sugar

150g (5oz) dried cranberries

125g (4½oz) light tahini

Equipment

33 x 23cm (13 x 9in) Swiss roll tin

Preheat the oven to 180°C (350°F), Gas mark 4. Line the Swiss roll tin with baking parchment, leaving a little hanging over the edges for easy removal.

Place the oats, sesame seeds and flour in a large bowl and mix together.

Place the butter and honey in a saucepan on a medium heat. Stir together until melted and mixed, then stir in the sugar until it has dissolved. Add the cranberries and tahini and mix well.

Pour the butter mixture over the dry ingredients and mix very well. Tip into the prepared tin, spread out evenly, then place in the oven and bake for 20–25 minutes until golden and just set in the centre.

Remove from the oven and allow to cool in the tin, then cut into bars to serve.

FRESH & FRUITY

Blueberry jelly and milk ice cream

Middle-Eastern orange, pistachio and
pomegranate

Pink grapefruit and raspberries
in a light cinnamon syrup

Yoghurt and elderflower cream
with poached rhubarb

Watermelon with mangoes and
apricots in ginger

Lemon verbena sorbet

Sweet labneh with honey, pistachios and
orange blossom water

Ivan's strawberries in red Burgundy syrup

Prosecco and raspberry jelly

Watermelon ginita

Poached peaches with raspberry sherbet

Jelly and ice cream: a classic twosome – and for very good reason, too. As the cool, refreshing ice cream starts to melt into the thick, wobbly jelly, it's hard not to feel a little nostalgic for 1980s birthday parties! This delicious combination isn't just for the children, though.

Blueberry jelly and milk ice cream

SERVES 4

For the milk ice cream

150g (5oz) caster or granulated sugar

Big pinch of salt flakes

500ml (18fl oz) milk

2 egg whites

250ml (9fl oz) double or regular cream

For the blueberry jelly

250g (9oz) blueberries

Juice of 1 lemon

75g (3oz) caster or granulated sugar

1 sheet of gelatine

Equipment

Ice-cream machine

Place the sugar, salt and milk in a saucepan over a medium heat. Stir together until the sugar has just dissolved, then set aside.

In a clean, dry bowl, whisk the egg whites until slightly fluffy (a minute or two is fine). Add the cream to the milk mixture, then combine with the egg white.

Freeze in an ice-cream machine according to the manufacturer's instructions.

Place the blueberries and lemon juice in a blender and whiz for a good few minutes until very smooth. Then push through a sieve and set aside.

Place 50ml (2fl oz) water and the sugar in a saucepan over a medium heat. Stir just until the sugar has dissolved, then remove from the heat and set aside.

Place the gelatine in a bowl of cold water and leave to sit for 3–5 minutes until softened. Remove the gelatine sheet from its soaking water and squeeze out any excess liquid. Transfer the softened gelatine to the warm syrup and stir until dissolved. Add some 4 or 5 tablespoons of the blueberry-lemon liquid to the gelatine syrup and stir together. Then pour the mixture into the remaining blueberry liquid.

Stir everything together well, then divide among four glasses or moulds and place in the fridge to set. This should take 3–4 hours.

Serve the blueberry jelly with the milk ice cream.

Fresh, fragrant and delightfully simple, this little concoction is a delicious way to start the day or, indeed, to end a meal.

Middle-Eastern orange, pistachio and pomegranate

SERVES 4

4 oranges

30g (1¼oz) icing sugar

2 tbsp orange blossom water

2–3 tbsp crème fraîche or sour cream

½–1 pomegranate, seeds removed

25g (1oz) pistachios, toasted (see tip on page 28) and chopped

Cut the top and bottom off the oranges, just down as far as the flesh. Peel the oranges with a knife, either from the top to bottom or in a spiral around the Equator. Cut the oranges into slices horizontally.

Place the oranges in a bowl, then sprinkle the icing sugar and the orange blossom water over the top. Place in the fridge for at least 1 hour (or even the whole day) to chill.

When ready to serve, put on plates, spoon a blob of crème fraîche over the oranges and sprinkle with the pomegranate seeds and the pistachios.

I remember the American mum of one of my school friends used to eat a half grapefruit sprinkled with cinnamon for breakfast every morning. This is not only a very healthy way to start the day, it's also a really good flavour match, which gave me the inspiration for this recipe. The cool, tangy flavours from the pink grapefruit and raspberries are injected with a sunny warmth from the sweet cinnamon.

Pink grapefruit and raspberries in a light cinnamon syrup

SERVES 4

75g (3oz) caster or granulated sugar

½ cinnamon stick or ⅛ tsp ground cinnamon

2 pink grapefruit

125g (4½oz) raspberries

Heat the sugar and 75ml (3fl oz) water with the cinnamon until the sugar has dissolved, then reduce the heat and simmer for a few minutes. Remove from the heat and set aside for about an hour to allow the cinnamon to infuse.

Meanwhile, peel and segment the grapefruit. Using a small, sharp knife and working over a bowl to catch the juices, cut off the ends, then carefully cut away the peel and pith in a spiral until you have a peeled grapefruit with only flesh and no pith. Next, carefully cut along the edge of each segment, leaving behind the membrane and freeing a segment of flesh from the pith. Repeat for all the segments and place the flesh in a bowl with the raspberries, squeezing over every last bit of juice from the peel and the membrane.

Remove the cinnamon stick from the syrup, if using, then pour the syrup over the fruit and chill in the fridge.

Serve chilled in little bowls or glasses as a delicious and refreshing dessert.

Nature is the perfect matchmaker. Think tomato and basil, blackberry and apple, and pea and mint. This recipe, which is a wonderfully refreshing take on an Italian panna cotta, gives a nod to the late spring/early summer elderflowers and rhubarb.

Yoghurt and elderflower cream with poached rhubarb

SERVES 6

150ml (5fl oz) milk

130ml (4½fl oz) double or regular cream

120g (4oz) caster or granulated sugar

2 sheets of gelatine

280ml (9½fl oz) yoghurt

120ml (4fl oz) elderflower cordial

For the poached rhubarb

225g (8oz) caster or granulated sugar

225ml (8fl oz) water

450g (1lb) trimmed rhubarb stalks, sliced 2cm thick

350g (12oz) hulled, sliced strawberries

Place the milk, cream and sugar in a saucepan on a medium–low heat. Warm, and stir until the sugar has just dissolved, then remove from the heat.

Soften the gelatine in a bowl of cold water for 3–5 minutes, then remove the gelatine sheet from its soaking water and squeeze out any excess liquid. Add the softened gelatine to the warm milk mixture and stir until dissolved.

Combine the yoghurt and elderflower cordial in a bowl, then gently whisk in the warm milk mixture. Transfer to a bowl or individual glasses and place in the fridge to set for about 3 hours.

Meanwhile, poach the rhubarb. Place the sugar and water in a saucepan over a medium–high heat. Stir as it comes to the boil to dissolve the sugar. Once it is boiling, tip in the rhubarb and stir gently. Bring the syrup back up to a gentle boil, cover with a lid and cook for just 1 minute, stirring gently once or twice without breaking up the rhubarb. Take off the heat, leave the lid on and set aside to cool. It will carry on cooking as it sits, but hopefully the rhubarb will hold its shape.

When the rhubarb is soft, with no bite, gently tip it and all the juices into a serving bowl. Add in the sliced strawberries, barely stirring them in. Set aside for at least half an hour before serving. The poached rhubarb is also divine served with meringues and cream.

Truly refreshing, this colourful combination is a great way to finish off a rich or heavy meal with some added ginger to kick-start the digestion.

Watermelon with mangoes and apricots in ginger

SERVES 4–6

100g (3½oz) caster or granulated sugar

50g (2oz) root ginger, peeled and sliced finely

4 apricots

1 mango

¼ watermelon

Place 200ml (7fl oz) water, the sugar and ginger in a small saucepan on a medium heat. Bring to the boil, then reduce the heat, simmer for 2 minutes and set aside to cool.

Slice the apricots towards the stone to form about eight segments per fruit. Peel the mango and slice into nice thin slices, again towards the stone. Cut the flesh of the watermelon off the skin, then slice into segments, then into chunks, removing any seeds. Place all the fruit in a bowl and pour over the syrup.

Chill in the fridge and serve as a lovely refreshing dessert.

If you don't have some lemon verbena in a pot by a sunny window or planted up against a south-facing wall, then may I please recommend you go out and get one right now? My favourite of all the summer herbs to infuse in boiling water for a refreshing tissane, lemon verbena comes into its own when made into a sorbet. And for a proper celebration, a dash of something pink and bubbly over the top will have you jumping for joy!

Lemon verbena sorbet

SERVES 8

225g (8oz) caster or granulated sugar

2 sprigs of lemon verbena

Juice of 3 lemons

1 egg white (optional)

Equipment

Ice-cream machine or sorbetière (optional)

Place the sugar, 600ml (1 pint) water and the lemon verbena sprigs in a saucepan over a medium–low heat. Bring slowly to the boil and simmer for 3 minutes. Remove from the heat and take out the lemon verbena sprigs. Allow the syrup to get quite cold, then add the strained juice of 3 lemons.

Strain and freeze in an ice-cream machine or sorbetière. If you don't have an ice-cream machine or sorbetière, simply freeze the sorbet in a freezable bowl. When it is semi-frozen, whisk until smooth and return to the freezer. Whisk again when almost frozen and fold in the stiffly beaten egg white.

If you have access to a food processor, you can simply freeze the sorbet completely in a tray, then break up and whiz for a few seconds in the processor. Drop the slightly beaten egg white down the tube, whiz and freeze again. Keep in the freezer until needed.

Serve in chilled glasses or chilled bowls. If you like, you can splash over a little pink prosecco.

Rachel's Tip: Lemon balm or mint could be used in place of the lemon verbena.

Labneh is a Middle-Eastern delicacy that is simply strained yoghurt, though sometimes it is called yoghurt cheese. Because of the fact that a lot of the whey has gone in the straining, it can be cooked without curdling. But it is like this that I love it most: as a completely simple dish to have at the end of the meal, or even for breakfast, with just some honey, nuts and, if you wish, a drizzle of fragrant orange blossom or rose water.

Sweet labneh with honey, pistachios and orange blossom water

SERVES 3-4

600g (1lb 5oz) natural yoghurt

2 tsp honey

25g (1oz) pistachios, toasted (see tip on page 28) and chopped

1 tsp orange blossom water

Place a sheet of kitchen paper in a sieve sitting over a bowl, then tip the yoghurt into it. Place in the fridge and allow to drip for 3 hours or overnight. It will thicken as it sits and the liquid drips through.

Next, discard or drink the liquid in the bowl, then tip the thick yoghurt (labneh) into the bowl. Stir in half of the honey, then put it on a large plate or individual plates and drizzle the remaining honey over the top. Scatter with the pistachios and orange blossom water and serve.

Rachel's Tips: You could use rose water instead of orange blossom water and add a few pomegranate seeds over the top.

Another gem from Isaac's cousin Ivan, this recipe came back to Ireland with him from France in the late 1980s after he spent a few months learning French in Tours. The ripe red berry and sweet black cherry notes from Burgundy's Pinot Noir wines work so well with strawberries. Pinot Noirs from other parts of the world will be successful here, too.

Ivan's strawberries in red Burgundy syrup

SERVES 4

75g (3oz) caster or granulated sugar

150ml (5fl oz) light, fruity red Burgundy, other Pinot Noir or maybe a Beaujolais

300g (11oz) strawberries, sliced

Place the sugar and 100ml (3½fl oz) water in a saucepan on a medium heat. Stir together until just dissolved, then allow to cool for a few minutes. Next, stir in the Burgundy and chill in the fridge for at least 2 hours. Add the sliced strawberries and leave for a further 2 hours in the fridge before serving.

Rachel's Tip: To set as a jelly, soften 1½ sheets of gelatine in cold water for 3–5 minutes, then dissolve the squeezed-out sheets of gelatine in 100ml (3½fl oz) of the warm Burgundy syrup. Keep this syrup out of the fridge while the rest of the syrup chills. When the syrup in the fridge is cold, pour 100ml (3½fl oz) of the cold syrup into the gelatine syrup mix and mix it all back in with the cold syrup. Add the strawberries into the syrup and transfer into pretty glasses to set.

Prosecco and jelly: two of my favourite things. And when combined with raspberries, they make a wickedly celebratory concoction. The reason for putting this in the freezer for the first half an hour is to help set the prosecco bubbles in the jelly. It also works very well with cava.

Prosecco and raspberry jelly

SERVES 4

3 sheets of gelatine

50g (2oz) caster or granulated sugar

375ml bottle of prosecco

125g (4½oz) raspberries

Place your chosen glasses or bowls in the freezer for half an hour. Soften the gelatine sheets in a bowl of cold water for 3–5 minutes.

Place 2 tablespoons of water and the sugar in a saucepan over a medium-low heat. Stir until the sugar dissolves, then remove from the heat.

Remove the gelatine sheets from their soaking water and squeeze out any excess liquid. Transfer the softened gelatine to the hot syrup and stir until dissolved. Set aside to cool for 5 minutes, then pour the prosecco into the syrup. Remove the glasses or bowls from the freezer, pour in the jelly mixture and return to the freezer for half an hour.

Take the glasses out of the freezer and place 8–10 raspberries in each jelly, pressing down slightly. Chill the jellies in the fridge for 2–3 hours until fully set.

Rachel's Tip: The two freezing stages help keep the prosecco bubbles in the jelly. If you prefer, you can use normal white wine and skip these steps.

A granita with gin – what could be more divine?! If you love a slice of cucumber in your gin and tonic, then be sure to include it here. Delicious before or after a meal or simply as a little refreshment on a balmy evening.

Watermelon ginita

SERVES 4–6

500g (1lb 2oz) watermelon flesh (about ¼ watermelon)

30g (1oz) peeled and seeded cucumber (optional)

Juice of 1 lime

100ml (3½fl oz) gin

1–2 tsp sugar, to taste (optional)

Pick out the seeds from the watermelon and discard. Place the flesh in a food processor with the cucumber, if using. Blitz with the lime juice and gin until smooth, then push through a sieve. Taste, and if necessary, add a teaspoon or two of sugar.

Transfer to a freezable container and freeze. Whisk the mixture several times during the freezing process.

Rachel's Tips: Ring the changes on a summer's day and add peaches, nectarines or apricots to the ginita. You can also leave out the gin for a non-alcoholic granita.

Possibly my favourite recipe in the book, this takes its inspiration from the classic Peach Melba, which was created by the King of Chefs, Frenchman Auguste Escoffier, for the Australian opera singer Dame Nellie Melba. Peaches and raspberries are a match made in heaven and this sherbet, which is neither a sorbet nor an ice cream but something in between, is the perfect accompaniment.

Poached peaches with raspberry sherbet

SERVES 4

For the raspberry sherbet

150g (5oz) raspberries, fresh or frozen

150ml (5fl oz) milk

60g (2½oz) caster or granulated sugar

4 tbsp lemon juice

For the poached peaches

100g (3½oz) caster or granulated sugar

4 peaches

Equipment

Ice-cream machine (optional)

To make the sherbet, place the raspberries, milk, sugar and lemon juice in a blender and whiz until smooth. Push through a fine sieve. Taste and add more sugar or lemon juice if necessary – you're tasting for a balance between sweet and sharp.

Freeze in an ice-cream machine according to the manufacturer's instructions. Alternatively, freeze in the freezer and take out three times during freezing to beat with a whisk or fork (to break up the ice crystals) before covering again and placing back in the freezer.

Place the sugar and 100ml (3½fl oz) water in a saucepan and bring to the boil, stirring to dissolve the sugar. Cut the peaches in half, remove the stones and tip the peaches into the syrup. Cover with a lid and cook on a medium heat for 10–12 minutes, until the peaches are tender but not yet falling apart. Then remove from the heat and allow to cool. The skins will have come off during cooking, so remove them completely and discard.

Serve with the raspberry sherbet.

MINI MOUTHFULS

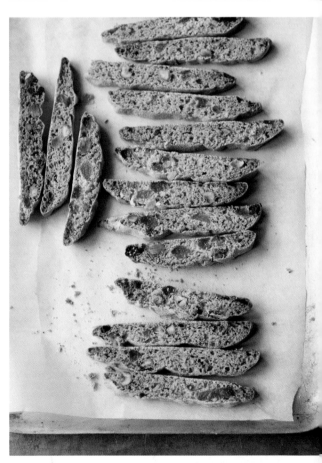

Ginger crunch

Cinnamon cigars

Chocolate and candied orange dates

JR's rose water marshmallows

Ballymaloe vanilla fudge

Chocolate fruit and nut clusters

Baklava

Pistachio, apricot and cardamom biscotti

Sesame and honey halva

A New Zealand classic, these divine little treats are the perfect accompaniment to a great cup of coffee. The crunchy, gingery shortbread base and the smooth ginger fudge topping take no time to throw together, but happily last very well for over a week. They can be cut into squares, fingers or little morsels that you'll just keep going back to, time and time again.

Ginger crunch

MAKES ABOUT 50 MINI TREATS OR 28 SLICES

For the base

225g (8oz) plain flour

100g (3½oz) caster sugar

2 tsp ground ginger

1 tsp baking powder

150g (5oz) butter, cut into cubes

For the topping

150g (5oz) butter

100g (3½oz) golden syrup

300g (11oz) icing sugar

2 tbsp ground ginger

Equipment

23 x 33cm (9 x 13in) tin

Preheat the oven to 180°C/350°F/Gas 4. Line the tin with baking parchment.

Place the flour, caster sugar, ginger and baking powder in a food processor and whiz to mix, then add in the butter and whiz again until it almost comes together. Alternatively, rub the butter into the dry ingredients by hand until the mixture resembles coarse breadcrumbs.

Tip into the prepared baking tin and press to evenly cover the base. Bake for 20 minutes until light golden.

About 5 minutes before the pastry is ready, place the butter and golden syrup in a saucepan on a medium–high heat and melt together. Add in the icing sugar and the ground ginger and cook for just 1–2 minutes until combined.

Pour the warm topping over the cooked base just after it comes out of the oven and allow to cool. Cut into slices or small squares to serve.

Puff pastry, icing sugar and cinnamon – just three simple ingredients. But believe me, these are much more than a sum of their parts. All you need is a pot of coffee and a few friends.

Cinnamon cigars

MAKES 12 CIGARS

1 tsp ground cinnamon

25g (1oz) icing sugar

200g (7oz) puff pastry

Preheat the oven to 220°C (425°F), Gas mark 7. Line a baking tray with baking parchment.

In a small bowl, mix together the cinnamon and icing sugar.

Roll out the puff pastry into a neat rectangle about 20 x 30cm (8 x 12in). Cut it into 12 rectangles, each about 5 x 10cm (2 x 4in). Sprinkle each small rectangle with about ½ teaspoon of the cinnamon sugar, then roll into a little cigar shape. Dust the outside with a little more cinnamon sugar, then place on the baking tray. Place in the fridge to chill for 15 minutes.

Place the tray in the oven and bake for 8–12 minutes until puffed and golden brown.

Rachel's Tip: Perfect for using up scraps of puff pastry.

I absolutely adored visiting the date market in Abu Dhabi, and literally ate my way around. I was intrigued by the huge variety of dates, from small and intense-tasting to plump and toffee-flavoured. There were dates stuffed with everything from caramelised nuts to candied fruit and some were dipped in chocolate, too. I made these when I returned home to give me a little taste of the exotic Middle East.

Chocolate and candied orange dates

MAKES 12 DATES

125g (4½oz) dark chocolate (55–70% cocoa solids), chopped or in pieces/drops

12 dates (Medjool dates are fabulous for this)

12 pieces of candied orange peel, about 1 x 2cm (½ x ¾in) in size, so they fit snugly in the dates

Place the chocolate in a bowl sitting over a saucepan with a few centimetres of water. Bring the water up to the boil, then take off the heat and allow the chocolate to melt slowly.

Meanwhile, place a piece of baking parchment on a baking tray.

Split the dates in half, but not all the way through. Remove the stones and discard, then stuff the dates with a piece (or a few small pieces if that's the size of your peel) of candied peel. Close the dates again, pinching the edges to seal.

Using two forks, dip each date in the melted chocolate, then transfer each one (so they're not touching each other) to the paper-lined tray. Place somewhere cool for the chocolate to set.

JR Ryall is the fabulously talented and super-lovely pastry chef at Ballymaloe House. He creates the most delicious sweet things for the dessert trolley, all with the same sensitivity and elegant touch as that of my husband's grandmother, Myrtle Allen, who opened the restaurant in 1964 and who still presides over the place today. Petits fours are served at the end of every evening meal at Ballymaloe and this recipe is just one of JR's gems.

JR's rose water marshmallows

MAKES ABOUT 90 MARSHMALLOWS

75g (3oz) icing sugar

75g (3oz) cornflour

455g (1lb) caster or granulated sugar

1 tbsp liquid or powdered glucose

9 sheets of gelatine or 9 tsp powdered gelatine

2 egg whites

2 tbsp rose water

Few drops of red food colouring (optional)

Equipment

30 x 20cm (12 x 8in) baking tray and a sugar thermometer

Line the baking tray with baking parchment. Sift the icing sugar and cornflour together.

Place the sugar, glucose and 200ml (7fl oz) water in a heavy-based saucepan. Stir to ensure all of the sugar is wet. Using a pastry brush dipped in water, remove any sugar crystals from the side of the saucepan. Place the saucepan on a medium heat and bring to the boil. Once boiling, do not stir, simply tilt the pan from side to side to ensure that the solution heats evenly until it reaches 127°C (261°F).

Meanwhile, soak the gelatine in 140ml (5fl oz) cold water for 3–5 minutes.

When the boiling syrup reaches 110°C (230°F), start whipping the egg whites in the bowl of an electric food mixer until stiff peaks form.

Add the gelatine and its soaking liquid into the syrup when it reaches 127°C (261°F) and stir with a wooden spoon. The mixture will foam slightly – this is normal. Whisking constantly, pour the hot syrup onto the egg whites and whip on full speed for 5–10 minutes until the marshmallow thickens and the bowl of the mixer has cooled to a tepid heat. Add the rose water and food colouring, if using, and continue to mix just until mixed through.

Cont. overleaf

Spoon the marshmallow mix into the lined baking tray and smooth with a palette knife. Allow to set for about 1–2 hours.

Dust the marshmallows with one-third of the icing sugar and cornflour mix. Turn out onto a work surface, cut into 2cm (¾in) squares and toss in the remaining icing sugar and flour.

These marshmallows will keep for up to 1 week.

Variation: **Raspberry marshmallows**
Omit the rose water and red food colouring and add 1 tsp vanilla extract instead. When you tip the mixture onto the tray, only pour out half, then scatter 250g (9oz) fresh raspberries evenly over the mixture, pour over the other half and allow to set. These are best eaten within 24 hours.

Another variation (too good not to include!): **Coconut marshmallows**
Omit the rose water and red food colouring and add 70ml (3fl oz) Malibu instead. Toast 150g (5oz) desiccated coconut by spreading out on a baking tray and cooking at 170°C (325°F), Gas mark 3 for 4–7 minutes until light golden. Toss the cut marshmallows in the toasted coconut instead of the icing sugar and cornflour.

This is the original fudge recipe that has been made at Ballymaloe House for more than a few decades now. When something is so good, why change it? Crumbly, wickedly sweet and with just the perfect amount of vanilla, this recipe is a knock-out.

Ballymaloe vanilla fudge

MAKES ABOUT 96 SQUARES

225g (8oz) butter

1 x 410g (14½oz) tin of evaporated milk

900g (2lb) caster sugar

3 tsp vanilla extract

Equipment

23 x 33cm (9 x 13in) Swiss roll tin and a sugar thermometer (optional)

Melt the butter in a heavy-based saucepan over a low heat. Add the evaporated milk, 200ml (7fl oz) water, sugar and vanilla extract and stir with a whisk until the sugar is dissolved. Turn up the heat to simmer and stir often for about 35–45 minutes. It's ready when it reaches 115°C (239°F). If you have a sugar thermometer, use it as soon as the mixture boils. If you don't have one, test for the soft ball stage (to do this, place a blob – ½ teaspoon or so – in a small bowl of cold water; as it cools, it will form a soft ball).

Pull off the heat and stir until it thickens and reaches the required consistency, with the saucepan set in a bowl of cold water. Allow to set for 2 minutes and then stir to break up any sugar crystals. Pour into the Swiss roll tin and smooth out with a spatula.

Allow to cool a little, then cut before completely cold.

The simplest of all mini treats to make, these are just a slightly more grown-up version of the birthday party staple: chocolate Rice Krispies cakes. Feel free to play to your heart's content with different filling combinations. Absolutely divine with a cup of coffee or a glass of liqueur at the end of a meal, or just a quick treat on the run.

Chocolate fruit and nut clusters

MAKES 25 SMALL CLUSTERS

125g (4½oz) dark chocolate (55–70% cocoa solids),

50g (2oz) toasted nuts, chopped (see tip on page 28)

50g (2oz) dried fruits, chopped

Place a sheet of baking parchment on a baking tray.

To melt the chocolate, place the chocolate in a bowl sitting over a saucepan with a few centimetres of water. Bring the water up to the boil, then take off the heat and allow the chocolate to melt slowly.

Stir in your chosen nuts and dried fruit, then use two teaspoons to make small clusters on the paper. Place somewhere cool to set.

Combinations that work well are

Pecan and cranberry
Hazelnut and fig
Pistachio and apricot
Almond and date
White chocolate, candied orange peel and stem ginger

Ever since I backpacked around a few of the Greek islands when I was twenty, I have adored baklava. Sweet, a little bit spicy and oh-so-nutty, this is well worth making for the baklava-lover in your life. Even if that person is you.

Baklava

MAKES ABOUT 28 BAKLAVA

110g (4oz) caster sugar

200g (7oz) ground almonds

3 tsp ground cinnamon

150g (5oz) butter, melted

200g (7oz) filo pastry

For the syrup

340g (12oz) caster or granulated sugar

200g (7oz) honey

½ cinnamon stick

8 cloves

Equipment

20cm (8in) square tin

Preheat the oven to 180°C (350°F), Gas mark 4.

In a bowl, mix together the sugar, almonds and cinnamon.

Line the base and sides of the tin with baking parchment. Brush the lined tin with some of the melted butter. Cut the filo the same size as the tin, then place four layers of filo in the base of the tin, brushing more melted butter over each layer.

Sprinkle half of the almond mix on top of the last buttered sheet, place one more sheet on top and butter it, and then sprinkle over the remaining half of the almond mix. If you have any offcuts of filo pastry, use these in the first four layers of pastry.

Set another four to six layers of filo on top, buttering between each layer. Cut the baklava diagonally into 3–4cm (1¼–1½in) diamonds in the tray.

Sprinkle with a teaspoon of water, then place in the oven and bake for 1½ hours until golden.

While the baklava bakes, make the syrup. Mix all of the ingredients together with 175ml (6fl oz) water in a saucepan and place over a medium–high heat. Bring to the boil and boil for 10 minutes.

When the baklava is baked, pour over the boiling syrup.

Cut down through the baklava where you have cut before baking. Set aside and allow to cool for a few hours or overnight.

Rachel's Tip: If the square tin has a removable base, the baklava in the tin should be placed on a baking tray in case it seeps a little as it cools.

Biscotti are such good-humoured little biscuits. This recipe makes loads, you can play around with the different fruit, nuts and spices, and they last for weeks in an airtight box or jar. I particularly love the dried apricot, pistachio and cardamom combo here and, of course, they can also be dipped in melted chocolate.

Pistachio, apricot and cardamom biscotti

MAKES ABOUT 40 BISCOTTI

100g (3½oz) plain flour, plus extra for dusting

100g (3½oz) caster sugar

1 tsp baking powder

½ tsp ground cardamom seeds

1 egg, beaten

50g (2oz) shelled, roasted and salted pistachios

50g (2oz) dried apricots, sliced into 6 pieces

Preheat the oven to 170°C (325°F), Gas mark 3.

Sift together the flour, sugar and baking powder into a large bowl. Stir in the ground cardamom, then mix in the beaten egg to form a soft dough. Next, mix in the pistachios and apricots.

Flour your hands, then turn the dough onto a lightly floured work surface and form into a sausage about 30cm (12in) long and 3cm (1¼in) wide. Place on a baking tray and bake for about 25 minutes, then remove and allow to cool on a wire rack for 5 minutes.

Cut into slices about 5mm (¼in) thick, then lay flat on the tray and bake for a further 10 minutes. Turn all the biscotti over on the tray, then return to the oven and continue to bake for 10 minutes more. They should be a light golden colour on both cut sides.

Cool on a wire rack, then transfer to an airtight container where they will keep for up to three weeks.

Halva, which in Arabic means 'sweet' or 'desserts', is made in many parts of the world, including the Middle East, Asia, North Africa and Eastern Europe. There are a few different types, but perhaps the most well-known one is that made from the über-nutritious sesame seed paste, tahini. The last time I was in Istanbul I ate nearly my body weight of the stuff! Happily, it's very easy and quick to make, too.

Sesame and honey halva

SERVES 8–10

300g (11oz) honey

250g (9oz) light tahini paste (stirred well to mix in any excess oil)

Equipment

900g (2lb) loaf tin

Sugar thermometer (optional)

Line the base and sides of a loaf tin with baking parchment.

Place the honey in a small to medium saucepan on a high heat and bring up to the boil. Continue to boil for 8–10 minutes, stirring regularly. It's ready when it reaches 115°C (239°F). If you have a sugar thermometer, use it as soon as the honey boils. If you don't have one, test for the soft ball stage (to do this, place a blob – ½ teaspoon or so – in a small bowl of cold water; as it cools, it will form a soft ball).

Cool for 3 minutes off the heat, then stir in the tahini paste and pour into the lined tin.

When completely cool, cover and place in the fridge. Leave to sit for 36 hours to allow the small sugar crystals that give halva its distinctive texture time to develop.

Cut into chunks or slabs to serve.

SOMETHING FOR THE AFTERNOON

Cinnamon spiral buns

Vanilla custard slice

Lavender sponge cake with rhubarb curd

Double chocolate pecan blondies

Sinead's Louise slice

Banana, ginger and golden syrup bread

Mango and lime drizzle cake

Salted caramel cupcakes

Lemon slab cake

Orange and almond cake

Lemon yoghurt polenta cake

Pear and nutmeg cake

Afternoon fruit brack

If ever I open a cute little tea shop, these will always be on the menu. A large 'cake' of individual buns, each their own spiral around sweet, sticky cinnamon butter, all topped with a drizzle of icing.

Cinnamon spiral buns

SERVES 10

80g (3oz) butter, plus extra for greasing

15g (½oz) fresh yeast or 1 x 7g (¼oz) sachet of fast-action yeast or 2 tsp of dried yeast

150–200ml (5–7fl oz) tepid water

450g (1lb) strong white flour, plus extra for dusting

Pinch of salt

35g (1¼oz) caster sugar

1 egg, beaten

For the cinnamon butter

125g (4½oz) butter

125g (4½oz) icing sugar

1 tsp ground cinnamon

For the icing

100g (3½oz) icing sugar

Equipment

23cm (9in) spring-form cake tin

Line the base of the cake tin with baking parchment and butter the sides. Dissolve the yeast in 50ml (2fl oz) of the water. Allow to sit for a few minutes.

In a separate bowl, sift together the flour and salt and add in the sugar. Rub in the butter with your fingers, then add in the egg. Add the yeast and combine with enough water to form a fairly soft dough. Knead well for 5–10 minutes until the dough becomes smooth and springs back when pressed – this will only take 5 minutes if using a food mixer with a dough hook. Place in a bowl and cover with cling film, then allow to rise until doubled in size (about 1½ hours). Knock back by kneading for 1–2 minutes, then rest briefly before rolling into a 30 x 40cm (12 x 16in) rectangle on a floured work surface.

Next, make the cinnamon butter. Beat the butter until very soft, then add in the icing sugar and cinnamon. Spread this cinnamon butter over the surface of the dough rectangle. Starting at the long end, and using two hands, roll the dough away from you. When it's rolled, cut ten slices, each about 3cm (1¼in) wide (the dough will have shrunk back a little). Place cut side up in the tin, with nine around the edge and one in the centre. Cover with a tea towel and place somewhere warm to rise for about 1 hour (or in the fridge overnight) or until the buns are doubled in size and when you press gently with your finger, your mark stays indented.

Preheat the oven to 180°C (350°F), Gas mark 4. When the buns have risen, take off the tea towel and place in the oven for 30–40 minutes until cooked in the centre. Allow to sit for 5 minutes before taking out of the tin and placing on a wire rack.

Make the icing by mixing together the icing sugar with 1–1½ tablespoons water, adding just enough water to form a drizzling consistency. Finish the buns by drizzling over the icing in a criss-cross pattern, then allow to set.

Probably the most 'retro' recipe in the book – two layers of buttery puff pastry sandwiching sweet vanilla custard and topped with a white glacé icing. Bring back the custard slice, I say!

Vanilla custard slice

MAKES 8 SLICES

300g (11oz) puff pastry

For the crème pâtissière (pastry cream)

375ml (13fl oz) milk

1 vanilla pod, split down the middle, or 1 tsp vanilla extract

75g (3oz) caster sugar

3 egg yolks

40g (1½oz) cornflour

Pinch of salt

25g (1oz) butter, cut into small cubes

For the icing

150g (5oz) icing sugar

50g (2oz) dark chocolate (55–70% cocoa solids), roughly chopped

First, make the crème pâtissière. Pour the milk into a saucepan and add the split vanilla pod, if using. If using the vanilla extract, add it in with the butter at the end. Bring the milk mixture to the boil, then remove from the heat.

Whisk the sugar, egg yolks and cornflour together in a large bowl for about 2–3 minutes using a hand-held electric beater or electric food mixer until pale and light.

Next, pour the hot milk onto the egg mixture, whisking continuously, then return the mixture to the saucepan. Cook the mixture over a low heat, stirring continuously, until the mixture boils and becomes thick. It will just come to the boil. If it boils unevenly or too quickly, it may become lumpy, in which case use a whisk to mix until smooth again.

Remove the custard from the heat and pour into a bowl (push the mixture through a sieve if there are any lumps). Add the pinch of salt and the butter and stir until melted and thoroughly combined.

Leave to cool, cover with cling film and then chill before using.

Preheat the oven to 220°C (425°F), Gas mark 7. Line two baking trays with baking parchment.

Divide the pastry into two equal pieces and roll out both pieces to 20cm (8in) square and 3mm (⅛in) thick. If you're using a sheet of ready-rolled pastry, the chances are it may be a rectangle measuring 18 x 46cm (7 x 18in). In which case, cut it in half so that you have two 23 x 18cm (9 x 7in) pieces, then roll each piece to about 20cm (8in) square. Place each pastry sheet on a lined baking tray, prick each piece a few times with a fork and chill for 10–15 minutes.

Bake the pastry sheets for 10–15 minutes or until golden brown and crisp. Set aside to cool.

Place one pastry sheet on a lined baking tray (reserve the prettiest piece for the top).

Spread the crème pâtissière evenly over the pastry on the baking tray, then place the other piece of pastry on top. Refrigerate while making the icing.

For the icing, sift the icing sugar into a bowl. Stir in 3–4 teaspoons cold water – just enough to give you a thick, drizzling consistency – and set aside.

Place the chocolate in a bowl sitting over a saucepan with a few centimetres of water. Bring the water up to the boil, then take off the heat and allow the chocolate to melt slowly. Once cooled slightly, transfer the melted chocolate into a piping bag fitted with a very small, plain nozzle.

Take the custard slice from the fridge and spread the icing over the top layer of pastry. A palette knife or spatula dipped into boiling water is handy for helping the icing to spread.

Using the piping bag, draw ten parallel lines with the melted chocolate along the top of the icing in one direction. Using the top of a toothpick, 'drag' the lines of chocolate across the icing in alternating directions at about 2cm (¾in) intervals to create a feathered effect. Place the slice back in the fridge to set. It will be easier to cut if it's been in the fridge for at least 2 hours.

Cut the finished custard slice into eight pieces, trimming the edges if you wish. Using the foil, carefully lift the portioned vanilla slices out of the tray and serve.

Rachel's Tip: If you prefer, you can just drizzle the icing and leave out the chocolate.

A gorgeously light and perfumed sponge with a seriously rhubarby curd, this has all the flavours of early summer.

Lavender sponge cake with rhubarb curd

SERVES 8

For the lavender sponge

6 eggs

175g (6oz) caster or granulated sugar

Pinch of salt

150g (5oz) plain flour

2 tsp lavender buds, finely chopped (off the stems)

125g (4½oz) butter, melted, plus extra for greasing

For the rhubarb curd

550g (1lb 3oz) rhubarb, cut in to 1cm (½in) slices (weigh when sliced and trimmed)

200g (7oz) caster or granulated sugar

75g (3oz) butter

3 eggs, whisked

Icing sugar and chopped lavender buds, to decorate

Cont. opposite

Preheat the oven to 180°C (350°F), Gas mark 4. Line the base of three 18cm (7in) cake tins and butter the sides.

To make the sponge, place the eggs, sugar and salt in a bowl and, using an electric whisk, beat for 5–8 minutes until tripled in volume, light and fluffy. Sift in the flour and fold into the light mousse-like mixture with the lavender and the melted butter, working quickly so that not too much air escapes.

Divide the cake mixture among the three tins and place in the oven. Bake for 22–25 minutes until light golden and a skewer inserted into the centre comes out clean. Take out of the oven and let sit in the tin for a few minutes before taking out and cooling on a wire rack.

Next, make the curd. Place the rhubarb and 50g (2oz) of the sugar in a saucepan on a medium heat, stirring every so often. Cook for 6–8 minutes until the rhubarb has softened, broken up completely and the mixture has thickened to a pulp.

Pour into a sieve sitting over a bowl and push the mixture through the sieve into the bowl, making sure to scrape the underside of the sieve to get every last bit.

Next, place the butter in the cleaned saucepan on a low–medium heat and allow to melt. Take off the heat and add in the eggs, the rest of the sugar and the rhubarb purée. Put back on a low heat and stir continuously for 5–7 minutes until thickened. Take off the heat, tip into a bowl and allow to cool.

Equipment

3 x 18cm (7in) cake tins with 3cm (1¼in) sides

When ready to assemble, place one cake (save the cake with the best-looking top for the top) upside down on a plate or cake stand. Place half of the curd on top and spread it out (I like to allow the curd to drip slightly over the edges). Put the next cake, right side up, on top, then cover with the second half of the curd, as before. Finally, top with the third (and best-looking) cake. Dust with icing sugar and decorate with some more chopped lavender, if you wish.

Rachel's Tip: If you wish, you can also put whipped cream between the layers with the rhubarb curd, though only if the cake is all going to be eaten on the day it's made. Otherwise, serve it with some softly whipped cream on the side. Use the pinkest rhubarb you can find to get this beautiful colour.

Nearly as famous as both Debbie Harry and Marilyn Monroe put together, blondies, or blond brownies as they're sometimes known, have a base of brown sugar rather than melted chocolate through them. Soft, fudgy and oh-so-sweet, these will definitely make you sing.

Double chocolate pecan blondies

MAKES 16 BLONDIES

115g (4oz) butter

200g (7oz) soft light brown sugar

1 large egg

1 tsp vanilla extract

125g (4½oz) plain flour

Pinch of salt

75g (3oz) dark chocolate drops (or chopped chocolate)

50g (2oz) white chocolate drops (or chopped chocolate)

75g (3oz) pecans, chopped

Equipment

20cm (8in) square cake tin

Preheat the oven to 180°C (350°F), Gas mark 4. Line the base and sides of the cake tin with baking parchment.

Melt the butter, pour into a mixing bowl, then add the sugar and the egg and whisk to mix together. Next, add in the remaining ingredients and stir to mix. Tip into the prepared tin and bake for 25–28 minutes until dry on top, but still ever so slightly unset in the centre under the crust.

Allow to cool for at least 20 minutes before cutting into squares.

My friend Sinead Doran used to live in New Zealand. Since she's come back, she has been making these delicious biscuits with a shortbread base, jam filling and meringue topping. Every time I mentioned I loved them, she always said they were 'Louise slice'. I kept meaning to ask her for the actual recipe, as I didn't know who Louise was anyway. It turns out that Louise slice, or Louise cake as it's sometimes called, is a New Zealand national treasure. The recipe varies hugely, but this is Sinead's version and I love it.

Sinead's Louise slice

MAKES ABOUT
32 SLICES

75g (3oz) soft butter

35g (1¼oz) caster sugar

2 eggs, separated

150g (5oz) plain flour

1 tsp baking powder

175g (6oz) raspberry jam

For the topping

115g (4oz) caster sugar

35g (1¼oz) desiccated coconut

Equipment

23 x 30cm (9 x 12in) Swiss roll tin

Preheat the oven to 180°C (350°F), Gas mark 4. Line the Swiss roll tin with baking parchment.

Place the butter in a bowl and beat until soft, then add in the caster sugar, then the egg yolks (keep the whites for the topping).

Sift in the flour and baking powder and bring together to form quite a dry, crumbly dough. Spread out in the lined tray and press down to even it out. Spread the raspberry jam over the top.

Using a hand-held electric beater, whisk the sugar for the topping and the egg whites until they hold stiff peaks, then fold in the coconut and spread over the jam, being careful not to disturb the jam.

Bake in the oven for 25–30 minutes until light golden and crisp on top.

I think my love for this comfortingly sweet and delicious tea-time loaf has superseded that of banana bread. If you're a banana-bread lover, then this one is for you.

Banana, ginger and golden syrup bread

SERVES 8

110g (3½oz) butter

50g (2oz) soft brown sugar

125g (4½oz) golden syrup

2 eggs

125g (4½oz) plain flour

2 tsp baking powder

2 tbsp ground ginger

2 medium bananas, mashed

Equipment

900g (2lb) loaf tin

Preheat the oven to 180°C (350°F), Gas mark 4. Line the base and sides of the loaf tin with baking parchment.

In a bowl, cream the butter until soft, then beat in the brown sugar and golden syrup. Beat in the eggs one at a time. The mixture will look sloppy and curdled, but don't worry. Sift in the flour, baking powder and ginger and fold together.

Next, mix in the mashed bananas to form a soft, wet dough. Pour into the loaf tin, place in the oven and bake for about 45 minutes until risen, golden brown and a skewer inserted into the centre comes out clean.

When you think of how much just a small squeeze of lime transforms a juicy chunk of exotic mango, it's not surprising that this cake works so well. A delicious drizzle cake with a totally tropical taste.

Mango and lime drizzle cake

SERVES 6–8

100g (3½oz) butter, plus extra for greasing

200g (7oz) caster sugar

Finely grated zest and juice of 1 lime

2 eggs

125g (4½oz) plain flour

1 tsp baking powder

250g (9oz) mango flesh, finely chopped (from 1 medium-sized mango)

75g (3oz) granulated sugar

Equipment

20cm (8in) spring-form cake tin

Preheat the oven to 170°C (325°F), Gas mark 3. Rub the base and the sides of the spring-form cake tin with soft butter. Do not line with a disc of baking parchment and make sure the base is upside down so there is no lip and the cake can slide off easily when cooked.

In a bowl, cream together the butter and caster sugar with the lime zest. Add the eggs one by one, stirring well after each is added. Then sift in the flour and baking powder and mix to combine. Stir in the mango flesh and transfer to the prepared tin. Place in the oven and bake for 50–60 minutes until a skewer inserted into the centre comes out clean.

Meanwhile, mix together the granulated sugar and the juice of the lime in a little bowl.

When the cake is cooked, take it out of the oven, use a skewer to make holes all over the top of the cake, then spoon over the sugary lime juices. As the cake cools, this will form a zingy, crunchy top.

When the cake has cooled down to room temperature, run a small sharp knife around the outside of the cake, then unclip and remove the sides of the tin. Use a palette knife to slide the cake off the base of the tin and onto your chosen plate or cake stand.

As you bite into these cupcakes, you get three different textures all at once: salted caramel frosting sitting over a buttery, crumbly bun oozing with a sweet-and-salty toffee sauce. What's not to love?

Salted caramel cupcakes

MAKES 12 CUPCAKES

For the salted
caramel sauce

225g (8oz) caster or
granulated sugar

75g (3oz) butter

100ml (3½fl oz) double
or regular cream

1 tsp salt

For the cupcakes

150g (5oz) plain flour

25g (1oz) cornflour

1 tsp baking powder

150g (5oz) caster sugar

Pinch of salt

100g (3½oz) butter, cut
into cubes

100ml (3½fl oz) milk

1 tsp vanilla extract

2 eggs

Cont. opposite

Preheat the oven to 170°C (325°F), Gas mark 3.

First, make the salted caramel sauce. Place the sugar in a saucepan on a medium heat. Allow to heat up. As it gets quite hot you'll notice the sugar melting and starting to caramelise around the sides of the saucepan. Swirl or gently shake the pan every so often until all the sugar turns a deep golden brown and is smooth and glossy. You might need to stir it a little bit with a wooden spoon to bash out any sugary lumps. Stir in the butter and the cream and keep stirring until it is smooth again – it might take a minute or so. Add in the salt and remove from the heat.

Next, make the cupcakes. Place 12 paper cases in a cupcake/muffin tray. Sift the flour, cornflour and baking powder into a bowl, then mix in the sugar and salt. Rub in the butter. Place the milk, vanilla extract and eggs in a separate bowl and whisk to mix. Pour into the dry ingredients and bring together with a wooden spoon. Fill each paper case about two-thirds or three-quarters full, then bake in the oven for about 20–25 minutes until cooked in the centre. There should be a light spring when you gently press the centres with your finger. Take out of the oven and allow the cupcakes to cool.

While the cupcakes are cooling, make the salted caramel buttercream icing. Place all the ingredients in a mixing bowl with 175g (6oz) of the salted caramel sauce (reserving any remaining sauce for later) and beat for 10–20 seconds to mix together until light and fluffy. Set aside.

When the cupcakes have cooled, using a small, sharp knife, cut a piece out of the centre of each cupcake, measuring about 1–2cm (½–¾in) in size. Discard (or eat!) the cut-out bits of cake, then fill the 'holes' with some of the reserved salted caramel sauce.

For the salted caramel
buttercream icing

475g (1lb 1oz) icing sugar

200g (7oz) butter, at
room temperature

¼ tsp salt

½ tsp vanilla extract

Equipment

12-hole cupcake/muffin
tray and a piping bag with
a plain or fluted nozzle
(or even a plastic bag
with the corner cut out)

Place the salted caramel buttercream icing in the piping bag and pipe in a
swirl over each cupcake. Drizzle any remaining salted caramel sauce over
each iced cupcake to decorate.

Rachel's Tip: If the cooled, salted caramel sauce is too thick to drizzle over
the cupcakes, you can thin it out by stirring in a tiny trickle of water.

This is the perfect picnic treat – delicious lemon sponge topped with an intensely citrussy icing. All you need is a blanket and flask of tea.

Lemon slab cake

MAKES ABOUT
24 'SLABS'

225g (8oz) butter

300g (11oz) caster or granulated sugar

2 eggs

250g (9oz) crème fraîche

Juice and finely grated zest of 1 lemon

225g (8oz) plain flour

2 tsp baking powder

For the icing

225g (8oz) icing sugar

Juice of ½ lemon

Equipment

23 x 30cm (9 x 12in) Swiss roll tin

Preheat the oven to 180°C (350°F), Gas mark 4. Line the base and sides of the tin with baking parchment.

Melt the butter on a low heat, then pour into a mixing bowl. Add in the sugar and whisk to combine, then mix in the eggs, crème fraîche, lemon juice and zest.

Sift in the flour and baking powder and fold in to mix, then tip into the prepared tin. Place in the oven and bake for 25–30 minutes or until a skewer inserted into the centre comes out clean. Allow to cool completely before icing.

To make the icing, sift the icing sugar into a bowl and add the lemon juice gradually – you may not need it all. If it's still too stiff when you've added it all, then add a tiny bit of water to bring it to a spreadable consistency.

Spread the icing over the top of the cooled cake, allow to set (about 20 minutes), then cut into slices to serve.

This is one of my favourite cakes. The ground almonds bring a wonderful moistness to the sponge, which is made even more delicious with the rich orange curd lying seductively over the top.

Orange and almond cake

SERVES 6–8

For the cake

225g (8oz) butter, plus extra for greasing

225g (8oz) caster sugar

3 large eggs

Juice and finely grated zest of 1 orange

115g (4oz) plain flour

1 tsp baking powder

115g (4oz) ground almonds

For the curd

50g (2oz) butter

Juice and finely grated zest of 2 oranges

110g (4oz) caster or granulated sugar

2 eggs

2 egg yolks

Equipment

23cm (9in) spring-form cake tin

Preheat the oven to 180°C (350°F), Gas mark 4. Line the base of the tin with baking parchment and grease the sides.

Place the butter and sugar in a bowl, then use a wooden spoon or the paddle attachment of an electric food mixer to cream together until light and fluffy. Beat in the eggs one by one, along with the orange juice and zest. Sift in the flour and baking powder, then gently fold in with the ground almonds.

Tip into the tin, then bake for 20–25 minutes until the centre feels springy to the touch. Place on a wire rack to cool, then remove from the tin.

To make the curd, place the butter in a medium pan on a medium–low heat. When melted, whisk in the orange juice and zest, sugar, eggs and egg yolks. Cook, stirring constantly, until thick enough to coat the back of a spoon. Pour into a jug and serve with the cake.

I'm always intrigued by the texture that different ingredients bring to a cake. In this Italian-inspired recipe, the natural yoghurt gives a lovely soft crumb and an ever-so-slightly tangy flavour, while the fine polenta lends a distinctly gritty bite. If you plan on keeping this cake for more than one day, then I would recommend replacing the mascarpone icing with the lemon glacé icing from the Lemon slab cake recipe (see page 147).

Lemon yoghurt polenta cake

SERVES 8

75ml (3fl oz) sunflower oil, plus extra for greasing

2 eggs

125g (4½oz) natural yoghurt

Juice and finely grated zest of 2 lemons

175g (6oz) plain flour

300g (11oz) caster sugar

175g (6oz) fine polenta (cornmeal)

2 tsp baking powder

Pinch of salt

For the lemon mascarpone icing

250g (9oz) tub of mascarpone

Juice of 1 lemon

75g (3oz) icing sugar

Equipment

23cm (9in) spring-form cake tin

Preheat the oven to 180°C (350°F), Gas mark 4. Line the base of the cake tin with baking parchment and brush a little sunflower oil around the inside.

First, make the cake. Crack the eggs into a bowl with the natural yoghurt, oil, lemon juice and zest. Whisk together to mix well, then stir in the flour, caster sugar, fine polenta, baking powder and salt.

Tip into the prepared tin and bake for 35–40 minutes until a skewer inserted into the centre comes out clean. When cooked, remove from the oven and allow to sit in the tin for 20 minutes before taking out of the tin to finish cooling.

To make the icing, whisk all ingredients together in a bowl and set aside until the cake is cool.

When ready to ice the cake, use a long-bladed (and serrated if possible) knife to split the cake in half and place the bottom half on a plate or cake stand. I find the base of the cake tin handy for sliding under and transporting each half. Spread enough of the icing to cover the bottom half (like generously buttering a piece of bread), then cover with the top half. Ice the top of the cake.

This cake can be stored (if you're keeping it any longer than a day) covered in the fridge to keep the mascarpone fresh, but make sure you bring it up to room temperature before eating it.

This recipe is inspired by a version of an old classic Dutch apple cake that's been made at Ballymaloe for nearly half a century. It's brilliant as a dessert or a perfect accompaniment to a tea or coffee.

Pear and nutmeg cake

Serves 8

2 eggs

175g (6oz) caster sugar

½ tsp vanilla extract

75g (3oz) butter

75ml (3fl oz) milk

125g (4½oz) plain flour

½ tsp ground nutmeg

2 tsp baking powder

2 pears, peeled, cored and sliced

25g (1oz) caster or granulated sugar, for sprinkling

Equipment

900g (2lb) loaf tin

Preheat the oven to 200°C (400°F), Gas mark 6. Line the base and sides of the loaf tin with baking parchment.

Using a hand-held electric beater, whisk the eggs, caster sugar and vanilla extract in a large bowl until the mixture is thick and mousse-like (this will take about 5 minutes).

Melt the butter in a saucepan with the milk, then pour onto the eggs, whisking all the time. Sift in the flour, nutmeg and baking powder and fold carefully into the batter so that there are no lumps of flour. Pour the mixture into the prepared tin and smooth the surface.

Arrange the pear slices over the batter. They will sink to the bottom (this is meant to happen!). Sprinkle with the remaining sugar and bake in the oven for 10 minutes.

Reduce the oven temperature to 180°C (350°F), Gas mark 4, and bake for a further 30–35 minutes or until well risen, golden brown and a skewer inserted into the centre comes out clean.

Allow to sit in the tin for 20 minutes before taking out. Cut into slices to serve.

This takes its name from the traditional Irish Barmbrack, or Bairín Breac, a sweet yeast bread with dried fruit that's served at Halloween. While this version contains no yeast, it is jam packed with lots of lovely dried fruit that will keep it delicious for more than a week

Afternoon fruit brack

SERVES 8

Juice and finely grated zest of 1 orange

25g (1oz) dried apricots, chopped into roughly 5mm (¼in) pieces

25g (1oz) dried cranberries, cut in half

25g (1oz) dried figs, chopped into roughly 5mm (¼in) pieces

25g (1oz) dried dates, chopped into roughly 5mm (¼in) pieces

25g (1oz) crystallised or stem ginger, finely chopped

150g (5oz) caster or granulated sugar

200g (7oz) butter

3 eggs

250g (9oz) plain flour

1 tsp baking powder

Equipment

900g (2lb) loaf tin

Preheat the oven to 180°C (350°F), Gas mark 4. Line the base and sides of the loaf tin with baking parchment.

Pour the juice of the orange into a small saucepan and add all the dried fruit. Place over a medium heat and bring just to the boil, then remove from the heat and transfer to a small bowl to cool.

Place the orange zest in a large bowl with the sugar and butter. Cream together the butter and sugar, then add the eggs one by one, beating all the time. Sift in the flour and baking powder and fold just to mix, then stir in the juice and the fruit.

Transfer the mixture to the prepared loaf tin, place in the oven and bake for about 50 minutes until golden and a skewer inserted into the centre comes out clean.

INDULGENT
& DECADENT

Honey soufflés

Chocolate and hazelnut praline ice cream

Lavender and honey panna cotta

Apple crumble ice cream

Gooey date and stem ginger pudding

Chocolate coconut cake

Layered mocha mousse coffee meringue

American chocolate fudge pie

Honey semifreddo with butter toffee figs

Double chocolate mousse cake

Pistachio and saffron kulfi

Date and almond tart

Date, cardamom and ginger upside-down cake

Drops au chocolat

People seem to think soufflés are extremely difficult to make, but really they are not. It's more about the timing. In this recipe, I show you how to cook them in advance for entertaining, which makes them a deliciously convenient dessert. I adore the contrast of textures and temperatures that you get here, with the cold, creamy Milk ice cream sitting on top of the hot, light, fluffy soufflé.

Honey soufflés

SERVES 4

For the moulds

15g (½oz) butter

25g (1oz) caster sugar

For the soufflés

125ml (4½fl oz) milk

Finely grated zest of
1 small lemon

2 eggs

50g (2oz) honey

1 tbsp cornflour

Pinch of salt

25g (1oz) caster sugar

For the top of
the soufflés

15g (½oz) caster sugar

Equipment

4 x 100ml (3½fl oz)
capacity soufflé moulds
or ovenproof cups

Cont. overleaf

Rub the 15g (½oz) butter around the insides of the soufflé moulds, then dust with the 25g (1oz) sugar. This will create a lovely light crust on the outside of the soufflés. Set aside until later.

Place the milk and the lemon zest in a saucepan on a low–medium heat and bring to the boil, then set aside.

Meanwhile, separate the eggs and place the whites in a mixing bowl and the yolks in another bowl. Into the yolks add the honey, cornflour and salt and whisk until thoroughly mixed. Pour the milk through a sieve and onto the egg yolk mixture, whisking as you pour and making sure it's properly mixed. Pour back into the milk saucepan and place on a medium heat, whisking all the time. It will thicken as it heats up. Don't stop whisking or you'll get a lumpy custard. Once it's thickened and smooth, take it off the heat and transfer into a bowl to cool a little until it's tepid. This may take up to about 10 minutes. Stir it regularly to cool it faster. If there are any lumps, push the custard through a sieve.

When the custard has cooled, you can start whisking the egg whites. Whisk for a minute or two until they turn frothy, then add the caster sugar gradually, whisking all the time until they form stiff peaks. Take a quarter of the egg white mixture and, using a large metal spoon or a spatula, fold it into the custard. When it is thoroughly mixed in, tip the remaining egg white into the custard and fold in very gently, trying not to knock out any air.

Divide the mixture into the four prepared soufflé moulds, making sure you smooth over the tops with a spatula or palette knife. Run your thumb and index finger around the edges to 'clean' the sides. This helps the soufflé to rise evenly. Clean off any mixture that may have dripped onto the sides of the moulds.

The soufflés can now either be baked, stored for later in the fridge for up to 3 hours or stored in the freezer for up to 1 week (cover them with cling film once they're frozen or place them in a plastic storage box).

To bake the soufflés, preheat the oven to 180°C (350°F), Gas mark 4, and place a baking tray in the oven to preheat, too. If using frozen soufflés, remove them from the freezer 1 hour before baking.

Scatter the 15g (½oz) of sugar over the top of the soufflés and bake for 10–15 minutes until they are golden brown on top and have risen 1–2cm (½–¾in) above the tops of the moulds. The baking time will vary depending on the size of the soufflé moulds, but when you gently press the centre of a soufflé with your finger, it should have a very light spring.

Remove from the oven and place on plates. Dust the tops of the soufflés with icing sugar and carefully place a scoop of Milk ice cream (see page 77) on top. Serve immediately.

Rachel's Tip: A baked soufflé waits for nobody, so make sure your guests are sitting at the table before the soufflés are served. This is because the beautiful light soufflés will start to sink 1 or 2 minutes after they come out of the oven!

A no-holds-barred rich chocolate ice cream with crunchy, caramelised hazelnuts swirled throughout. A delicious combination of textures and flavours in one bowl.

Chocolate and hazelnut praline ice cream

SERVES 10–12

For the praline

100g (3½oz) caster or granulated sugar

100g (3½oz) hazelnuts

For the ice cream

600ml (1 pint) double or regular cream

100g (3½oz) caster or granulated sugar

4 egg yolks

1 tsp vanilla extract

150g (5oz) dark chocolate (55–70% cocoa solids)

Equipment

Sugar thermometer (optional)

First, make the praline. Line a baking tray with baking parchment and set aside. Place the sugar in a frying pan and scatter the hazelnuts over the sugar. Place on a medium heat, not stirring but swirling the pan every so often to caramelise the sugar evenly. Cook until the sugar has completely melted and is a deep golden colour. Swirl the pan again so that the hazelnuts are coated in the caramel.

Transfer the coated nuts to the prepared baking tray and allow to cool completely. Once cool, break up the praline using your hands, then place in a food processor and whiz until it resembles coarse breadcrumbs.

Next, make the ice cream. Whisk the cream until it is just holding a soft peak. Place in the fridge until later. Combine the sugar and 200ml (7fl oz) water in a small saucepan, then stir over a medium heat until the sugar is completely dissolved. Remove the spoon and boil the syrup until it reaches the 'thread' stage, 106–113°C (223–235°F). If you don't have a sugar thermometer, the mixture should look thick and syrupy, and when a metal spoon is dipped in, the last drops of syrup will form thin threads.

Meanwhile, place the egg yolks in the bowl of an electric food mixer and whisk until pale and fluffy. When the syrup is at the correct temperature, gradually, and on a slow speed, pour the boiling syrup over the egg yolks, whisking constantly. Once all the syrup is incorporated, turn the speed up to high, add the vanilla extract, and continue to whisk until the mixture is a thick, pale mousse. It will hold a figure of eight.

While you are whisking the egg mousse, place the chocolate in a heatproof bowl over a saucepan of water on a medium heat. Bring the water just up to the boil, then take off the heat and allow the chocolate to melt slowly.

Allow to cool slightly, then add some of the mousse to the chocolate and stir quickly; add more, then combine them together thoroughly. Don't panic if it starts to seize – keep mixing and it will loosen. Now fold in the softly whipped cream. Place in a freezable container, cover and put in the freezer.

After an hour and a half, as the ice cream is just beginning to set, stir in three-quarters of the praline, then return to the freezer to set completely for about 6 hours or overnight. Serve with the remaining praline over the top.

A delicious and elegant dessert to serve on a balmy evening or, indeed, at any time of the year. Lavender, honey and cream are a most delicious combination. This is summer on a plate.

Lavender and honey panna cotta

SERVES 4

10 stalks of lavender (2 tsp buds if already off the stalk)

300ml (½ pint) double or regular cream

40g (1½oz) honey

1 sheet of gelatine

Fresh raspberries or poached peaches (page 96), to serve

Pick the flower buds from the lavender stalks and place in a saucepan with the cream and honey. Place on a medium heat and bring just to the boil, then remove from the heat and allow to infuse for 10 minutes.

Place the gelatine sheet in a bowl of cold water for 3–5 minutes, until softened. Remove the gelatine from its soaking water and squeeze out any excess liquid.

Rewarm the cream mixture and drop in the softened gelatine, stir to dissolve, then strain through a sieve and divide into four serving glasses or little pots. Leave in the fridge to set for about 3 or 4 hours.

Serve with fresh raspberries or poached peaches.

When you think of how delicious a freshly baked apple crumble tastes when it has a scoop of vanilla ice cream slowly melting into it, it's not surprising that this works so well.

Apple crumble ice cream

SERVES 8-10

50g (2oz) butter

50g (2oz) brown sugar

2 eating apples, peeled, cored and cut in to 1cm (½in) chunks

For the ice cream

3 egg yolks

75g (3oz) caster or granulated sugar

1 tsp vanilla extract

800ml (1½ pints) softly whipped cream (measured when whisked)

For the crumble mix

50g (2oz) plain flour

25g (1oz) brown sugar

25g (1oz) rolled (porridge) oats

25g (1oz) butter, cut in to 1cm cubes

Equipment

Sugar thermometer (optional)

To make the ice cream, place the egg yolks in a bowl and whisk until light and fluffy. Combine the sugar and 150ml (5fl oz) water in a small saucepan, then stir over a medium heat until the sugar is completely dissolved. Remove the spoon and boil the syrup until it reaches the 'thread' stage, 106–113°C (223–235°F). If you don't have a sugar thermometer, the mixture should look thick and syrupy, and when a metal spoon is dipped in, the last drops of syrup will form thin threads. Pour this boiling syrup in a steady stream onto the egg yolks, whisking all the time. Add the vanilla extract and continue to whisk until it becomes a thick, creamy white mousse. Fold in the softly whipped cream, place in a container, cover and place in the freezer for an hour.

Next, cook the apples. Place the butter in a pan on a medium heat. When melted, stir in the sugar just until dissolved, then add the apple and cook, stirring occasionally, for about 10 minutes until the apple is soft. Remove from the heat and set aside to cool.

Preheat the oven to 160°C (320°F), Gas mark 3.

To make the crumble, in a bowl, mix together the flour, sugar and rolled oats, then rub in the butter to form a crumbly consistency. Spread out on a piece of baking parchment on a baking tray. Place in an oven and bake for about 15 minutes until golden and crisp, then set aside and allow to cool.

Remove the ice cream from the freezer and mix together the semi-frozen ice cream with the crumble and apple in a bowl, then return to the freezer to freeze all the way through. This should take 3–4 hours.

A real family favourite. The dates bring a rich unctuousness to this pudding, while the ginger stops it from being too sweet and provides a nice little kick. This is completely divine with lots of custard or some softly whipped cream.

Gooey date and stem ginger pudding

SERVES 6

75g (3oz) stoned dates, chopped

75g (3oz) butter

1 egg

250ml (9fl oz) milk

40g (1½oz) stem ginger in syrup

125g (4½oz) plain flour

1½ tsp baking powder

125g (4½oz) dark brown sugar

½ tsp salt

Softly whipped cream or custard, to serve

For the sauce

125g (4½oz) dark brown sugar

150ml (5fl oz) boiling water

50g (2oz) butter

2 tbsp stem ginger syrup from the jar

Equipment

1 litre (1¾ pint) capacity pie dish

Preheat the oven to 180°C (350°F), Gas mark 4.

Place the chopped dates in a small saucepan with the butter over a medium heat and allow the butter to melt, then take off the heat. Whisk the egg in a bowl, then add in the milk, the butter and date mixture. Drain the ginger, reserving the syrup, chop very finely and add to the bowl.

Place the flour, baking powder, brown sugar and salt in a mixing bowl. Mix, then make a well in the centre. Pour in the wet ingredients and stir to combine. Pour into the pie dish.

Next, make the sauce. Place the dark brown sugar, boiling water, butter and ginger syrup in a saucepan on a high heat and bring to the boil, stirring to melt the butter. As soon as it comes to a rolling boil, pour it evenly over the batter in the dish and place in the preheated oven (this may look a little strange, but it will create the beautiful sauce at the bottom). Cook for 40–45 minutes until just set in the centre.

Remove from the oven, allow to cool very slightly, then serve with softly whipped cream or custard.

It's no coincidence that the two primary flavours in this cake are so good together, as this recipe is inspired by what was, and perhaps still is, my very favourite chocolate bar ever! As a treat after church every Sunday, my sister and I were allowed to run down to the local shop to choose a bar, and the chocolate-covered one with the sweet, creamy coconut inside won hands down every time.

Chocolate coconut cake

SERVES 8–10

175g (6oz) butter, softened, plus extra for greasing

300g (11oz) ground almonds

100g (3½oz) desiccated coconut

50g (2oz) cocoa powder

½ tsp salt

1 x 400ml (14fl oz) tin of full-fat coconut milk

75g (3oz) dark chocolate (55–70% cocoa solids)

250g (9oz) caster sugar

3 eggs

For the ganache

200g (7oz) dark chocolate (55–70% cocoa solids)

50ml (2fl oz) Malibu (optional) or a few drops of coconut extract

Equipment

23cm (9in) spring-form cake tin

Cont. overleaf

Preheat the oven to 180°C (350°F), Gas mark 4. Line the base of the tin and grease the sides.

In a bowl combine the almonds, coconut, cocoa powder and salt. Pour half the coconut milk into a saucepan and bring to the boil. Take off the heat and stir in the chocolate until melted, then set aside.

Place the butter in a bowl and beat until soft, then add the sugar and beat for another minute until light and creamy. Add the eggs while beating, one by one. Next, stir in the chocolate and coconut milk mixture and the dry ingredients. Pour into the prepared tin and bake for 40–45 minutes until a skewer inserted into the centre comes out clean. Allow to sit in the tin for 10–20 minutes before taking out (remove the sides, then tip upside down to remove the base and paper). Tip back upright and cool.

While the cake cools, make the chocolate coconut ganache. Place the remaining 200ml (7fl oz) of coconut milk in a saucepan and bring to the boil, then remove from the heat, tip in the chocolate and stir to melt. Add in the Malibu, if using, or a few drops of coconut extract and place in the fridge, stirring every 20 minutes or so, until stiff enough to spread over and around the cooled cake.

Serve scattered with the coconut crumb (see overleaf). This cake keeps really well for days and days.

For the coconut crumb

75g (3oz) caster or granulated sugar

35ml (1fl oz) water

75g (3oz) desiccated coconut

Coconut crumb

Preheat the oven to 180°C (350°F), Gas mark 4. Place a sheet of baking parchment on a baking tray. Place the sugar and water in a saucepan over a medium heat and stir to dissolve the sugar before it comes to the boil. Once the syrup boils, stop stirring and continue to boil for 1 minute. Take off the heat and pour into a bowl with the coconut. Mix thoroughly and spread out evenly over the baking parchment. Bake in the oven for 4–7 minutes until golden. Take out halfway through cooking and mix it up so that it browns evenly, as the coconut around the outside will turn golden first.

Take out of the oven and allow to sit on the tray until cool. Break it up as it cools, then transfer to a jar or bowl. This will keep for 2–3 weeks.

From the fifteenth to the seventeenth centuries, Mocha, the Yemeni port on the Red Sea, was famous for being a major marketplace for coffee. The Mocha coffee beans are known for their distinctive rich chocolate flavour, which gives inspiration to this show-stopping meringue and mousse-layered cake.

Layered mocha mousse coffee meringue

SERVES 10–12

For the meringue

20g (¾oz) freshly ground coffee

250g (9oz) caster sugar

4 egg whites

¼ tsp cream of tartar

For the mocha mousse

100g (3½oz) dark chocolate (55–70% cocoa solids)

20g (¾oz) freshly ground coffee

2 eggs + 1 egg white

Pinch of salt

Cont. overleaf

Preheat the oven to 150°C (300°F), Gas mark 2 (I use a fan oven at 135°C for this). Line two baking trays with baking parchment.

To make the meringue, place the coffee, 3 tablespoons water and 50g (2oz) of the sugar in a small saucepan and bring up to the boil, stirring to dissolve the sugar, then take off the heat and let the coffee infuse.

Place the egg whites in the bowl of an electric food mixer with the whisk attached, add the cream of tartar and whisk until frothy. Add in the remaining caster sugar gradually and continue to whisk until it holds stiff peaks.

Once the egg white mixture is stiff, stop whisking and pour in every bit of the coffee mixture through a sieve. Fold it through carefully, then divide out between the two trays and spread into four ovals, two on each tray, about 20cm (8in) wide and 26cm (10in) long. Make sure the mixture is about 7.5mm (¼in) thick and not too thin around the edges as they can crack and break when cooled.

Place in the oven and cook for 50 minutes, then turn off the oven and allow to cool for at least 1 hour in the oven. If cooking in an Aga, just take them out of the oven and place on top at the side to cool down gently. Once the meringues have cooled, you can assemble the dessert, although stored in an airtight box they will keep for one or two weeks.

For the whipped cream layers

200ml (7fl oz) double or regular cream (measure before whisking)

Cocoa powder, to decorate

Start making the mocha mousse at least 2 hours in advance, so that it can set in the fridge before you assemble the dessert. Place the chocolate in a bowl sitting over a saucepan with a few centimetres of water. Bring the water up to the boil, then take off the heat and allow the chocolate to melt slowly.

Meanwhile, place the coffee and 3 tablespoons water in a small saucepan and bring up to the boil, stir, then remove from the heat and set aside for 5–10 minutes for the coffee to infuse. When the chocolate has melted, pour the coffee through a sieve into the chocolate.

Separate the two eggs and stir the yolks into the chocolate. Whisk all three egg whites with a pinch of salt until stiff, then fold into the chocolate mixture. Place in the fridge to set.

Whip the cream until just stiff, and place in the fridge until you are ready to assemble the meringue.

When ready to assemble, place one meringue oval on your serving plate. Spread over half of the mocha mousse, then top with a second meringue oval. Cover with half the whipped cream, then a third layer of meringue, then cover this with the second half of the mousse, the final meringue and the second half of the cream. Dust with cocoa powder and serve.

Rachel's Tip: For an extra coffee hit you can, if you wish, fold 3 tablespoons of a coffee liqueur through the whipped cream.

If this fudge pie were a person, I reckon it would be Roseanne Barr from the 1980s sitcom *Roseanne*. Big, brash and very sweet, this is not for the faint hearted.

American chocolate fudge pie

SERVES 10–12

For the base

75g (3oz) butter, cut into cubes, plus extra for greasing

115g (4oz) plain flour

25g (1oz) caster sugar

30g (1oz) pecans, chopped quite finely

For the chocolate layer

45g (1½oz) cornflour

30g (1oz) cocoa powder

Pinch of salt

175g (6oz) caster sugar

3 large egg yolks

450ml (16fl oz) milk

25g (1oz) butter

2 tsp vanilla extract

For the creamy layer

250ml (9fl oz) double or regular cream

200g (7oz) cream cheese

150g (5oz) icing sugar

Equipment

23cm (9in) spring-form cake tin

Preheat the oven to 180°C (350°F), Gas mark 4. Butter the sides and the base of the cake tin. Make sure the base is upside down, so that there's no lip and the cake can slide off easily when cooked.

To make the base, place the flour and sugar in a bowl, then rub in the butter until the mixture resembles coarse breadcrumbs. Mix in the pecans, then form a soft dough. Spread evenly into the cake tin.

Place in the oven and bake for 25 minutes until golden. Leave the base in the tin and place on a wire rack to cool.

Meanwhile, make the chocolate layer. Sift the cornflour, cocoa powder and salt into a bowl, then add the sugar and mix well. Beat in the egg yolks and milk and mix together. Transfer to a saucepan, place on a medium heat and cook, whisking continuously, until the mixture boils and becomes very thick. It is at the right thickness when it holds a figure of eight traced into the surface. Whisk in the butter and vanilla extract, then set aside to cool.

Now make the creamy layer. Whisk the cream until quite stiff. Beat the cream cheese and icing sugar to become soft and then fold in the cream.

To assemble, use a dessertspoon to blob all the cream cheese mix onto the biscuit base. Smooth it out a bit, then blob on the chocolate mix. Swirl with the handle of a teaspoon for a marbled effect, then place in the fridge to set. This should take a few hours or could be done overnight.

To serve, unclip the sides of the tin and remove. Using a palette knife or fish slice, slide the cake off the tin base onto a serving plate.

Rachel's Tip: This can be frozen, covered, for 2–3 weeks. It's delicious eaten straight from the freezer.

Literally meaning 'half cold', or 'half frozen', a semifreddo can be anything from a frozen cake to a mousse, but one that does not harden completely in the freezer. This delicious honey-sweetened, almost soft, ice cream is the perfect match for the indulgent and oh-so-good butter toffee figs.

Honey semifreddo with butter toffee figs

SERVES 6–8

For the semifreddo

2 eggs + 2 egg yolks

100g (3½oz) honey

250ml (9fl oz) double or regular cream

For the butter toffee figs

50g (2oz) soft light brown sugar

200g (7oz) fresh figs (about 6–8 figs)

50g (2oz) butter

50g (2oz) honey

50ml (2fl oz) double cream

Equipment

20cm (8in) spring-form cake tin

Cont. overleaf

Line the cake tin with a double layer of cling film.

First, make the semifreddo. Place a saucepan with a few centimetres of water on a medium heat. Put the eggs, egg yolks and honey into a bowl and sit over the saucepan so that the water is not touching the bottom of the bowl. I use a heatproof glass bowl for this (a stainless-steel one is not a good idea, as it will get too hot and scramble the eggs).

Using either a hand whisk or a hand-held electric beater (this is not difficult to do by hand), whisk the eggs and honey over the simmering water for about 5–10 minutes until the mixture is pale, light and will hold a figure of eight. Once it's holding a figure of eight, take the water off the heat and continue to whisk the honey and egg mixture for about 8–10 minutes until it has cooled down to room temperature.

Whip the cream in a mixing bowl until just holding stiff peaks – too stiff and it will go grainy, too soft and it won't be able to hold the honey mousse mixture. Tip one-quarter of the cream into the honey mousse and fold to combine, then tip this mixture into the remaining cream and fold lightly to completely mix, but keeping it light and airy. Tip into the prepared tin, cover with cling film and place in the freezer to freeze.

To make the butter toffee figs, place a frying pan on a medium – high heat and allow to get hot. Scatter the brown sugar on a plate. Cut the figs into wedges from top to bottom, either sixths or eights, depending on the size of the figs. Dip the cut sides of the wedges in the brown sugar so that they're covered with brown sugar (so that it sticks) and put them cut side down into the pan. Allow to caramelise on one cut side before turning to the other cut side.

Once all the figs are cooked and caramelised, take them out, set aside and add the butter, honey and cream to the pan. Stir over the heat and allow to boil for a minute or two until the sauce thickens to a thick butter sauce. Tip the figs back into the pan (this will keep for a few days, just reheat to serve).

When ready to serve, take the semifreddo out of the freezer, remove the cling film, cut into wedges and serve with the warm butter toffee figs over the top, the sauce oozing down the sides.

Rich, flour-free chocolate mousse cake covered with a thick blanket of, yes, rich chocolate mousse. This is a no-holds-barred onslaught of chocolate deliciousness. I recommend using a dark chocolate with somewhere between 55 and 70 per cent in cocoa solids.

Double chocolate mousse cake

SERVES 8–10

For the chocolate mousse cake

50g (2oz) butter, plus extra for greasing

200g (7oz) dark chocolate (55–70% cocoa solids), chopped or in pieces or drops

5 eggs

150g (5oz) caster sugar

Pinch of salt

For the chocolate mousse coating

100g (3½oz) dark chocolate (55–70% cocoa solids)

2 eggs

50g (2oz) butter

Equipment

2 x 18cm (7in) cake tins with 3cm (1¼in) sides

Preheat the oven to 180°C (350°F), Gas mark 4. Line the base of the two cake tins with baking parchment and grease the sides with butter.

To make the mousse cake, place the chocolate and butter in a bowl sitting over a saucepan with a few centimetres of water. Bring the water up to the boil, then take off the heat and allow the chocolate to melt slowly.

Separate the eggs. Place the yolks in a bowl with the sugar and whisk for a few minutes until pale and light. Beat the chocolate mixture into the egg yolk mixture. Whisk the egg whites with the pinch of salt in another bowl until they form stiff peaks, then fold into the chocolate mixture.

Divide the mousse between the two tins and bake in the oven for 30–35 minutes. A skewer inserted into the centre should just come out clean, but remember the mixture should remain moist – it's not a sponge. Take out of the oven and allow to sit for 30 minutes before taking out of the tins.

Next, make the mousse coating. Place the chocolate in a bowl sitting over a saucepan with a few centimetres of water. Bring the water up to the boil, then take off the heat and allow the chocolate to melt slowly.

Separate the eggs and beat the yolks into the warm chocolate, then beat in the butter. Whip the egg whites until stiff peaks form, then fold a quarter into the chocolate mixture, followed by the remainder, which should be folded in gently.

Place in the fridge for 1–2 hours until stiff enough to 'ice' the cake without it falling off. When ready to ice, put one cooled cake upside down on a plate or cake stand. Spread a couple of heaped tablespoons of the mousse over the top as though generously buttering a slice of bread. Cover with the second cake, then ice the top and sides of the cakes.

I remember the very first time I tasted a proper homemade kulfi. It was 1991 and I had just started working in the cookery school at Ballymaloe when Madhur Jaffrey came to teach. I was thrilled to get the opportunity to assist the beautiful, iconic Indian cookery writer. She made this rich Indian ice cream in the traditional way by boiling milk, uncovered, so that it evaporated over time, before adding sugar, nuts and spices. This recipe is close to the version Madhur cooked at Ballymaloe and never fails to bring me back to that lovely day.

Pistachio and saffron kulfi

Serves 6

2 litres (4¼ pints) milk

8 green cardamom pods

½ tsp grated or ground nutmeg

Good pinch of saffron strands

65g (2¼oz) sugar

75g (3oz) pistachios, chopped

Equipment

Ice-cream machine

Moulds (optional)

Place the milk, cardamom pods and nutmeg in a saucepan on a medium heat. Once the milk comes up to a simmer, turn the heat down so that the milk continues to simmer without boiling over. Cook for about 1 hour – the time will vary depending on your pan and the heat, but the milk has to reduce to one-third of its original amount (about 675ml/1¼ pints). Keep stirring regularly as it cooks. It browns a little on the bottom of the saucepan, so don't scrape this bit into the milk.

Pour through a sieve into another saucepan, add the saffron, sugar and half of the chopped pistachios and cook for 2 minutes more. Pour out into a bowl and allow to cool.

Pour into an ice-cream machine or cover and place the bowl (if not using an ice-cream machine) in the freezer. Take out of the freezer after about 2 hours and stir vigorously, then cover and put back into the freezer. Take out again another 2–3 hours later and repeat.

When the kulfi is nearly frozen you can, if you wish, transfer it to individual moulds, then pop back in the freezer overnight, or for at least a couple of hours, until frozen.

Turn out the kulfi and scatter with the remaining pistachios. This is wonderful served just as it is, or with some chopped or sliced ripe mango.

I always think that dates don't quite taste as they look. Brown, a bit wrinkly, not necessarily appetising, but one bite into the sweet, chewy, almost toffee-like dried fruit and it's hard to stop. A favourite since the Garden of Eden, dates really are the food of the gods and have the nutritional benefits to match. They absolutely love being paired with almonds, a match that's showcased to perfection in this rich, decadent tart. Good, plump dates works best for this tart, especially the Medjool date, which comes from Morocco originally and, in my opinion, is the king of dates.

Date and almond tart

SERVES 6-8

For the pastry

200g (7oz) plain flour

1 tbsp icing sugar

Pinch of salt

100g (3½oz) chilled butter, diced

1 egg, beaten

For the frangipane filling

100g (3½oz) butter

100g (3½oz) caster sugar

2 eggs

125g (4½oz) ground almonds

10–12 Medjool dates or 16–20 smaller ones (such as deglet nour), stoned and halved

Cont. overleaf

Sift the flour, icing sugar and salt into a bowl and rub in the butter until the mixture resembles coarse breadcrumbs. Add half the beaten egg and, using your hands, bring the dough together, adding a little more egg if it is too dry.

If you are making the pastry in a food processor, sift in the flour, icing sugar and salt and add the butter. Whiz for a few seconds, then add half the beaten egg and continue to whiz for just a few more seconds until it comes together. You might need to add a little more egg, but don't add too much – it should just come together. Don't over-process the pastry or it will be tough and heavy. Reserve the remaining beaten egg for brushing over the finished pastry.

Without kneading the dough, carefully shape it into a 1–2cm (½–¾in) thick round, using your hands to flatten it. Cover with cling film and place in the fridge to chill for about 30 minutes.

Meanwhile, preheat the oven to 180°C (350°F), Gas mark 4.

Take the pastry out of the fridge and place it between two sheets of cling film (each bigger than your tart tin). Using a rolling pin, roll out the pastry to about 3mm (⅛in) thick. Make sure to keep it in a round shape and large enough to line the base and sides of the tin.

For the apricot glaze

50g (2oz) apricot jam

Juice of ⅛ lemon

Equipment

23cm (9in) loose-bottomed tart tin

Removing just the top layer of cling film, place the pastry upside down (cling-film side facing up) in the tart tin (there's no need to flour or grease the tin). Press the pastry into the edges of the tin, with the cling film still attached to the dough, and using your thumb 'cut' the pastry along the edge of the tin for a neat finish. If there are any holes or gaps in the pastry, simply patch them up with some of your spare pieces of dough.

Remove the cling film and chill the pastry in the fridge for 15 minutes or in the freezer for 5 minutes.

Remove the pastry from the fridge or freezer and line with greaseproof paper or baking parchment, leaving plenty of paper to come up over the sides. Fill the lined tart case with baking beans or dried pulses (you can use these over and over again), and bake 'blind' for 20–25 minutes or until the pastry feels just dry to the touch on the base.

Remove the paper and beans, brush with a little of the remaining beaten egg and return to the oven for 3 minutes. Again, if there are any little holes or cracks in the pastry, patch them up with any leftover raw pastry so that the filling doesn't leak out during cooking. Once the pastry has been baked blind, take it out of the oven and set it aside in the tin.

Next, make the frangipane filling. Cream the butter, gradually beat in the sugar and continue beating until the mixture is light and soft. Gradually add the eggs, beating well. Stir in the ground almonds until just mixed, then pour the frangipane into the pastry case, spreading it evenly. Arrange the dates on top of the frangipane in concentric circles. Bake for 30–35 minutes until golden and just set in the centre.

Meanwhile, to make the apricot glaze, pour the jam and lemon juice into a saucepan and put on a medium heat. Stir together well, then remove from the heat and push the mixture through a sieve. The glaze can be stored in an airtight jar and reheated to melt it before using.

When the tart is cooked, remove it from the oven and brush generously with the apricot glaze while warm.

I'm such a fan of upside-down cakes. I think there is a recipe for at least one in every book of mine. This particular cake has a few of my favourite ingredients: toffee-like dates, warming ginger and its close relative, the cardamom pod. An easy-to-throw-together cake, but still deliciously rich and indulgent.

Date, cardamom and ginger upside-down cake

SERVES 6–8

75g (3oz) butter

200g (7oz) (stoned weight) lovely plump dates (such as Medjool dates), coarsely chopped

75g (3oz) brown sugar

50g (2oz) stem ginger in syrup, finely chopped

3 tbsp stem ginger syrup from the jar

For the cake batter

150g (5oz) butter, cut into cubes

175g (6oz) caster sugar

200g (7oz) plain flour

1 tsp baking powder

1 tsp ground cardamom

3 eggs

Equipment

25cm (10in) ovenproof frying pan

Preheat the oven to 170°C (325°F), Gas mark 3.

Place an ovenproof frying pan over a medium heat and allow to warm up. Add in the butter, allow to melt, then tip in the dates, brown sugar, ginger and the syrup. Stir together and allow to bubble for just about 1 minute until slightly thickened, but don't let it darken. Take off the heat, set aside and make the cake batter.

In the bowl of a food processor, place the butter, sugar, flour, baking powder and ground cardamom. Pulse a few times to mix, then add in the eggs and whiz until it forms a soft dough. Alternatively, place the butter in a bowl and beat until soft, then add in the sugar and beat again; next add the eggs one at a time, and lastly stir in the dry ingredients.

Place tablespoonful blobs of the cake batter over the sticky date mixture in the ovenproof frying pan, carefully spreading to cover, but trying not to disturb the dates, and place in the oven.

Bake for 25–30 minutes until a skewer inserted into the centre comes out clean. Once out of the oven, allow it to sit for just 2 minutes before placing an upturned plate over the pan and flipping out upside down.

A nifty little French recipe for using up scraps of puff pastry, these are heavenly little swirls of buttery, chocolaty deliciousness.

Drops au chocolat

MAKES 12 DROPS

350g (12oz) puff pastry

A little icing sugar, for rolling out

75g (3oz) dark chocolate (55–70% cocoa solids) chopped, or dark chocolate chips or drops

Preheat the oven to 220°C (425°F), Gas mark 7.

Roll the pastry out into a 20 x 30cm (8 x 12in) rectangle, using icing sugar to dust the worktop and the top of the pastry.

Sprinkle the chocolate chips evenly over the whole sheet then, with the long end closest to you, roll up tightly into a log. Place in the fridge to chill for 15 minutes. When chilled, cut into twelve even slices. Place on a baking tray lined with baking parchment and bake for 10–12 minutes until puffed up and golden brown around the edges. Transfer to a wire rack to cool.

CLASSICS
WITH A TWIST

Cinnamon custard tarts

Puff pastry

Rhubarb meringue pie

Salted caramel crème brûlée

Raspberry and white chocolate meringue roulade

Apricot fool with cardamom shortbread fingers

Meringues with pink grapefruit curd and cream

Blueberry bread and butter pudding

Apple and cinnamon baked cheesecake

Strawberry Victoria mess

Pear and maple crumble

Nectarine custard tarts

Orange caramel choux puffs

My agent sometimes calls with strange requests – not strange in a weird way, but just slightly different to the average magazine article or food festival gig. One day she called and said, 'Fancy going to Lisbon for the day and eating Portuguese custard tarts for a TV crew?' Well, no one needs to ask me twice to, number one, go to a beautiful city for the day and, number two, eat custard tarts. So off I went to check out the iconic Portuguese custard tarts, and eat them I did. Nearly every single one of them. This recipe is inspired by those classic Portuguese tarts.

Cinnamon custard tarts

MAKES 12 TARTS

375g (13oz) puff pastry (see page 206), rolled out to 3mm (⅛in) thick and placed in the fridge to chill

Icing sugar, to decorate

For the cinnamon custard

20g (¾oz) plain flour

350ml (12fl oz) milk

225g (8oz) caster sugar

¼ tsp ground cinnamon

5 egg yolks

Equipment

12-hole bun tray (smaller than a cupcake or muffin tray)

Preheat the oven to 230°C (450°F), Gas mark 8.

Make the cinnamon custard. Place the flour, 50ml (2fl oz) of the milk, the caster sugar, cinnamon and the egg yolks in a bowl and whisk for 10 seconds.

Place the remaining 300ml (½ pint) milk in a saucepan and bring to the boil. Pour onto the egg yolk mixture, whisking all the time, and continue to whisk until thoroughly mixed. Pour back into the saucepan, place on a medium heat and stir all the time until it thickens – it needs to boil for 2 minutes. I use a wooden spatula for this, but if it goes lumpy you can use a whisk. Take off the heat.

Take the pastry out of the fridge and cut into twelve 9cm (3½in) discs. Take the bun tray and press the discs into the cups. Divide the custard out among the cups and bake for 8–12 minutes until the pastry is golden. Allow to cool and dust with icing sugar to serve.

Puff pastry takes a little time and effort to perfect, but it's worth having a go and the results are so delicious. If you're pressed for time, you can buy puff pastry from supermarkets – though look for one that contains butter and no oils. This recipe makes generous quantities, so you can store any leftover pastry in the fridge for 48 hours or in the freezer for up to three months.

Puff pastry

MAKES APPROXIMATELY 1.15KG (2½LB)

450g (1lb) strong white flour

Pinch of salt

1 tbsp freshly squeezed lemon juice

200–275ml cold water (the amount of water will depend on the absorbency of the flour)

450g chilled butter, still in its wrapper

Step 1: Sift the flour and salt into a large bowl. Mix the lemon juice with 200ml (7fl oz) water, pour into the flour and, using your hands, mix to a soft but not sticky dough, adding more water if necessary. This dough is called détrempe (a mixture of flour and water). Flatten it slightly and cover with a plastic bag, cling film or greaseproof paper and allow to rest in the fridge on a baking tray (which aids the chilling process) for 30 minutes.

Step 2: Roll the détrempe into a rectangle about 1cm (½in) thick. Remove the butter from the fridge, still in its wrapper and, using a rolling pin, 'beat' it until it forms a slab about 1.5–2cm (⅝–¾in) thick. Remove the wrapper, place the butter in the centre of the dough rectangle and fold the dough over the edges of the butter to make a neat parcel, covering the butter.

Step 3: Turn the dough over and, dusting the work surface with flour to stop the dough from sticking, roll it gently out into a rectangle approximately 40cm (16in) long and 20cm (8in) wide, positioned so that one narrow end is facing you. Brush off the excess flour with a pastry brush, then fold neatly into three by lifting the end furthest away from you and placing it on the rectangle, so that only one-third of the pastry is left uncovered, and aligning the sides as accurately as possible. Fold the other end on top. Seal the edges with your hands or a rolling pin.

Step 4: Give the dough a one-quarter turn (90 degrees), so that the folds are running vertically in front of you (it should look like a closed book) Roll out away from you, again into a rectangle (to roughly the same measurements as before), brush off any excess flour and fold in three again. Seal the edges, cover with cling film or greaseproof paper and allow to rest in the fridge for another 30 minutes.

Repeat steps 3 and 4 twice more (always ensuring that you start the process with the folds in the pastry running vertically, i.e. looking like a closed book), so that in the end the dough has been rolled out six times and has rested in the fridge three times for 30 minutes each time.

Chill for at least 1 hour before using.

One of my fail-safe Sunday lunch puddings is poached rhubarb with meringues and cream. Tart rhubarb is the ideal foil for sugary meringues, and whipped cream perfectly bridges the gap between them. This recipe is a delightful amalgamation of this and another classic: lemon meringue pie. Use the pinkest rhubarb you can for a pretty pink curd.

Rhubarb meringue pie

SERVES 6

For the sweet shortcrust pastry

200g (7oz) plain flour

Pinch of salt

100g (3½oz) butter

25g (1oz) icing sugar

1 egg, beaten

For the rhubarb curd

550g (1lb 3oz) rhubarb, cut in to 1cm (½in) slices (weigh when sliced and trimmed)

200g (7oz) caster or granulated sugar

75g (3oz) butter

3 eggs, whisked

Cont. overleaf

First, make the sweet shortcrust pastry. Place the flour, salt, butter and icing sugar in a food processor and whiz briefly until the butter is in small lumps. Add half the beaten egg and continue to whiz for just another few seconds until the mixture looks as though it may come together when pressed (prolonged processing will only toughen the pastry, so don't whiz it up until it is a ball of dough). You might need to add a little more egg, but not too much as the mixture should be just moist enough to come together.

If making by hand, rub the butter into the flour, salt and icing sugar until the mixture resembles coarse breadcrumbs then, using your hands, add just enough beaten egg to bring it together.

With your hands, flatten out the ball of dough until it is about 2cm (¾in) thick, then wrap in cling film or place in a plastic bag and leave in the fridge for at least 30 minutes.

Preheat the oven to 180°C (350°F), Gas mark 4.

Remove the pastry from the fridge and place between two sheets of cling film (each bigger than your tart tin). Using a rolling pin, roll the pastry out to no thicker than 5mm (¼in). If the tin is round, keep the pastry in a round shape and make sure it is large enough to line both the base and the sides of the tin.

Remove the top layer of cling film, place your hand, palm facing up, under the cling film underneath, then flip the pastry over, cling-film side facing up, and into the tart tin. Press the pastry into the edges of the tin, with the cling film still attached to the pastry, and, using your thumb, 'cut' the pastry along

For the meringue

4 egg whites (about 150–170g/5–6oz)

110g (4oz) caster sugar

110g (4oz) icing sugar

Equipment

23cm (9in) loose-bottomed flan ring or tart tin

the edge of the tin for a neat finish. Remove the cling film and, if you have time, chill the pastry in the fridge for another 30 minutes or in the freezer for 10 minutes (it can keep for weeks like this, covered, in the freezer). If the pastry has remained cold while rolling it out, there is no need to chill it again.

Next, line the pastry with baking parchment, leaving plenty to come up the sides. Fill with baking beans or dried pulses (all of which can be reused again and again). Place in the oven and bake 'blind' for 20–25 minutes until the pastry feels dry on the base. Remove from the oven, take out the baking beans and paper and brush the base of the pastry with any leftover beaten egg, then cook in the oven for another 3 minutes. When completely blind baked, take out of the oven and set the pastry aside. Turn the oven down to 150°C (300°F), Gas mark 2.

Next, make the curd. Place the rhubarb and 50g (2oz) of the sugar in a saucepan over a medium heat and cook for about 5–6 minutes, stirring every so often, until the rhubarb has softened, broken up completely and the mixture has thickened to a pulp.

Pour into a sieve sitting over a bowl and push the mixture through the sieve into the bowl, making sure to scrape the underside of the sieve to get every last bit.

Next, place the butter in the cleaned saucepan on a low–medium heat and allow to melt. Take off the heat just while you add in the eggs, the remaining sugar and the rhubarb purée. Put back on a low heat and stir continuously for about 6–8 minutes until thickened. Take off the heat, tip into a bowl and allow to cool.

Place the egg whites for the meringue in the bowl of an electric food mixer with the whisk attachment (or use a hand-held electric beater). Whisk at full speed for a few minutes until the egg whites hold fluffy, stiff peaks when the whisk is lifted.

Continue whisking and add the caster sugar one tablespoon at a time, but with a few seconds between each addition. Once all the caster sugar is added in, stop the whisk. Sift in one-third of the icing sugar and fold in carefully, using a spatula, then fold in the second third, and finally the last third. The mixture should be fluffy and light.

Spread the curd all over the tart base, then tip the meringue on top, making peaks with the back of a spoon. Place the tart in the oven and bake for 35–45 minutes until the meringue topping is crisp and lightly browned on the outside.

Take out of the oven and allow to sit in the tin for 5 minutes before removing from the tin. I do this by sitting the tin on a small bowl and allowing the sides to fall down, then carefully sliding the shortcrust pastry crust off the base of the tin, using something flat like a palette knife. Allow to cool before cutting into slices to serve.

The English, French and the Spanish all like to think that they originally created the crème brûlée, and indeed each country has recorded versions of the recipe dating as far back as the 1600s. Whoever was the initial instigator of the burnt-sugar-topped custard pudding we cannot be exactly sure, but what is certain is that crème brûlée loves to take on other flavours, and this salted caramel variation works a treat.

Salted caramel crème brûlée

SERVES 4

For the custards

50g (2oz) caster or granulated sugar

250ml (9fl oz) double or regular cream

⅛ tsp salt

2 egg yolks

For the caramel topping

100g (3½oz) caster or granulated sugar

Few pinches of sea salt flakes, such as Irish Atlantic Sea Salt, Oriel, Maldon or Halen Mon

First make the custards. Place the sugar in a small saucepan on a medium heat and leave for a few minutes. When the sugar starts to caramelise around the edge of the pan, give it a shake and swirl and return to the heat. Repeat once or twice more until it is all caramelised with no sugar left. It will be smoking and a deep golden brown when ready. Too light and you won't get the deep caramel flavour. Too dark and it'll taste bitter. Immediately pour in the cream and the salt, then turn the heat down to low and allow the caramel to dissolve completely in the cream. Set aside off the heat.

Place the egg yolks in a bowl and pour over the warm caramel, whisking all the time. Pour this back into the saucepan and stir over a low heat, using a flat-bottomed wooden spoon (to get into the edges) until the mixture coats the back of it. You need to be careful – if it gets too hot it will scramble; you might need to take it off the heat every so often if it starts to catch. As soon as it's ready, and while still hot, pour the mixture into four cups or bowls and set aside. You need to allow a 'skin' to develop on each custard, so do not shake them or cover them while warm. When cool, place in the fridge to set.

Next day, take the custards out of the fridge. Place the 100g (3½oz) of sugar in a saucepan and caramelise as before. Spoon it over the custards, then immediately sprinkle a tiny pinch of salt flakes over each before the caramel hardens. Allow to sit for 5 minutes before serving.

Rachel's Tip: If you have a blowtorch, instead of making caramel, scatter over the custards a 2mm (⅛in) layer of caster or granulated sugar. Wave the blowtorch slowly over the sugar, from about 10cm (4in) away, until it is deep golden and caramelised. Allow to sit for 5 minutes before serving.

Coming from the French verb *rouler*, meaning 'to roll', a roulade can be applied to anything, be it a slice of meat or a thick sheet of soft marshmallow meringue. Though ever so slightly 1980s, a roulade never fails to please, and I particularly love this version with raspberries and white chocolate.

Raspberry and white chocolate meringue roulade

SERVES 6–8

For the coulis

Juice of ½ lemon

100g (3½oz) raspberries, fresh or frozen

1–2 tbsp icing sugar

For the meringue

50g (2oz) hazelnuts

4 large egg whites

200g (7oz) caster sugar

1 tsp cornflour

1 tsp vinegar (such as white wine vinegar) or lemon juice

Cont. overleaf

First, make the coulis. Place the ingredients in a food processor or blender, whiz for a few minutes until smooth, then pour through a sieve into a bowl.

Preheat the oven to 160°C (320°F), Gas mark 3.

Place the hazelnuts on a baking tray and toast in the oven for 5–6 minutes until golden, then remove from the oven. Tip into a tea towel and rub to loosen the skins. Pick out the nuts from the skins, then roughly chop.

Next, line the Swiss roll tin with an oiled piece of foil so that there's enough to come up the sides by about 4cm (1½in), as the meringue will rise as it cooks.

Using a hand-held electric beater or food mixer, whisk the egg whites until almost stiff, then pour in (while still whisking) the sugar gradually and whisk until stiff. Add in the cornflour and vinegar or lemon juice, then whisk again just for a few seconds until mixed. Lastly, fold in the chopped, toasted hazelnuts.

Spread out in the lined tray and bake for 18–20 minutes until light golden and softly springy in the centre. Take out of the oven and let sit for about 5 minutes before turning out onto another sheet of foil. Allow to cool completely.

For the filling

100g (3½oz) white chocolate, broken into pieces or drops

200ml (7fl oz) double or regular cream

1 tsp vanilla extract

150g (5oz) fresh raspberries

Equipment

23 x 37cm (9 x 15in) Swiss roll tin

Place the white chocolate in a bowl sitting over a saucepan with a few centimetres of water. Bring the water up to the boil, then take off the heat and allow the chocolate to melt slowly over the water (I find this is the best way to melt white chocolate to prevent it 'blocking'). Once the chocolate has melted, take the bowl off the saucepan and allow to cool.

Meanwhile, whip the cream – but stop whisking just before it reaches the stiff-peak stage. Once the white chocolate has cooled, fold it into the cream with the vanilla extract, then spread out to cover the surface of the meringue. Scatter with raspberries.

With the larger end of the meringue facing you (and using the foil to help) roll the meringue away from you to form a roulade. Turn out onto a plate (with the join underneath) and serve with the raspberry coulis.

Cardamom and apricot have long been paired together in everything from Danish pastries to jams, and this great little match continues to work its magic in a fluffy light fool with crumbly shortbread fingers.

Apricot fool with cardamom shortbread fingers

SERVES 6

For the fool

6 large fresh ripe apricots (about 450g/1lb with stones)

125g (4½oz) caster or granulated sugar

200ml (7fl oz) double or regular cream (measured before whisking)

For the cardamom shortbread fingers

150g (5oz) plain flour

50g (2oz) caster sugar

½ tsp freshly ground cardamom seeds (from about 16 green cardamom pods)

100g (3½oz) butter, cubed

Cut the apricots in half and remove the stones. Place in a saucepan with the sugar and 2 tablespoons water over a medium heat. Stir to dissolve the sugar, then cook, covered, for 10–15 minutes until the apricots are completely soft. If there is any liquid in the bottom of the pan, continue to cook, uncovered, to allow it to evaporate until the juices are thick. Place in a blender and whiz, then allow to cool. The mixture should be quite a thick purée. If it's not thick enough, put it back on the heat and cook, uncovered, and stirring regularly, until it's a bit thicker. If it's too liquidy, the fool will not be fluffy. Remove from the heat and allow to cool completely.

While it's cooling, you can whisk the cream until not quite, but almost, stiff. Fold the cream into the apricot purée. Store in the fridge until ready to serve.

Preheat the oven to 180°C (350°F), Gas mark 4.

To make the cardamom shortbread fingers, place the flour in a bowl with the sugar and the cardamom and mix, then rub in the butter and squeeze in your hands to bring it together to form a dough. Alternatively, you could bring the ingredients together very briefly in a food processor.

Roll the dough out until 5mm (¼in) thick, keeping it in a square or a rectangle. Pierce it all over with a skewer or fork, then cut it into twelve fingers about 10 x 2cm (4 x ¾in) in size.

Place on a baking tray (no need to grease or line) and bake for 5–8 minutes until light golden. Take out and let stand on the tray for 2 minutes before transferring to a wire rack.

Serve the shortbread fingers with the apricot fool.

I love experimenting with different-flavoured curds and the unique balance of the pink grapefruit's sweetness and tang is ideal for accompanying meringues and cream. The meringue recipe works a treat: half caster and half icing sugar, with a hint of vanilla for flavour, these are generous, big cushions of fluffy sweetness.

Meringues with pink grapefruit curd and cream

MAKES 10 MERINGUES

For the meringues

4 egg whites

110g (4oz) caster sugar

110g (4oz) icing sugar

1 tsp vanilla extract

250ml (9fl oz) double or regular cream

For the grapefruit curd

75g (3oz) butter

Juice and finely grated zest of 1 pink grapefruit

75g (3oz) caster or granulated sugar

2 eggs + 1 egg yolk

Preheat the oven to 110°C (225°F), Gas mark ¼ (or use a fan oven at 100°C for this).

Line two baking trays with baking parchment. Place the egg whites in the bowl of an electric food mixer with the whisk attachment (or use a hand-held electric beater). Whisk at full speed for a few minutes until the egg whites hold fluffy, stiff peaks when the whisk is lifted.

Continue whisking and add the caster sugar one tablespoon at a time, but with a few seconds between each addition. Once all the caster sugar is added in, stop the whisk. Sift in one-third of the icing sugar and fold in carefully, using a spatula, then fold in the second third and finally the last third and the vanilla extract. The mixture should be fluffy and light.

Scoop a heaped tablespoonful of the mixture onto a baking tray, using a second tablespoon to help ease it off, to form blobs (or if you prefer, make a little dip or well in the centre to hold the whipped cream and curd). Repeat with all the mixture, place in the oven and cook for 1½ hours until the meringues are crisp on the outside and will lift off the baking parchment.

Place the butter in a saucepan on a medium–low heat and when melted, whisk in the juice, zest, sugar, eggs and egg yolk. Turn the heat down to low and cook, stirring constantly, until thick enough to coat the back of a spoon. Then remove from the heat and allow to cool.

Softly whisk the cream, then place generous blobs on the meringues and drizzle with the grapefruit curd.

A bread and butter pudding is a classic – and for good reason, too. White bread soaked in sweet vanilla-scented custard and baked in the oven, what's not to love? There are countless variations on the theme and this is one of my favourites. Use fresh or frozen blueberries.

Blueberry bread and butter pudding

SERVES 6–8

50g (2oz) butter, softened, plus extra for greasing

12 slices of good-quality bread, crusts removed

250g (9oz) blueberries

675ml (1¼ pints) double or regular cream

325ml (11fl oz) milk

6 eggs

225g (8oz) caster sugar

2 tsp vanilla extract

2 tbsp granulated sugar

Softly whipped cream, to serve

Equipment

2 litre (4 pint) capacity gratin dish

Preheat the oven to 180°C (350°F), Gas mark 4. Rub the bottom and sides of a gratin dish with butter.

Butter the bread slices on one side. Arrange a single layer of bread in the gratin dish, butter side up. Scatter a good handful of blueberries over the layer, then use more bread to make another layer in the dish. Scatter another handful of blueberries over this layer, then make another layer of bread. Continue in this way until you have used all of your bread and blueberries. I like to have neat, overlapping triangles of bread on the top layer.

Place the cream and milk in a saucepan and bring to just under the boil.

While it's heating up, in a separate bowl whisk the eggs, caster sugar and vanilla extract, then pour the hot milk and cream into the eggs and whisk to combine. Pour this custard over the bread and leave to soak for 10 minutes.

Sprinkle the granulated sugar over the top, then prepare a bain-marie. Place the gratin dish in a large, deep-sided roasting tin and pour in enough boiling water to come about halfway up the sides of the dish. This regulates the heat in the oven and ensures that the eggs don't scramble.

Carefully transfer the dish and bain-marie to the oven and cook for 1 hour. The top should be golden and the centre should be just set. Serve with softly whipped cream.

Part Bavarian, part American, this is equally as good enjoyed at the end of a meal as with a cup of coffee. The ginger nut biscuits bring a lovely warmth to the cheesecake base, but feel free to use whichever type of biscuit you like. Make sure you just cook the cheesecake until it has a thick wobble. If it cooks for too long, it will crack all over, which is not the end of the world, but not exactly what you're looking for!

Apple and cinnamon baked cheesecake

SERVES 8

200g (7oz) caster sugar

3 eating apples, peeled, quartered and cores removed

75g (3oz) butter, melted, plus extra for greasing

175g (6oz) ginger nut biscuits

450g (1lb) cream cheese

1 tsp ground cinnamon

4 eggs, lightly beaten

Equipment

24cm (9½in) spring-form cake tin

Place 50g (2oz) of the sugar and 2 tablespoons water in a saucepan and dissolve the sugar over a medium heat. Arrange the apples in the saucepan cut side down and cover with a cartouche (a circle of baking parchment) and a lid. Cook for 2 minutes – there should be a couple of tablespoons of liquid; if there is more, remove the apples and boil to reduce. Take off the heat and leave for 5 minutes with the lid on. Remove the lid and cool.

Preheat the oven to 180°C (350°F), Gas mark 4. Butter the sides and base of the cake tin. Make sure the base is upside down, so that there is no lip and the cake can slide off easily when cooked.

Place the biscuits in a food processor and whiz until quite fine, or place them in a plastic bag and bash with a rolling pin. Mix the crushed biscuits with the melted butter and evenly press them into the base of the tin. Arrange the apple mixture on top and chill in the fridge while you make the topping.

Beat the cream cheese, remaining sugar, cinnamon, eggs and cooking juices together in a large bowl until smooth and creamy. Pour over the top of the apple, then bake in the oven for 40 minutes or until it is set around the outside but still has a wobble in the centre.

Allow to cool completely, then run a knife around the edge to loosen it and carefully remove the cheesecake from the tin by sliding it off the base using a palette knife or fish slice. Transfer to a serving plate. Cut into slices to serve. This cheesecake is best eaten when it is at room temperature.

A simple little twist on the classic Eton mess, but instead of using meringues, this recipe uses Victoria sponge. A delicious quick recipe to assemble on a summer's day.

Strawberry Victoria mess

SERVES 6-8

For the sponge

100g (3½oz) butter, plus extra for greasing

100g (3½oz) plain flour, plus extra for dusting

100g (3½oz) caster or granulated sugar

2 eggs

¾ tsp baking powder

1 tbsp milk

For the strawberries

450g (7oz) strawberries, dehulled

100g (3½oz) caster or granulated sugar, plus 1 tbsp for the purée

Juice of 2 lemons

250ml (9fl oz) double or regular cream

Few sprigs of mint, to decorate

Equipment

1 x 18cm (7in) sandwich tin with 3cm (1¼in) sides

Preheat the oven to 180°C (350°F), Gas mark 4, then butter and flour the sides of the tin and line the base with a disc of baking parchment.

Cream the butter until soft in a large bowl or in an electric food mixer. Add the sugar and beat until the mixture is light and fluffy.

Whisk the eggs in a small bowl for a few seconds until just mixed, then gradually add them to the butter mixture, beating all the time. Sift in the flour and baking powder, then add the milk and fold in gently to incorporate.

Tip the mixture into the tin and place in the centre of the oven. Bake for 18–25 minutes or until golden on top and springy to the touch.

Remove from the oven and allow to cool in the tin for 10 minutes, then loosen around the edges of the cake using a small, sharp knife and carefully remove from the tin. Leave on a wire rack to cool down completely.

Take 100g (3½oz) of the strawberries and place in a food processor with 1 tablespoon of the sugar and the juice of ½ lemon. Whiz for a few minutes, then push through a sieve and set aside.

Slice the remaining strawberries and mix together in a bowl with the 100g (3½oz) of sugar and the remaining lemon juice. Set aside and allow to sit for about an hour or so to become juicy.

Strain off the juices and place in a bowl. Next, cut the sponge in to 1–1.5cm (½–⅝in) pieces and add to the bowl. Mix together well to make sure each sponge piece is moistened.

In a bowl, whisk the cream.

To serve, add in layers to serving glasses first a few pieces of sponge, then some sliced strawberries, a spoonful of cream and finish with a drizzle of the puréed strawberries and a sprig of mint.

This is a decidedly autumnal treat, perfect for enjoying at the end of a long, lazy Sunday lunch. For a deliciously crunchy crumble, make sure to just rub the butter into the flour and sugar so that it's still coarse.

Pear and maple crumble

SERVES 6-8

8 small pears (about 800g), peeled, cored and cut into 1.5cm (⅝in) chunks

50g (2oz) caster or granulated sugar

120ml (4fl oz) maple syrup

For the crumble

100g (3½oz) caster or granulated sugar

150g (5oz) plain flour

75g (3oz) butter, cubed

Equipment

1 litre (1¾ pint) capacity pie dish

Preheat the oven to 180°C (350°F), Gas mark 4.

Place the cut pears in the pie dish, then sprinkle over the sugar and pour over the maple syrup.

In a bowl, mix together the sugar and flour, then rub in the cubes of butter until the mixture looks like coarse breadcrumbs.

Tip the crumble mix over the fruit, then place in the oven and bake for about 30 minutes until the crumble mixture is golden brown. Remove from the oven and allow to cool slightly before serving with softly whipped cream or vanilla ice cream.

Light, buttery puff pastry sitting under vanilla-scented custard and topped with juicy, almost caramelised nectarine slices – divine. This recipe also works very well with apricots, peaches, apples, bananas or rhubarb.

Nectarine custard tarts

MAKES 6 TARTS

For the custard

175ml (6fl oz) milk

100ml (3½fl oz) double or regular cream

½ vanilla pod, split down one side, or 1 tsp vanilla extract

2 egg yolks

50g (2oz) caster sugar

2 tbsp plain flour

375g (13oz) puff pastry (all butter or homemade)

3 ripe nectarines, halved, stones removed and each half sliced into 6 wedges

2 tbsp caster or granulated sugar

First, make the custard. Place the milk, cream and the vanilla pod, if using, in a saucepan and bring to the boil. Set aside to infuse for 5–10 minutes.

Meanwhile, using a hand-held electric beater, whisk together the egg yolks, sugar and flour until pale in colour and thick. Reheat the milk and cream, removing the vanilla pod (this can be wiped clean and reused another time), then pour, while whisking, onto the egg yolk mixture.

Tip back into the saucepan (with the vanilla extract, if using), and stir over a low–medium heat for a few minutes, stirring all the time with a wooden spatula, until thickened (you can use a whisk if it gets lumpy). It will need to boil for about 2 minutes to really thicken. It should coat the back of a spoon. Take out of the saucepan, put into a bowl (or onto a plate if you need to cool quickly) and allow to cool.

Preheat the oven to 220°C (425°F), Gas mark 7. Roll the pastry out on a floured worktop until just 4–5mm (¼in) thick. Trim the edges with a knife, then cut into six rectangles or squares.

Turn each one upside down (so that the cut edges are now cut upwards, which will encourage the pastry edges to rise well), then score (about halfway down through the pastry) a 1cm (½in) border around each (like a picture frame, this will rise and hold in the custard).

Leaving the borders free, spread out a generous heaped tablespoon or two of custard to thickly cover the pastry, then arrange the nectarine slices over the top and sprinkle each pastry with the sugar. Bake for 20 minutes until the pastry is puffed up and golden.

Rachel's Tip: The puff pastry trimmings can be used for the Cinnamon cigars (page 104) or the Drops au chocolat (page 198).

Admittedly one of the more involved recipes in the book, but also one of the most delicious things to eat. Ever. Thin, crisp, burnt sugar caramel coating light choux pastry stuffed with creamy orange-scented custard; these are a real treat.

Orange caramel choux puffs

SERVES 8–10

For the choux pastry

100g (3½oz) strong white or plain flour

Pinch of salt

75g (3oz) butter

3 eggs, beaten

For the crème pâtissière (pastry cream)

4 egg yolks

100g (3½oz) caster sugar

30g (1¼oz) plain flour

1 vanilla pod, with a line scored down the side, or ½ tsp vanilla extract

350ml (12fl oz) milk

100ml (3½fl oz) double or regular cream

Grated zest of 1 orange

Cont. overleaf

For the choux pastry, please see method on page 54.

Preheat the oven to 220°C (425°F), Gas mark 7.

Line a baking tray with baking parchment. Put the choux pastry into the piping bag fitted with the large nozzle and pipe the dough into twenty rounds about 4cm (1½in) in diameter, spaced about 4cm (1½in) apart on the tray to allow for expansion. Use a small wet knife to stop the dough coming out when you have finished piping each puff. If you don't have a piping bag, you can use two dessertspoons, scraping the dough off one with the other to make rounds of a similar size.

Brush the puffs gently with some of the remaining beaten egg and bake in the oven for 15–20 minutes or until they are puffed up, golden and crisp. Remove the puffs from the oven and, using a skewer or the tip of a small sharp knife, make a hole in the side or the base of each puff. Return to the oven and bake for a further 5 minutes to allow the steam to escape. Allow the puffs to cool on a wire rack.

For the crème pâtissière, in a bowl, whisk the egg yolks with the sugar until light and thick, then sift in the flour and stir to mix.

Place the vanilla pod, if using, in a saucepan with the milk and bring it slowly just up to the boil. Remove the vanilla pod and pour the milk onto the egg mixture, whisking all the time. Return the mixture to the pan and stir over a low to medium heat until it comes up to a gentle boil (it must boil for it to thicken). Continue to cook, stirring all the time (or use a whisk if it looks lumpy), for 2 minutes or until very thick.

For the caramel sauce

225g (8oz) caster or granulated sugar

110g (4oz) butter

175ml (6fl oz) double cream

Pinch of salt

Icing sugar, to dust

Equipment

Piping bag fitted with a large and small nozzle (optional)

Remove the saucepan from the heat, add the vanilla extract, if using, and pour into a bowl. If the mixture goes a little lumpy while cooking, remove the saucepan from the heat and whisk well. If it is still lumpy when cooked, push it through a sieve. Place in a bowl and allow to cool completely.

Pour the cream into a bowl, whisk until stiff, then fold into the cooled pastry cream with the orange zest. Use the piping bag with a small nozzle attached to pipe the orange cream into the choux puffs in the hole that you made while they were baking.

To make the caramel sauce, dissolve the sugar in 75ml (3fl oz) water in a pan over a medium heat. Stir in the butter, raise the heat a little, and bubble, stirring occasionally, for about 8–10 minutes until it turns a light toffee colour. Turn off the heat and stir in half the cream. When the bubbles die down, stir in the rest of the cream and a pinch of salt.

To finish, place the choux puffs on serving plates, dust with icing sugar, then pour over the warm caramel sauce to serve.

Rachel's Tips: The crème pâtissière can be frozen or maybe made a couple of days in advance and stored in the fridge before using.

The caramel sauce can be stored in the fridge for up to two weeks and reheated when necessary.

FESTIVE TREATS

Easter chocolate meringue cake

Sweet wine syllabub

Spiced plum tarte tatin

Festive fruity steamed pudding

Mulled port pears with port jelly

Negroni jelly with clementine sorbet

Iced pumpkin cake

Spiced cranberry, white chocolate and
orange biscotti

Nectarine and sloe gin jelly trifle

Eggnog crème brûlée

Chocolate and vanilla swirl biscuits

Cinnamon, apple and raisin pastries

This is a variation of a cake that my sister makes. It has an unusual method, where two layers of meringue and chocolate cake are baked together in the oven before being sandwiched together with whipped cream. The three different textures come together, resulting in a perfectly festive Easter treat. Feel free to put raspberries or sliced strawberries in with the cream, too.

Easter chocolate meringue cake

SERVES 8–10

For the cake

100g (3½oz) butter, softened, plus extra for greasing

350g (12oz) caster sugar

2 eggs

225g (8oz) plain flour

50g (2oz) cocoa powder

¾ tsp baking powder

¼ tsp bicarbonate of soda

Pinch of salt

225ml (8fl oz) buttermilk or sour milk

For the meringue

3 egg whites

150g (5oz) caster sugar

275ml (9½fl oz) double or regular cream

Icing sugar, for dusting

Equipment

2 x 23cm (9in) spring-form cake tins

Preheat the oven to 165°C (325°F), Gas mark 3. Brush the sides of the tins with melted or soft butter and dust with flour. Make sure the bases are upside down, so there is no lip and the cakes can slide off easily when cooked.

To make the cake, place the butter in a mixing bowl and beat until very soft. Add the sugar and one of the eggs and beat again, then add the other egg and mix. Sift the flour, cocoa powder, baking powder, bicarbonate of soda and salt into a separate bowl and set aside. Measure the buttermilk and set aside also.

Now, start the meringue. Place the egg whites in a bowl and whisk until frothy using an electric food mixer or hand-held electric beater. Add in half the sugar and continue whisking until the mixture holds stiff peaks. Turn off the whisk and fold in the remaining sugar.

Next, go back to the cake. Fold in the sifted dry ingredients and the buttermilk, then divide the mixture between the two cake tins, making sure they are level. Divide the meringue between the two cakes and spread out evenly over the cakes.

Cook in the oven for 1 hour or until a skewer inserted into the centre comes out clean. Take out of the oven and allow to sit in the tin for 15–20 minutes before loosening around the sides with a small, sharp knife, removing the cakes from the tins and allowing to cool completely, meringue side up.

When ready to assemble, whip the cream until it just holds stiff peaks, then place one of the cakes (save the best cake for the top) on a cake stand. Spread the whipped cream over the top, then sit the second cake on top of the cream. Dust with icing sugar and serve.

The classic syllabub, which dates back as far as the early 1500s, is something of a cloud-like mousse, but as it contains no egg, it's even lighter again. Described by the *Oxford English Dictionary* as, 'A drink or dish made by milk or cream curdled by the admixture of wine, cider or other acid, and often sweetened and flavoured,' it was apparently made by the milkmaid, who would milk a cow directly into a jug of cider. This particularly festive version uses sweet dessert wine for a wonderfully decadent treat.

Sweet wine syllabub

SERVES 6

300ml (½ pint) double or regular cream

50g (2oz) caster sugar

125ml (4½fl oz) white dessert wine

Whip the cream very softly – it should not even hold soft peaks. In a separate bowl, stir the sugar into the wine until it has dissolved, then gently fold into the cream.

Divide into six small glasses and chill for 2 hours to softly set.

Serve with shortbread biscuits and the rest of the bottle of dessert wine.

Plums have a rich and complex flavour that stands up to, and even embraces, spices very well. This is a gorgeous dessert, perfect at Christmas or New Year. Make sure you pack in as many plum halves as possible, as when cooked they'll have shrunk in size.

Spiced plum tarte tatin

SERVES 6

For the pastry

150g (5oz) plain flour

Pinch of salt

75g (3oz) butter

65g (2½oz) crème fraîche or sour cream

For the filling

175g (6oz) caster or granulated sugar

25g (1oz) butter

½ tbsp mixed spice

8 ripe plums, halved lengthways and stones removed

Equipment

24cm (9½oz) ovenproof frying pan

Preheat the oven to 200°C (400°F), Gas mark 6.

First, make the pastry. Place the flour, salt and butter in a food processor and whiz briefly. Add two-thirds of the crème fraîche or sour cream and continue to whiz. You might add a little more, but not too much as the mixture should be just moist enough to come together. If making by hand, rub the butter into the flour and salt until it resembles coarse breadcrumbs then, using your hands, add just enough crème fraîche or sour cream to bring it together.

With your hands, flatten out the ball of dough until it is about 2cm (¾in) thick, then wrap in cling film or place in a plastic bag and leave in the fridge for at least 30 minutes.

Place the sugar, butter and mixed spice together in the ovenproof frying pan. Stir together and boil, uncovered, for 5–8 minutes, until the mixture turns into a golden brown caramel. Place the plums cut side down in the pan of syrupy caramel. Cook for 3 minutes, then remove from the heat.

Roll out the pastry to the same size as the inside diameter of the pan and place it on the plums, tucking it into the edges. Bake it in the oven for 20–25 minutes or until golden brown on top. Take out of the oven and allow to sit for 1 minute before placing a plate over the top and carefully flipping it over, holding tightly.

Serve in slices with softly whipped cream.

A very jolly Christmas pudding; this one is seriously citrussy with the addition of orange liqueur and lots of marmalade. Feel free to chop and change the dried fruit; dates or sultanas would work well, too.

Festive fruity steamed pudding

SERVES 6–8

For the fruit topping

100g (3½oz) orange marmalade

100ml (3½fl oz) orange liqueur, such as Cointreau, Grand Marnier or triple sec

50g (2oz) dried cranberries, roughly chopped

50g (2oz) dried apricots, chopped

For the pudding

200g (7oz) butter, plus extra for greasing

200g (7oz) caster sugar

3 eggs, lightly beaten

250g (9oz) plain flour

1 tsp mixed spice

½ tsp baking powder

¼ tsp bicarbonate of soda

75ml (3fl oz) buttermilk

Equipment

1.7 litre (3 pint) pudding basin and kitchen string

To start, place the marmalade, liqueur, cranberries and apricots in a small saucepan, bring to the boil and simmer for 2–3 minutes until the mixture becomes slightly stickier, then set aside to cool.

Next, make the pudding batter. Cream the butter in a large bowl or in an electric food mixer until soft. Add the sugar and beat until the mixture is light and fluffy. Gradually add the beaten eggs, beating well between each addition.

Sift in the flour, mixed spice, baking powder and bicarbonate of soda and mix into the batter until just incorporated. Next, add the buttermilk and mix together to make a dropping consistency.

Lightly butter the pudding basin. Pour the fruit mix into the base of the prepared pudding basin and spoon in the sponge batter.

Cut out a sheet of baking parchment at least 8cm (3in) larger than the top of the basin, fold a crease in the middle (this allows the paper to expand as the pudding cooks) and tie the sheet over the lip of the bowl with heatproof string.

Place the pudding in a saucepan not much larger than the basin and carefully pour in enough hot water to come three-quarters of the way up the basin. Cover and boil for approximately 1½ hours until a skewer inserted in the centre of the pudding comes out clean and it feels spongy to the touch. Keep the water topped up in the saucepan during cooking.

Carefully remove the basin from the pan and turn out onto a warmed serving plate, allowing the fruit to fall down the sides. Serve with lightly whipped cream.

I love how some old-fashioned cookery terms find their way into our everyday language today. One example of this is the phrase to 'mull things over', meaning to slowly think and consider an idea or thought. This is most likely derived from the very slow and deliberate process of infusing juices, brandies or wines with spices over a low heat.

In this recipe, pears are poached in a sweet port syrup infused with cardamom, cinnamon and star anise. The poaching liquid is then given another star turn and set with gelatine to make a truly festive feast.

Mulled port pears with port jelly

SERVES 6

225ml (8fl oz) port

225g (8oz) caster or granulated sugar

7 green cardamom pods, bashed

1 cinnamon stick

2 star anise

2 strips of orange rind (removed with a peeler)

6 pears, peeled

2 sheets of gelatine

Place the port, 225ml (8fl oz) water, the sugar, spices and orange rind in a saucepan that will just fit the pears. Place on a medium heat and stir until the sugar has dissolved. Place the pears neatly in the saucepan with the port syrup. Cover with a disc of baking parchment and a lid, then simmer for 20 minutes. Turn over the pears, then cook for a further 20–30 minutes until the pears are soft.

Remove the pears and strain the juices into a measuring jug. Add enough water to make up to 475ml (16fl oz). Pour 75ml (3fl oz) of this liquid back over the pears and keep aside in the saucepan, then set aside.

Place two sheets of gelatine in a bowl of cold water for 3–5 minutes to soften, then remove from the water and squeeze out any excess liquid. Add the softened gelatine sheets to the warm syrup, stirring to dissolve. If the syrup has cooled too much, the gelatine will not dissolve, in which case, heat the syrup again.

Divide the liquid into six small glasses or moulds lined with cling film and chill in the fridge for 3–4 hours until set.

To serve, warm the pears gently in the syrup, then turn out the jellies onto plates, place a warm pear on the side and drizzle over some of the syrup. Serve with softly whipped cream. These are just as delicious cold.

I was trying to work out how I could incorporate my favourite cocktail, the negroni, into this book. It was either going to be a sorbet or a jelly, but seeing as how a negroni is basically just alcohol, the chances of a negroni sorbet freezing properly weren't very high. So a negroni jelly it is, and it goes superbly with the clementine sorbet. Be warned, though: just the one will do, otherwise you'll be under, or on top of, the table.

Negroni jelly with clementine sorbet

MAKES 4

For the sorbet

Juice of ½ lemon

Juice and zest of 4 clementines, tangerines or satsumas

50g (2oz) caster or granulated sugar

For the jellies

45ml (1½fl oz) gin

45ml (1½fl oz) Campari

45ml (1½fl oz) Martini Rosso

1 sheet of gelatine

45ml (1½fl oz) orange juice

25g (1oz) caster or granulated sugar

Equipment

Ice-cream machine or sorbetière

To make the sorbet, mix together the lemon juice, clementine juice, zest and sugar, stirring to dissolve the sugar. Then freeze in an ice-cream maker according to the manufacturer's instructions.

To make the jellies, in a bowl mix together the gin, Campari and Martini. Soften a sheet of gelatine in cold water for 3–5 minutes, then squeeze out any excess liquid. Pour the orange juice into a saucepan, add the sugar and place on a low heat. Stir just until the sugar has dissolved, then remove from the heat.

Add the softened gelatine to the warm orange juice, then mix everything together well. Strain through a sieve into the alcohol mixture, then pour into four glasses or lightly greased moulds.

Place in the fridge to set for at least 3 hours, then turn out and serve with a scoop of the clementine sorbet.

Rachel's Tip: If you don't have an ice-cream machine, transfer the mixture to a freezerproof bowl and place in the freezer. After 30 minutes, remove from the freezer and run a spatula around the edge of the container, where ice crystals will have formed. Stir the sorbet like this every 30 minutes until all the juices have frozen.

A great recipe to make at Halloween time with the scooped-out pumpkin. This has the North American flavours that I adore: sugar and spice and all things nice.

Iced pumpkin cake

SERVES 8–10

425g (15oz) pumpkin, peeled, deseeded and cut into roughly 2cm (¾in) chunks (300g/11oz when prepared)

250g (9oz) plain flour

2 tsp baking powder

250g (9oz) caster sugar

¼ tsp ground cloves

½ tsp ground ginger

½ tsp ground nutmeg

½ tsp ground cinnamon

½ tsp salt

2 eggs

150g (5oz) butter, melted

For the icing

200g (7oz) icing sugar

2–3 tbsp orange juice

Equipment

23cm (9in) spring-form cake tin

Line the spring-form cake tin with baking parchment.

First, cook the pumpkin. Place in a saucepan with 200ml (7fl oz) water, bring to a simmer and cook for 20–25 minutes until tender. Allow to cool, then mash well or whiz in a food processor to form a pulp.

Preheat the oven to 180°C (350°F), Gas mark 4.

In a bowl, sift the flour together with the baking powder, then mix in the rest of the dry ingredients. In a separate bowl, thoroughly mix together the eggs, butter and pumpkin. Combine with the dry ingredients and place in the cake tin.

Bake for 45 minutes until a skewer inserted into the centre of the cake comes out clean. Remove from the oven and place on a wire rack to cool for 10 minutes before turning out of the tin.

As the cake cools, make the icing. Place the sugar in a bowl and mix in just enough orange juice to make a spreadable icing, making sure it's not too wet. If there's too much orange juice, the icing will fall off the sides of the cake, but if there's not enough, it will be difficult to spread.

For the icing, I like to use a palette knife that I regularly dip into a jug of boiling water, as this helps to spread it out. So, using the palette knife, spread the icing over the top of the cake. Allow the icing to set (this takes about 15 minutes), then cut into slices to serve.

This cake keeps well for a week (the pumpkin seems to prevent it from drying out).

While these are a very welcome treat to have in a jar over Christmas, they're actually delicious any time of the year. I adore the white chocolate, orange and dried cranberry trio, but other dried fruit and chocolate also work well.

Spiced cranberry, white chocolate and orange biscotti

MAKES ABOUT 40 BISCOTTI

100g (3½oz) plain flour, plus extra for dusting

100g (3½oz) caster sugar

1 tsp baking powder

½ tsp ground cinnamon

½ tsp ground nutmeg

80g (3oz) white chocolate, chopped

50g (2oz) dried cranberries, roughly chopped

50g (2oz) candied orange peel, roughly chopped

1 egg, beaten

Preheat the oven to 160°C (320°F), Gas mark 3.

Sift together the flour, sugar, baking powder and spices into a large bowl. Add the chocolate, cranberries and candied orange and mix well, then mix in the beaten egg to form a soft dough. Flour your hands, then turn the dough out onto a lightly floured work surface and form into a sausage about 30cm (12in) long and 3cm (1¼in) in diameter.

Place on a baking tray and bake for about 25 minutes until browned and just set, then remove and allow to cool on a wire rack for 5 minutes.

Cut into slices about 5mm (¼in) thick, then lay flat on the tray and bake for a further 10 minutes.

Turn all the biscotti over on the tray, return to the oven and continue to bake for 10 minutes more. They should be a light golden colour on both cut sides. Cool on a wire rack, then transfer to an airtight container where they will keep for up to two weeks.

A very grown-up trifle. Sloe gin is a quintessential Christmas ingredient as, if you've made it yourself, you'll know that happily it matures perfectly by mid-December. The nectarines, while not a seasonal local fruit where I live, are a little festive treat to make this trifle truly delicious.

Nectarine and sloe gin jelly trifle

SERVES 8

For the jelly

100g (3½oz) caster sugar

75ml (3fl oz) sloe gin or grenadine

Juice of ½ lemon

2 sheets of gelatine

400g (14oz) nectarines

For the sponge

50g (2oz) caster sugar

50g (2oz) butter

1 egg, beaten

50g (2oz) plain flour

½ tsp baking powder

Cont. opposite

To make the jelly, place the sugar and 150ml (5fl oz) water in a saucepan on a high heat, stir and simmer for just 2 minutes to dissolve the sugar. Remove from the heat, stir in the sloe gin and lemon juice and set aside. At this stage, remove 5 tablespoons of syrup and keep to drizzle over the sponge.

Next, place the gelatine in a bowl and cover with cold water, then let stand for 3–5 minutes to soften. Remove the gelatine from the water and squeeze out any excess liquid, then add the softened gelatine to the warm syrup and stir to dissolve. If the syrup has cooled, gently reheat.

Slice the nectarines thinly and add to the syrup. Divide evenly among eight glasses, filling them not more than halfway, then place in the fridge to set. This should take 3–4 hours.

Preheat the oven to 160°C (320°F), Gas mark 3.

To make the sponge, place the sugar and butter in a bowl and use a wooden spoon or the paddle attachment of an electric food mixer to cream together until light and fluffy. Add the beaten egg and mix in, then sift in the flour and baking powder, folding together just until combined.

Divide the batter into four paper bun cases in the bun tray, then place in the oven and bake for 15–20 minutes until risen and springy to the touch. Remove from the oven and place on a wire rack to cool then, when cool, slice each bun in half horizontally.

For the custard

150ml (5fl oz) single, whipping or regular cream

4 strips of orange rind (removed with a peeler)

150ml (5fl oz) milk

2 egg yolks

25g (1oz) caster or granulated sugar

Equipment

6-hole bun tray (smaller than a cupcake or muffin tray)

To make the custard, place the cream, orange rind and milk in a small saucepan and place on a medium heat. Bring up to just before the boil, then remove from the heat. In a bowl, whisk together the egg yolks and sugar. Pour the hot creamy milk over the sugar and egg yolks and whisk together. Return to the saucepan, discarding the orange strips, then cook on a low heat, stirring constantly until the mixture starts to thicken. Be careful that it doesn't get too hot or else you will have sweet scrambled eggs. Transfer the custard to a bowl to cool slightly.

To assemble the trifles, remove the jellies from the fridge, place a disc of sponge on top of each one and drizzle a spoon of the retained syrup over each sponge disc. Divide the custard out evenly to cover each disc of sponge and return it to the fridge to allow the custard to set.

To serve, add a good spoonful of softly whipped cream on top of each trifle and decorate with a mint or sweet geranium leaf if you wish.

Rachel's Tips: Replace the sloe gin with orange juice for an alcohol-free version. Raspberries also work really well in place of the nectarines. This recipe can be doubled or tripled to make one large trifle.

A centuries-old drink recipe containing eggs, alcohol and cream, eggnog was often used in toasts to good health and prosperity. It's long been associated with Christmas and is especially festive when turned into a celebratory crème brûlée.

Eggnog crème brûlée

SERVES 4

2 egg yolks

1 tbsp caster or granulated sugar

240ml (8fl oz) double or regular cream

60ml (2½fl oz) brandy

½ cinnamon stick

½ vanilla pod, split and scraped

For the caramel topping

110g (4oz) caster sugar

Ideally, make the custard the day before the crème brûlée is needed, or at least 8 hours beforehand. Mix the egg yolks together with the sugar. Place the cream, brandy, cinnamon and vanilla pod in a saucepan. Place on a medium heat and warm just until 'shivering', but do not boil.

When hot, remove the cinnamon and vanilla pod (these can be rinsed, dried and used again) and pour the cream slowly over the egg yolks, whisking all the time. Return to the saucepan and cook on a low heat, stirring constantly, just until it is thick enough to coat the back of a spoon. It must not boil or the egg yolks will scramble. Pour into four cups, glasses or ramekins. Allow to cool, then place in the fridge to chill overnight. Be careful not to break the skin that forms.

The following day, or 8 hours later, make the caramel topping. Dissolve the sugar for the caramel topping in 75ml (3fl oz) water. Place in a saucepan and on a medium–high heat. Bring to the boil and cook until the sugar caramelises and turns a chestnut-brown colour. Do not stir while it is boiling or the sugar will crystallise, though you can swirl the pan when it starts to brown a little at the edges. Remove from the heat and immediately spoon a thin layer of caramel over the top of the custards, making sure not to 'swirl' them to help spread the caramel. Doing this can break the skin on top of the custard, which will cause the caramel to sink.

Allow to cool and set for at least 15 minutes, then serve. The crème brûlées will sit in a dry atmosphere for 2–3 hours.

Rachel's Tip: If you have a blowtorch, instead of making caramel, scatter over the custards a 2mm (⅛in) layer of caster or granulated sugar. Wave the blowtorch slowly over the sugar, from about 10cm (4in) away, until it is deep golden and caramelised. Allow to sit for 5 minutes before serving.

I like the *Charlie and the Chocolate Factory*-esque look of these. A delicious swirl made up of two of the best-suited flavours in baking: chocolate and vanilla. You can cook a few or all of these biscuits at one time.

Chocolate and vanilla swirl biscuits

MAKES ABOUT 36 BISCUITS

150g (5oz) butter, softened

110g (4oz) caster sugar

1 egg

Icing sugar, for dusting

For the vanilla swirl

2 tsp vanilla extract

150g (5oz) plain flour

¼ tsp baking powder

For the chocolate swirl

35g (1¼oz) cocoa powder

115g (4oz) plain flour

¼ tsp baking powder

Preheat the oven to 180°C (350°F), Gas mark 4. Line a baking tray with baking parchment.

Cream the butter with the sugar and beat until it is light and fluffy, then beat in the egg. At this point, divide the mixture evenly between two bowls. There should be about 160g (5½oz) mixture in each. Into the vanilla swirl bowl, add the vanilla extract, then sift in the flour and baking powder and mix to a soft dough. Into the chocolate swirl bowl, sift the cocoa powder, flour and baking powder. Mix this to a soft dough as well.

Dust two sheets of baking parchment with icing sugar (make sure you use enough, so that the dough doesn't stick). Roll out each ball of dough on a different sheet of parchment, dusting the top with icing sugar too, to a rectangle of 20 x 30cm (8 x 12in). Both rectangles need to be the same size.

Slide one onto the other layer evenly and, starting from the long 30cm (12in) end, roll tightly into a swirled log. Be careful, as the dough is quite fragile. Wrap in the paper and place in the fridge to chill for at least 15 minutes (they can sit in the fridge for up to two weeks).

Cut into slices about 7.5mm (¼in) thick. Bake for 15 minutes until the underside is golden on the outside and just dry to the touch. Transfer carefully to a wire rack to cool.

Rachel's Tip: The log will keep in the fridge for two weeks. Simply cut and cook as many swirls as you need.

Another gorgeous way to use puff pastry. These are deliciously moreish, sweet and spicy, and just perfect with a cup of coffee.

Cinnamon, apple and raisin pastries

MAKES 6 PASTRIES

3 small eating apples, peeled, cored and cut into 1cm (½in) chunks

100g (3½oz) caster or granulated sugar

40g (1½oz) raisins

½ tsp ground ginger

1 tsp ground cinnamon

250g (9oz) puff pastry

1 egg, beaten

3 tsp demerara sugar

Preheat the oven to 220°C (425°F), Gas mark 7. Line a baking tray with baking parchment.

First, prepare the spiced apple filling. Place the apples in a saucepan with the sugar, raisins, spices and 3 tablespoons water. Cover and cook for about 10 minutes until the apples are soft. Take the lid off and cook, uncovered, for another 1–2 minutes until there's no liquid left in the pan. Tip the mixture onto a plate and allow to cool.

Roll the pastry into a rectangle about 35 x 25cm (14 x 10in). The pastry should be about 3mm (⅛in) thick. Trim the edges of the pastry (not too much, as this will be discarded) and cut the pastry into six squares.

Divide the spiced apple mixture among the six squares, placing it in the centre of the squares. With each one, fold in each of the four corners so that they almost meet in the middle. Brush the tops with beaten egg, then sprinkle with demerara sugar.

Lift the pastries carefully onto the prepared tray and bake for 10–12 minutes until golden and crisp. Allow to cool slightly before eating.

Index

Acknowledgements

It is with a mixture of emotions that I write the acknowledgements, as this is the final and last chapter of the book. One half of me is sighing with relief that I've got this far and somehow managed not to lose all my recipes in that cloud up there, while the other half of me is almost sad, as it's like saying goodbye to a friend. And in this case it's a really lovely, sweet friend.

As is always the case, there were many people involved in making this book come to fruition. At HarperCollins, where the project turned from an idea into delicious reality, I was lucky enough to work with Georgina Mackenzie, Martin Topping, James Empringham, Carole Tonkinson, Virginia Woolstencroft, Hannah Gammon.

A huge thank you to photographer Tara Fisher and also to Mario Sierra, Joss Herd, Jordan Bourke, Rachel Webb, Kathryn Morrissey, Tabitha Hawkins and Liz MacCarthy for doing stunningly stellar work on the shoot for the book.

A huge hug and sincere thanks to Ivan Whelan for the enormous contribution he made to this book and all his help testing the recipes with me.

While the final editing for this book was taking place I was also working on filming the *All Things Sweet* television series. David Nottage of Liverpool Street Productions, Karen Gilchrist, Michael Connock, Annabel Hornsby, Rob Partis, Sam Jackson, Ed Beck, Ivan Whelan, Jette Vindi, Gail O'Driscoll, Rebecca Bullen, Al Blaine, Scott Breckenridge, Duncan Hart, Ewan Henesy, Richard Hobbs: you are all incredible at what you do and somehow managed to make our relentless shoot schedule not only painless, but really good fun, too!

A big thanks also to everyone at Ballymaloe House and Cookery School, Fiona Lindsay and all at Limelight Management, Ardmore Pottery, Article, and Eden (two beautiful homeware shops in Dublin), Nougat, sphere One by Lucy Downes (for the divine cashmere), JR Ryall, Diarmaid Falvey, Conor Pyne, Brian Walsh of RTE , my wonderful parents Brian and Hallfridur O'Neill, my also wonderful parents-in-law Tim and Darina Allen, and my super-fabulous sister and brother-in-law Simone and Dodo Michel.

Isaac, thank you for everything. You make everything run smoothly at home and in work, you think outside the box (which I don't), you're the most wonderful cook, and most importantly you are my gorgeous and lovely husband.

I dedicate this book to my children and godchildren who are, without doubt All Things Sweet: Josh, Lucca and Scarlett Allen, Lola and Rosa Michel, Matilda Cuddigan-Eck, James Whyld and Sophie Gleeson.